Alan

Many thanks for
your help.

May'19

DUNDEE LAW 1865-1967:

THE DEVELOPMENT OF A LAW SCHOOL IN A TIME OF CHANGE

Robin M White LLB, LLM, Cert Soc Anth

Honorary Research Fellow

School of Law

University of Dundee

Dundee

2018

For Cherry

and, of course, the rest of the family, past, present and future

CONTENTS

List of Illustrations   vi

Preface   viii

Introduction   1

Chapter One – The Setting: 19th-century reforms to the legal profession and the universities   7

Chapter Two – 1865-1898: The Early Days: Repeated attempts to launch a Law School   53

Chapter Three – 1899-1938: Challenging Decades: Limited teaching and further reform   109

Chapter Four – 1938-1949: Blighted Success: A BL Degree and a Scots Law chair, but war-time woes   175

Chapter Five – 1950-1955: A Fair Breeze: An LLB degree, a chair in Conveyancing, and a Law Faculty   249

Chapter Six – 1956-1967: A Modern Law School Achieved: Full-time staff, a chair in Jurisprudence, and an Honours degree   289

Coda   357

Annex on Sources of Information on Students   365

Bibliography   371

Index   395

LIST OF ILLUSTRATIONS

Front cover – Detail of a letter from Thomas Thornton to Principal Peterson, 23 April 1890

Frontispiece – Thomas Thornton   iii

1 – Mary Ann Baxter of Balgavies   233
2 – John Boyd Baxter LLD   233
3 – Sir William Peterson KCMG   233
4 – 3rd Marquess of Bute   233

5 – David S Littlejohn   234
6 – William C Smith   234
7 – James Allison CBE   234
8 – Hugh Carlton   234

9 – Lord Trayner LLD   235
10 – Sir James Irvine KBE, FRS, FRSE, FEIS   235
11 – Thomas Mackay Cooper, 1st Baron Cooper of Culross PC, KC, FRSE   235
12 – Arthur William Tedder, 1st Baron Tedder of Glenguin GCB   235

13 – Arthur Alexander Matheson QC   236
14 – Alexander (Alastair) John McDonald   236
15 – Bernard (Ben) Clifford Bowman OBE   236
16 – Ian Douglas Willock   236

17 – James Joseph Robertson   237
18 – Dennis Ferguson Collins   237
19 – Sir Neil MacCormick QC, FBA, FRSE   237

20 – Report in *Dundee Courier & Argus* 4 August 1865   238
21 – Advertisement in *Dundee Courier & Argus* 13 December 1890   238

22 – Dundee Sheriff Court exterior   239
23 – Dundee Sheriff Court interior in the 19th century   239

24 – The houses acquired for University College Dundee in 1881   240
25 – 'Front Buildings' in the mid-20th century   240

26 – Free Kirk of St John's, Small's Wynd   241
27 – Ellenbank and Union Mount   241

28 – Plan of University College Dundee buildings in c.1892   242
29 – Plan of University College Dundee buildings in 1911   242

30 – Nethergate frontage in the 1950s before the Tower was built   243
31 – The Master's Room in the Front Buildings in 1966   243

32 – The Princess Cinema in (Old) Hawkhill   244
33 – St Mary Magdalene church and hall, off (Old) Hawkhill   244

34 – The Tower Building   245
35 – Bonar House   245

36 – Interior of the old Library in Union Mount   246
37 – Interior of the ncw Library in the Tower   246

38 – The Charter of Incorporation of the University of Dundee   247
39 – The entrance to the 'Terrapins'   247

40 – The Scrymgeour Building   248

Illustrations are reproduced by courtesy of the following: Frontispiece, Dundee City Archives; 1, 9, 13, University of Dundee Museum Services; 2, Dundee City Council (Dundee's Art Galleries and Museums); Front cover, 3, 4, 11, 14, 16, 24-25, 27-38, 40, University of Dundee Archive Services; 5, 7-8, 15, 20-21, by kind permission of DC Thomson & Co Ltd; 6, private collection; 10, University of St Andrews Museum Collections; 12, Imperial War Museums; 17, Mrs A Robertson; 18, Mrs E Collins; 19, Special Collections, University of Edinburgh Library; 22-23, 26, Libraries, Leisure and Culture Dundee; 39, the author.

PREFACE

The idea of a history of law teaching in Dundee had swirled about the Law School for some years before the observation in late 2012 that, if I did not write one, no-one else would. Although this sounded like the minor premise of a syllogism which lacked a major premise, it seemed a good enough reason to do so.

When I did embark upon the enterprise, I had very little idea of what the final product might look like. Contacting former students on the alumni database produced a few replies. Contacting some former colleagues produced some more. I am grateful to all the respondents, but (though the students invariably said they had enjoyed their time in the law school) there was too little material for even the briefest of histories. The project therefore became essentially archival, supplemented by a trawl through 19th-century law journals, and delving into some exotic legislation. The bibliography shows the results. On the other hand, I was also able to have numerous interesting and informative conversations with some former colleagues, to whom thanks are given below.

What has emerged is a history of law teaching in Dundee from 1865 to 1967, that is, from the first recorded law lectures, to the near simultaneous foundation of the University of Dundee and introduction of the modern law degree (and, incidentally, my LLB graduation). The book seeks to locate its narrative within revolutionary changes in both the universities and the profession, and the concentration upon one institution allows a better understanding of those changes than a broader brush would allow, and counteracts the focus on such bodies as the Writers to the Signet and Faculty of Advocates, which tend to dominate accounts.

In consequence, it is hoped that this book will be useful to legal historians interested in law teaching and the legal profession. And, as the period covered includes the years when University/Queen's College was part of St Andrews University, it contributes to the history of that

University as well as Dundee. And, further, as the institution variously known as University College Dundee, Queen's College Dundee, and the University of Dundee, has been rooted within the City of Dundee, it is hoped that it will be valuable to local historians.

Numerous debts were incurred along the way. Firstly, I must thank my wife, Cherry, for her enormous forbearance of my preoccupation during the researching and writing. I must also thank colleagues and former colleagues, and others, who provided help in many different ways. It is always invidious to identify individuals, but approximately chronologically, the list must include Colin Reid, who implanted the idea of the book, and watered it by reading and commenting upon more than one draft of every Chapter; Alan Page, who initiated and renewed the Honorary Fellowship which enabled me to research and write the book, even though he had expected the time to be spent doing work on civil penalties (and his successor, Stuart Cross, who continued the Fellowship); Mark Cargill, who always willingly sorted out IT problems which too easily derailed me; Kenneth Baxter who unfailingly helpfully pointed me at archival sources and shared his encyclopaedic knowledge of the history of the University of Dundee, and indeed Caroline Brown, Jan Merchant, Keren Guthrie and all the other staff of the University of Dundee Archives, who ever cheerfully supplied me with materials, often obscure (not to mention also the staffs of St Andrews University Library Special Collections, of the National Library of Scotland and of the Privy Council Office, who did likewise, and Martin Allan of Dundee City Archives, David Powell of D C Thomson's archives, Sally McIntosh of The McManus: Dundee's Art Gallery & Museum, Claire Robinson of the University of St Andrews Museum Collections, Denise Anderson of Edinburgh University Library special Collections and Mrs A Robertson and Mrs E Collins, who helped with the illustrations); Sheila Smith who volunteered her research skills in the early stages and found useful information; Ross Macdonald who deployed his historian's skills and ferreted out material that I would not have discovered; Iain Gillespie and David Hart, who helped me with University of Dundee Library matters; Elizabeth McGillivray, then Secretary of the Faculty of Procurators &

Solicitors in Dundee, who gave me access to the FPSD Minutes; Catriona Thomson of the Faculty of Advocates, who helped me with advocates' bio-data; Alastair McDonald, Jim Ryan, Ian Willock and, most particularly, Dennis Collins, who provided personal recollections and more, but all of whom sadly died before publication; Alastair McDonald and Dennis Collins (again), who both read several drafts of every Chapter; and Pamela Ferguson who also read some drafts, though hard-pressed with other work.

Also, I must thank Hector MacQueen and Mark Godfrey (and their anonymous reader) for their enthusiasm for a manuscript that turned up out of the blue with a title probably reminiscent of Beachcomber's "List of Huntingdonshire Cabmen", even though, in the end, their Grand Plan did not succeed.

Even more, must I offer grateful thanks to Matthew Jarron and the Abertay Historical Society for undertaking most of the editing and other work involved in the actual publication of a work a good deal larger than usual, and whose plan therefore did succeed.

Further, for financial assistance in publishing this book, I must thank both a number of alumni (listed alphabetically), that is, Billy Boyle (Boyles Solicitors), Stewart Brymer (Brymer Legal Limited), Lady Clark of Calton, Elizabeth McGillivray (again) (Bowmans Solicitors), Dr J Morrow (Lord Lyon), Lord Turnbull, and another alumnus who wishes to remain anonymous; and others (again listed alphabetically), that is, the Clark Foundation, the Faculty of Advocates, Alastair McDonald (again), and Thorntons Solicitors.

And finally, I must thank the late Myra Porter, without whom I would never have entered St Andrews University in the first place.

INTRODUCTION

This book traces the evolution of law teaching in Dundee from 1865 to 1967. It does so primarily in terms of processes, structures and curricula. Starting from the earliest recorded teaching, which was *ad hoc*, aimed chiefly at clerks and apprentices, and started at their instance, it continues through the major events of the following near-century, including institution of the first University College Dundee (UCD) law classes, which were specifically for professional examinations; the introduction in UCD of the Bachelor of *Law* (BL) degree; the founding of its first Chairs; the introduction of the more prestigious Bachelor of *Laws* (LLB); and the creation of a Law Faculty. It concludes with the ending of the BL, but the introduction of the radically different modern LLB, which remains in broadly the same form today. On the way, it considers various other events, including the Railway Lectures, the Bachelor of Commerce (BCom) debacle, war-time difficulties and the Polish "soldier-students", and the creation of "unique selling points" for the Law Faculty.

But it also does so in terms of the people involved. It looks at those instrumental in initiating and delivering law teaching, their identities and careers; but also, no less important, those receiving the teaching, the identities of at least some of the more noteworthy, and their numbers, gender, and achievements. In the course of this, it examines matters such as the role of local legal practitioners in, the nature of, and the post-Second World War burgeoning of, law teaching.

The account is largely derived from material in the University of Dundee Archives[1], supplemented by contemporary legal periodicals[2] and the press[3]. However, it seeks to locate the evolution within the changes in higher education and the legal profession which were roughly contemporaneous with it. These changes are best seen as three specific contexts. The first is the development of UCD into the University of Dundee. This commenced with the founding of UCD, reflecting the growth of "civic universities" throughout the United Kingdom. It continued through the College's troubled "affiliation" to the University of St Andrews, including the interesting role of the University Principal, and both an official inquiry[4] and a Royal Commission[5] to examine the "affiliation". It carried on through UCD's consequential translation into Queen's College Dundee (QCD), but also through its reaction to the 'Robbins Report'[6], which produced the post-war expansion of student numbers and thus the physical "campus". It ended with QCD's transformation into the University of Dundee, incidentally almost simultaneously with the introduction of the modern LLB.

The second context is the series of changes in university legal education, initiated by establishment of two new, separate, law degrees in the 19th century, that is, the initially rather unsuccessful LLB, and then the rather more successful BL. By the early 20th century, both degrees were taught in all the then-existing Universities, save for St Andrews (which caught up in mid-century), but always largely by part-time practitioner staff, to part-time students, usually on concurrent apprenticeships. At least in St Andrews, these undergraduate students only constituted a small group, however, sharing the classes of the already-existing larger contingent of non-graduating students, also usually on concurrent apprenticeships (accountancy as well as law), but qualifying through professional examinations. Though there was remarkably little analytical discussion published on the issues, there were various attempts over the years, successful and otherwise, to reform the two degrees. These attempts culminated in abolition of the BL, but creation of the modern LLB. This was taught in all the then-existing Universities, substantially by full-time career academic staff, to full-time students, with Honours options, and usually with a consecutive apprenticeship. Its introduction was also more or less simultaneous with the near-disappearance of non-graduating students.

The third context is the linked, but institutionally separate, history of changes in legal professional qualification, whereby, out of a number of disparate organisations, the legal profession in its current form was created. This process involved, for the first time, a national legal practitioner status, initially termed "procurator", but shortly thereafter "law agent", which in effect absorbed all other statuses (such as "notary"), except membership of the Faculty of Advocates, so necessitated national admission requirements. It also involved various iterations of these requirements, all of which included examinations in both general knowledge and law, and apprenticeships of varying lengths, finally producing the current status of "solicitor", with the Law Society of Scotland as its professional body. (The position of women is an interesting theme within this).

The first of these contexts provides the backdrop against which the evolution of law teaching in Dundee took place. The other two provide an explanation of why that evolution took the course that it did. All three are introduced in Chapter One, and in the following Chapters they either provide an initial introduction, or are interwoven through the body of the text.

But to understand these contexts, it is necessary to know something of the state of the universities and the legal profession in the mid- to late-19th century, both in general, and in relation to Dundee. The description which follows depends largely upon standard published sources. Unfortunately, however, these sources are somewhat thin in relation to certain central questions. They are thin in general, for example, in relation to the third context, that is, the emergence of a recognisable modern legal profession in the 19th century, for though there are relevant books (including monographs)[7], chapters in books[8], and periodical articles[9], there is no full account, and some reliance has to be placed upon the often scattered references in the sole general history of Scots Law[10], and the current major legal encyclopaedia[11] and its predecessors[12]. They are also especially thin in relation to Dundee, for no history has been written of the Faculty of Procurators and Solicitors in Dundee (FPSD), and its early records have disappeared[13], though there are occasional mentions in the literature[14].

They are less thin, however, in relation to the first context, that is, the emergence of UCD, and its later incarnations. The two standard histories of St Andrews, of which it formed part for some 75 years, give only occasional references, and a very brief account, respectively[15]. But there is a comprehensive published account, and a separately published illustrated summary[16].

Because of the thinness of some of these sources, the description given here of all three contexts seeks to offer some greater depth and coherence in relation to the mid- to late-19th century than is found in them. It seeks to do so in part through more detailed examination of the relevant legislation[17] (including delegated legislation, some of an unusual type[18]); in part through a comprehensive trawl through the legal periodical literature of the time; and in part through a greater focus on institutions other than those, such as the Faculty of Advocates and Society of Writers to the Signet, to which most attention has been usually paid. It also seeks to offer some reinterpretation of the account provided in the standard sources, by underlining the magnitude of the changes to university legal education and professional legal qualification in the 19th century. Indeed, given the equivalent magnitude of the mid-20th century change from "old" to "modern" LLB, it is argued that the period from 1865 to 1967 not only covers a neat near-hundred years, but seems to run from one revolution to another.

---

[1] Principally St Andrews University Court and Senate Minutes, University College Council and Queen's College Council Minutes, and St Andrews University and Dundee College Calendars, all referred to below, as required, and listed in the Bibliography.

[2] Principally the *Journal of Jurisprudence (JoJ)*, *Scottish Law Review (ScLR)*, *Juridical Review (JR)* and *Scots Law Times (SLT)*.

[3] Principally the *Dundee Courier*.

[4] Report of the Inquiry Appointed in February 1949 to Review and Report on the Organisation of University Education in Dundee and its Relationship with St Andrews University (1949) (the "Cooper Inquiry").

[5] Report of the Royal Commission on University Education in Dundee 1951-52 (Cmnd 8514: 1952) (the "Tedder Commission").

[6] Higher Education: report of the Committee appointed by the Prime Minister under the Chairmanship of Lord Robbins 1961-63 (Cmnd 2154: 1963).

[7] E.g. the invaluable J Henderson Begg, *A Treatise on the Law of Scotland relating to Law Agents ...* 1st ed (1873) and 2nd ed (1883), but see also John Finlay, *Men of Law in Pre-reformation Scotland* (2000), John Finlay, *The Community of the College of Justice ...* (2012) and J Finlay, *Legal Practice in Eighteenth Century Scotland* (2015). The still standard primer, Various Authors, *An Introduction to Scottish Legal History,* Stair Society vol 20 (1958), is almost silent, and there is little more in O F Robinson, T D Fergus & W M Gordon, *European Legal History: sources and institutions* 3rd ed (2000), however.

[8] E.g. Alan A Paterson, "The Legal Profession in Scotland: an endangered species or a problem case for market theory?", in Richard L Abel and Philip S C Lewis, *Lawyers in Society* 2 vols (1988) vol i 'The Common Law World', various contributions in D L Carey Miler & R Zimmerman (eds), *The Civilian Tradition and Scots Law: Aberdeen Quincentenary Essays* (1997), John Finlay, 'Lawyers in the British Isles', in B Dolemeyer (ed) *Anwaelte und Ihre Geschichte,* (2011), and J Finlay, "Legal Education, 1650-1850", in Robert Anderson, Mark Freeman & Lindsay Paterson, *The Edinburgh History of Education in Scotland* (2015).

[9] Referred to below, as required, and listed in the Bibliography.

[10] David M Walker, *A Legal History of Scotland* 7 vols (1988-2004) (which is not universally admired). Andrew R C Simpson & Adelyn L M Wilson, *Scottish Legal History* vol 1: 1000-1707 (2018) appeared too late for consideration.

[11] Sir Thomas Smith & Robert Black (Gen. Eds.), Hamish McN Henderson, Joseph M Thomson & Kenneth Miller (Dep. Gen. Eds.), *Stair Memorial Encyclopaedia of the Laws of Scotland* (various dates), chiefly in vol 'Legal Profession', Reissue.

[12] *Green's Encyclopaedia of the Law of Scotland* 1st ed (1896-1904), 2nd ed (1909-14), 3rd ed (1926-35), & Supplement (1949-51).

[13] An Index to Minutes for the mid-19th century, and actual Minutes from the late 19th century, survive.

[14] E.g. Begg, *Law Agents* (see note 7) 2nd ed 379.

[15] I.e. Ronald Gordon Cant, *The University of St Andrews: a short history* 3rd ed (1992), and Norman H Reid, *Ever to Excel: an illustrated history of the University of St Andrews* (2011).

[16] Donald G Southgate, *University Education in Dundee: a centenary history,* (1982) and Michael Shafe, *University Education in Dundee 1881-1981: a pictorial history* (1982), respectively.

[17] Principally the Procurators (Scotland) Act 1865, Law Agents (Scotland) Act 1873, and Acts of Sederunt thereunder, and the Universities (Scotland) Acts 1858 and 1889 and Ordinances thereunder.

[18] Conventionally, Parliament is said to have a (near) monopoly of legislative power, exercised through Acts of Parliament, but in a "parent Act", it may delegate some of that power to others, typically to the Government, which typically exercises it in "statutory instruments" . However, there may be delegation to the courts, typically exercised in "Acts of Sederunt", and to other bodies. An unusual type in the 19th century, figuring largely below, was to "executive Commissions", exercised in "Ordinances".

CHAPTER 1

THE SETTING:

19th-CENTURY REFORMS TO THE LEGAL PROFESSION AND THE UNIVERSITIES

The State of the legal profession: in general

Before the mid-19th century, with little exaggeration, one could say that there was no legal profession[1]. Instead, there had emerged over the centuries what appears as an anarchic array of groups of practitioners, variously named, at various times, "notaries", "procurators", "forspeakers" (and "forespeakers"), "prolocutors" (and "prelocutors"), "attorneys", "writers", "agents", "advocates", and "solicitors" (and "solicitors-at-law"), not to mention "men of law", and even simply "doers"[2].

This list does in fact somewhat exaggerate the diversity, for some of the terms used are actually near synonyms, and in any case, the groups were not wholly discrete[3]. Nevertheless, it remains that, in the mid-19th century, there was a considerable diversity of such groups, not only functionally, but also geographically (and socially) differentiated, commonly each with its own monopolies, institutions and educational requirements, subject only to the ultimate jurisdiction of the courts[4].

The oldest group (and the one of lowest social status), "notaries public", had a monopoly of certain notarial functions, that is, broadly, officially authenticating or executing documents with legal effect, possibly on oath, and with a public written record (which was of particular importance in conveyancing and burgh affairs, for instance)[5]. They did not create any professional organisation, but became subject to national control and, though practice and standards varied over time, in essence, admission was effected by the judges, and came to require apprenticeship and examination, as prescribed in sundry legislation[6]. No law degree was required, if only because until 1862, there were no law degrees to be had (save honorary doctorates of law - LLDs), and for some years thereafter, such degrees were only available in Edinburgh University (as discussed below). Nor was attendance at non-graduating law classes (which predated degrees, as also discussed below), if only because such classes were held only in Aberdeen, Edinburgh and Glasgow Universities, and were thus not readily available to those elsewhere wishing to become notaries.

The title "procurator" (for which "forspeaker", "forespeaker", "prolocutor" and "prelocutor" were probably near synonyms, and "attorney" closely related), however, was commonly applied to those appearing in the "inferior courts" such as the Sheriff Court and Burgh Court (though, notoriously, in Aberdeen, they called – and call – themselves "advocates"[7], and in Dundee, at least for a time, they may have called themselves "writers"). "Procurators" became generally organised into self-governing local bodies, commonly called Faculties or Societies (of which, in the mid-19th century, there were some 30[8]), probably with an effective monopoly of representation in their local "inferior courts", and control of their own admission requirements (though Sheriffs, and judges of other inferior courts, actually admitted applicants). These requirements also probably involved an apprenticeship, though not necessarily examinations, and might be of varying standards. As with notaries, and for the same reason, neither a law degree nor, probably, attendance at law classes were required[9].

"Writer", "(law) agent", "man of law", and even "doer", however, were used at different times as generic titles for practitioners, however qualified (or unqualified), though with the implication (save perhaps in Dundee) that they did not appear in court, but only in "chamber practices", undertaking conveyancing, writing wills, carrying out executries, and the like. "Solicitor", though known from the sixteenth century (primarily as a term of disparagement for those soliciting clients in the courts), became general only later.

Three unusual Faculties or Societies, accorded higher social status, require mention. They are admittedly of great importance, but the literature on them unfortunately tends to crowd out consideration of all others. The Faculty of Advocates[10] (collectively called "the Bar", and accorded the highest status) comprised, and comprises, those procurators in the "superior" civil and criminal courts, that is, the Court of Session and the High Court of Justiciary, respectively (both considered part of the "College of Justice"[11]). They acquired the monopoly of representation in those Courts which defined, and still defines, them, and until recently, in practice, they provided the pool from which judges and sheriffs were exclusively drawn. They also acquired self-governance, with their own admission requirements, which did not include an apprenticeship, however, though did involve examination requirements, some surprising to modern eyes, and placed a high premium upon a broad university Arts education[12]. The Society of Solicitors in the Supreme Courts[13] (SSC) comprised practitioners who had acquired a near-monopoly of acting as intermediaries between clients and members of the Faculty of Advocates, when advocates ceased to deal directly with the public, and thus had some claim to be part of the "College of Justice". They, too, achieved self-governance, with their own admission requirements. The Society of Writers to the Signet[14] (WS) commenced as a group of medieval civil servants who were clerks to the central courts, thereby acquiring a monopoly over certain stages of Court of Session litigation, and forging a symbiotic relationship with the Faculty of Advocates as part of the "College of Justice". Increasingly, however, they undertook private work for clients, and they, again, achieved self-governance, with their own admission requirements. For the same reason as with notaries and ordinary procurators, none of these unusual Faculties or Societies required a law degree for admission, though they might require attendance at university law classes (readily available to them, since all were based in Edinburgh).

The radical, even revolutionary, changes in the mid- to late-19th century, largely merged all these diverse groups of practitioners into a single profession, with a single set of educational requirements.

For most purposes, this unification started with the Procurators (Scotland) Act 1865[15]. The original Bill ambitiously sought functional and geographical (though not necessarily social) unification by complete amalgamation of all "Procurator[s], Solicitor[s], Writer[s], Conveyancer[s], or Law Agent[s], or any other designation implying [that a person] is qualified or entitled to act as such ..." into a single status to be termed "Procurator"[16]. It also made "acting as, or assuming" a listed "Name or Title", in effect, an offence, though the penalty was expressed as a "forfeit". Notaries public and advocates were not included, though.

However, during its passage through Parliament, for unclear reasons (as the Bill passed all its stages on the nod[17]), this ambition was diluted[18] to simple geographical unification of only "procurators", with a monopoly of "inferior court" work only within the county[19] in which they were admitted[20]. (Also, though a prohibition upon use of the title by the unqualified remained, the "forfeit" for so doing was dropped). Nevertheless, "procurator" became the first country-wide professional legal qualification with, at first sight, unified admission arrangements.

These arrangements were convoluted, requiring of all applicants a four year apprenticeship (or three for Arts graduates of any United Kingdom university, and some others), and examinations in both general knowledge and law[21]. The various Faculties and Societies of procurators, if incorporated, and subject to the Sheriff's approval, were required to impose preliminary examinations in general knowledge for entrance to the apprenticeship, and might also impose interim examinations in law at the end of its second, third and fourth years[22].

Actual admission as a "procurator" remained for the Sheriff, but required passing new final ("Entrance") general knowledge and law examinations first. The syllabuses and examination arrangements for these examinations were delegated (subject to approval, under a complicated procedure, of both sheriffs and judges) to a new General Council of Procurators set up by the Act, and representing the incorporated Faculties and Societies[23]. (The Act also rendered it easy for unincorporated Faculties and Societies to incorporate, and thereby, among other things, participate in the General Council[24]). The new national law syllabus encompassed a "procurators' triad" [25] of subjects, comprising[26] the simple and comprehensive (but not further defined) list of "Scots Law (including Criminal Law and Evidence)", "Conveyancing" and "Forms of Process" (i.e. evidence and procedure).

Neither the Faculties and Societies, nor the General Council, were required to offer classes for the examinations, but admission now also required that all applicants had attended "at least the classes of Scots Law and Conveyancing, in a Scotch [sic] University" before taking the final law examination[27]. No requirement for a law degree was imposed although, as noted above and discussed further below, the LLB had been instituted in Edinburgh in 1862. But this attendance requirement clearly seemed to create a novel and onerous obligation upon those outside the three cities in which universities offered such classes, such as those in Dundee.

However, even this merely geographical unification was considerably circumscribed. Firstly, the Act simply exempted WS and SSC applicants[28], and holders of the new LLB, from its final examination requirements[29]. Secondly, it declared that the "Rights and Privileges" of those two societies, and of all other already-incorporated Faculties and Societies[30], should not be "limit[ed] or prejudice[d]", thereby preserving both their admission requirements and their monopolies[31]. They might replace their admission requirements with those under the Act, but none appears to have done so. Thus, rather than one single set of admission requirements for all "procurators", there remained several[32].

One consequence of this was of present importance. Because the Faculty of Procurators and Solicitors in Dundee was already incorporated, the preservation of its "Rights and Privileges" meant that the university class attendance requirement did not apply to its admissions. In consequence, the legislation had no significance for law teaching there (though, as we shall see, the odd and complicated subsequent history of the obligation did)[33].

Unsurprisingly, in 1869 a Royal Commission[34] found the Act unsatisfactory, and recommended reform which emerged in further legislation a few years later. But before that further legislation was enacted, some functional unification was achieved by a side-wind. The country-wide professional legal qualification created by the 1865 Act, and associated monopolies, related only to court work.

Thus, exclusively "chamber practices" were unaffected, and could continue to exist outside any Faculty or Society, as long as they did not call themselves "procurators" or the like. However, the Stamp Act 1870[35] provided that anyone who "draws or prepares any instrument relating to ... heritable or personal [*sic*] estate" (subject to certain exceptions, including "wills or other testamentary instruments"), and does so "either directly or indirectly, for, or in expectation of fee, gain or reward", in effect committed an offence (though again the penalty was expressed as a "forfeit"), unless he was "... a notary public, writer to the signet, agent, [or] procurator..."[36].

Thus, it remained perfectly lawful to do one's own conveyancing, or another's gratuitously (subject to a certain ambiguity about "agent", a term coming into fashion, as we shall shortly see). But to do so by way of business now required joining one of the formally controlled practitioners' associations; what is often termed the lawyers' "conveyancing monopoly" was thereby created (though no "testamentary monopoly" was); and something approaching more closely to the functional unification intended by the original 1865 Bill was achieved. (Indeed, the "conveyancing monopoly" was formalised when the provision was re-enacted in the Solicitors (Scotland) Act 1933[37], which made "solicitor" the national professional legal qualification).

But functional (and social) unification remained incomplete, for not only could professional will-writing continue unregulated, but also the process of unification still did not include notaries public or advocates.

The first attempt to enact legislation at least partly effecting the 1869 Royal Commission recommendation, noted above, seems to have been a

Courts of Law (Scotland) Agents Bill, introduced in 1872[38]. Though never enacted, its provisions offer insights into the unification process (and the considerable lobbying which accompanied it).

In its original form, it did not seek to repeal the 1865 Act, but to replace the term "procurator" with "law agent" and to allow such "law agent", if "enrolled" as a member of a Faculty or Society, to practise, not just in his county, but in any inferior court in Scotland[39]. More significantly still, any enrolled law agent would have been able to apply to be admitted as a notary public without further educational requirement. Thus, being a "law agent" would have been a pre-condition of being a notary, in effect unifying the two groups of practitioners (though notarial functions which a law agent, *tout court*, could not undertake, would remain)[40].

The Bill would also have extended the apprenticeship to five years (though still reduced to three for Arts, but now also Scottish LLB, graduates, and others), and amended admission arrangements. The power to admit would be transferred from Sheriffs to the Court of Session; the General Council might still operate a preliminary general knowledge examination and interim law examinations; but the final examination (from which advocates and LLB graduates were, however, exempt) would now be operated by a Board of Examiners, representing the WS and SSC Societies, the Royal Faculty of Procurators of Glasgow, the General Council of Procurators, and the Court itself (whose representative would be Chair), with the power (subject to the approval of the Court) to make rules as to curricula and examinations[41]. (No requirement to attend university classes was mentioned, but that does not indicate any intention to drop it, since it would be expected in an Act of Sederunt[42] under the Act). Yet the Bill would still have partly exempted the WS and SSC Societies and incorporated Faculties and Societies[43].

Thus, further geographical and, more importantly, functional, unification was sought, though the Bill did not fulfil the 1869 Royal Commission's recommendation. It was heavily amended in Parliament[44]. In particular, the right of "law agents" to practise was further extended to include the Court of Session[45]; the right to apply to be a notary public preserved[46]; and the exemptions in favour of the WS and SSC Societies fully restored[47]. But the Bill was withdrawn, seemingly on the understanding that a new one would be presented in the following Session, after better consultation[48].

That new Bill was introduced, and became the Law Agents (Scotland) Act 1873[49]. Its contents were similar to those of the 1872 Bill (though completely redrafted, going further, and actually repealing the 1865 Act). "Procurator" was again replaced by "law agent", but if "enrolled" as a practitioner in any Sheriff Court, such "law agent" might now practise "in any court of law in Scotland", thus including the Court of Session, and do so without being a member of any Faculty or Society[50].

It also included the right of an "enrolled law agent" to apply to be a notary public but, interestingly, on the one hand, it added a one-year transitional provision for any notary public of seven years standing, and "engaged in actual practice as a Law Agent or Conveyancer", to be admitted as an enrolled law agent, at the Court's discretion while, on the other, it dropped the precondition for a notary public of being a law agent[51].

It was also similar to the 1872 Bill in extending the apprenticeship to five years, but further centralised admission in the Court of Session by dispensing with any Board of Examiners[52]. Thus, the Court itself was given powers to "examine and inquire, by such ways and means as they [sic] shall think proper, touching the ... fitness and capacity of" anyone petitioning to become a law agent[53]. These powers were exercised in Acts of Sederunt, which continued examinations in both general knowledge and law covering the (now "law agents'") "triad" [54]. Also, as part of the odd and complicated history of that obligation, the requirement to attend university classes was enhanced to include a requirement to also "take part in"[55] the university examinations[56]. This enhanced obligation still applied to all applicants for admission outside the three cities with university law teaching, but as the SSC, WS and incorporated Faculty and Society exemptions were not re-enacted, this now included those in

Dundee with (unlike the 1865 Act) obvious repercussions for law teaching there (discussed in Chapter 2).

But by the same token, the Act seemingly fulfilled the 1869 Royal Commission's recommendation, entirely removing the Faculties' and Societies' local monopolies, and partly including notaries public, thereby achieving a high level of functional and geographical (and social) unification of the legal profession. It was, however, still an incomplete one, for it failed to include advocates, and by creative interpretation of the Act, the judges backtracked and continued to treat the WS Society as partly exempt[57].

That was not the end of late 19th century legislation on the matter. In 1886, an Act of Sederunt under the 1873 Act amending the original Act of Sederunt under that Act, unexpectedly (and as part of the odd and complicated history of that obligation) completely dropped the university attendance requirement, which had obvious significance for law teaching in Dundee[58]. This was seemingly because it was deemed *ultra vires* (that is, beyond the powers delegated by the parent Act) and therefore void[59]. A Bill to Amend the Law Agents Act 1873[60], introduced in 1887, once again, part of the odd and complicated history of that obligation, sought to restore the requirement, albeit in a modified form to allow approved non-university classes, which would have had equally obvious significance for law teaching in Dundee. However, it was a Private Member's Bill and appears to have fallen[61].

In 1891, the "forfeit" provisions for impersonating a law agent, found in the 1865 Act but omitted from the 1872 Bill and 1873 Act, were finally restored in the Law Agents and Notaries Public (Scotland) Act of that year, buttressing the law agents' monopoly[62]. This Act made it an offence, prosecutable by a procurator-fiscal, an incorporated Faculty or Society, or an individual law agent or notary public, for an unqualified person to "wilfully and falsely pretend to be" a law agent or notary public, or to act as one[63].

As yet a further part of the odd and complicated history of the obligation, it also gave the power to restore the university attendance requirement in something like the modified form sought by the 1887 Bill (though it remained unused until well into the 20th century, as discussed below).

Finally, in 1896, the provision which made being a law agent a precondition of being a notary public (dropped from the 1872 Bill and omitted from the 1873 Act) was restored in the Law Agents (Scotland) Act Amendment Act of that year[64], which also extended the transitional power in the 1873 Act by allowing the court to admit as law agents existing notaries public of seven years standing, without further educational requirement[65]. Thereby, law agents finally, in effect, absorbed notaries public (though notarial functions which a law agent, *tout court*, could not undertake, continued[66]).

Thus, after a halting progress over a generation, by the end of the 19th century, the diversity of particularistic, if non-discrete, groups of practitioners, differentiated functionally, geographically and socially, which included notaries, some 30 geographically defined varieties of procurator (each controlling its own admission requirements and exercising a local monopoly), and other law agents and writers undertaking conveyancing, had been substantially unified into a single legal profession, with centralised admission requirements and a national monopoly, whose members might be members of a local Faculty or Society, but need not be.

Nevertheless, unification remained incomplete. Firstly, the Faculty of Advocates remained a functionally (and socially) differentiated exception, retaining control over its admission requirements, and exercising its own monopoly. Secondly, professional will-writing remained an uncontrolled activity. And thirdly, late-19th century complaints about "unqualified" or "unlicensed" practitioners persisted, though it is not always clear who is being described. It might be "chamber practitioners" exclusively concerned with will-writing and other uncontrolled activities, or it might be bank agents and the like undertaking legal work at the margins of the law, though in either case subject to no admission requirements, and exercising no monopoly[67].

Four other matters related to the process of unification require further attention. Two were alluded to above, that is, the odd and complicated history of the obligation to attend law classes, and the Faculty of Advocates' avoidance of the process of unification. Two others were not, that is, the creation of Incorporated Society of Law Agents, and the position of women.

The history of the obligation to attend law classes had considerable importance for law teaching in Dundee. It is discussed fully in Chapters 2 and 3, but requires brief rehearsal here, and is best seen in seven stages. In the first, it was imposed (with an exemption applying to Dundee and some other places) by an Act of Sederunt under the 1865 Act, and in the second, was enhanced by a requirement to take examinations (with no Dundee exemption) in an Act of Sederunt under the 1873 Act. But in 1886, in the third stage, the obligation was entirely removed by Act of Sederunt under the same Act. In the fourth stage, in 1887, a Bill seeking to re-impose a version of it was made, but fell. In the fifth stage, in 1891, the Law Agents and Notaries Public Act (Scotland)[68] clearly gave a power to impose a modified form of it by Act of Sederunt. Yet the Act of Sederunt under that Act in 1893 (replacing the 1873 one, as amended in 1886), did not include it[69]. Indeed, to stray into the 20th century, no such obligation was imposed until 1926[70], the sixth stage, and that was dropped in 1938, the seventh[71].

The Faculty of Advocates avoided the process of unification. In itself, in contrast, this is a fact of limited interest for law teaching in Dundee[72]. But, long regarding itself as an elite, intellectually and otherwise, this continued social, as much as functional (or geographic), differentiation is a tribute to its political power. However, it did not exclude itself from reform. During the mid- to late-19th century, it strengthened its equivalent of the procurators' and law agents' general knowledge examination, that is, its "general scholarship" requirement (though exempting MA graduates), and imposed increasingly exiguous

17

law examination requirements[73]. Initially, only Civil Law[74] and Scots Law had been required, but later, Private International Law (i.e. the law on disputes with a foreign element between individuals) was added, and by the end of the century, also Jurisprudence (i.e. legal theory), Public International Law (international law as commonly understood), Constitutional Law & History, Medical Jurisprudence (now usually called Forensic Medicine) and Conveyancing (Procedure – equivalent to the law agents' "Forms of Process" being included in Scots Law[75]). In addition, from 1866 (almost simultaneously with the 1865 Act requirement upon procurators), attendance at the equivalent university law classes became compulsory and, from 1874, LLB graduates (though not BL graduates, discussed below) were exempted from all subjects (though a law degree, as such, remained unnecessary). Also, an apprenticeship was still not required, though intrants commonly spent a year in a legal office, and at the end of the century, the practice grew up of "devilling", that is, learning the job by assisting a practising advocate, unpaid[76].

The creation by Royal Charter of the Incorporated Society of Law Agents in Scotland, in 1883[77], open to all law agents and, later, to notaries public, was clearly a result of unification. Although (unlike the General Council of Procurators under the 1865 Act) it had no role in admission to the legal profession, it was intended as a representative body, and can be seen as a forerunner of the Law Society of Scotland[78].

Finally, as to the position of women, we can note that, while the 19th century changes in the profession were revolutionary, the revolution did not reach women, for no woman became a lawyer in that century. The first to qualify as a law agent, Madge Easton Anderson, did not do so until 1920, and the first as an advocate, Margaret Henderson Kidd, not until 1922. Nor was their path to qualification straightforward. Detail is provided in the Appendix to this Chapter.

The State of the legal profession: in Dundee

How the mid- to late-19th century revolution in the legal profession played out in Dundee is the substance of the next Chapter. But it is useful to look here at the arrangements in Dundee upon which it was played out[79].

There was an unincorporated Society or Faculty called the Society of Writers in Dundee from the late 18th century, among other things collecting funds for widows and orphans (a typical activity for such bodies), with its first public event a dinner in 1817. In 1819, by Royal Charter, it became incorporated, inserting that word into its title[80]. The petitioners for the charter were the Town Clerk (William Small), Clerk to the Dean of Guild Court and Depute Clerk of the Peace (Alexander Christie), and seventeen "writers in Dundee and Procurators of the Baillie Court and Dean of Guild Court"[81] (but not, seemingly, of the Sheriff Court, possibly because it then normally sat only in Forfar, the county town[82]).

By that time, the Society had some 30 members, and a substantial library of over 200 books including titles on English and Civil Law, as well as Scots Law. As an incorporated Society, it was one of the bodies exempted from the admissions requirements of the Procurators (Scotland) 1865 and, under powers in that Act, changed its name to the still-used title of Faculty of Procurators and Solicitors in Dundee (FPSD)[83]. By 1883 it had 55 members, the usual committee structure, and was open to law agents practising in the Sheriff Court of Forfarshire, with entry money of £10 and annual subscription of £1/5/-.[84]

In the 1860s, it became midwife to the first law classes in Dundee, as discussed, along with its admission requirements, in the next Chapter.

The State of the universities: in general

However flourishing they might once have been, and how open to the lad o'pairts they might remain, by the mid-19th century all the universities were in considerable need of reform, as two Royal Commissions revealed[85]. They were essentially closed corporations of professors, each with a monopoly on his subject, and paid largely from class fees. These professors taught a wide range of subjects, but to a superficial level, almost entirely by professorial lecture to large classes of remarkably young students. Moreover, they were geared principally to producing ministers for the Church of Scotland, who did not actually need to graduate[86].

All, moreover, had been founded with the ability to teach law, but over the centuries had ceased to do so systematically, or possibly at all. Thus, students seeking university law tuition had to go abroad (as they had before the universities had been founded), until new chairs were created in Edinburgh, Glasgow and Aberdeen (but not St Andrews) in the 18th and 19th centuries[87]. Even then, the traditional method of rote-learning by lectures (albeit sometimes punctuated by oral "examinations" and "exercises"), commonly in Latin[88], and given by professors sometimes of indifferent ability and considerable unreliability, remained[89]; few students attended; numbers of staff were tiny[90]; and there were no law degrees, save honorary ones.

Just as radical, even revolutionary, change took place in the legal profession in the mid- to late-19th century, so too, it did such change take place in the universities. In relation to universities as a whole, it was effected largely by the Universities (Scotland) Acts 1858[91] and 1889[92] (prompted, respectively, by the two Royal Commissions referred to above[93]), and Ordinances thereunder[94]. These Acts and Ordinances transformed university governance, finance, and curricula (not least, by permitting women to graduate[95], and amalgamating King's College and Marischal College into Aberdeen University).

In particular, with only minor differences between universities, while maintaining the traditional Senates (comprising Principal and Professors, and intended to "superintend and regulate" teaching and discipline, and "administer" property and revenues), the 1858 Act introduced both University Courts and General Councils. The former, chaired by a student-elected Rector and representing the various university interests, were to "control and review" Senates and perform a long list of specific functions. The latter, comprising all former students, whether they had graduated or not[96], had powers to require University Courts to "take into consideration" their questions about the functioning of the university, and to receive representations about such matters.

Again with only minor differences between universities, the 1889 Act retained the Senates' responsibility for teaching and discipline, but transferred their responsibility for property and revenue to expanded Courts, and enhanced the General Councils' powers to meet and to investigate[97].

In relation to law teaching, revolution occurred through the introduction of a law degree[98]. As noted above, a revival had started in the 18th century, but without benefit of degrees. The first new degree, the LLB, was introduced by Ordinance in 1862[99] (quite shortly after the 1858 reforms), but initially only in Edinburgh, the other universities having insufficient staff (a telling limitation). Glasgow introduced it a decade later, but no other university did so in this form. An MA was a prerequisite, and the degree itself required passes in six law subjects[100], over three years and (for unclear reasons[101], though thereby allowing students to work in legal offices concurrently) it was part-time.

It largely reflected the wishes of the Faculty of Advocates (the MA prerequisite expressing its traditional desire for a broad liberal education among its members) and, as noted above, from 1866, the Faculty required attendance at relevant university classes, and from 1874 allowed LLB graduates exemption from its law examinations (though not requiring a degree). However, the LLB was not a success as, despite the Faculty of Advocates' influence, few students took it[102].

Probably in consequence of this, in 1874, by amendment of the Ordinance[103], Edinburgh and Glasgow (with some variations between them) also introduced another new degree, the BL[104]. This substituted one or two year's study of four Arts subjects for the MA pre-requisite, required only four law subjects[105] over two years, but was also part-time. It fulfilled neither the Faculty of Advocate's requirements, nor the law agents', yet (despite chronic dismissiveness in the literature), was marginally more popular than the LLB[106].

Revolution continued, in that both BL and LLB were recast in 1893[107] (shortly after the 1889 university reforms), in a form that was to last, albeit with some modification, until the 1960s.

The recast BL had the prerequisite of a year's study of only three Arts subjects and more choice, but still required four law subjects over two years, and remained part-time[108]. Like its predecessor, it was at least as popular as the LLB[109], and was adopted in Aberdeen in 1895 and St Andrews in 1939 (as discussed in Chapter 4).

The recast LLB continued the MA prerequisite but, while also giving more choice overall, required two more law subjects than before, though still over three years, and also remaining part-time[110]. As noted, it was no more popular than its predecessor[111], but was adopted in Aberdeen in 1908 and (finally, and after further amendment) St Andrews in 1961 (as discussed in Chapter 5).

But the paucity of graduating students should be emphasised. Over the 19th and first half of the 20th centuries, the great majority of law students were non-graduating[112].

Also, the revolution in the legal profession may not have reached women in the 19th century, but that in universities did, insofar as, from 1892, they might be allowed to graduate, as noted above. However, the first women law students, Eveline MacLaren and Josephine Gordon Stuart, were only recorded in 1906. Detail is again provided in the Appendix to the Chapter.

The State of the universities: in Dundee

A surprisingly infrequently asked question is why there was not a university institution in Dundee before the late 19th century. St Andrews

(1411), Glasgow (1451), Aberdeen (twice, King's College in 1495 and Marischal College in 1593, merged in 1860) and Edinburgh (1583) had all managed to acquire one centuries earlier, and there was even an attempt in Fraserburgh (1592), not to mention the somewhat more successful one in Glasgow, which produced Anderson's Institution/University/College (1796: part of Strathclyde University from 1964).

The existence of St Andrews University, and lack of a bishop[113], adequately explain the absence before the Reformation. But in the 16th century Dundee was "still the second wealthiest town in Scotland"[114], so thereafter, it is more difficult to explain. Bishops became unnecessary, as the creation of "the Tounis College" in Edinburgh, Marischal College in Aberdeen and "the Andersonian" in Glasgow indicate, and the propinquity of another University was a surmountable barrier, as the latter two also demonstrate. In any event, though there were other initiatives in "tertiary education" in Dundee[115], no attempt to found a university institution before the mid-19th century appears recorded. And when it was attempted, it was against the background of the movement in England and Wales for "civic universities", and the decay of St Andrews, seemingly without any reference to the "Andersonian" (arguably already a "civic university"), nor to the further, contemporaneous, attempt to create another in the guise of St Mungo's College, also in Glasgow[116].

What was this movement for "civic universities"? In England and Wales, there were only two universities at the beginning of the 19th century, both in quiet midland towns, and both chiefly concerned with producing Church of England clergy. Some new establishments emerged in the 1820s and 1830s, all but one, however, in the Oxbridge image, and commonly far from the major industrial cities which had grown up[117].

These cities therefore started setting up non-denominational colleges providing useful, especially scientific, tertiary education. Such colleges later blossomed into the "civic universities" such as Birmingham, Bristol, Leeds, Liverpool, Newcastle and Sheffield. The precedent for Dundee was obvious. However, there were important distinctions between the English and Scottish situations. Scotland did not have an underprovision of universities, and its universities were already in, or near, major industrial cities.

At the same time, St Andrews University was in serious decay. It had two Colleges, which were separate corporate bodies, each with their own property and revenue. These were United College (formed in 1747 from the medieval, separately-founded, St Leonard's and St Salvator's Colleges), effectively coincident with the Arts Faculty, and St Mary's College (founded in 1538 out of a medieval "Pedagogy"), effectively coincident with the Divinity Faculty. Yet its total student numbers were down to 130 by 1876 (out of almost 5,000 in Scotland as a whole, thus less than 3%), and it had seriously reduced revenue from rents and teinds[118]. But it did have degree-awarding powers and the curious prestige endowed by age, while Dundee had the potential students and the money. Mutual assistance would seem obvious[119].

Though the idea may have been floating sound for some time, formal discussions on a "civic university" type of college in Dundee appear to have first occurred in the early 1870s[120], but then fell foul of difficulties over the nature of its relationship with St Andrews University. Dundee sought a college teaching a full range of subjects; St Andrews University jealously guarded its Arts teaching[121]. And then industrial depression reduced the likelihood of Dundee money, so nothing eventuated.

The 1878 Royal Commission, the second of the two mentioned above[122] nevertheless considered the matter, and adumbrated four suggestions: (i) move St Andrews University to Dundee; (ii) strengthen St Andrews University and have Dundee students commute; (iii) found a college in Dundee teaching a full range of subjects (possibly including Law), but "affiliated" to St Andrews University; and (iv) found a college in Dundee teaching only Science and Medicine, with Arts students commuting to St Andrews[123].

The last-mentioned was recommended, but members of the Baxter family[124] intervened. In 1880, John Boyd Baxter, long involved in attempts to set up a college (and at 80, an old man in a hurry), and Mary Ann Baxter, possibly long interested in such an enterprise (and almost 80), demanded an independent college, albeit one which might later "affiliate" to another institution, teaching a full range of subjects, and which also, notably (and in step with the new English foundations), should not discriminate on grounds of sex or religious opinion. This was substantially the Royal Commission's third option, though expressed by John Boyd Baxter as founding "a College similar, or nearly similar, to Owens College, Manchester"[125] (arguably the leading 'civic university'). The Baxters carried their demand through the power of the purse. Their proposal was costed at £125,000, and John Boyd Baxter ultimately put up £20,000, and Mary Ann Baxter, £130,000. It was effected by a Deed of Endowment and Trust (possibly drafted by Thomas Thornton[126]), dated 30 & 31 December 1881, containing its governmental arrangements[127].

These arrangements were later, not inaccurately but perhaps slightly, described as resembling those of a joint-stock company[128]. The "Supreme Governing Body" (or "Governors") included, *ex officio*, local magnates, such as the Lord Lieutenant, local MPs, the Sheriff (in modern parlance, "Sheriff-Principal") of Forfarshire and the Dean of Guild, together with individual and corporate donors and subscribers of money (the shareholders?)[129]. The "Managing Body", however, was the College Council, which comprised the Provost of Dundee, the Dundee MPs, the Sheriffs-Substitute (in modern parlance "Sheriff") of Forfarshire, and representatives of the Governors, of the Principal and Professors, and of others (the directors?)[130]. This College Council appointed the Principal, Professors and Lecturers, and was specifically given the power to "affiliate or unite" the College with any other educational institution. There was, further, an Education Board to "organise and direct the education [i.e. teaching policy] of the College", and which might make by-laws (a committee of the directors?)[131].

Such arrangements, so obviously different from those under the Universities (Scotland) Act 1858 which governed the universities (discussed above) were strongly insisted upon by the Baxters, indeed becoming a great source of contention during the setting up of the college, when it appeared to them that they were losing control of the enterprise[132]. Unsurprisingly, in the light of John Boyd Baxter's words, they were based on the experience of Owens College, Manchester[133].

The land between Small's Wynd and Park Place (still core of the campus, and now occupied by the Tower Building) was bought[134], and on 5 October 1883, UCD was inaugurated, some eighteen months after the Deed of Endowment and Trust but sadly, just after John Boyd Baxter, and shortly before Mary Ann Baxter, died[135]. The new College had no degree-awarding powers, relying upon "external" degrees from London University (incidentally of little use for Scots Law), but did have an exceptional group of professors, and was strong in science teaching, especially Chemistry. However, higher expenditure than expected, lack of successor philanthropists to the Baxters, and fewer students than hoped for, gave it a lasting debt burden. Further, the insistence upon teaching Arts, the governmental arrangements and the nature of the "affiliation" to St Andrews University (discussed below), all caused continuing difficulties.

Negotiations on a connection between UCD and St Andrews University commenced in the 1880s, but dragged on acrimoniously, while a series of Bills designed to effect the 1878 Royal Commission recommendations were introduced and failed, finally culminating, however, in the Universities (Scotland) Act 1889. This, as noted above, significantly altered university governance generally. But it also contained both general provisions for "affiliating new colleges" to universities and, separately, a specific provision to "affiliate the University College, Dundee to, and make it form part of, the University of St Andrews, with the consent of the University Court[136]."

Against this backdrop, the negotiations produced an Agreement[137], drafted by Thomas Thornton (his St Andrews LLD no doubt his reward). It was effected in 1890 by purported delegated legislation in the form of an "Order" (rather than an Ordinance, which involved elaborate procedural requirements) of the 1889 Commissioners intended (carefully reproducing the precise terms of the Act) to "affiliate … University College, Dundee to, and make it form part of, … University of St Andrews", and declaring the resulting "Union" to be "permanent and dissoluble only by an Act of Parliament"[138].

Thomas Thornton's experience (discussed in the next Chapter) should have produced a watertight document. But it did not resolve the inherent difficulty of the University as a whole operating under the 1858 Act constitution (as amended by the 1889 Act), while UCD retained its own 1883 constitution under the Deed. In particular, the College Council thereby kept control over UCD finances and, in general, decision-making was split not only between University Court and Senate (as the legislation intended), but also between both of them and the College Council (as the Agreement presumably intended). This created, as it was later put[139], an *imperium in imperio* – a "state within a state".

Turf wars soon broke out, especially in relation to Medicine, and in a series of events too complicated to recount fully here[140], University authorities in St Andrews questioned the validity of the affiliating "Order", and pursued the matter through the Courts for some years, ultimately successfully in 1895[141], thereby generating institutional chaos[142]. These University authorities' change of heart from acceptance to rejection of the "Union" was greatly re-inforced by a couple of uncovenanted events. One was the election as Rector in 1893 of the Marquess of Bute[143], who disliked UCD. Though one of the 1889 Commissioners, and thus party to the "Order" containing the Agreement (albeit dissenting on this issue from their General Report published a few days after the "Order"[144]) he saw no conflict of interest in then seeking to nullify it. He was also immensely rich and very generous towards the rest of St Andrews. The other was the unexpected receipt by the University of the "Berry Bequest" of £100,000 (seemingly paid in instalments in the 1890s) which, together with Bute's contributions, removed the University's financial frailty[145].

Nevertheless, by further delegated legislation, this time in the form of an Ordinance (again challenged in the courts, though unsuccessfully[146]), the relationship was restored in 1897 on essentially the original conditions[147], and remained thus until UCD (by then renamed Queen's College Dundee) regained its independence as the University of Dundee in 1967.

Numerous people were involved in setting up UCD, but two stand out: John Boyd Baxter and Mary Ann Baxter. They were members of a family which became enormously rich through the establishment, by William Baxter of Balgavies (1764-1854), of Baxter Brothers & Co., which introduced power looms to linen manufacture, and whose Dens Works[148] became the biggest linen works in the world. The family practised a good deal of philanthropy. Which of the two Baxters was the prime mover in founding UCD is unclear, so they are considered alphabetically.

John Boyd Baxter LLD (1796-1882)[149] saw Dundee grow from a town of moderate size to an industrial conurbation. He lived latterly at Craigtay, a large house in the Broughty Ferry Road (now the Craigtay Hotel). His portrait by Daniel Macnee, painted in 1881, shortly before he died, is owned by Dundee Art Galleries & Museums.

He was a Dundonian, the son of W W Baxter, "one of the principal merchants of the town" and a distant cousin and friend of Mary Ann Baxter. He attended the Grammar School (one of forerunners of the present High School of Dundee), and probably served part of his apprenticeship as a procurator in Dundee, part in Edinburgh, since he attended classes "in Scotch law" at Edinburgh University in 1815-16 (which was unlikely to have been a requirement of the Dundee Society of Writers, and thereby perhaps a sign of ambition).

Returning to Dundee, he went into practice, presumably about 1816, with an uncle, John William Baxter (one of the signatories of the petition for incorporation of the Society of Writers in Dundee) and later on his own account, and by 1822 was seemingly a successful court practitioner. In the following year he was involved in the dispute between the then-corrupt Town Council and the Guildry, but was admitted as burgess "by privilege of his father".

In 1824, thus, surprisingly, only about 28 years of age, he was appointed a Procurator Fiscal for Forfarshire. The procurator-fiscal's role today is essentially similar (though much work is now delegated to the police). At that time fiscals did not need to be legally qualified, but might also be in private practice if they were (as Baxter was[150]), and were appointed by the Sheriff, and originally paid by fees (though, by the time he retired, by salary).

At this time, the Sheriff normally sat only in Forfar, the county town[151], but Baxter became the first Procurator Fiscal for the Dundee area, as its rapid expansion took place, with the Sheriff coming to sit in Dundee from time to time, in the "Guild Hall" (that is, the "Guildry Room" in the Town House[152]), the present Sheriff Court House only being commenced in 1833. He held office for 57 years, retiring in 1881, the oldest, and longest serving, in the country. After retiral, he was appointed an Honorary Sheriff (an office sometimes conferred upon prominent local practitioners, and sometimes involving some judicial work) by Sheriff Trayner (who also figures later in this history).

Obituaries display their usual uncritical praise, though there is other evidence of his repute. He was Preses (the title then used) of the Faculty of Procurators and Solicitors in Dundee continuously from 1867 till his death. (One obituary, describing him as Vice-Preses at the time of its incorporation in about 1821, presumably confuses him with his uncle). Though in his 70s, he was two or three times elected President of the General Council of Procurators under the Procurators (Scotland) Act 1865, was a member of the Royal Commission on the Scottish Law Courts, whose report generated the Law Agents (Scotland) Act 1873, and in 1874 was one of the first examiners appointed under that Act.

Obituaries also suggest numerous educational interests of long-standing, though their fruition was achieved only in his later years. He was Chairman of the company promoting, by private subscription, the Albert Institute (1865-67: the first phase of what is now The McManus: Dundees Art Gallery & Museum) which "embraced a free Library,

Museum, Picture Gallery and Lecture Room", and was donated to the Dundee Corporation in 1881.

Of more immediate interest, he may have been "the first to advocate the establishment of a College in Dundee" (though others credit Dean Stanley and Rev Dr Watson, who may have coined the word "affiliate" in relation to St Andrews University, the cause of so much woe, in the UCD context[153]). He had participated in the series of law lectures in 1867 (discussed in the next Chapter), but his efforts in the early 1870s were the first recorded move towards the founding of UCD, and were the probable reason for his receipt of an LLD from St Andrews University in 1874.

These moves were unsuccessful, but almost six years to the day after his 1874 plan was unveiled, at a meeting of the directors of the High School of Dundee, he produced the ultimately successful plan for a College (and promises of the necessary funds).

Presumably the £20,000 he donated was inherited wealth, since his father was a successful merchant, and he could not have generated it himself from being a Procurator Fiscal, or from private practice. Most unfortunately, he died two months before the College opened, having worked to within a month of his death.

A son predeceased him and, had that son survived, Baxter might not have donated the money to UCD. His widow inherited a life rent in his estate, though only surviving him by a few months, dying ten days after UCD was opened. He made numerous bequests, including a residuary power for his executors to make further donations to UCD, which they do not appear to have exercised.

Mary Ann Baxter (1801-84)[154] of Balgavies (near Forfar) and Ellengowan (the site now occupied by Ellengowan Drive, off the Broughty Ferry Road), also saw the enormous growth of Dundee but, as a Victorian woman had little opportunity to pursue any career and "lived a quiet, retired, life". Her portrait, by Edward Hughes, painted in 1883 shortly before she died, is owned by the University of Dundee, where it hangs.

As noted above, obituaries must always be viewed with suspicion, but they suggest she was "unostentatious [though] eminently hospitable ... [and with] a keen sense of humour". Light is thrown on her character by the assertion that "[t]he statesman whom she most admired was John Bright [the Radical Quaker MP who founded the Anti-Corn Law League], her favourite author was Walter Scott [a prominent Tory], and her chosen book and daily companion was the Bible". She was one of the many children of William Baxter of Balgavies (founder of the Baxter fortunes), and her brother David (later Sir David, Bart. of Kilmaron, near Cupar), was later the driving force in the firm. She briefly outlived all her siblings, inheriting a life rent of Balgavies.

As one of the Baxter dynasty, she was very wealthy, and she seems to have put most of her energy into charity. She was a staunch Congregationalist, and a founder member of the Panmure Street Congregational Church, but cheerfully supported non-denominational causes (though "whatever savoured of ecclesiasticism or priestism was distasteful to her"). The non-denominational character of the founding document of UCD is a clear example of this.

Christianity naturally informed her charity. Though in post-colonial days, the chief objects may appear less morally secure than once they did, she was not a "telescopic philanthropist" like Mrs Jellyby[155], for obituaries, corroborated by letters between her and John Boyd Baxter[156], speak of her "high intellectual gift, soundness of judgment and independence of action", and "the cheerfulness of her liberality and ... conscientiousness". She strongly supported missionary work, donating large sums to the London Missionary Society for the purchase of a steamer (named *"Ellengowan"*) for a mission in New Guinea (and for its replacement), and to establish a Papuan Institute for training teachers. She also donated large sums for missions in Africa, China and India.

At home, she supported mission buildings in the Hilltown, paid the debt for founding the YMCA, financed an "independent chapel", school and teacher at Letham (near Balgavies), and gave substantial sums to the congregational Theological Hall[157].

Apart from religious charities, with her then-surviving siblings she acquired the land which became Baxter Park, Dundee, subscribed to the Sailors' Home in Dock Street, Dundee (now converted into flats), to a Children's Ward in the Dundee Royal Infirmary, and to a Convalescent Hospital in Barnhill.

But by far the biggest single donation she ever made, £130,000, was as "the munificent founder" of UCD. When she became interested in this project is unclear, but an obituary refers to the scheme "occup[ying] her thoughts for a long time", so it just might be that she aroused John Boyd Baxter's interest, rather than the reverse.

Had she lived longer, she might have given even more but, infirm for some years and affected by the death of her sister (the other surviving sibling) two days before the opening of the College, she died just over a year after that event. She was buried in Roodyards Cemetery, opposite Ellengowan, and adjacent to John Boyd Baxter's Craigtay. Her estate amounted to some £300,000, with legacies to local institutions and individuals, including small bequests to servants. The residuary legatees were probably nephews and nieces, but perhaps surprisingly did not include UCD.

She remains the only woman to have founded a university institution in Scotland, and one of the few in the United Kingdom.

APPENDIX

THE FIRST WOMEN LAWYERS, LAW STUDENTS AND LEGAL ACADEMICS

Who was the first woman lawyer? Whatever the position before the mid-19th century, the central provision of the Procurators (Scotland) Act 1865 stipulated that "no person shall ... act or practise as a Procurator ... unless ...he shall be admitted ... pursuant to the Directions and Regulations of this Act"[158]. The central provision of the Law Agents (Scotland) Act 1873 similarly stipulated that "no person shall be admitted as a law agent ... except in accordance with this Act"[159]. Thus, it could be argued that, after 1865, women, being "persons"[160], could become procurators, and after 1873, law agents, provided they fulfilled the requirements of those Acts.

Nevertheless, there appears no record of any woman seeking to do so before the turn of the century. The first recorded was Margaret Hall who, in 1900, sought to enrol for the law agents' examinations. The Secretary of the Board of Examiners declined to accede, on the grounds of her gender. She petitioned the Court of Session to "authorise and direct" the Board to do so. In a brief judgment, the Inner House concluded that, although "person" in the 1873 Act was "no doubt, equally applicable, to male and female", nevertheless it was "ambiguous", and "inveterate usage" had confined it to "male persons"[161]. The opinion of the Whole Court, even briefer, unanimously upheld the Inner House. (There may have been further, unsuccessful, attempts by a Miss Cave in 1903, and possibly others[162]).

This judicial prohibition was only overturned a decade later, by the Sex Discrimination (Removal) Act 1919[163], and the first woman to become a law agent (indeed probably the first woman lawyer in the whole United Kingdom) was in fact Madge Easton Anderson, who achieved this goal in 1920 (thus nearly 50 years after the 1873 Act and nearly 60 after the 1865 Act)[164].

By this time, opposition to women law agents appears to have evaporated. Madge Anderson only had to take the Forms of Process examination because, unlike Margaret Hall, she had a law degree (incidentally being the first Glasgow woman law graduate). But a problem was that she had served half her apprenticeship before the 1919 Act, which was not retrospective. In the light of Hall's case, the Registrar of Law Agents had declined to accept its validity.

The Inner House, upholding the Lord Ordinary, concluded that, Madge Anderson having fulfilled all the Act's other requirements, the only question was whether she had complied with the requirement for an apprenticeship, and she had done so, because the indenture under which it had been served was "an effectual and valid contract"[165]. Sadly, it seems unknown what career she then had.

The first woman advocate was Margaret Henderson Kidd. Though originally set on a career in the diplomatic service, she was called to the Bar in 1923, thus also shortly after the 1919 Act, but without need for litigation. Her career is well-known and distinguished, as she appeared before the House of Lords (the first woman advocate to do so), became King's Counsel in 1948 (again the first woman), and Sheriff-Principal in 1960 (once more, the first woman), initially for Dumfries and Galloway, and later for Perth and Angus, as well as undertaking various good works[166].

But, as has been pointed out, these straws in the wind were not closely followed by a gale. Madge Anderson was followed by Elizabeth Barnett in Aberdeen in 1921[167] and Christian Bisset (later Mrs Tudhope) in Dundee in 1930[168], and others. But Margaret Kidd remained the only woman advocate for 25 years; there was no woman judge until 1996; no woman Solicitor-General for Scotland or Lord Advocate until 2001 and 2006, respectively; no woman President of the Law Society of Scotland until 2005; and there has still been no woman Dean of the Faculty of Advocates[169].

Who the first women university law students were, is a different question. Law classes started in the 18th century, and though women could graduate in law from 1892, the power in the relevant Ordinance was permissive and depended upon universities invoking it and, until the 1919 Act, inability to qualify legally must have been a powerful disincentive.

There might have been earlier non-graduating women university law students, but the first women law graduates, in Edinburgh, in 1909 (a decade before the Act) were Eveline MacLaren and Josephine Gordon Stuart (nearly 50 years after the law degree was created, and following not litigation but change to the Edinburgh Law Faculty regulations). A good deal is known about them[170], but neither qualified legally.

As noted above, as well as being first woman law agent, Madge Anderson was the first Glasgow woman law graduate, and possibly first Glasgow woman university law student. Incidentally, she graduated BL in Glasgow just six weeks before the Sex Discrimination (Removal) Act 1919 received the Royal Assent[171], and also, oddly, graduated LLB just six months later. As also noted above, the first Aberdeen woman law agent, Elizabeth Barnett, was seemingly the first Aberdeen woman law graduate[172]. The earliest Dundee woman university law student, commencing in 1912, was Mary Ferguson, about whom regrettably little is known, though she does not seem to have become a law agent or advocate[173]. The first Dundee woman BL graduates, Jess M Page and Margaret Walker, who did become law agents, were not until 1945 and the first woman LLB graduate, whose later career is unknown, was Janet Hurst, in 1955[174].

A further question is who the first woman legal academic was. It is pleasant to record that it seems to have been Christian Bissett (later Mrs Tudhope)[175], an MA of St Andrews and LLB of Edinburgh, and noted above as the first as the first woman solicitor in Dundee. She was appointed to the Dundee Law School in 1939 (as discussed in Chapter 4).

[1] The notion of "legal profession" is, of course, not without difficulty (and, incidentally, judges are usually excluded from consideration). For a relevant discussion, see John Finlay, *Men of Law in Pre-reformation Scotland* ch 1.

[2] The Stamps Act 1785 (25 Geo III, c 80), which taxed those "admitted, enrolled or registered" in any court, lists in (unnumbered) s 1 "Solicitor, Attorney, Notary, Proctor, Agent [and] Procurator" (though this list covered England and Wales as well). Later Stamp Acts used slightly different lists, including "Writer to the Signet" (discussed below), but never "writer" (who might not appear in court), as such, nor "advocate" (who certainly did): see John Finlay, "'Tax the Attornies!' Stamp Duty and the Scottish Legal Profession in the Eighteenth Century" (2014) 34 *Journal of Scottish Historical Studies* 141-166. One might even include messengers-at-arms and sheriffs' officers (i.e. those enforcing court orders) which J Finlay, "The History of the Notary", in Martin Schmoekel & Werner Schubert (eds), *Handbuch zur Geschichte des Notariats der europaeischen Tradition* (2009) 410 and Ibid, *Legal Practice in Eighteenth Century Scotland* (2015) 360 (also 371-372) notes might, in the 18th and early 19th centuries, also be notaries and writers.

[3] Thus, a person might belong to more than one group. Several of the Court of Session's initial "general procurators" had been notaries: see Finlay, *Men of Law* ch 3, and next note.

[4] The most comprehensible account of this array, unfortunately unfootnoted, is J Spencer Muirhead, "Notes on the History of the Solicitor Profession in Scotland" (1952) *ScLR* 25-36 & 59-71 (two parts), though see now the more recent and detailed Finlay, *Men of Law* ch 1 *et passim*, whose analysis is broadly similar, though adding another group, "assessors" (legal advisers to lay judges): also Anon, "The Education of Scotch Lawyers" (1869) XIII *JoJ* 124, 177-131 & 177-187, John Finlay, "Pettifoggers, Regulation and Local Courts in Early Modern Scotland" (2009) 87 *Scottish Historical Review* 42, Finlay, "Lawyers in the British Isles" and Finlay, *Legal Practice* 1-3: and further *Green's Encyclopaedia* (*sub voc* "notary", "procurator", etc), *Stair Memorial Encyclopaedia*, Reissue 'Legal Profession', and Walker, *Legal History of Scotland* (various vols). It is interesting how willingly non-advocates accepted that they were the "lower branch" of the profession.

[5] For a history of notaries, see Finlay, "The History of the Notary", also John Durkan "The early Scottish notary", in Ian B Cowan & Duncan Shaw (eds) *The Renaissance and Reformation in Scotland* (1983) and Finlay, *Legal Practice* ch 11 (which admittedly commences "[n]otaries did not form a separate class of legal practitioners", an assertion depending, of course, upon the meaning attached to "legal practitioner").

[6] See Finlay, "The History of the Notary", 402-404, Finlay, *Legal Practice* 369-371, and J Henderson Begg, *A Treatise on the Law of Scotland relating to Law Agents* 1st ed (1873), 2nd ed (1883), 2nd ed 45-48.

[7] See John Alexander Henderson (ed), *History of the Society of Advocates in Aberdeen* Aberdeen University Studies No 60 (1912) (recording that the title "advocate" was only officially adopted in 1862, though used earlier), Anon, "The Advocates of Aberdeen" (1969) 14 *JLSS* 325: also Begg, *Law Agents* 2nd ed 12-13 & 378-79.

[8] Anon, "Notes on the Judicature Commission" (1869) XIII *JoJ* 13 identifies 31 distinct groups (noting Scotland's population to be the same as London's). Most were incorporated under the Procurators (Scotland) Act 1865, but probably existed well before incorporation, as is indicated by the description of their size and activities in Begg, *Law Agents* 1st ed. ch XXVI (and 13-22) & 2nd ed, ch XXVII (and 9-15). On their history and nature generally, see Finlay, *Legal Practice* 17-25 and ch 7.

[9] But see John Findlay, "Legal Education, 1650-1850" in Robert Anderson, Martin Freeman & Lindsay Paterson *The Edinburgh History of Education in Scotland* (2015) 125-127 in relation to Aberdeen, Dumfries, Glasgow and Forfarshire, and Finlay, *Legal Practice* 258, who asserts that by the 19th century "country practitioners" were surprisingly commonly in Edinburgh for part of their apprenticeships (and see references to Thomas Thornton below).

[10] See e.g. Robert Kerr Hannay, *The College of Justice: essays on the institution and development of the Court of Session* (1933), ch 9, John Finlay, "Lawyers in the British Isles", in B. Dolemeyer (ed), *Anwaelte und Ihre Geschichte* (2011), John Finlay, *The Community of the College of Justice: Edinburgh and the Court of Session 1687-1808* (2012), also Sir Thomas Smith & Robert Black (Gen Eds), Hamish McN Henderson, Joseph M Thomson & Kenneth Miller (Dep Gen Eds) *Stair Memorial Encyclopaedia of the Laws of Scotland* (various dates), Reissue paras 1239 *et seq,* and David M Walker, *A Legal History of Scotland* 7 vols (1988-2004) (various vols).

[11] The "College of Justice" was set up in 1532, comprising the Court of Session, and a slightly uncertain number of other groups, including the Faculty of Advocates and the Writers to the Signet. Advantages of membership included monopolies of certain activities, and exemption from some taxes.

[12] The "public examination" in law, conducted in Latin, a survival of the medieval *viva voce* examination, though purely formal at least by the mid-19th century. The Faculty of Advocates sought, not a banausic one suitable for the actual practice of law, but "a legal education suitable for gentlemen": John W Cairns "Importing our Lawyers from Holland ...", in Grant G Simpson (ed) *Scotland and the Low Countries 1124-1994* (1996) 136-153, at 146 (also 140-143). For the development of advocate's education, see John W Cairns, "Advocates' Hats, Roman Law and Admission to the Scottish bar, 1580-1812" (1999) 20 *Journal of Legal History* 24-61, J D Ford *Law and Opinion in Scotland* (2007) 2-7 *et seq.,* Finlay *Community of the College of Justice* 123-130, and Finlay, "Legal Education, 1650-1850" 118-120.

[13] See Anon, "The Society of Solicitors of the Supreme Courts of Scotland" (1970) 15 *JLSS* 66, and J B Barclay, *The SSC Story 1784-1984* (1984): also Begg, *Law Agents* 2nd ed 10-11 & 374-76 and Finlay *Community of the College of Justice* 178-179. In 1850, it absorbed another unusual Faculty or Society, the Advocate's First Clerks whose monopoly of acting as intermediaries it had broken: see J B Barclay, *SSC Story, 1784-1984* (1984) ch IV, also Begg, *Law Agents* 2nd ed 7-8.

[14] See Anon, *The Society of Writers to HM Signet, with a list of members ...* [etc] (1936) Introduction and "The Early History of the Scottish Signet", A R B Haldane, "The Society of Writers to Her Majesty's Signet" (1970) 15 *JLSS* 35, Finlay, *Community of the College of Justice* ch 6 and Finlay, "Legal Education, 1650-1850" 123-4: also Begg, *Law Agents* 2nd ed 8 & 370-77 and Hannay, *College of Justice* various entries.

[15] 28 & 29 Vict c 85. (According to Begg, *Law Agents* 1st ed. 18-19 & 2nd ed 15-16, two Acts of Sederunt, AS 12 November 1825 and AS 10 July 1839, were precursors. However, the Faculty of Advocates' Library cannot track down either: I am grateful to Iona Murphy of the National Library of Scotland for this information. The Medical Act 1858, introducing the General Council of Medical Education and Registration of the United Kingdom (i.e., the General Medical Council), may have prompted the Act, but note lobbying by the Glasgow Faculty of Procurators: see *Glasgow Herald* March 1 1862. For contemporary comment, see Anon, "The Proposed Procurators Act" (1865) IX *JoJ* 92 & 213, Anon, "Notes on the Judicature Committee" and "W.S." (letter), *Scotsman* March 16 1865, 4.

[16] H.C. Paper 1865 No. 87, cl 2 & 3, also 26 & 27.

[17] See HC Deb (3rd Series) vol 178, Friday 31 March 1865 (Second Reading); Thursday 18 May 1865, Thursday 25 May 1865 and Thursday 8 June 1865 (Committee Stage); and HL Deb (3rd Series) vol 180, Monday 19 June 1986 (Second Reading); and 20 June 1865 (Committee Stage).

[18] HC Paper 1865 No. 157, cl 2.

[19] Counties then broadly co-incided with Sheriffdoms.

[20] Ss 1 & 2. Section 1 specifically mentions "The Incorporated Society of Writers in Dundee" in the definition of "procurators", presumably because "writer" was then used, not "procurator".

[21] Procurators (Scotland) Act 1965, ss 4-12.

[22] *Ibid* s 16.

[23] *Ibid* ss 4, 11, 20 & 21.

[24] *Ibid* ss 14 & 15.

[25] This characterisation imitates, but modifies, the threefold "pattern of legal education" (Civil Law in first year, Scots Law in second and Conveyancing in third) impliedly referring only to university legal education, in Stephen D Girvin, "Nineteenth century reforms in Scottish legal education: the universities and the bar" (1993) 14 *JLH* 127-140, at 131.

[26] Curriculum and Regulations prepared by the General Council of Procurators in Scotland, Chapter 1 (Examinations, etc) para 6 (incidentally, signed by John Boyd Baxter at Dundee), appended to AS 26 June 1866: see also Anon, "The Education of Scotch Lawyers" (1869) XIII *JoJ* 124 ("Procurators of Inferior Courts") (which erroneously dates the AS to 22 June 1866).

[27] It was imposed not by the Act, but in delegated legislation thereunder, i.e. Curriculum and Regulations prepared by the General Council of Procurators in Scotland, Chapter 1 (Examinations, etc), para 3, appended to AS 26 June 1866: see also Anon, "Education of Scotch Lawyers" ("Procurators in Inferior Courts") (which erroneously dates the AS to 22 June 1866).

[28] The WS Society then required a five-year apprenticeship and attendance at university classes in Civil Law, Scots Law and Conveyancing but, seemingly, no actual Law examination until sometime later: see *Regulations Regarding Applicants for Indenture, Adopted by the Society of Writers to the Signet in 1851* and *Regulations of the Society of Writers to the Signet Relative to Entrants*, reproduced in Begg, *Law Agents* 1st ed 515-518 (cf *Regulations Respecting Apprentices and Intrants to the Society of Writers to the Signet* in Begg, *Law Agents* 2nd ed 412-415). The SSC Society then, seemingly, only required an apprenticeship: see Anon, "Education of Scotch Lawyers" ("Solicitors before the Supreme Courts").

[29] S 11.

[30] I.e. those in Edinburgh, Glasgow, Paisley and Aberdeen (all mentioned by name) and seemingly those in Perth, Dundee and Banffshire (all recorded as incorporated before the Act in Begg *Law Agents* 1st ed ch XXVI and 2nd ed ch XXVII, which also list, respectively, 23 incorporated under the 1865 Act with 3 unincorporated, and 18 incorporated under the 1865 Act with 5 "extinct").

[31] S 27. They were also given the power to change their names, and the Incorporated Society of Writers in Dundee took advantage, seemingly becoming the Faculty of Procurators and Solicitors in Dundee at this time.

[32] Seemingly ten, ie (i) under the Act's principal provisions (the "public door"); (ii)-(iii) by membership of the WS or SSC societies; (iv)-(vii) by membership of one of the four named incorporated Faculties or Societies, or (vii)-(x) by membership of one of the three unnamed incorporated Faculties or Societies (the "separate private doors" for "each of the nine old close monopolies"): c.f. Anon, "Law Agents' Bill" (1873) XVII *JoJ* 313.

[33] Though, as noted above, Finlay, *Legal Practice* 258 asserts that by the 19th century "country practitioners" were surprisingly commonly in Edinburgh for part of their apprenticeships (and see references to Thomas Thornton below).

[34] Fourth Report of the Royal Commission on the Courts of Law in Scotland (C-175:1869) 42-43 recommended that "there should be one general examination applicable to agents throughout all Scotland [and] that anyone who has passed that examination should be entitled to practise in all the Inferior Courts". John Boyd Baxter (of whom, much below) was a member of the Commission.

[35] 33 & 34 Vict c 97.

[36] S 60. The Act applied to Great Britain and, while "heritable estate" was the usual Scots Law term to describe (immovable) property in the form of land and buildings, "personal estate" is a term of English Law, so the Scots Law equivalent, "moveable property", to refer to all property not "heritable", appears to have been treated as implied. Other English Law professional statuses ("serjeant-at-law", "barrister"), were also exempted. The "forfeit" was £50.

[37] 23 & 24 Geo 5 c 21, s 32.

[38] HC 1872 Bill No 135.

[39] Cll 2-4 & 6. Those in the exempted Faculties and Societies under the 1865 Act retained their powers to appear within the county, but did not acquire the extended ones to appear elsewhere: cll 1 (*sub voc* "law agent") and 4

[40] Cl 7. After amendment in Committee (HC 1872 Bill No. 150) an amended version became cl 17.

[41] Cll 8-10, 14-19 & 23. Rather extraordinarily for a Bill with "(Scotland)" in the Short Title, s 11 facilitated advocates to become attorneys or solicitors in England.

[42] Acts of Sederunt are legislation by the courts under powers delegated by Parliament.

[43] Insofar as Cll 5 & 12 allowed existing members of those bodies, and new members admitted according to their rules, to exercise the same rights and privileges as they had, or would previously have had, but not the newly extended ones under the Act, such as to practise in any inferior court in Scotland.

[44] HC 1872 Bill No. 150. Again, Second Reading and Committee Stage produced no debate: see HC Deb (3rd Series) vol 212, Monday 17 June 1872 & Tuesday 16 July 1872. For contemporary comment, see Anon, "Professional Reform" (1871) XV *JoJ* 201, Anon, "Uniform Rights for Law Agents in Scotland" (1871) XV *JoJ* 595, Anon, "Law Agents Bill" (1872) XVI *JoJ* 363 & 430, Anon, (report of discussion on Law Agents Bill in the Scottish Law Amendment Society) (1872)

XVI *JoJ* 369, Anon. "Law Agents' Bill", Anon (papers of the Scottish Law Amendment Society) "The Law Agents (Scotland) Bill" (1873) XVII *JoJ* 353, John H Begg "On the Law Agents Act 1873) (1873) XVII *JoJ* 449, and "Fiat Justitia" and "A Country Solicitor" (letters) *Scotsman* January 9 1873.

[45] Cl 2. "Practise" here means "act in relation to", since the advocates' monopoly was not breached.

[46] Cl 17.

[47] Cl 5.

[48] HC Deb (3rd Series), vol 212, Monday 22 July 1872. For representations by the Glasgow Faculty of Procurators (fearing loss of privileges): see *Scotsman* 27 November 1872 (an adjourned meeting six months after the Bill was withdrawn).

[49] 36 & 37 Vict c 63. There was some debate on this Bill: see HC Deb (3rd Series), vol 216, Thursday 5 June 1873 and Friday 6 June 1873 (House of Commons Committee Stage), and vol 217, Tuesday 24 June 1873 (Commons consideration of Lords' amendments), and HL Deb (3rd series), vol 246, Friday 4 July 1873 (Lords' Second Reading), vol 217, Friday 11 July 1873 (Lords Committee Stage) and Tuesday 15 July 1873 (Lords Report Stage).

[50] Ss 1-4, 16, 17 & 25. Begg *Law Agents* 2nd ed 19 noted that this last provision produced "a distinct falling off in the membership of all societies", such that by 1883, only 1700 out of 2350 enrolled law agents were members. S 19, incidentally, allowed Faculties and Societies to enrol members "on such terms as [they] may see fit".

[51] Ss 18 & 24.

[52] Ss 5 & 6.

[53] Ss 7-10.

[54] AS 20 December 1873 (as amended), reproduced in contemporary editions of *Parliament House Book,* and Begg, *Law Agents* 2nd ed, Appendix (and discussed in chs 1 & 2); also summarised in *Green's Encyclopaedia sub voc* "law agent". The 1873 Act, two relevant Acts of Sederunt of 1873, one of 1875 (extract only), one of 1878, and "Specimen" general knowledge and law examination papers, are also reproduced in William George Black, *The Law Agents Act 1873* ... (1884) Appendix.

[55] Though, presumably, not necessarily pass.

[56] AS 20 December 1873 s 4.

[57] *Petition, T Shaw Maclaren*, 18 July 1874 (unreported): the Court concluded that "by such ways and means as they shall think proper" included accepting WS admission examinations as an alternative: see Begg, *Law Agents* 2nd ed 39 (who, in the 1st ed 525, rehearses the contemporary WS admission requirements).

[58] AS 4 November 1886: "it shall not be necessary for the future, that any applicant for admission as a Law Agent shall have attended the classes of Scots Law and Conveyancing in a Scottish University". Confusingly, however, the Examiners might "take into account whether such Applicant has or has not attended such classes". Was attending regarded as advantage or disadvantage?

[59] Any delegated legislation may, in principle, be found *ultra vires*. The full oddity here lies in that the conclusion that the provision was *ultra vires* did not result from litigation, nor complaint, nor any formal process, and was arrived at by the same Lord President (Inglis) as had originally promulgated it, a dozen years before. Anon, "The New Act of Sederunt anent the Admission of Law Agents" (1886) XXX *JoJ* 644-648 adversely compared the amendment to a "decree of Nebuchadnezzar", declaring it "a severe blow both to the status of the legal profession and to the Law Faculties" (though largely on the ground that a "youth" could now practise in any court "without any knowledge of the world of men and manners other than is to be gathered in the back office of a local writer and banker in Wigtown or Thurso").

[60] HC 1887 Bill No 284.

[61] Private Members' Bills are those introduced by a back-bencher, rather than by a member of the Government. In the 19th century, such Bills had a chance of success, particularly if introduced by so weighty a proposer as, in this case, J B Balfour, formerly Solicitor-General for Scotland and Lord Advocate, and subsequently Lord President of the Court of Session.

[62] 54 & 55 Vict c 30.

[63] Ss 2 & 4.

[64] 59 & 60 Vict c 49.

[65] S 2. On the relationship between notaries and writers (and agents) in the 19th century, see John Finlay, "The History of the Notary" in Martin Schmoekel & Werner Schbert (eds) *Handbuch zur Geschichte des Notariats der europeanischen Trdation* (2009) 410-411.

[66] See now the Solicitors (Scotland) Act 1980 s 57(1), entitling any solicitor with a practising certificate to be admitted as a notary public.

[67] See eg "Mr Shaw" and others, "Unlicensed Practitioners" (annual meeting of Incorporated Society of Law Agents" AGM) (1885) XXIX *JoJ* 381, and Anon, "Country Agents' Grievances" (letters) (1893) IX *ScLR* 148-150 & 173-174, also Begg, *Law Agents* 1st ed. ch III & 2nd ed, ch IV.

[68] Law Agents and Notaries Public Act (Scotland) 1891 (54 & 55 Vict c 30) s 5.

[69] AS 18 March 1893, essentially identical in relation to the law examination, but exempting those with a LLB or BL degree from the Scots Law and Conveyancing parts. However, it split the general knowledge component into "First" and "Second" examinations.

[70] AS 12 March 1926.

[71] See *Regulations for Examination and Admission of Solicitors … 19th March 1937*', in force 1 January 1938.

[72] Aspiring advocates from Dundee would have had to move to Edinburgh, as did Thomas Thornton (see references below).

[73] In addition to the purely formal "public examination", noted above, on the mere formality of which by this time, see Harold F Andorsen [*sic*] (ed), *Memoirs of Lord Salvsesen* (1949) 20 and Lord Macmillan, *A Man of Law's Tale* (1952) 30-31.

[74] "Civil law" here refers to a revision and compilation of Roman Law (the *Corpus juris civilis*), regarded as a Platonic ideal, and the basis of most Continental ("civil law") legal systems, as opposed to home-grown English and English-based ("common law") systems. Thus, Civil law

was the basis of university legal study for centuries. Scots law, as a "mixed system", is said to partake of "civil" and "common" law.

[75] For details of the late 1860s, see Anon, "Education of Scotch Lawyers" (1869) XV *JoJ* 124 ("Faculty of Advocates"), and for the end of the century, Faculty of Advocates *Regulations as to Intrants* 21 November 1894, reproduced in contemporary *Parliament House Books*, and summarised in *Green's Encyclopaedia sub voc* "advocate".

[76] For the late 19th century development of the Faculty of Advocates as a whole, see "Legal Profession", in *Stair Encyclopaedia*, Reissue paras 1278-1283. Arguably, "devilling" revived the previous practice frowned upon by the Faculty of Advocates because not involving a university education.

[77] *Green's Encyclopaedia sub voc* "law agent".

[78] For its origins, see Begg, *Law Agents* 2nd ed 388-89.

[79] Sources are meagre, in particular because, as noted above, early records of what became the Faculty of Procurators and Solicitors in Dundee are lost. However, the Index to FPSD Minutes 1846-87, and actual Minutes 1887-present, have survived and are held by the FPSD. (I am grateful to Elizabeth McGillivray, then Secretary of the FPSD, for access to them). There are occasional references in the literature, including Begg, *Law Agents* 1st ed 19, 401 and 2nd ed 16, 379, Anon, "Notes on the Judicature Commission" (1869) XIII *JoJ* 13, Anon, "The Education of Scotch Lawyers" (1869) XIII *JoJ* 124, and Anon, "Dundee Faculty Dinner Dance" 1950 *SLT* 227: also *Regulations and Catalogue of the Library belonging to the Society of Writer in Dundee* (1826), National Library of Scotland GD 16/57/58. There is also specific reference to the Society in the Procurators (Scotland) Act 1865, s 1, as noted above.

[80] A copy of the petition for a Royal Charter, dated 10 March 1821, is in the FPSD Index to Minutes, 1846-87, 4-5.

[81] John Ogilvie, James Ogilvie, John William Baxter [uncle of John Boyd Baxter, of whom much more later], David Cobb, Thomas Adamson, William Rodger, William Barrie, James Simpson, David McEwen, William Reid, David Jobson, David Mitchell, Christopher Kerr, George Milne, Thomas Walker, John Anderson, and James Brown. "Writer" and "procurator" are both used in this list, seemingly disjunctively. Nevertheless, the Society, while representing "Procurators", explicitly chose the "Writer" for its name, possibly suggesting that the two terms were interchangeable. There had been, seemingly, eight "licensed practitioners" in 1804, and twelve in 1813: see Finlay, *Legal Practice* 227.

[82] A Sheriff (or Sheriff-Substitute) appears to have first sat regularly in Dundee in 1832: see Anon, "Additional Sheriffs for Dundee ..." (1860) IV *JoJ* 135-137. The present Dundee Sheriff Court House was commenced in 1833, though only completed in 1863: see Charles McKean & David Walker, *Dundee: an illustrated architectural guide* (1984) 55.

[83] *Dundee Courier and Argus* 2 February 1866.

[84] See Begg, *Law Agents* 2nd ed 379, also 1st ed 401-02.

[85] Report made to His Majesty by a Royal Commission of Inquiry into State of the Universities of Scotland 1826-30 (1831), and Report of the Commissioners appointed to inquire into the Universities of Scotland 1876-78 (C.1935: 1878) (the former seemingly generated by internal disputes in all the Universities precipitated by "[t]he new forces of Evangelism and Whiggish

liberalism", and the latter by internal disputes, largely over the breadth of the curriculum: see R D Anderson, *Education and Opportunity in Victorian Scotland* (1983) 38-49 & 92-101). Note also the follow-up reports to the 1831 Royal Commission reports (e.g. Report of the St Andrews Commissioners (Scotland) (1845)).

[86] See Anderson, *Education and Opportunity* 27, also John Malcolm Bulloch *A History of the University of Aberdeen* (1895), J D Mackie *The University of Glasgow 1451-1951* (1954) and D B Horn *A Short History of the University of Edinburgh 1556-1889* (1967).

[87] See e.g. Findlay, "Legal Education, 1650-1850" 115-118 and 120-122, also Stephen D Girvin, "Nineteenth century reforms in Scottish Legal Education" (1993) 14 *Journal of Legal History* 127, 128-131, Finlay *Community of the College of Justice* 168-171, and especially in relation to St Andrews, John W Cairns, "The Law, the Advocates and the Universities in Late Sixteenth Century Scotland" (1994) LXXIII *Scottish Historical Review* 171-190 and John W Cairns, "Academic Feud, Bloodfeud, and William Welwood: legal education in St Andrews, 1560-1611" (1998) 2 *Edinburgh Law Review* 158-179 & 255-287 (2 parts), and for the complicated position in Aberdeen, John W Cairns, "Lawyers, Law Professors and Localities": the Universities of Aberdeen 1680-1750" (1995) 46 *Northern Ireland Legal Quarterly* 304-331.

[88] John W Cairns, "The Origins of the Glasgow Law School: the Professors of Civil Law 1714-1761", in Peter Birks (ed), *The Life of the Law: Proceedings of the Tenth British Legal History Conference, Oxford 1991* (1993), notes that Hercules Lindesay in Glasgow was the first person to teach Civil Law in English, seemingly in the mid-18th century.

[89] See e.g. David M Walker, *A History of the School of Law, the University of Glasgow* (c.1990), chs 2 & 3, John W Cairns & Hector L MacQueen, *Learning and the Law: a short history of Edinburgh Law School* (2013) chs I & II, also Cairns, "Origins of the Glasgow Law School" in Birks *Life of the Law*, and John W Cairns, "From 'Speculative' to 'Practical' Legal Education: the decline of the Glasgow Law School 1801-1830" (1994) 62 *Tijdschrift voor Rechtsgeschiednis* 331-356.

[90] As late as 1887, Edinburgh had only seven chairs (including ones in the fringe subjects of Medical Jurisprudence, and Commercial and Political Economy), and a lectureship in Procedure (though the subject was not on the syllabus for either BL or LLB); Glasgow had only two chairs (one covering both Roman Law and Scots Law) and two lectureships; Aberdeen had only one chair and no lectureships: Anon, "Bill to amend Law Agents (Scotland) Act" (1887) XXXI *JoJ* 386. Cf similar figures given in Anon, "University Legal Education" (1889) 1 *JR* 194 (which understandably asserts that only Edinburgh could properly be called a Law Faculty), and Girvin, "Nineteenth century reforms" (1993) 14 *JLH* 127.

[91] 21 & 22 Vict c 83.

[92] 52 & 53 Vict c 5.

[93] See Anderson, *Education and Opportunity* chs 2 & 7. For Royal Commission comment on law teaching, see Report of Royal Commission 1826-30 (1830) 53-55 and Report of Royal Commission 1876-78 (1878), and for "executive" Commission activities (see next note) see General Report of the Commissioners under the Universities (Scotland) Act 1858 ... (1863) xxxv-xxxvi, and General Report of the Commissioners under the Universities (Scotland) Act, 1889 ... (Cd 276: 1900) xxi-xxii.

[94] Both set up "executive Commissions" (chaired by senior judges) which heard evidence and issued (subject to consultation and Privy Council approval) Ordinances amending the law. The

Ordinances under the 1858 Act are reproduced in General Report of the 1858 Commissioners (1863), and those still in force at its time of publication are reproduced in Alan E Clapperton (ed), *Universities (Scotland) Act 1858 together with Ordinances of the Commissioners under said Act ...* (1916). Those under the 1898 Act still in force at their times of publication are reproduced in General Report of the 1889 Commissioners *(*1900) and Alan E Clapperton (ed), *Universities (Scotland) Act 1889 together with Ordinances of the Commissioners ... and University Court Ordinances* (1915). Those made thereafter, up to their dates of publication, are reproduced in Alan E Clapperton (ed), *University Court Ordinances made and approved between 1ˢᵗ January 1915 and 31ˢᵗ December 1924 under the Universities (Scotland) Act 1889 ...* (1925), and W A Fleming, *University Court Ordinances from 1ˢᵗ January 1925 to 31ˢᵗ July 1947 ... and Emergency Ordinances ... with a General Index* (1948). As both 1858 and 1889 Commission Ordinances run from a "No 1", it is important to distinguish them by the year of promulgation.

[95] Ordinance No 18 (General No 9) of 1892, Regulations for the Graduation of Women and for their Instruction in the Universities. The 1858 Act also amalgamated King's College and Marischal College into Aberdeen University.

[96] Until well into the 19th century, it was common to attend university, but not to graduate.

[97] Donald G Southgate, *University Education in Dundee: a centenary history* (1982) 9 suggests that, at least in the early days, the St Andrews General Council was "controlled" by London-based medical graduates who had never attended the University, but had acquired degrees from it, essentially through simple purchase on the basis of references, as was then possible. However, it seems clear from later Minutes that it took its role seriously after this enhancement as, for instance, it discussed much of the relevant proposed legislation, including that in particular Ordinances, some in great detail: see University of St Andrews Archives ("UStAA") UY/615 University of St Andrews General Council Minutes 1859-1883. Indeed, given the large proportion of professors attending, it may have operated as a revising chamber for Senate rather than a version of HM Loyal Opposition.

[98] For a description of the process, see "Legal Profession", in *Stair Memorial Encyclopaedia,* Reissue para 1281, also Report of Royal Commission 1876-78 (1878) xxxv-xxxvi. LLDs were awarded as honorary degrees by all universities (even St Andrews), but also possibly by thesis in Glasgow: see Walker, *History of the School of Law* 29.

[99] Ordinance No 75 (General No 8) of 1862, reproduced in General Report of the 1858 Commissioners and Clapperton (ed), *Universities (Scotland) Act 1858...* 206, and summarised in General Report of the 1889 Commissioners xxi-xxii. Its co-incidence with the Procurators (Scotland) Act 1865 is probably just that. Walker, *History of the School of Law* 48 notes that LLB is short for "Baccalaureus Legum", that is, Bachelor of *Laws* (plural), i.e. presumably Civil Law and Scots Law (rather than Civil Law and Canon Law).

[100] Civil Law, Law of Scotland, Conveyancing (all at least 80 lectures: the unit of account), Public Law [probably in modern parlance Public International Law], Constitutional Law & History, and Medical Jurisprudence (all at least 40 lectures). This limited range (not, for example, including Mercantile Law or Private International Law, presumably reflected the range of the professoriate in Edinburgh (on which, see Cairns & MacQueen, *Learning and the Law* 13-14, 20 and ch IV). From 1884, Commercial and Political Economy might be taken instead of Conveyancing in Edinburgh: Note of Alteration [of Ordinance No 75, General No 8] of 1884, reproduced in

Clapperton (ed), *Universities (Scotland) Act 1858...* 209. For the evolution of the LLB, see Chapter 3, Appendix 2.

[101] The literature does not discuss the reasoning. The MA prerequisite was clearly intended to show that law students were well-educated.

[102] Anon, "Graduation in Law" (1871) XV *JoJ* 246-248 asserted that, by that time, while 300 students had taken Scots Law and Conveyancing, only 15 had graduated. David M Walker, "Legal Studies in the Scottish Universities" 1957 *JR* 21-41 & 151-179 (two parts) cited 24 graduates in the first decade.

[103] Notes of Alteration of [Ordinance 75 (General No 8)] of 1874, reproduced in Clapperton (ed), *Universities (Scotland) Act 1858...* 207-09.

[104] Walker *History of the School of Law* 48 notes that "BL" is short for "Baccalaureus Legis", that is Bachelor of *Law* (singular), i.e. presumably Scots Law, although the degree also included Civil Law.

[105] Civil Law, Law of Scotland, Conveyancing and one out of the three other LLB subjects.

[106] Walker, *History of the School of Law* 46 records an average of seven BL graduates a year from 1878 to 1900, compared with an average of fewer than six LLB.

[107] Ordinances 39 (General No 11) and 40 (General No 12) of 1893 reproduced in Clapperton (ed), *Universities (Scotland) Act 1858...* 206 and xxx, and General Report of the 1889 Commissioners 69 & 70.

[108] The drafting is complex but, essentially, included the same list of subjects as before, but allowing a "half-course" in Civil Law, provided a "half-course" in Jurisprudence (i.e. legal theory - the joint first time this subject emerges), Public International Law, Constitutional Law & History, Mercantile Law or Administrative Law was also taken, and requiring a "half-course" in Forensic Medicine or another from the new "half-course" list of Jurisprudence, etc.

[109] In the 35 years from 1918, in Edinburgh, there were almost exactly the same number of BLs as LLBs (averaging about twenty a year each), and in Glasgow, one and a half times more BL than LLB (averaging about 27 and seventeen a year, respectively): Alistair R Brownlie, "The Universities and Scottish Legal Education" 1955 *JR* 26-61, at 55 (Table 2). For the evolution of the BL, see Chapter 3, Appendix 2.

[110] That is, Jurisprudence, though (again with somewhat complex drafting) increasing Public Law, and Constitutional Law & History, to 80 lectures, but allowing International Private Law, Political Economy or Administrative Law in place of Medical Jurisprudence (renamed "Forensic Medicine"). The increasing similarity to the Faculty of Advocates' requirements, discussed above, is evident. For the evolution of the LLB, see Chapter 3, Appendix 2.

[111] Alistair R Brownlie, "The Universities and Scottish Legal Education" 1955 *JR* 26 at 55 (Table 2) shows that the number of law graduates in Glasgow did not reach twenty a year until 1928, nor in Edinburgh until 1931.

[112] Compare the number of law graduates, BL and LLB, footnoted above with the total numbers of law students 1893-1913 in Anderson, *Education and Opportunity* Appendix 1(C), which shows for Edinburgh 252 to 455 law students a year; for Glasgow, 175 to 236 (and for Aberdeen, fifteen to 51).

[113] St Andrews, Glasgow and Aberdeen were founded by Bishops Wardlaw, Turnbull and Elphinstone (all, incidentally, holders of law degrees), respectively.

[114] Southgate, *University Education* 1, c.f. Charles McKean & Patricia Whatley, with Kenneth Baxter, *Lost Dundee: Dundee's lost architectural heritage* (2008) x.

[115] E.g. the Watt Institution: see J V Smith *The Watt Institution Dundee 1824-49* (1977).

[116] Also, the initial constituent of what is now Queen Margaret University, as the Edinburgh School of Cookery and Domestic Economy, was founded in 1875 to provide women with access to tertiary education.

[117] St David's College Lampeter, King's College London and Durham University, were all essentially for Church of England or Wales clergy, and only University College London was a counterblast. St David's College could hardly be further from industry, and Durham was well-insulated from Tyneside and Teeside.

[118] Anderson, *Education and Opportunity* 39 (noting that it had earlier been reduced to selling medical degrees) and 252, Table 3.1 and Appendix 1(B) (at 351). See also Report of Royal Commission 1876-78, Evidence vol IV, and Report of the St Andrews Commissioners.

[119] This account summarises Southgate, *University Education* chs 1 & 2, Ronald Gordon Cant, *The University of St Andrews: a short history* (1992), and Norman H Reid *Ever to Excel: an illustrated history of the University of St Andrews* (2011) 160-165.

[120] See Southgate, *University Education* 6 ff., but also UStAA UY 615/1 General Council of St Andrews University Minutes, Meetings of 28 November 1872, 27 March & 28 November 1873 (though the discussions referred to appear to have run into the sand).

[121] A contingent within it clearly preferred to be "ivy-covered professors, in ivy-covered halls": see Tom Lehrer, "Bright College Days" (c.1959) (song). As noted above, the St Mungo's College precedent appears unmentioned in recorded discussions, as does the "Andersonian" (and, perhaps less surprisingly, though devoted to women's tertiary education, the Edinburgh School of Cookery and Domestic Economy).

[122] I.e. Report of Royal Commission 1876-78.

[123] *Ibid* 57-8.

[124] Discussed below.

[125] Quoted in Southgate, *University Education* 22. For a justificatory account of the thinking behind the founding, including the desire on the one hand for University College to prove itself before seeking any link with St Andrews University, but on the other to expand into Arts, written in the light of later contentions, see Principal Peterson's *St Andrews and Dundee: a retrospect* (1893). As noted above, no reference appears to have been made to St Mungo's College, "the Andersonian" (or the Edinburgh School of Cookery and Domestic Economy).

[126] Discussed in the following Chapter. He had drafted the motion "[t]hat a Committee be appointed to devise a scheme for the establishment of a College in Dundee, to confer with the University of St Andrews with a view to the incorporation of the proposed College ... with that University ...", at the public meeting in 1874 which arguably initiated the project: see William Angus Knight, *A Biographical Sketch with Reminiscences of Thomas Thornton (including several estimates of him)* (1905) 35. On the other hand, by 1880, John Boyd Baxter and Mary Ann Baxter regarded

him with suspicion, as too friendly towards St Andrews University: Southgate, *University Education* 23 & 25.

[127] Reproduced at the beginning of Dundee University Archives ("DUA") Recs A/38 University College Dundee, Council Minute Book, and commencing by recording that the two Baxters "resolved to establish a College in Dundee for the purposes hereinafter particularly set forth ...". The other trustees included some of the great and the good of the area, e.g. Alexander Moncur (Provost of Dundee), Rt. Hon. William Baxter (MP for Montrose Burghs: small burghs were then commonly grouped to form a constituency: he was a nephew of Mary Ann Baxter, and in government under Gladstone), George Armitstead and Frank Henderson (MPs for Dundee: large burghs commonly then had two MPs: George Armitstead, later first and last Baron Armitstead, was a local business man who married into the Baxters, was a friend of Gladstone's, and made many charitable donations in Dundee), Alexander Robertson (Sheriff-Substitute for Forfar, and Alexander Henderson (Dean of Guild in Dundee).

[128] The "Cooper Inquiry" (discussed in Chapter 4) para 25.

[129] They included, *int al,* several of the Trustees of the Deed of Endowment and Trust, the Earl of Strathmore, representatives of the Dundee Chamber of Commerce, Dundee School Board, and "all Members of the [College] Council" (described below).

[130] *Int al,* the Earl of Dalhousie and Thomas Thornton as two of the Governors' representatives, all the Trustees, and representatives of Owens College Manchester, and of the Lord President of the [Privy] Council (in effect, the Government).

[131] In practice, the professoriate.

[132] Southgate, *University Education* 23-29 (noting, at 28 & 29, that John Boyd Baxter confessed to having little "University experience").

[133] As noted above, one member of College Council was a representative of that institution (initially, H E Roscoe, Professor of Chemistry at Owens College and later Principal, also MP and Vice-Chancellor of London University), who was credited with reviving that College when it was failing some years earlier). Southgate, *University Education* ch. 1 Appendix, notes later reliance upon Roscoe in planning the curriculum of University College. P J Hartog (ed), *The Owens College ... a Brief History ...* (1900) 21 n2, also observes that University College Dundee was "founded expressly upon the model of Owens College".

[134] The "piece of ground in Nethergate Street ... bounded on the west by Small's Wynd; on the north by the lands formerly belonging to the heirs and successors of James Johnston ...; on the east by a wall separating the said piece of ground from Park Place ... comprising an acre or thereby ...". On the acquisition by the Baxters of this land, then the westernmost extension of the Burgh of Dundee, and the inhabitants of the four houses thereon, see Southgate, *University Education* 33. The simultaneous propensity of all proprietors to sell seems extraordinary, but might be explained by noting that the four villas on the land (later known collectively as "Front College") built a century earlier in rural surroundings, were by then suffering from the encroachment of industry in the ["Old"] Hawkhill: see McKean, Whatley & Baxter, *Lost Dundee* who note the four houses were collectively called "Whiteleys". The names of some of the selling proprietors are given in Southgate, *University Education* 33, and in the caption to a contemporary photograph of them in Michael Shafe, *University Education in Dundee 1881-1981: a pictorial history* (1982) 15.

[135] See Anon, *University College, Dundee: the opening ceremony, Professor Stuart's Address, Description of the College Buildings* (1883).

[136] S 16. As noted below, arguably the apparent equation of "affiliate" and "make part of" was the underlying cause of later difficulties.

[137] Reproduced in General Report of the 1889 Commissioners 186, as a Schedule to the Commissioners' Order of 21 March 1890 (see next note); and is quoted in Southgate, *University Education* 74-76.

[138] Order Affiliating University College, Dundee (1890): reproduced in General Report of the 1889 Commissioners 185. Use of an Order rather than an Ordinance (the subject of the later litigation) was explained in an undated Memorandum, reproduced at 284. Essentially, Parliament intended that affiliation, if agreed to, should occur rapidly, without the lengthy period of consultation Act required for Ordinances, and the constitutional changes which the Act made should be brought into effect simultaneously in all universities, requiring affiliation to be complete beforehand.

[139] The "Cooper Inquiry" para 53.

[140] But discussed lengthily in Southgate, *University Education* chs 2 & 3, forthrightly in Peterson, *St Andrews and Dundee, passim,* (which suggested St Andrews University needed University College more than *vice versa,* distinguished "incorporation" from "absorption", and pointed the finger at the Marquess of Bute – see below – and St Andrews' "monopolists at heart" who "think that Dundee is a very inferior sort of place, which got a college by a kind of accident ..."), though only briefly in Cant, *University of St Andrews* 148-154, and even more briefly, though with more insight, in Reid, *Ever to Excel* 161-162 (which observed that "[i]n an effort to overcome the [difference between 'affiliate' and 'form part of'] the nineteenth century negotiators had left a vagueness in the agreement which boded ill for the future". See also the Commissioners' account in General Report of the 1889 Commissioners xliii-lxii, to which the undated Memorandum referred to above is, in effect, annexed.

[141] See *Metcalfe & Others v University of St Andrews & Others* (1894) 2 SLT 139 (OH), (1894) 2 SLT 371 (Court of Seven Judges), (1894) 22R 210 (Court of Seven Judges), (1895) 22R (HL) 13, (1896) 23R (HL) 60, (1896) 23R 559 and [1896] AC 647. (Courts of Seven - or other enhanced number of - Judges, are convened in cases where important principles are at stake, but the law unclear law or ripe for re-consideration).

[142] At this time, University of St Andrews Senate Minutes are littered with objections by some St Andrews professors to the presence of Dundee ones. See also the University College Principal's Reports in the Dundee Calendar for these years: DUA Recs A/814/6-14.

[143] John Patrick Crichton-Stuart, 3rd Marquess of Bute (1847-1900), medievalist and architectural dilettante (responsible for Mount Stuart House on the Isle of Bute), millionaire and philanthropist (whose fortune flowed from ownership of the Cardiff Docks and adjacent coalfields, and who funded Glasgow University's Bute Hall and St Andrews University's Bute Chair of Anatomy, together with many other gifts: though comparison with his near-contemporary, Andrew Carnegie, is interesting). According to Southgate *University Education* 112 n4 he "loathed ugly, industrial Dundee, politically Radical, with an upstart plutocracy [an odd opinion, if true, for one with wealth built on docks and coal], and despised its College, which he well-nigh ruined, not without damage to St Andrews itself", and described University College as "this abortion by the late Miss Baxter", as vituperative a comment upon a respectable Victorian spinster as it is possible

to imagine (quoted by Southgate, ibid, 97, from a private letter to the Earl of Rosebery, 21 May 1894, cited as Rosebery Papers [presumably Rosebery Estate Papers, NLS GRH.9. (175)] 10094 fs 129-130]). For a more sympathetic view, see Rosemary Hannah, *The Grand Designer: Third Marquess of Bute* (2012) especially chs 14 & 15, who (at 358) regards him as saving St Andrews University from the clutches of UCD, concluding that his interventions through the litigation of the 1890s were justified by the emergence of the University of Dundee (70 years later), and explains (at 301) the "abortion" remark as meaning that UCD was "stillborn, or rather, that it was dying before ever being fully-formed", though (at 297) displaying an uncertainty of touch by describing John Boyd Baxter and Mary Ann Baxter as siblings (seemingly citing Southgate as authority), and (at 298, 309, 315 & 358) variously describing UCD as "United College Dundee", "Queen's College Dundee", and "Dundee College".

[144] General Report of the 1889 Commissioners at lxi-lxii, asserting that "the union of St Andrews and Dundee, if established at all ... would have been wiser [if] of the nature of an incorporation or else the nature of an affiliation".

[145] Cant, *University of St Andrews* 147 fn2 and 151 fn1, concedes that "the financial position of St Andrews, which underlay some of the most serious doubts about its viability, was immensely improved by the great Berry Bequest". However, accounts of this bequest are surprisingly meagre. The fullest appears to be Reid, *Ever to Excel* 118-19 & 122-23 (also conceding the financial weakness as "represent[ing] a very real threat to the University's continued existence", at 134-135), recounting that it was bequeathed by Alexander Berry, from Cupar, who left without a degree in 1799, was employed as a ship's surgeon, emigrated to Australia and "became the massively wealthy owner of an estate in New South Wales", published scientific papers, entered politics, dying in 1873, seemingly with a will directing his brother to make the bequest (although no money appears to have been received for years). Anderson, *Education and Opportunity* 287 shows the bequest to be equal to the total sum that the Carnegie Trust for the Universities of Scotland (which distributed more than the Government did) shared out in 1901 among all Scottish universities, of which St Andrews was by far the smallest

[146] *M'Gregor & Others v University Court of St Andrews & Others* (1897) 5 SLT 102 (OH), (1897) 5 SLT 215 (IH) and (1898) 25 R 1216 (IH).

[147] Ordinance No 46 (St Andrews No 5) of 1894 (approved by the Privy Council on 15 January 1897), misleadingly entitled "Regulations as to the Application of Parliamentary Grants, as to Salaries, and for the Institution of a Fee Fund, and for Other Purposes", reproduced in General Report of the 1889 Commissioners 81. (Only Article 4 of the Agreement was changed from the original version).

[148] Upper Dens Works, on the north side of Princes Street, Dundee, is now converted to flats. Lower Dens Works, on the south side, is being converted into an hotel at the time of writing.

[149] This account, and the quotations reproduced, are taken chiefly from the various obituaries collected in the Dundee City Library Family and Local History Centre *Obituaries Notices 1885-1909*, 13-15, but see also Anon, *Roll of Eminent Burgesses of Dundee 1513-1886* (1887) 261-262 (available at http://www.fdca.org.uk/1823_JohnBoydBaxter.html, last accessed 27 July 2018), and FPSD Minutes.

[150] He had an "extensive Private practice besides acting as Procurator Fiscal": Dundee *Obituaries Notices 1885-1909* 47 (obituary of W B Dunbar).

[151] Anon, "Additional Sheriffs for Dundee" (1860) IV *JoJ* 135.

[152] See *Dundee Directories* for the period, McKean, Whatley & Baxter, *Lost Dundee* 55 & 58, Annette M Smith, *The Guildry of Dundee* (2005) 31-32, and *Dundee Advertiser* 9 January 1855 (recounting that Sheriffs had, for unclear reasons, on numerous occasions been denied use of the Guildry Room for their Court, and that on the occasion in question, Sheriff Logan had consequentially held his Court in - presumably Room - "No 45 of the British Hotel". I am grateful to Kenneth Baxter for this last reference).

[153] Southgate, *University Education* 6, 10-12.

[154] This account, and the quotations reproduced, are taken chiefly from the various obituaries collected in Dundee *Obituaries Notices 1895-1909* 15-18: she appears only in passing in Anon. *Eminent Burgesses of Dundee* but see also Matthew Jarron (ed), *Ten Taysiders* Abertay Historical Society No 51 (2011) ch 6.

[155] See Charles Dickens, *Bleak House*.

[156] Quoted in Southgate, *University Education* 23-30.

[157] Having later become the Scottish Congregational College, this is now the Scottish United Reformed and Congregational College, or Scottish College, West Regent Street, Glagow: see http://archiveshub.ac.uk/data/gb237-coll-737 (last accessed 27 July 2018). Mary Ann Baxter also endowed scholarships for the Hall (still operating as bursaries for ordinands matriculated at the College, and administered by the Dundee Congregational Church) and a Professorship of Systematic Theology, and financed acquisition of a property in George Square, Edinburgh, for the original Hall. I am grateful to Rev. Jack Dyce, Principal of the College, for this information..

[158] 28 & 29 Vict c 85, s 2.

[159] 36 & 37 Vict c 63, s 2.

[160] Lord Brougham's Act 1850 (13 & 14 Vict c 2) s 4, in force at the time of both 1865 and 1873 Acts, stipulated that "in all Acts importing the masculine gender it shall be deemed ... to include females", and the Interpretation Act 1889 (52 & 53 Vict c 63) s 1(a), in force at the time of the litigation, stipulated that "... in every Act ... words importing the masculine gender shall include females".

[161] *Hall v Incorporated Society of Law Agents* (1901) 3F 1059, (1901) 9 SLT 150 (IH, Whole Court). The Court ignored both Lord Brougham's Act 1850, and the Interpretation Act 1889, although both were raised in argument: *cf Nairn v University of St Andrews and Edinburgh University Courts* 1909 SC(HL) 10. There is a brief reference to Margaret Hall in Anon, "News" (1901-02) 9 *SLT* 13, and Anon, "Ladies in the Legal Profession" (1903-04) 11 *SLT* 114-115: see also Anon, "Lady Lawyers" (1900-01) 8 *SLT* 126.

[162] See Anon, "Undaunted ..." (1906-07) 14 *SLT* 106, which also refers appears to refer to Eveline MacLaren and Josephine Gordon Stuart, discussed below.

[163] 9 & 10 Geo V c 71 s 1, which provided that: "A person shall not be disqualified by sex or marriage from the exercise of any public function, or from being appointed to or holding any civil or judicial office or post, or from entering or assuming or carrying on any civil profession or vocation, or for admission to any incorporated society ...". S 2 additionally provided that "A woman shall be entitled to be admitted and enrolled as a solicitor after serving under articles for

three years only if ... she has taken such a university degree as would have so entitled her had she been a man ...".

[164] See "the Glasgow University Story" at www.universitystory.gla.ac.uk/biography/?id=WH1693&type=P (last accessed 27 July 2018) and Hector L MacQueen, "Scotland's First Women Law Graduates: an Edinburgh centenary", Edinburgh Law School Working Papers Series, No. 2009/22, 1-14 (2009). The former, incidentally, observes in passing that "Anderson" was her married name, "Easton" her *nom de jeune fille*. This is surprising given that women then usually gave up any employment upon marriage, but she was presumably thus the first married woman law agent, as well. Walker, *History of the School of Law* does not refer to her. The first woman solicitor in England seems to have been Carrie Morrison, in 1922: see http://first100years.org.uk/carrie-morrison-2/ (last accessed 27 July 2018).

[165] *Anderson, Petitioner* [not, incidentally, "Anderson or Easton", the usual style for married women] 1921 1 SLT 48 (IH). It was observed that s 2 was drafted in terms of English Law, but was readily applicable to Scotland, *mutatis mutandis*, though anyway irrelevant, as no law degree entitled anyone to be admitted as a law agent, because graduates still had to pass the Forms of Process examination. But why did she start the apprenticeship at a time when she could not have qualified?

[166] H C G Matthew & Brian Harrison, *Oxford Dictionary of National Biography* (2004). She was awarded a LLD by Dundee University in 1982. The first woman barrister, Ivy Williams, briefly preceded her: see Matthew & Harrison, *Oxford Dictionary of National Biography*.

[167] MacQueen, "Scotland's First Women Law Graduates ...".

[168] See Chapter 3. She was MA (St Andrews) LLB (Edinburgh), and seemingly the first woman MA LLB in Dundee.

[169] MacQueen, "Scotland's First Women Law Graduates ...".

[170] See MacQueen, "Scotland's First Women Law Graduates ...", also Anon, "Undaunted ..." 14 SLT 106, and Anon, "Admission of Women to Law Classes" (1906-07) SLT 161. In England, Elizabeth Orme was possibly the first woman law student, as she was seemingly "the first women to attain the LLB degree at the University of London (and in the British Empire) in 1888" (having already "opened a law office in Chancery Lane in the 1870s, after a short apprenticeship at Lincoln's Inn"): see Mary Jane Mossman, "Women Lawyers and Legal Equality: reflection on women lawyers at the 1893 World's Columbian Exposition in Chicago" (2012) 87 *Chicago-Kent Law Review* 503-591, at 507 (though no authority is cited). See also Mary Jane Mossman *The First Women Lawyers: a comparative study of gender, law and the legal profession* (2006), ch 3.

[171] I.e. 8 November 1919, and 23 December 1919, respectively.

[172] MacQueen, "Scotland's First Women Law Graduates ...".

[173] See Chapter 3. As discussed there, at least in her *nom de jeune fille,* she received no obituary in the *Scots Law Times*, nor in any newspaper covered by the Dundee City Library Family and Local History Centre *Obituaries Notices*, nor appears as a law agent in the *Dundee Directories* for likely years. If married, she would be unlikely to have taken or continued employment, though, as noted above, Madge Anderson appears to have done so.

[174] See Chapters 4 & 5.

[175] I am grateful to Peter Robson for this information.

CHAPTER 2

1865-1898: THE EARLY DAYS:

REPEATED ATTEMPTS TO LAUNCH A LAW SCHOOL

There were four sets of attempts in the 19th century to institute law teaching in Dundee The first of these, indeed seemingly the first ever recorded, was in the 1860s, preceded the founding of University College Dundee (UCD), and was at the instance of law clerks and apprentices, with the assistance of Thomas Thornton (whose activities dominate these developments), after inconclusive action by the Faculty of Procurators and Solicitors in Dundee (FPSD). It had limited success. The second, in the 1880s, followed the founding of UCD, but was once more at the instance of law clerks and apprentices, though under the auspices of UCD and the FPSD. It was even less successful. The third took place in the early 1890s, again under the auspices of UCD (by then "affiliated" to St Andrews University), and was seemingly largely at Thornton's instance. It was somewhat more successful. The fourth, in 1899, yet again under the auspices of UCD, and probably again at Thornton's instance, was finally successful, but discussion of it is reserved for the next Chapter.

Collectively, these various attempts spanned the period of the changes in the legal profession and in universities described in Chapter 1 as arguably "revolutionary". These changes included the near-unification of the legal profession and near-standardisation of legal education. They also included reform of the universities and the institution of law degrees and, not least, the founding of UCD, its affiliation to St Andrews, the rupture of that affiliation, and finally its restoration. Collectively, they shed light upon the development of law teaching, but also in part explain why the earlier attempts petered out.

This Chapter also considers those involved in the law teaching which took place in the first three attempts, whether as instigators, teachers, or students.

1865-70: The First Set of Attempts: Overture

Law teaching in Dundee seems to have started as a result of the external pressure of legislation, albeit indirect, mediated less through any initiative of the Faculty of Procurators and Solicitors in Dundee[1], than through pressure from law clerks and apprentices.

The first recorded steps occurred in 1865, clearly triggered by the Procurators (Scotland) Act of that year (rather than by the introduction of the LLB in Edinburgh three years earlier). As discussed in Chapter 1, for entry to the new national status of "procurator", this Act required, subject to exceptions, a four year apprenticeship, both general knowledge and law examinations to a national syllabus, and (in the first stage of the odd and complicated history of that obligation, also discussed in Chapter 1) attendance at University classes[2]. There was thus a law teaching requirement which could not be fulfilled in Dundee, and which appeared to be onerous for anyone outwith Aberdeen, Edinburgh or Glasgow.

However, as also discussed in Chapter 1, a major exception to these requirements was that local Faculties and Societies, if incorporated (as the FPSD was), were exempted (though they might opt in)[3]. We know broadly what the FPSD admission arrangements were, at least a few years later (and though it is possible that they had been amended in the light of the 1865 Act by then, the Index to the FPSD Minutes offers no suggestion that they were). With one major exception, they were in fact similar to those under the Act, including an apprenticeship of at least four years, and general knowledge, and law, examinations[4]. The major exception was that, unsurprisingly, there was no requirement to attend university classes[5]. Thus the exemption for incorporated local Societies and Faculties exempted Dundee apprentices from that obligation.

Nevertheless, while there was no direct pressure to institute law teaching, the new situation must have called out for at least a review of current practice. Although the contemporary Minutes of the FPSD are lost, a press report indicates that, shortly after the Act came into force, this new situation was discussed, and a committee set up to "consider the various duties imposed upon the Society, and the powers conferred on it by the Procurators' Act and to report [and also] to meet with Sheriff Oglivy[6] to consider the course of law lectures proposed to be instituted in Dundee[7]."

Unlike the Minutes themselves, the Index to the FPSD Minutes for this period has survived and, in clear reference to this event, records a "Committee to Consider the Propriety of Instituting Law Lectures in Dundee"[8]. The press report and Index entry seem to be the first recorded references to the possibility of law teaching in Dundee.

The committee's report was discussed inconclusively at the AGM of the FPSD in the following February, though it is clear that the FPSD did not opt in[9]. There was discussion led by Mr Grant[10], who quoted Sheriff Ogilvy as to "the propriety" of a course of twenty, admittedly superficial, law lectures, every two or three years for apprentices "before proceeding to University classes"[11]. However, that discussion was also inconclusive, and there is no record of any classes resulting.

No doubt because nothing eventuated from the FPSD deliberations, and clearly with shrieval approval, the clerks and apprentices took matters into their own hands, for later that year a "well-attended meeting of law clerks" in the newly-completed Sheriff Court, agreed that lectures would be of great advantage to clerks and apprentices[12]. Messrs More and Ogilvie (solicitors), Moffat (Depute Sheriff Clerk), Thain jnr. and Petrie (presumably clerks or apprentices) took the lead, and an *ad hoc* Committee was formed, reporting two weeks later[13]. It reported that Sheriff (in modern terms, Sheriff-Principal[14]) Heriot[15] was busy, but that Sheriff-Substitute (in modern terms, Sheriff) Guthrie Smith[16] had secured the services of "James" [*scil.* William] Guthrie, clearly an up-and-coming advocate with academic interests[17], to give a lecture on "Law Studies" in January 1867, and of "one of the members of the local Bar – Thomas Thornton, Esq"[18] to give two lectures on "The History and General Principles of Conveyancing" thereafter. Use of an advocate, who would presumably expect a fee, first class return rail fare from Edinburgh, and overnight accommodation[19], is surprising, and perhaps intended to show that the classes should be taken seriously. There is no hint as to the financing of the classes but, in the light of later events, it seems likely that Thornton provided the funds.

At the same meeting, possibly sensing unwillingness on the part of the FPSD to organise matters, the *ad hoc* Committee also recommended founding a Law Clerks & Apprentices Society (LCAS) to arrange lectures "with a view of advancing the facilities whereby law clerks may be better prepared for [examinations]." This suggests a hope for more than occasional lectures by guest advocates or local practitioners, and might suggest that classes equivalent to university ones were intended. Indeed, though this was some years before formal discussions on a Dundee College (linked to St Andrews University or otherwise) started, the idea was "floating about", and it is clear that some people might be turning their thoughts towards a free-standing law school[20], or a revived St Andrews University Law Faculty, located in Dundee.

Sheriff Heriot was elected Honorary President of the Society[21] on the spot; Sheriff Guthrie Smith, President; Mr Thain jun., Vice-President; and Messrs H Jamieson, J Robertson, W McCall, D Duncan, P McIntyre and J W Leslie, Committee members (though it is not clear that the Sheriffs were actually present: presumably the others were clerks or apprentices)[22].

That expectations were high for something more than preparatory lectures was evident at the first of these LCAS lectures, given by William Guthrie on 18 January 1867, in the Sheriff Court[23]. It was chaired by Sheriff Guthrie Smith, who hoped it "would not be an inappropriate beginning to … the commencement of a permanent law school in Dundee [Applause]."

Just as the discussion at the 1866 AGM of the FPSD seems to have been the first reference to law teaching in Dundee so, just a year later, this event seems to have been the first actual law teaching there, which also provided the occasion for the first explicit public suggestion of a Dundee law school (made, incidentally, without any hint of co-operation with St Andrews University). William Guthrie himself was "very eloquent and instructive", wide-ranging[24] and encouraging[25]. During comments and questions afterwards, and entering into the spirit of the meeting and of Sheriff Guthrie Smith's hopes, Thornton enjoined law clerks to take notes in the future lectures, suggested lecturers provide references, found it "delightful" that there were upwards of 70 law clerks (and apprentices?) there. He further proposed a sort of tutorial after each lecture run by the Sheriff, and suggested the local profession might supply "three prizes of some value" for performance in them.

Thomas Thornton gave his own two lectures on Conveyancing in mid-February 1867[26]. More lectures were reported in the press later that month[27], including ones on "Sale" by Mr J D Grant[28]; "the Administration of Justice" by Bailie Hay[29]; "Changes on [*sic*] our Mercantile Law introduced by the Mercantile Law (Amendment) (Scotland) Act 1856" by John Trayner, advocate[30]; "Our Law as a System of Equity" by George Thoms, advocate[31]; and "the Law of Partnership and Joint Stock Companies" by Francis W Clark, advocate[32]. Clearly, the enthusiastic participation of several members of the FPSD countered its earlier hesitancy. However, the predominance of further up-and-coming advocates is equally interesting. Thomas Thornton may have had to draw further his privy purse, as well as his contacts.

However, despite the ambition shown, clearly these lectures did not in fact go far towards preparing for the FPSD examinations described above (or, alternatively, for the "law agents' triad" of professional examinations[33]), though an axe-grinding letter eighteen months later, considered below, suggested otherwise. Still less did they go far towards "the permanent establishment of a law school", most particularly when one recalls that the university law teaching tradition was one of professors reading out notes on the whole of Scots Law and Conveyancing (or as much as could be covered), which the students copied and learned, and were then examined on.

Nevertheless, ambition for a law school was undimmed, for an anonymous article in a legal journal at this time constituted a manifesto for one[34]. The anonymous author, praising the law clerks and apprentices for their initiative, observed that in the first year, lectures "must necessarily be desultory and unsystematic", but might amount to preparation for "more methodical and sustained exertion ... next winter".

And further:

if there is to be 'a permanent law school in Dundee', we must be allowed to express a hope that the Society of Procurators [*sic*] there will do much more than present a few prizes to be competed for at the end of the course of lectures ... [and will] follow up the beginning which has successfully been made by establishing, in co-operation with the Society of Law Clerks [*sic*], a permanent lectureship [thus paralleling the foundation of the Chairs of Scots Law and Conveyancing in Edinburgh[35]].

Most remarkably, yet further:

[w]e believe that it has been in the minds of influential persons in Dundee to endeavour to effect the removal to that city of a part at least of the University of St Andrews ... and of adding a Faculty of Law which is now wanting in that University. Such a scheme may probably be realized, and it would materially contribute to this result if a law school should already be in successful operation in Dundee, originated and supported by the voluntary efforts of the legal profession [though it would] be impossible for a single lecturer to include within any reasonable number of lectures the whole law of Scotland.

Guthrie was editor of the journal in which this appeared. John Boyd Baxter[36] might already have been nurturing thoughts of a University College, and of a link to St Andrews, and was later among those giving lectures in Dundee (and might have been among the "influential persons"[37]). But the article has the stamp of Thornton on it.

A further, second, set of lectures, given by members of the local profession (including a sheriff), and presumably under the auspices of LCAS, took place over the winter of 1867-68, though none by advocates, as such. The first was on "the Principles of Jurisprudence", delivered by Sheriff Guthrie Smith, followed by nine on Civil Law[38] delivered, it is interesting to note, by John Boyd Baxter (by then Preses of the FPSD)[39].

Civil Law was an odd choice, since it was not required by the FPSD examinations, and nor was it part of the "law agents' triad". Perhaps it was designed, like the earlier use of advocates as lecturers, to show the seriousness of the enterprise, and indicate intellectual weight. Another anonymous article, certainly from the same pen as first, recorded (so fulsomely that one suspects ulterior motives, and clearly excluding the possibility of Baxter's authorship) that "[t]hough Mr Baxter [then 72] started late in life as a lecturer … these lectures are but a foretaste of what may be expected from his mature though unobtrusive literary and legal acquirements. He is the Nestor of the legal profession in Dundee"[40]. However, it was followed by at least five further lectures on the more obviously useful topic of "personal and domestic relations" in Scots Law[41], delivered by Grant (again)[42], and other topics, delivered by William Bell[43] and (again) Thornton[44].

Overall, the second anonymous article applauded the LCAS's "vigorous existence" and flattered the FPSD by describing it as "set[ting] an example to the rest of the profession in Scotland in the performance of the duties which they owe to their apprentices who, as students, are too much left to shift for themselves." It also suggested that the lectures were an example which might profitably be followed "in other towns not favoured with a legal chair"[45].

There was also a series of lectures by Henry Gibson[46] on "The Law of Cautionary Obligations" started in March 1868 in the Burgh Court-room[47], presumably as part of the Society's series.

But in the winter of 1868-69, lectures appeared to be abandoned. Attendance at the second series of lectures had not been as good, and the LCAS was in decline, as revealed in the lengthy, and somewhat axe-grinding, Letter to the Editor in May 1868, referred to above, from James

Thain, joint-initiator and first Vice-President of the Society[48]. (He also claimed, implausibly, that there were 200 law clerks in Dundee[49]).

No response to this letter appears to have been published, and there is no record of any law lectures over the winter of 1868-69. Indeed, another Letter to the Editor in December 1868, this time pseudonymously signed "Lex", and apparently from a member of the LCAS who attended the lectures of the previous winter, indicated that he was "anxious to know if [they] are to be continued this year"[50], to which, again, no response appears to have been published. The idea of a "permanent law school" was clearly losing momentum.

Nevertheless, undaunted, and clearly not dead, in October 1869, the LCAS convened a meeting to consider a third series of lectures[51]. The meeting, with continuing ambitions, explicitly expressed hopes that, given by a "properly qualified person", such lectures "should be conducted as nearly as may be on the footing of the university law classes, so that attendance at the lectures might to a certain extent come in place of or be equivalent to attendance at the University[52]."

Further lectures were indeed arranged[53]. These commenced with one from Sheriff Guthrie Smith (again) on "The Legal Theory of the State"; followed by "The Principles and Practice of the Criminal Law" by W B Dunbar, Procurator-Fiscal[54]; Andrew Hendry, solicitor[55], on either "The Practical Object of the Profession" or "Legal Oaths" (reports vary); Grant (again) on "Land Rights"; possibly a Mr More on an unknown topic; and finally Thornton (again) on "The Law of Succession"[56].

A yet further anonymous article, seemingly from the same pen as before, and published halfway through the series, simply recorded pleasure[57]. But this series of lectures, however interesting and well-delivered, still did not constitute preparation for the examinations, and a continuing loss of momentum can be detected.

In April 1870 the law clerks were still sufficiently organised to meet in order to consider means of shortening their hours in summer[58], and the

LCAS had its "first annual gathering" ("in the Cafe Royal") in October of that year[59]. But thereafter, no record of lectures, or of the LCAS, appears.

Whether or not enthusiasm was waning, one specific event, the second stage of the odd and complicated history of the obligation to attend law classes, may have seemed the end of the line for law lectures in Dundee.

As discussed in Chapter 1, the Law Agents (Scotland) Act 1873 replaced the Procurators (Scotland) Act 1865, and not only removed the automatic exemption of incorporated Societies and Faculties from the statutory admission requirements, but also continued, indeed enhanced, the attendance requirement, by obliging all those seeking admission not only to have attended, "the Classes of Scots Law and Conveyancing in a Scottish University ... in two separate Winter Sessions" but also "[to have] taken part in the Examinations" in them[60]." Clearly, Dundee classes could never fulfil this requirement, so any hopes for them seemed to have been sunk[61].

However, could it be that this attendance requirement (and perhaps the introduction of the BL in 1874, as discussed in Chapter 1) helped to set John Boyd Baxter's mind turning towards the possibility of a university institution in Dundee? As noted in Chapter 1, it was at this time that thoughts of a Dundee College, connected with St Andrews University, and therefore in line to offer university classes and examinations, was being considered. In any case, this enhanced obligation turned out not to be the last word on the university attendance requirement. So any reports of the death of law lectures would have proved premature.

1883-87: The Second Set of Attempts: Beginners I

A law school had been in the minds of some from at least 1865, as we have seen, and one retrospective account of the debates in the 1870s which led to the foundation of UCD, by someone closely involved, records numerous suggestions for law teaching at that time (presumably in the knowledge of the attempts of the 1860s), though, unfortunately, the references are usually anonymised and undated[62].

One, a contribution to the press[63], principally addressed to St Andrews University, observed that "there might be the rudiments of a Legal School established in Dundee", and asked "why should not the solicitors of the future be taught at least part of their profession within the walls of the College of Dundee?", ambitiously suggesting that there "might be Chairs for the teaching of Scots Law, of Roman Law, and of Conveyancing; [and] others might be added, as the College advanced in endowments[64]." Another contribution observed that in "the course of time, Medical and Legal Schools might gather round a [science-based] Academic Foundation when once fairly laid[65]." Slightly less anonymously, "a Fellow of the Royal Society of Edinburgh" made similar remarks[66].

Presumably, all these considered that removal of the exemption from the university class and examination requirement, which had seemingly sunk law teaching in 1873 (in the second stage of the odd and complicated history of the obligation), in fact presented no problem because, as hinted in the suggestions quoted above, either the proposed College would be treated as a University, or there would be a sufficient link with St Andrews University to allow fulfilment of the obligation. Indeed, the requirement could now be turned to advantage, for in either case, the College would join the oligopoly offering accredited classes. However, as noted in Chapter 1, the hopes of the early 1870s for a Dundee College fell foul of difficulties in relations with St Andrews University and industrial depression, delaying any opportunity to found a College.

Nevertheless, as discussed in Chapter 1, the recommendations of the Royal Commission of 1878, together with the intervention of the Baxters, resulted in the founding of UCD in 1881, and, two decades after the first law classes, with the possibility of fulfilling the requirement to attend university classes and examinations, this might have been thought a propitious moment for considering law teaching there[67]. Indeed, in

October 1883, as UCD finally opened, the Principal of St Andrews, John Tulloch[68] observed in a letter "to a citizen friend in Dundee" that "nothing could be more likely than the speedy growth of a Medical School, and also indeed of a Law School"[69].

Certainly, the principal participants in the founding of UCD might have been expected to favour the idea. John Boyd Baxter was a law agent, Procurator Fiscal, Preses of the FPSD, member of the Royal Commission on the Scottish Law Courts whose recommendations produced the Law Agents (Scotland) Act 1873 (as discussed in Chapter 1), and had been directly involved in the 1866-70 law lectures. Thomas Thornton was also a law agent. Mary Ann Baxter, though clearly not a law agent, sought to encourage advanced study of trades useful in a growing industrial and commercial city, which might include the law.

Yet law was not even on the Baxter/Thornton wish-list of subjects for the College, and any opportunity was seemingly lost. All that is recorded is Thomas Thornton's observation that a Latin class would be useful to law students[70]. In the light of Principal Tulloch's views quoted above, the silence cannot have been for fear of conflict with St Andrews University. More likely, the lack of success with the earlier classes suggested that law was just too great a risk, at least in the short term. Nevertheless, with a UCD link to St Andrews University a distinct possibility, Thomas Thornton was probably just biding his time.

However, not long after, there were attempts by others, in the light of the founding of UCD, to get law lectures restarted. The complicated sequence of events can be reconstructed from UCD Council Minutes and related papers, newspaper reports and the Index to FPSD Minutes[71]. Thus, we know a surprising amount about this episode. It does not shed very favourable light upon either the FPSD or UCD, and Thornton's involvement is remarkable for its absence.

The renewed attempts were again triggered by law clerks and apprentices, though not, seemingly, as a revived LCAS, fifteen years after its presumed demise. In the summer of 1885, they sent to the FPSD "a

Memorial… praying [it] to institute a law lectureship in connection with Dundee University College[72]."

The timing and purpose of this Memorial are interesting. Possibly it reflected disappointment at the failure of UCD to institute law lectures itself. Probably it was in expectation that any UCD lectures would count as "university classes". Presumably it was in ignorance of the fact that the obligation to attend university lectures would, to great surprise, be removed the following year.

The FPSD called a meeting on 3 July 1885 to consider the Memorial[73]. Unhelpfully putting cart before horse, it seemingly suggested that "no benefit would result from the movement unless a law lecturer were appointed". However, it did send a letter to Messrs Shiell & Small[74], then UCD's "Secretaries", recounting that:

> [u]pwards of 100 of the Law Clerks and Apprentices in town have presented a Memorial to the [FPSD] urging the institution of a course of Law Lectures and suggesting that the [FPSD] should communicate with the authorities of University College with the view of obtaining a Room in the College in which the Lectures might be delivered[75].

It added that this proposal was "favourably entertained by the [FPSD]", who had set up a Committee "to obtain information on the subject".

UCD Council reacted slowly. A couple of months later, a meeting was requisitioned to consider the letter, but was inquorate, so recalled for October 1885[76]. The recalled meeting (Thornton, though a member, absent, perhaps diplomatically) suggested a Joint Committee with the FPSD to consider the matter, and appointed three of its members (Sheriff Campbell Smith[77], Mr Robertson[78] and Mr Cunningham), also requesting the Principal (not then a member of the UCD Council) to be present.

The Principal, however, was keen on the idea, seeing expansion into this area as a way out of other difficulties. His letter to the next UCD

Council meeting noted the fragility of student numbers in the College as a whole and, rather sanguinely, hoped the discussions with FPSD would be concluded in time for law classes to commence in the New Year[79].

The FPSD, also acting slowly, appointed members to the Joint Committee shortly after that[80]. This Committee met in November (though without Sheriff Campbell Smith), but merely sub-delegated to Messrs Pattullo[81] and Agnew[82] (the Secretary) for the FPSD, and Principal Peterson (who was also absent) for UCD, the task of enquiring to how many students were likely, how much the lecturer should be paid, and who might be lecturer[83].

A month later the Joint Committee met again[84], and considered a letter from Peterson (read into the Minute) which included a proposal by himself and Pattullo (Agnew nevertheless largely concurring), dealing with these questions.

The first thing to notice about this proposal is that, whatever the hopes of the Memorialists, it clearly did not seek to institute "university classes" for the purposes of qualification as a law agent, at least in the short term. Indeed, there is no hint in the discussions outlined above that any representations had been made to achieve that.

The second, however, is that it was nevertheless ambitious. After consultation with the Memorialists, the Joint Committee decided that the lectures should cover contracts generally, and sale, employment, hire, promissory notes, partnerships "and the like" in particular. Nevertheless, all this was to be covered in just twelve lectures[85], partly because of shortage of time, partly because of cost. Also, Peterson suggested that the lecturer would have to bear in mind that the students would "have little or no experience in the study of law and ... will require a deal of guidance to the textbooks and cases they ought to read up." Moreover, underlining their non-qualifying nature, but possibly seeking to maximise the income from them, the proposal suggested that the lectures might be available the general public.

"Mr McLennan of Edinburgh"[86] was suggested as a suitable lecturer, and he would be content with "Fifty or Sixty Guineas". Law clerks should be charged 7/6d, "outsiders" 10/6 but, significantly: "[h]alf of any balance required to meet the Lecturer's fee would probably be got from the [FPSD] or at all events from [its] individual members". Optimistically, Pattullo thought "no great difficulty would be experienced in raising the balance".

Peterson's letter also advised, however, that "additional enquiries" and further consultation[87] (presumably after the proposal had been drafted), had suggested that thirteen or fourteen lectures was a more appropriate number, and (aiming high) that a more suitable lecturer would be "Mr Shaw MA, LLB, advocate"[88], who would also give the lectures for "from fifty to sixty pounds", and that 60[?][89] law clerks would attend on the terms suggested.

But the FPSD and College were ambivalent, producing failure. There was "considerable discussion" of the Joint Committee's proposal at a well-attended FPSD General Meeting on 23 December 1885[90]. It was approved, but with a complicated sequence of amendments, making it abundantly clear that (contrary to Henry Pattullo's expectations) there was strong opposition to financial support from the FPSD. A further motion that "individual members of the [FPSD] contribute towards" a guarantee of the lecturer's fee, despite a further complicated sequence of amendments, was carried.

UCD Council also remained unconvinced, and clearly did not want to run the lectures itself, though agreeing to the request for house room[91]. Nevertheless, Principal Peterson remained enthusiastic, and in January 1886 the press reported that, when introducing a series of public lectures on Political Economy, he had assured the audience that "there would be no danger of this College ever becoming merely a College of Physical Science ... [and] spoke particularly of two subjects - law and economics – the former more or less special, the latter more widely popular." Most significantly, he added that "he was glad to know that many members of the legal profession [present] were alive to the importance of the proposal to institute a course of law lectures as being possibly the first step towards securing the privilege now possessed by Aberdeen of having university teaching in law recognised by the Faculty of Advocates and the Court of Session[92] (Applause)." On the other hand, it does not appear that the lectures ever took place.

In 1886 (in the third stage of the odd and complicated history of the requirement to attend university classes), seemingly to considerable surprise, the obligation was removed by Act of Sederunt[93]. This breaking of the university oligopoly might seem a god-send to those promoting law classes in Dundee. Apprentices taking the examinations would want, possibly need, them, therefore it would not be necessary to argue whether they were university classes or not.

However, mysteriously, the dog did not bark. There is no record of the law clerks and apprentices, the FPSD or UCD even considering this opportunity. Perhaps all were too worn down by the repeated failures, and anyway expected the position to be reversed in the near future (rather than 40 years later, as was in fact the case)[94], and Thornton was no doubt still biding his time.

A couple of years later, a spark of hope was struck by a Bill to amend the Law Agents (Scotland) Act 1873, which the Principal's Report for 1887-88 suggested "might hasten the addition of Law Teaching to our curriculum of study"[95].

Presumably he was referring to the Bill to Amend the Law Agents Act 1873, of 1887[96], the Private Member's Bill discussed in Chapter 1 which (in the fourth stage in the odd and complicated history of the obligation) sought to restore the requirement to attend university classes, but did so in a particularly usefully extended form. It would be fulfilled not only by classes "conducted by professors or lecturers in a Scotch [*sic*] University", but also by those conducted by lecturers in any other "School of Law" approved by the judges of the Court of Session, and even in ones "not connected with any University or School of Law", if so approved. Unsurprisingly, the Principal added that it was "gratifying to note that the promoters of the Bill point out that University College is 'pre-eminently a place where the provisions of the Bill could and should be taken advantage of'[97]."

But this is paradoxical. While the breaking of the university oligopoly in 1886 had not been treated as an opportunity, its possible reintroduction with UCD as one of the oligopolists in 1887 was. Nevertheless, even this opportunity slipped away. No doubt because it came in the middle of tricky negotiations with St Andrews University about the "affiliation" of UCD, the Principal cautiously added that anything "done in this direction would no doubt be undertaken in co-operation with St Andrews, which has no Faculty of Law at present[98]."

Whether any discussion of law teaching occurred in these negotiations is unknown. Thornton's involvement in them, but silence on the possibility of law classes at this time, might suggest it did not. On the other hand, his remarks three years later, discussed below, about "try[ing] to get a Chair of Law founded" suggest that it did, but that he did not get his way. In any event, even the paradoxical spark of hope was extinguished as the Bill appears to have fallen[99].

1890-98: The Third Set of Attempts: Beginners II

Nevertheless, demand was not dead, and in 1890, there were attempts to start law lectures upon the occasion of the "affiliation" of University College Dundee to St Andrews University.

An anonymous Letter to the Editor in August 1888 had lamented the lack of such lectures[100]. Another in December 1889 had suggested that economies of scale might allow joint classes for bank clerks and law clerks[101]. And in 1890, the "Order" of the "executive Commissioners" under the Universities (Scotland) Act 1858, and the formal Agreement, affiliating UCD to St Andrews University (discussed in Chapter 1), were promulgated. Although the university class attendance requirement had not been restored, an impetus was provided. In what can hardly be a coincidence, three attempts, almost simultaneous (though not all, on the face of it, linked), were made at that time to restart law lectures.

However, the first, limited, attempt to restart lectures comprised an unknown number given by Mr Littlejohn, a prominent member of the local profession[102]. They commenced in March 1890, just a week before the affiliating "Order" was made[103].

We know a good deal more about the content of these lectures than that of the earlier ones for, later that year, they were published as a book[104]. This book indicates that they did not simply deal with a number of specific, but disparate, topics as the earlier lectures had done. Rather, it seems, they sought to cover the whole of Scots Law, as traditionally conceived, in the traditional categorisation (stemming from Civil Law) of the "law of persons", "law of actions" and "law of things". As the original book was 70 pages long, it seems implausible that there were only the two lectures suggested by the press report advertising them[105].

How far the lectures were organised by the FPSD is unclear. There is no reference to them in the Index to their Minutes, but the Preface to the First Edition of the book recounted, with barely disguised disappointment (and slightly confusing grammar), that:

> this address [*sic*] ... was delivered on the understanding that it would be followed by similar addresses from other members of the Local Bar, [despite doubt as to] whether a sufficient number of gentlemen would be found willing to prepare lectures, [notwithstanding which] I resolved to prepare and deliver this address as I had promised, and other gentlemen had, I believe, undertaken to prepare lectures against next winter.

It is worth noting that the third edition was twice that length of the first, in order, according to its preface:

> to include various new subjects not usually found in law books but which have come under the author's observation in the course of an extensive and varied legal practice [including]

references to the Lunacy Acts, the Income Tax Acts, the Electoral Franchises, the Corrupt Practices Acts, the Marriage Laws, the Law of Copyright, the Joint-Stock Company Laws, and [a] short account of the constitution of the different Courts of Law in the United Kingdom ... [and though] originally intended to be only a general treatise, [it] has gradually extended itself into a book of reference.

This edition was described in Littlejohn's obituary as "unambitious, but useful and very readable" but nevertheless (with perhaps permissible exaggeration, and presumably intentionally commenting on the state of legal writing) as "being accepted by the profession as one of their most useful books of reference, containing, as it does, so many authorities for the statements made – a feature which has been wanting in so many of its predecessors[106]."

A second, aborted, attempt in that year emerged in an FPSD General Meeting on 23 April 1890 (a date of great significance, as we shall see). One of the matters discussed (without specific reference to Mr Littlejohn's recent lecture, but corroborating his assertion that there would be "similar addresses from other members of the Local Bar") was "whether it would be advisable that arrangements should be made for Members of the [FPSD] delivering a course of Law Lectures during the ensuing Winter[107]." However, this second attempt did not survive that meeting, being overtaken by a third, successful, attempt, disclosed in the same Minute.

In that Minute, the Secretary noted that he had received a letter from Thornton (so conspicuously absent from initiatives of the 1880s) revealing a new scheme for lectures, involving UCD, but clearly developed without reference to the FPSD[108]. The FPSD (possibly with a collective sigh of relief) "highly approved of and expressed their great satisfaction" with this, and set up a Committee to assist him[109].

In what cannot be a coincidence[110], also on 23 April 1890, Thornton wrote another letter on the subject, this time to Principal Peterson[111]. In a clear reference to the lectures of 1866-70, he recounted that:

[m]any years ago, I delivered to the law clerks and apprentices of Dundee lectures on the feudal law and principles of conveyancing and a year or two after that on the law of succession and kindred subjects [and the] late Mr A J [sic] Grant and others of my friends followed with lectures on other subjects[112].

Modestly, he went on to confess that "our lectures failed to produce any practical results", and offered his conclusion that "systematic instruction would alone promote the study of law". In other words, he concluded that largely *ad hoc* lectures on a variety of topics, which had characterised previous attempts, were pointless. A formal series of lectures addressing the "law agents' triad" of Scots Law, Conveyancing (and possibly Forms of Process[113]) for the professional examinations was required.

Thomas Thornton's ambition produced the founding declaration of the School of Law. Revealing his scheme, and shedding some light on his silence on law classes during the 1880s, he declared that "I have for many years desired to see a Lectureship in Law established" and indeed that "since our University College was created, I have again tried to get a Chair of Law founded"[114]. If true, this can hardly have been news to Principal Peterson, so the letter was no doubt intended for publication.

But if true, with whom had he had negotiations, for what, and when? Answers must be speculative, but possibly they had been with local philanthropists to fund a Chair: possibly (as speculated upon above) with St Andrews University, in the course of the affiliation negotiations, to accede to its institutional location there, but its physical location in Dundee, and its intellectual location within the Baxters' vision of the purpose of tertiary education; possibly with the Faculty of Advocates to find a suitable candidate; possibly all three. In any event, the lack of success in either of the first two might explain the proposal which emerged.

This founding declaration (faintly echoing Sheriff Guthrie Smith's hopes for "a permanent law school", expressed at the very first LCAS lecture nearly 25 years before, and the anonymous "manifesto" of a dozen years before), continued:

> subject to the approval of the Council of University College and to the sanction of the University Court of St Andrews I have now resolved to establish a law lectureship for two or three years with a view to encouraging young men desiring to follow the profession ... [and] to test the likely success of a Law Chair, should it afterwards be found possible to endow one[115].

In brief, Thornton would go it alone, and organise and fund the lectureship himself, as he had with earlier lectures, but with the hope that others would take up the baton thereafter. He related that he was raising the matter with the FPSD, suggesting a Committee to liaise with the UCD Council, and asking for co-operation (as he had done in the letter considered by it on the very same day, noted above). To provide extra weight, he added (suggesting the negotiations with the Faculty of Advocates, hypothesised above, unlike the others, might have had some success) that "I have already elicited the views of some highly valued friends, both on the bench and at the bar, and they heartily approve of the proposal[116]."

The proposal needs to be looked at in detail. The letter went on to explain that his aim was to have the law students matriculate at UCD, but for a "very moderate" matriculation fee, and class fee of 10/6d, "in order to encourage every young man, however poor, to take advantage of the course of study". Explicitly noting that the frequency of trains would increase with the opening of the Forth Bridge[117] (presumably with a thought for advocates, living in Edinburgh) and also relying on the rest of the local rail network (with a thought for students, living in a variety of locations), he:

contemplate[d] that the lectures should be on such days and such hours as might best suit the general convenience, and if possible the hour should suit not only Dundee clerks and apprentices, but those of the other towns of Forfarshire, and say Perth, Cupar and St Andrews[118].

Clearly, he was fitting his plan within the Baxters' philanthropic intentions, preserved in the Agreement between UCD and St Andrews University. Anticipating financial objections, he added that "the nominal class fee will entail more expense upon me, but that is of no matter". Indeed, he hoped "to obtain a lecturer of eminence and position, and I shall most willingly pay him an ample salary in addition to the small class fee, which will of course, be his own."

Equally clearly aiming at the professional syllabus for law agents, he also proposed "three winter sessions" from October to March[119]. The first would deal with "Scots law properly so called"[120], the second with "Scotch [sic] Conveyancing" and the third with "Commercial and Company Law"[121]. By this means, "young men attending for the three sessions should ... acquire as good a legal education as is now obtained at Edinburgh or Glasgow, and be able to pass their law examinations[122]." There should be no dilatoriness as "with your assistance the Lectureship might be opened next session [though] there is little time to lose as the lecturer should have ample time to prepare his course."

The University College response was encouraging. At the UCD Council meeting, again on 23 April 1890, Peterson read out the letter, and the Council "cordially accepted" the proposal, appointing a Committee (with Thornton himself, though absent, as Convenor)[123]. At its next, May, meeting, Thornton was again absent, but recorded his thanks[124], and at its June meeting, a further letter from him (seemingly by-passing the Committee[125]) was read, nominating as lecturer Mr William C Smith, Advocate, Edinburgh[126], and the UCD Council unanimously approved[127]. This was sufficient for the Principal to record in June 1890, in his Report in UCD Calendar for 1890-91, that:

[t]hrough the liberality of Mr Thomas Thornton to whom the College is under a deep obligation for the services which he rendered in connection with the union with St Andrews, we are to have the opportunity next session of breaking new ground in the department [i.e. discipline] of Law. Mr W C Smith, advocate, Edinburgh, has been asked to deliver the course for which various indications of the needs of the district seem to guarantee a large measure of success ...[128].

In September, Thornton (conspicuously absent yet again) asked the UCD Council by letter what the registration fee for the classes might be, and was told there would be none, as they counted as evening classes[129]. This could have been a disappointment to him, as evening classes might be less likely to count as "university classes" if the requirement to attend them were re-imposed, and might not attract all the privileges of a student, such as access to the Library. Thornton might well have had advance knowledge that the power to require university attendance was (in the fifth stage of the odd and complicated history of the obligation) shortly to be enacted[130], though he can hardly have foreseen it would not be invoked until 1926. There is later evidence that they were, in fact, treated as day classes[131].

In the same reply, UCD Council added, somewhat greedily under the circumstances, that it would retain one third of the class fee to meet its expenses, which appear to have been limited to heating and lighting. Nevertheless, it showed rather more enthusiasm than it had for the proposal of five years before.

The FPSD dragged its feet again, however. A couple of days after his 23 April 1890 letter, Thornton wrote once more to its Secretary, referring to a conversation on the previous day which "has induced me to go forward"[132], and enjoining him to do what he must have known from that conversation had already been done, that is, get a small committee appointed. But he added mysteriously (as noted above) that "There is no need for secrecy now". It is not clear what this referred to, unless the Secretary had kept the FPSD, or the public at large, in the dark about the plans, but it is evidence that Thornton had been negotiating with various parties.

Nevertheless, the FPSD still moved slowly, for at its next Meeting, three and a half months later, in August (well after the UCD Council had approved the choice of lecturer), further communications with Thornton were produced and remitted to the existing committee[133], and more than a month after that, the Committee's Report (tellingly "revised by Mr Thornton") was read to the September Meeting[134] (well after details of dates and lecturer had been reported in the press[135]).

Giving substance to the phrase "revised by Mr Thornton", the Committee's Report makes it clear that he simply told them his plans, and asked for co-operation, largely to be supplied by agreement to a Circular to FPSD members, already drafted.

That Circular[136] made clear that Thornton had effected all the arrangements, and that there would be 60 lectures commencing on 6 October 1890, "embracing the most prominent and useful subjects for legal practitioners" and "specially intended [for] apprentices and clerks [in] different law offices in the Town and Neighbourhood"[137], therefore fixed for 6.30pm. Although they were seemingly designed to help apprentices "to pass their law examinations", that was not made explicit and, perhaps as insurance against small attendance, but risking falling between stools, they were asserted to be "of such a character as to be useful even for young men outside the profession".

Nevertheless, it was declared that the "success of the lectures [would] depend on the attendance of those for whom they are specifically intended", as the Circular recorded that "the [FPSD] desire earnestly to impress upon members of the profession, to urge upon their clerks and apprentices the advantage to themselves of regular attendance" (and might find it convenient to attend themselves)[138]. Most significant of all, "[s]uccess now may mean permanence of a Law Lectureship in Dundee". Further, it expressed the hoped that the Lecturer would be introduced by Lord Trayner[139]. Thomas Thornton had prepared his ground.

The lectures were to be delivered (as anticipated) by William C Smith, Advocate[140]. We do not know why he was lit upon, but his academic interests and achievements, and political predilections[141], might have suggested him to Lord Trayner, who was presumably one of Thornton's "highly valued friends".

Remarkably, given the time scale, and providing hard evidence of his abilities as a fixer, Thornton got the lectures advertised in the St Andrews University Calendar for 1890-91 (along with Peterson's encomium), where they were described as covering Scots Law "with special reference to Personal Status, Contract, Property, and Succession"[142].

The original commencement date having been found "impractical" (but with no hint of the nature of the impracticality), the lectures were delayed until January 1891[143]. Notices advertising them appeared on the front page of the *Dundee Courier*.

The FIRST of the COURSE of LECTURES on SCOTS LAW, previously advertised, will be delivered by W.C. Smith, Esq, Advocate, on Monday 5th January, 1891, at 6.30pm.

The LECTURES will be continued on MONDAYS, WEDNESDAYS and FRIDAYS at the same hour.

Fee (including College Registration), 10s. 6d.

G.W. ALEXANDER, M.A. Secretary[144]

Further advertisements added that "The Hon. Lord Trayner will preside and introduce the Lecturer", whose opening subject would be "The Sources of Scots Law"[145]. Unfortunately, there was no indication of where in the College the lectures would be held (but the most likely location was the original College Hall[146], where the College's inaugural ceremony had taken place).

Some 50 people attended. There is no record of the content of the lecture, but in his inaugural speech from the chair, Lord Trayner:

took the occasion to briefly indicate the responsibilities and duties of a student of Law [and said that he] ... had been a hard student [and] impressed upon his hearers the assurance that this most difficult of Sciences could not be acquired without sedulous application[147].

No less significantly in terms of ambitions for UCD, he described William Smith as a "Professor", and Thomas Thornton as having established a "Chair", declaring that UCD was:

> no longer a mere independent school ... [but] ... an integral part of the oldest of the Scottish Universities ... [a fact which would] ... infuse into the minds of the students an academic spirit ... to add lustre to their *alma mater* by their learning and probity in the world (*Applause*)[148].

Smith continued lecturing until April 1891 (though, again, we do not know where in the College), covering the law of husband and wife, guardianship, master and servant, property, and landlord and tenant, but in only 35-40 lectures instead of the proposed 60, because of undefined "untoward circumstances"[149]. Up to 70 students enrolled, and there was an average attendance of about 50. There were five written examinations (the first in April), and some 60 students took them[150], and marks ranged from 3 to 38 out of a possible 40[151]. The lecturer himself recorded that "[s]everal students were insufficiently prepared to follow the lecturer with advantage; but the competition for prizes was keen and highly creditable"[152].

In the following winter, on Mondays to Fridays at 7-8pm[153], starting on 16 October 1891, the lectures covered Conveyancing including deeds in general; deeds relating to personal rights, including co-partnery; deeds relating to heritable rights, including feu-charter, sasine, disposition, assignation, completion of title, marriage contract, entail and heritable securities[154]. Class attendance was down somewhat on the previous year, with 55 enrolling and an average attendance of 35 over the winter, and "a portion of the course was postponed till summer" , though "[t]he competition for prizes was again well-sustained" [155].

And in the winter after that, at the same times, and starting on 21 October 1892, the lectures dealt with Mercantile Law, including bankruptcy, maritime law, fire and life insurance, goodwill and trade marks, principal and agent, joint stock companies, and sale of goods[156]. Class attendance was down further, with 47 enrolments, and average attendance "considerably less". In addition to class prizes, there were two prizes "for Essays upon a title in Bankruptcy Law"[157]. Thus, Smith lectured on, in effect, all of the "law agents' triad", save for criminal law within Scots Law, and Forms of Process on which lectures were not generally given anywhere[158].

What students were recommended to read is unrecorded. The contemporary drafting of the law agents' Scots Law requirement specified Erskine's *Institute*[159], Bell's *Principles*[160] and Hume's *Commentaries*[161], though Erskine's *Principles*[162] was the standard student text, and was just out in a new edition[163]. However, as Smith himself was the editor of Bell's *Principles*, it is likely that this was relied on, and since there were no criminal law lectures, possibly students were simply told to read Hume's *Commentaries* by themselves. Students may have had access to firms' copies of these works but, in any event, early in 1891, Thornton applied for students to use the FPSD Library[164].

While we know the identity of the lecturer, what was lectured upon, and what examinations there were, we do not know anything directly about the style of teaching or examinations. It is likely that the classes were delivered in straight lecture style[165], possibly with some form of "quiz" in certain lectures, as this seems to have been the practice elsewhere. Tutorials are extremely unlikely to have taken place as there is no reference to them, and they were not common at the time. The relevant Ordinances used lectures as the unit of account for the relative sizes of courses, and tutorials would have taken up a good deal more of Smith's time. Examinations were presumably standard written essay type[166].

It seems unlikely that there was any final examination (leaving that for the actual professional law examination), as there was no mention of payment for setting exams, marking them or finding external examiners, and the students were not getting a degree, or any other university qualification, as a result of their labours.

In relation to fees, there has survived an intriguing letter[167] dated just at the beginning of the third cycle of lectures, from G W Alexander, former UCD Secretary, to R N Kerr, his replacement, confirming Thomas Thornton's generosity. It recounts that:

> In former years the Law Class counted [*scil.* as] a Day Class because Dr Thornton thought the students might have a little more privilege eg the Library. He pays all the Reg. fees and he pays the whole fees of his own Clerks. Usually I got the class fees from his cashier early in the Session and the Reg. fees of all the students towards the close of the Class. Surely he paid them to you for last Session if I remember rightly.
>
> You had better ask the Principal which Reg. fee is to be charged this year. Dr Thornton was anxious for Univ. Reg [illegible] and thus hoped that a 5/- fee would enable students for such a class to matriculate. I expect though he will just pay the 3/6 each as before. I dare say he'll pay for the non-lawyers too. He never asks who the students are.

There is a PS: "The Law Students used to sign the <u>Day</u> Album [illegible] of the College and get Day Cards". This is obscure, but probably referred to the Day Matriculation Register, implicitly classifying them as not evening classes[168]. But overall, the whole exchange may reflect concerns as to the acceptability of UCD lectures counting as "university classes", if the need arose.

There was even icing on the cake for, just as these lectures were getting under way (in the fifth stage of the odd and complicated history of the obligation, as noted above), the power to require law agents' apprentices to attend university classes, not restored by the unsuccessful 1887 Private Members' Bill, was about to be restored by another, more successful Bill (as Thornton no doubt expected)[169], seemingly promoted by the Incorporated Society of Law Agents[170]. Thornton's cup might have overflowed.

But not completely, for the resulting Law Agents and Notaries Public Act 1891[171], while drafted differently from the 1887 Bill, was if anything more generous towards providers of classes. The power given was to require, by Act of Sederunt, attendance at "university *or other* classes" and accepting "university degree *or other* certificates" as exempting from the 1873 Act requirements[172]. This generosity might be employed by an independent UCD, reducing any benefit of affiliation to St Andrews University. Entry to the oligopoly would now be easier. (Moreover, though presumably unforeseen at the time, even this power was not exercised until 1926, as described in Chapter 3, in the sixth stage of the odd sequence of events described in Chapter 1).

In any case, in the end, the lectures only lasted the three sessions, 1890-91 to 1892-93. The benefit of being affiliated to St Andrews University having been reduced can hardly account for this, since it clearly constituted no drawback to attendance at the classes. Indeed, paradoxically, at just this time, two possibly linked events might have encouraged continuation.

Firstly (as noted in Chapter 1 and above), St Mungo's College in Glasgow also branched out into "extra-mural" law classes in 1890, seemingly offering a full range of subjects, and certainly significantly wider than that available at Glasgow Law School[173]. Possibly it hoped to be validated by the School, but clearly it might also benefit from the extension to "other classes" and "certificates". (However, in fact, it may never have taught law, a failure conceivably acting as discouragement rather than encouragement). Secondly, the LLB and BL regulations were recast in 1893[174]. One of the changes permitted two years of the LLB, or one year of the BL, to be spent in a University or approved School of Law other than the University of graduation. Possibly this was intended for the benefit of St Mungo's College[175], but in principle would also allow a transfer from UCD to obtain a law degree elsewhere after one more year's study (irrespective of whether attendance at university classes was required or not).

But it is in fact easy to infer reasons for the ending. Firstly, Thornton's initial philanthropy, if designed to prime St Andrews University to continue law classes, and institute a BL and/or LLB, had failed to do so. Nor had it unbuttoned the purses of any successors to the two Baxters to fund at least a permanent lectureship. Secondly, in 1893, he became Town Clerk, a possible diversion of even his massive energy, and two years later, he resigned from the UCD Council. Thirdly, William Smith contested the Dundee Parliamentary constituency in 1892 (and 1895) which may have undermined the likelihood of continuation (even if his chances of election were slim), and indicated his greater ambitions[176]. And fourthly, 1893 saw the start of the unhappy period, discussed in Chapter 1, in which the Marquess of Bute and his allies sought, through years of litigation, to terminate the affiliation of UCD to St Andrews University.

In 1894, there is an obscure note in UCD Council Minutes authorising Principal Peterson to see Thornton (again absent) regarding Law Classes, which looks like an attempt to keep them going[177]. In the same year representatives of two unnamed "Legal Societies"[178] solicited financial support from the FPSD for a lectureship on criminal and civil procedure[179]. This is intriguing, particularly because, as noted above, despite "Forms of process civil and criminal" being compulsory for law agents, it is not clear that any institution offered lectures on the subject[180], and all law teaching in UCD had recently ceased. But no further information is recorded, and the "Legal Societies" were told that the FPSD "was precluded from applying any part of its Funds in this direction".

In the spring of 1896, there appear to have been half a dozen lectures by advocates in Dundee to "accountants, bankers, solicitors and their clerks and apprentices" on legal topics, presumably as a form of continuous professional development[181]. There is no indication that Thornton was involved in this, but it seems likely.

Also, there was correspondence in April 1897 between the UCD Council and Senate on a proposed letter from the UCD Principal to the University Commissioners under the 1889 Act, concerning certain Arts classes in Dundee, in which it is mentioned that "we anticipate being able ultimately to institute a Faculty of Law at Dundee, but we could hardly hope for success in this direction were English and Logic excluded from the list of qualifying classes [for the MA, then a prerequisite for an LLB][182]."

This was just after the restoration of the St Andrews University connection. It may have been simply a bargaining chip in the dispute about Arts teaching in Dundee, but does indicate the possibility of the renewal of a more ambitious scheme and is noteworthy as possibly the first official mention of an actual Faculty, alongside Arts and Divinity, in St Andrews University. In any case, once again, reports of the death of law lectures in UCD would have been premature, for undergraduate lectures recommenced in 1899, as discussed in the next Chapter.

1865-98: People

But before considering the lectures recommencing in 1899, we must first consider three who were involved in setting up, and teaching, law in UCD, Thomas Thornton, William Guthrie and William Smith.

The Baxters were considerably assisted by the towering personality of Sir Thomas Thornton LLD (1829-1903)[183], Dundee's "Great Panjandrum"[184], who had been one of the principal actors in setting up law teaching in the 1860s, and was the "onlie begetter" of the law school in the 1890s: indeed, he is clearly the "father of the law school". He was a remarkable man, even allowing for obituarists' and sketch-writers' exaggerations. One of them recorded, probably accurately, that "within the community of Dundee and county of Forfar … his influence for half a century was unique, commanding and many-sided … extend[ing] far beyond his profession …". More recently, he was described as "the lawyer who ran Dundee single-handedly between 1863 and 1893", and who "controlled most of the boards and trusts that ran the burgh"[185].

Yet he appears curiously uncommemorated in Dundee. His name does not appear in the *Roll of Eminent Burgesses of Dundee 1513-1886*[186], for example, and The McManus's presentation portrait of him by W Q Orchardson[187] is currently unavailable, on long term loan[188].

He was born in Jeanfield, Forfar, in 1829, his ancestors seemingly "for hundreds of years extensive landowners in Forfar and Kincardineshire, though lately fallen into decayed circumstances". He attended the Burgh School, from whence he went to work for the Town Clerk of Forfar.

But he then attended Edinburgh University with a view to qualifying for the Bar, achieving "a brilliant career … [being] prizeman in Scots Law and Conveyancing in two successive years", while working for a number of legal firms. (He took no degree, there being no LLB or BL, and no MA was recorded in obituaries, though he probably took Arts classes to fulfil the Faculty of Advocates' requirement of general scholarship). However, in 1851, at the age of 21, unspecified health problems caused him to come to Dundee, which became "the scene of his lifework and labours".

Initially, (and at a remarkably young age) he was managing clerk to the Town Clerk ("giving him a firm hold on the details of civic business", and other skills). In 1857, he married Helen Hean[189] and about that time left for private practice, being assumed as partner by James Pattullo[190] in Bank Street (though he did not join the FPSD until 1864[191]). The partnership lasted for 24 years under the name of Pattullo & Thornton. It appears the firm undertook a wide range of work, including parliamentary business[192] and litigation, because (subject always to the usual *caveat* on obituaries) "[f]rom his earliest years... [Thornton] was recognised as one of the foremost and ablest pleaders at the local Bar", and "a sound and able lawyer... marshall[ing] his facts with unerring precision in the many litigations in which he was engaged in the Supreme Court[193]".

At the end of that partnership, he started the firm of Thomas Thornton, Son & Coy[194] of 15 Albert Square[195] with his son William (and from 1898 also including a nephew, John Thornton, and Robert Still). However, this was as much as anything a springboard because, for "at least forty years he [was] closely identified with the public life of Dundee [so that] to trace the many parts he ... played and the influence he ... exerted in moulding and developing the corporate policy, would ... entail the writing a history of the community for that period". His mind (again not forgetting obituarist's exaggeration) was "framed for great undertakings, massive and logical", and he was "perhaps the strongest legal brain north of the Forth". Much involved in railway business, he acquired a "knowledge of ... Private Bill Legislation and Procedure [that] was unrivalled", and "no one had promoted a greater or more varied number of Bills, [including those of the Harbour Trust, Police Committee, and Gas and Water Trust], almost with complete success", and also the Bill merging the Town Council with the Police Commissioners to form a single local authority. It was "perhaps in the Parliamentary Committee Room that he was seen at his best".

Other large undertakings in which he was involved included not only promotion of the first Tay Bridge (of which he was "not the originator... but... was its chief promoter and successful organiser") but also, as solicitor to the North British Railway Company, the public inquiry which followed its fall[196]. His forensic strengths, and the ability to "fight hard when he believes he is right", but also to "compromise when he thinks this course more beneficial to his clients", enabled him to effect "such compromise on a gigantic scale on behalf of the railway company in the Tay Bridge disaster, where some eighty lives were lost [that] no claim arising from the accident found its way to Court" and (giving a check to any tendency to adulation, and clear evidence that his clients' interests "dominate[d] all other considerations"), the "total compensation paid was probably less than the expense of a few litigants would have reached".

His qualities were also evident both in the original creation of UCD, as one of those advising Mary Ann Baxter and John Boyd Baxter (though they initially regarded him as too friendly towards St Andrews University[197]), and in its affiliation to St Andrews (for which he probably received his LLD in 1891[198]), and he "rendered eminent service to the negotiators" after the affiliation became "troubled". In addition, from its inception, and for many years thereafter, he served on the UCD Council, and was a Governor of the College, *ex officio*, not only by virtue his membership of Council, but also by virtue of being one of seven subscribers each contributing £200 towards the Chair of Biology[199]. (It is worth noting that in his resignation letter from the Council in September 1895, while hoping to continue a "warm and active interest" in the College, he explicitly reiterated warnings to the Council about expenditure on salaries exceeding income, noting that members might "involve themselves in personal liability". This precipitated a note by another member of the Council, Sir John Leng[200], minuted with the accounts at the next Meeting, rejecting personal liability, and also hoping that any "further waste of money in litigation should also be stopped"[201]).

Having "an insatiable appetite for public work", Thornton was also at various times clerk to the Forfarshire Prison Board, the Forfarshire Lunacy Board, the Dundee Gas Corporation, the Dundee Police Commission, the Dundee School Board, legal adviser to the Harbour Trust, and Honorary Secretary to various charitable bodies[202]. He returned to full-time public service in 1893 by becoming Town Clerk, and in 1894 was knighted[203] ("in recognition of his fifty years' service to the Community and to his Country – socially, educationally, and politically"), after which (so late in his career) he was elected Preses of the FPSD[204]. A Gladstonian Liberal, he declined to stand for the Montrose Burghs parliamentary constituency in 1885.

As to his personality, he was "an ardent Scot", a "strong silent man … of few words, but deep convictions" and "a stalwart Calvinist who loved his Bible", with views that were "somewhat puritanical... [with] little love for instrumental music in the church" (though later he "took great delight in the reading and singing of hymns") and his habits were "almost stoic", though he enjoyed classical history and literature, logic and contemporary politics.

It is not surprising to learn that he created "among the members of the public boards with which he was associated a feeling of dependence, which unconsciously caused him to become the master-mind ... and undoubtedly created in him an attitude and manner which were somewhat intolerant of opposition or criticism". Equally unsurprisingly, he had "somewhat blunt and brusque speech" (reportedly once stating "all strong men are rude"), with "a somewhat hasty temper", indeed might state his views "with surprising frankness and freedom". ,

On the other hand, it was said that this manner concealed "a warm and generous heart", and one commentator asserted that he had "a great appreciation of humour", while another said that he liked "boisterous fun" and "to play blind man's buff, hide and seek" and other games with children, though his "chief delight was in charades". Overall, he had "indomitable energy and ... an insatiable love of work", but "never seemed to be flurried", and "[h]is friendships were few, but warm and enduring".

Having acquired Thornton Castle near Laurencekirk in 1893 (though "he did not lay claim to any direct connection with the Thorntons who formerly owned it"[205]), he also enjoyed long walks, apparently crossing the Cairn o' Mount on foot annually in later years (though returning by train)[206]. But after an unspecified "serious illness" in 1895, he became an "altered man". Nevertheless, his death "creat[ed] the greatest blank in the public life of Dundee experienced for many years" and there were numerous obituaries in a wide range of newspapers, including the London-based *Times* and *Morning Post*.

William Guthrie (1835-1908)[207] gave the very first, extra-mural, law lecture in Dundee in 1867. He was a native of Wigtownshire, called to the

Bar in 1861, in 1871 was made a Commissioner under the Truck Commission Act 1870 (in the course of which responsibility he took evidence in Shetland from 264 witnesses in 26 days, and produced a "valuable" report, although legislation did not follow until 1887) and was Registrar of Friendly Societies from 1872-74. He was appointed Sheriff-Substitute of Lanarkshire in 1874, thereafter becoming Sheriff from 1903 until his death.

Nevertheless, he never had an extensive practice, but "devoted himself to the pen", as he was a contributor to the *Journal of Jurisprudence*, and later editor from 1857 to 1874; editor of 6th-10th editions of Bell's *Principles*; editor of Erskine's *Principles*; and editor of *Select Sheriff Court Cases*. Further, in 1868, he produced an "excellent" translation of F v Savigny's *System in Public International Law*, and was the author of "a small book on trade unions". He received an LLD from Edinburgh University in 1881.

Also, he was known as an opponent of "double sheriffships" (presumably one sheriff holding two sheriffdoms), and most interestingly, proponent of transfer of the Outer House of the Court of Session (in other words, of major civil trials) to Glasgow, and it was suggested that had this occurred he "would be Lord Ordinary", i.e. Outer House judge).

William Charles Smith (1849-1915)[208] gave the first law lecture in UCD, in 1891. He was an Edinburgh man, who graduated MA, LLB, was called to the Bar in 1875, and made KC in 1902. In his career at the Bar, an obituarist wrote that "he gained the reputation of a strenuous worker and a lucid pleader, and acquired a good practice" appearing in "the famous Orr-Ewing case as to jurisdiction in Scotland, the Glen Doll right-of-way action, and the dispute between Sir William Mackinnon and the liquidators of the City of Glasgow Bank". He was appointed Sheriff of Chancery in 1896, Sheriff of Dumfries and Galloway in 1897[209], and Sheriff of Ross, Cromarty and Sutherland in 1898.

Clearly, he had academic inclinations, which might be one reason for his choice by Thornton. He was an Examiner in Edinburgh University, edited (like William Guthrie) Bell's *Principles* and, for the eleven years until 1900, the *Juridical Review* (long the only academic legal periodical in Scotland, and still one of its leading ones). He later applied unsuccessfully for the Chair in Law in Aberdeen in 1907 (when it was setting up its LLB)[210]. He also wrote two books, *Social Government for Scotland* and *The Secretary of State for Scotland,* and contributed the article on Cremation in the 10th edition of the *Encyclopaedia Britannica* (1902)[211].

But one obituary of him was headlined "A Familiar Figure in Scottish Politics", rather than "in Law", and another recorded that he "was more at home on the political platform than in the law Courts" and "[t]o hear him plead in Court, one would not have placed him highly as a counsel, but he was a different man altogether when on the platform, for on it his oratory was most delightful to hearken to". Thus, his chief love was clearly politics, and "no man more zealously served his party [though] there was no more unfortunate politician in Scotland", and "it has often been said here that his party treated him in a very shabby fashion, for no rewards came his way". He unsuccessfully fought seven general or by-elections as a Liberal Unionist, in constituencies seemingly "forlorn hopes" as "strongholds of Radicalism". These were Dundee itself[212] (against the Liberals, Sir John Leng and Edmund Robertson in 1892 – thus shortly after the inaugural law lecture in Dundee - and again in 1895), Wick Burghs (1896), South Aberdeen (for which he resigned his shrieval office, 1900), South Edinburgh (1906), Linlithgowshire (1910) and South Aberdeen again (1910, attacking the seat of the Lord Advocate "with as much wholeheartedness and enthusiasm as he showed at Dundee eighteen years before"). It may be that his politics provided a link to the Baxters.

But in addition to those involved in setting up, and teaching, law, clearly, we must look at those no less involved in early law teaching, that is, the students. All attended lectures which were no doubt very much in the traditional mode, and sat the examinations set, probably all working most of the time as apprentices in law offices. Beyond that, regrettably, we know nothing about most of them.

A couple of those involved in the attempts in 1866-68 to start law classes, Messrs Thain and Petrie, presumed to be law clerks or apprentices, no doubt attended the lectures which resulted. Those who did well in William Smith's lectures in the 1890s, some of whom merited obituaries, included the Scots Law prize-winners, as follows[213]:

1. J M Hodge
2. J M Irons
3. W D Allardice
4. G R Donald
5. (equal) F Lowe & A H Buglass.

In addition those obtaining 50% or more in the examinations were, in order:

1. W A Watterston (noted as having missed one examination through illness)
2. J Pearson
3. C R Beveridge
4. J Grant[214]
5. J G Lawson
6. J M Soutar[215]
7. A W Carlisle[216].

In the following year[217], W D Allardice and J M Hodge were first equal in Conveyancing, with F Lowe third, while J Fettes, J A Lang, W B Mount, J Pearson and G B Simpson were awarded Certificates. And in the year after that[218], the "Prizemen" for Mercantile Law were:

1. W D Allardice
2. John Miller
3. J A Lang
4. C J Bisset
5. (equal) A H Buglass & J Carmichael
7. A Lindsay.

In addition, J A Lang and J Nicol received prizes for an essay, and C J Bisset an Honourable Mention.

We do know a little more about half-a-dozen of these high achievers. George Reid Donald MBE (1870-1962)[219], described in his obituary as "Dundee's oldest lawyer", was the son of an accountant, attended the High School of Dundee, and was apprenticed to Ferguson & Stephen in Dundee, then Stoddart & Ballingall in Edinburgh. He was also described as "prizeman in Scots Law and Conveyancing" in Edinburgh. If accurate, this would indicate that he attended there after UCD.

When qualified, he worked for Smith & Bennet, Arbroath, then in 1902 as Donald & Ross, Whitehall Street, Dundee. In 1904, upon the appointment as Sheriff Clerk of Forfarshire of C J Bisset (see below) the firm took over Watt, Bisset & Co to become Watt, Donald & Co, and in 1909 that firm merged with J & H Pattullo[220] as J & H Pattullo & Donald.

In 1914 he joined up as a private in the Black Watch, but was shortly thereafter commissioned, was at the Somme, but then recalled to the War Office and promoted Captain. His work there merited the award (which he "resisted", and which became a "well-kept secret") of his MBE (Military Division).

Later, he was Secretary of the Dundee Chamber of Commerce, the Jute & Linen Merchants Society, and the Flax Spinners & Manufacturers Association of Great Britain, and President of the Association of British Chambers of Commerce. He was also Conservative agent 1904-10, Vice-President of the Scottish Mountaineering Society, President of the Grampian Club and one of the founders of the Dundee Ski Club.

John Pearson (1870-1961)[221] was possibly the most academically remarkable law student. He attended Glebelands Public School, leaving at the age of 12, and according to his obituarist, "had the distinction of passing the law entrance examination [presumably the general knowledge examination under the Law Agents (Scotland) Act 1873], but could not be found an apprenticeship until he was 14".

He actually qualified in Edinburgh in 1893, returned to Dundee and became a partner in Anderson, Gardiner, Hepburn & Co in Ward Road, and was Dean of the Faculty of Procurators and Solicitors in Dundee, Honorary Sheriff-Substitute and a Justice of the Peace. Also, "nearly all his life [he] rose early and began the day with a cold bath":

John Grafton Lawson (1870-1933)[222] attended Brown Street Public School, then the High School of Dundee, obtaining "many prizes", and entered the office of A W Cumming, rapidly becoming head clerk and cashier. He is recorded as taking classes in Edinburgh in 1891, but this may be an error, since the present record shows that he was doing so in Dundee in that year. He set up as a sole practitioner in Dundee, probably undertaking court work, much later taking on "Dr Dan Carmichael" as partner. In 1909 he had a column offering legal advice in Joseph Lee's short-lived Socialist periodical *The Tocsin*[223].

During the First World War, he was involved in the Association of Dependants of Deceased & Serving Soldiers & Sailors, was at various times Secretary of the Dundee branch of the National Farmers Union, of the Scottish Federation of Merchant Tailors, of the Dundee Safety First Council and of the Dundee Fish Traders Association (when he "conducted single-handedly their litigation with the Town Council in regard to markets").

Christopher Johnson Bisset OBE (1873-1944)[224] was son of C J Bisset CE, attended Victoria Road Public School and is recorded as taking law classes in St Andrews University (i.e. those presently recorded, though the obituary does not mention the prize obtained) and Edinburgh.

He became partner in Watt, Bisset & Co in 1897, and on Watt's death in 1907, succeeded him as Sheriff Clerk of Forfarshire for 40 years (the firm then becoming Watt, Donald & Co: see above in relation to G R Donald). He became Honorary Secretary of the Sheriff Clerks' Association, and Chairman of the Departmental Committee on Sheriff Clerks' Forms Etc (introducing standardisation). He was also Dean of the

FPSD, a Justice of the Peace for Dundee and Angus and Honorary Secretary of the Joint Conciliation & Arbitration Board of Dundee.

Further, he was Honorary Secretary of the Dundee Conservative Association and Tay Division of the National Union of Conservative Associations of Scotland, and also of the Dundee Soldiers & Sailors Families' Association, Convenor of the Nine Trades, and Lord Dean of Guild and Speaker of the Dundee Parliament.

Of particular interest, he was a member of the UCD Council and trustee and manager of the Technical College: Also, he was father of Christian J Bisset, one of the stalwart teachers of law appointed in 1939, as discussed in the following Chapter.

---

[1] Formerly the Incorporated Society of Writers in Dundee, and just renamed under the Procurators (Scotland) Act 1965.

[2] Sections 4-9, 11, 12, 20 & 21 and Curriculum and Regulations prepared by the General Council of Procurators in Scotland, Chapter 1 (Examinations, etc), para 3, appended to AS 26 June 1866: see also Anon, "Education of Scotch Lawyers" (1869) XIII *Journal of Jurisprudence* 124, 177 ("Procurators in Inferior Courts") (which erroneously dates the AS to 22 June 1866).

[3] Section 27. J Henderson Begg, *A Treatise on the Law of Scotland relating to Law Agents ...* 1st ed (1873) 2nd ed (1883) chs XXVI and XXVII, respectively, list those incorporated and unincorporated before 1865.

[4] Anon, "The Education of Scotch Lawyers" (1869) XIII *JoJ* 177-187 ("Faculty of Procurators of Dundee"). This records that the syllabus comprised: Solemnities of Deeds, Delivery, Homologation, Succession, and Domestic Relations, examined at the end of the first apprenticeship year; Minority and Guardianship, Bills, Prescription, Diligence and Land Rights, examined at the end of the third; and Securities over Land, Servitudes, Contracts, Quasi-Contracts, Extinction of Obligations, Jurisdiction and Actions, and Evidence, examined at the end of the fourth. Whether or not this constituted an integrated course of study, and how far it fulfilled the Act's "procurators' triad" (discussed in Chapter 1) of Scots Law (including Criminal Law and Evidence), Conveyancing and Forms of Process (which, admittedly, no law school taught at that time), are matters for discussion. The requirements of the Faculty of Procurators in Glasgow are also given in this article, in greater detail and with sample questions, and indicate that university attendance (easily achieved in Glasgow) was required there.

[5] Though it may long have been common. John Boyd Baxter (discussed in Chapter 1), had attended classes in Edinburgh.

[6] George Ramsay Ogilvy (1822-1866), advocate 1844, Sheriff-Substitute of Forfarshire at Forfar 1857-61, and at Dundee 1861-66: see Stephen P Walker, *The Faculty of Advocates: a Biographical*

Directory of Members Admitted from 1 January 1800 to 31 December 1986 (1987), and F J Grant, *The Faculty of Advocates in Scotland 1532-1943* ... (1944) (which give slightly different dates for his shrieval offices).

[7] *Dundee Courier and Argus* 4 August 1865. Following contemporary practice, the Act presumably came into force on its date on enactment, 5 July 1865. Reference to "the course of lectures proposed" begs the question of who actually proposed them but, unfortunately, no clue as to identity remains.

[8] Index to FPSD Minutes for 1846-87, 152, 157.

[9] *Dundee Courier and Argus* 2 February 1866.

[10] Presumably James David Grant (1828-81), native of Dundee, apprenticed to Walker & Ferguson, took law classes in Edinburgh, and "was for some time clerk to Mr More, advocate, Professor of Scots Law" (ie John Shank More, Professor of Scots Law, Edinburgh University 1843-61: see John W Cairns & Hector L MacQueen, *Learning and the Law: a short history of Edinburgh Law School* (2013) 11). He then managed an Elgin firm before acquiring "a large and lucrative business" in Dundee on his own account, specialising in maritime law, and obtaining retainers from the Board of Trade for representation at inquiries, including "the protracted inquiry into the fall of the Tay Bridge" (for which Thomas Thornton, discussed below, was solicitor to the North British Railway, and John Trayner, also noted below, was counsel). He was also Auditor of the Sheriff Court, and Procurator Fiscal of the JP Court and Burgh Court. See Dundee City Library Family and Local History Centre *Obituaries Notices 1869-94,* 54-55.

[11] *Dundee Courier and Argus* 2 February 1866. Clearly, this assumed that, despite the exemption, Dundee apprentices would attend such classes.

[12] *Dundee Courier and Argus* 14 December 1866. Apprentices were those seeking to qualify, clerks those already qualified but, because considerable stamp duty was exacted upon formal entry to the profession, commonly delayed this event until partnership approached. I am grateful to Dennis Collins for this information. (However, usage at this period seems to have been looser).

[13] *Dundee Courier and Argus* 28 December 1866. A further meeting was held ten days later: see *Dundee Courier and Argus* 8 January 1866. Regrettably, none of the members of the Committee appear to have received an obituary in the local press, nor appear in the *Dundee Directory* of that date, save that a George Ogilvie of J & J Ogilvie & Reid, solicitors, of 12 Meadowside, is recorded in the *Dundee Directory 1866-67*).

[14] As noted in Chapter 1.

[15] Frederick Maitland Heriot of Ramornie (1818-1881), advocate 1839, Advocate-Depute 1857 & 1859-62, Sheriff of Forfarshire 1862-81: Walker *Biographical Directory*, Grant *Faculty of Advocates*. Ramornie lies between Ladybank and Pitlessie in Fife.

[16] John Guthrie Smith (1831-1895), advocate 1855, Sheriff-Substitute of Forfarshire at Forfar 1860-62, and at Dundee 1866-70, Sheriff of Aberdeenshire 1870-95, sub-editor of *Caledonian Mercury* and author: Walker *Biographical Directory*, Grant *Faculty of Advocates*.

[17] For biographical details, see below.

[18] This appears to be the first mention of Thomas Thornton (much discussed below as "father of the law school") in connection with law classes. Though in practice in Dundee from 1851, working for the Town Clerk, and in partnership since 1857, he did not join the FPSD until 1864,

so this may have been his first foray into its activities, (and in any case marked the start of 40 years of involvement in law teaching), and may have been the occasion of the start of his involvement with what became UCD.

[19] For the significance of the difference between advocates and procurators or law agents, see Chapter 1. At that time, the trip from Edinburgh required crossing both Tay and Forth by ferry, as the bridges did not open until 1879 (and then briefly) and 1890, respectively. Coincidentally, Thornton had promoted the first (1863-64) and second (1865-66) unsuccessful Private Bills for the first Tay Bridge, on behalf of the North British Railway Company, and at this time was shortly to promote the third (1869-70), successful, one.

[20] Such "extra-mural" classes (in the parlance of the time, non-university classes recognised by universities for graduation) for medicine were already used in Edinburgh and Glasgow (see R D Anderson, *Education and Opportunity in Victorian Scotland* (1983) 72 & 261-3), and references to St Mungo's College in Chapter 1, and discussed below, show that they were considered for law. Edinburgh Law Faculty had earlier emerged from private teaching of law: Cairns & MacQueen *Learning and the Law* 1.

[21] Presumably a largely ornamental role, given Sheriff Guthrie Smith's title.

[22] Again, none of this Committee (save Sheriff Guthrie Smith), received obituaries in the local press, but a David Duncan jnr. appears as solicitor at 70½ High Street, and J W Leslie as a law clerk at 114 Hawkhill, in the *Dundee Directory 1866-67*.

[23] *Dundee Courier and Argus* 18 (advertisement) & 19 (report) January 1867.

[24] After initial remarks on the science of law and the necessity of historical knowledge of municipal law and connected systems, he referred to the origins of law, tracing its progress down the ages, then glancing at the sources of law and how a knowledge of law was best attained, sketching a course of study (and so on).

[25] In desiring a law school in Dundee the audience had shown their sense of the advantages of a deeper and wider learning and in supplementing the scanty provision the State had made (and so on).

[26] *Dundee Courier and Argus* 25, 26 January & 2 February 1867. The first was "erudite, interesting and instructive", the second "masterly".

[27] *Dundee Courier and Argus* 16 February 1867. The FPSD Index to Minutes 1846-1887 for the period reveals an 1867 Committee on Law Lectures (members including John Boyd Baxter, discussed in Chapter 1), in addition to the apparently abortive 1865 one, possibly for distributing these topics among the members who gave lectures.

[28] *Dundee Courier and Argus* 23 February 1867: presumably the same Mr Grant as had expressed qualified support for classes in 1865 (see note 10).

[29] *Dundee Courier and Argus* 1 March 1867. William Hay (1818-93), rivalled Thomas Thornton in influence. A native of Elgin, he was indentured to the Elgin Town Clerk, then attended Edinburgh University, after which he was Sheriff-Clerk-Depute of Forfarshire in 1840, admitted solicitor [*sic*] 1843, went into practice, undertook various duties and was elected Councillor in Dundee in 1863 (at time when councillors had personal responsibility for municipal debt and, as attempts were made to sequestrate the town, devised a scheme to avoid it). He undertook oversight of legal municipal business e.g. private Acts (the need for which in municipal government at this time is

noted below), and was begetter of Riverside Drive (the *corniche* of Dundee), elected First Bailie 1867 and Provost 1868, but then Town Clerk 1869 and was also Chairman of Governors of Morgan Hospital (his opinion on the dispute over the financing of which being later vindicated by the House of Lords), Director of the High School of Dundee, JP, Preses of FPSD, Commissioner of Supply, and Honorary Sheriff-Substitute. On retiral through ill-health he was voted a pension of £600pa by the Council, legal doubts upon which were stilled by his death: see Dundee *Obituaries Notices 1869-94* 136.

[30] *Dundee Courier and Argus* 9 March 1867. On John Trayner, see below.

[31] *Dundee Courier and Argus* 16 March 1867. George Thoms (1831-1903), native of Aberlemno, Advocate Depute 1862, and Sheriff of Caithness, Orkney and Shetland 1870-99: see Walker *Biographical Directory,* Grant *Faculty of Advocates.*

[32] *Dundee Courier and Argus* 22 March 1867. Francis William Clark (1827-1886), qualified as writer, admitted advocate 1851, and Sheriff-Substitute of Lanarkshire at Glasgow 1867-76 (thus, presumably, appointed shortly after the lecture), then Sheriff 1876-1886, LLD (Glasgow) 1877, and "author (legal)": see Walker *Biographical Directory,* Grant *Faculty of Advocates.*

[33] Ie Scots Law (including Criminal Law and Evidence), Conveyancing and Forms of Process (though no law school at this time offered classes in "Forms of Process"): see Chapter 1.

[34] Anon, "Proposed Law School in Dundee" (1867) XI *JoJ* 91-92; *Dundee Courier and Argus* 18 February 1867.

[35] Founded by the Town Council and the Society of Writers to the Signet, respectively: see Cairns & MacQueen *Learning and the Law* 2 & 9.

[36] For whom, see Chapter 1.

[37] And see the accounts, discussed below, of the debates on UCD in the 1870s, recorded in William Angus Knight, *Early Chapters in the History of the University of St Andrews and Dundee* (1902). The phrase "influential persons" seems have been a widely used code in this context: see e.g. University of St Andrews Archives UY/615 University of St Andrews General Council Minutes, Meetings of 28 November 1872 and 27 March & 28 November 1873, and c.f. Donald G Southgate, *University Education in Dundee: a centenary history* (1982) 9 *et seq.*

[38] That is, as noted in Chapter 1, a compilation of late Roman Law, regarded as a Platonic ideal legal system. Topics covered in these nine lectures included the laws and institutions of ancient Rome, sources, persons, property, succession, obligations, etc.

[39] Anon, "Lectures to the Dundee Society of Law Clerks" (1868) XII *JoJ* 97-98; *Dundee Courier and Argus* 21 & 29 November, 5 & 20 December 1867 and 13 January 1868.

[40] Anon, "Lectures to the Dundee Society" (see previous note). Nestor fought in the Trojan War at the age of 110.

[41] Covering husband and wife, parent and child, guardians and wards and master and servant.

[42] See notes 10 & 28. All seem to have been delivered in the Burgh Court room, which was the "Guildry Room" (also used by the Sheriff Court: see Chapter 1) in the Town House: see contemporary editions of *Dundee Directories.* The Town House also contained a gaol: see Charles McKean & David Walker, *Dundee: an illustrated architectural guide* (1984) 14-15.

[43] Possibly William Bell, died 17 December 1878: *Dundee Year Book 1878*, 49.

[44] Anon, "Lectures to the Dundee Society" (1868) XII *JoJ* 98.

[45] *Dundee Courier and Argus* 14 February & 21 March 1885 reported that Mr JA Maclean gave four or more lectures in Forfar and a copy of *Trayner's Latin Maxims* as a prize and, 8 September 1887, that the Law Agents' Society AGM referred to encouragement of local classes (even where tiny), noting one in Stirling in 1886-87.

[46] Henry Gibson (1837-95), from Brechin, entered law with D D Brown, was Town Clerk of Brechin, then went to Edinburgh, coming to Dundee around 1864 to Shiell & Small as managing clerk, later in partnership with Thomas Walker, then on his own account: Dundee City Library Family and Local History Centre *Obituaries Notices 1895-1909,* 100.

[47] *Dundee Courier and Argus* 1 April 1868. The Burgh Court met in the Town House: see contemporary editions of *Dundee Directories*. This seems to have been in the same "Guildry Room" as the Sheriff Court used, as discussed in Chapter 1.

[48] *Dundee Courier and Argus* 4 May 1868. It was written from Edinburgh, to which he had presumably removed, possibly to attend university classes.

[49] But note the Memorial of 1885, discussed below. *Dundee Directory 1864-65* lists 55 Procurators and Notaries Public in Dundee, though law clerks and apprentices are not listed, as such.

[50] *Dundee Courier and Argus* 19 December 1868.

[51] *Dundee Courier and Argus* 11 & 12 October 1869.

[52] *Dundee Courier and Argus* 13 October 1869.

[53] *Dundee Courier and Argus* 13, 16 & 20 October 1869. The events of 1869-70 do not figure in the Index to the FPSD Minutes.

[54] William Bishop Dunbar (1835-1887), a Dundonian, apprenticed to John Boyd Baxter, and later procurator fiscal in Perthshire, then in Dundee as assistant to Baxter, whom he succeeded as Procurator Fiscal, and frequent contributor to the *Journal of Jurisprudence* and other publications: Dundee *Obituaries Notices 1895-1909* 47.

[55] Probably brother of John M Hendry, much discussed in the following Chapter.

[56] Anon, "Dundee Law Lectures" (1869) XIII *JoJ* 688: *Dundee Courier and Argus* 19 & 20 November 1869, 8 & 12 January and 23 February 1870.

[57] Anon, "Dundee Law Lectures" (see previous note).

[58] *Dundee Courier and Argus* 14 April 1870.

[59] *Dundee Courier and Argus* 28 October 1870.

[60] AS 20 December 1873 s 4, amended by AS 28 January 1874 s 1 (both reproduced in Begg, *Law Agents* Appendix, and (with "Specimen" general knowledge and law examination papers) in William George Black, *The Law Agents Act 1873: its operation and results as affecting legal education in Scotland* (1884) Appendix. It will be recalled that the Courts of Law (Scotland) Agents Bill 1871, discussed in Chapter 1, did not mention the requirement, no doubt because it would have appeared in an Act of Sederunt.

[61] By the same token, institution of the BL in the following year was of no interest.

[62] Knight, *Early Chapters.* William Angus Knight (1836-1916) was a Dundee minister, much involved in these debates, and appointed to the chair of Moral Philosophy at St Andrews in 1876. As a participant-observer familiar with both sides, his views might provide unrivalled insights. However, the book was published many years after some of the events described, and is something between an *apologia pro sua vita* and an "I told you so". Moreover, it is not always clear what are Knight's views and what are others'.

[63] I.e. the *Dundee Advertiser*, a supporter of UCD: see references to Sir John Leng, its proprietor, below.

[64] Knight, *Early Chapters* 139.

[65] Ibid., 85.

[66] Ibid., 23.

[67] The Report of the Royal Commission into University Education in Dundee 1951-52 (Cmnd 8514: 1952) (the "Tedder Report", discussed in Chapter 5) para 40, referred to law teaching being envisaged in 1878. However, it may be a misprint for 1887 when, as noted below, there was activity on this front. Southgate, *University Education* does not consider the point.

[68] John Tulloch (1823-86), Principal of St Mary's College and therefore, as senior to the Principal of United College, Principal of St Andrews University, under the terms of the Universities (Scotland) Act 1858.

[69] Knight, *Early Chapters* 116. It would, admittedly, be linked to a chair of Constitutional Law "in fact necessary to complete the equipment of the study of History": see also 109. Southgate, *University Education* 57-9 at 59, records that this letter was in fact an updated version of one sent in 1876, probably to Knight himself (though the reference is difficult to follow). Also, at 68, in a discussion of the internal structures of the University, he records that the "public attitude" of Principal Donaldson, who followed John Tulloch, "was to welcome a Medical School and a Law School in Dundee, if formed into colleges managed by the Court".

[70] Knight, *Early Chapters* 80-81.

[71] Confusingly, references there are indexed under the general heading of "1865 Committee to Consider the Propriety of Instituting Law Lectures in Dundee". However, some sub-headings (e.g. "Petition of Law Clerks") have page numbers significantly higher than the others, and cross-references from entries concerning members (e.g. "Agnew, Alexander"), in conjunction with the UCD Council Minutes, and the various archived papers, make it clear that they refer to 1885.

[72] *Dundee Courier and Argus* 4 July 1885, *Dundee Courier & Argus and Northern Warder* 7 July 1885. The Memorial itself seems not to have survived.

[73] Ibid. No equivalent entry can be identified in FPSD Index to Minutes 1846-87.

[74] David Small (1810-85), partner therein, like Hay, a rival to Thornton in influence. Son of William Small, Town Clerk, apprenticed to a later Town Clerk, afterwards working in an Edinburgh firm and studying at Edinburgh University, he returned to Dundee to set up with John Shiell in 1832, initially in New Inn Entry, then in Reform Street, and Bank Street around 1860, undertaking "lucrative and extensive" business, in particular (like Thornton and Hay) Parliamentary work in connection with railways (so "there were few undertakings of an extensive nature … which the firm was not instrumental in carrying out"). The firm was also agent for local landowners, including the Panmure Estate, owned by the Earls of Dalhousie, and for numerous

local concerns and utilities, including the Dundee and Perth Railway and the Dundee and Arbroath Railway. He was also active in various public offices, and as Preses of the FPSD several times. Unsurprisingly, as a cousin of Mary Ann Baxter, he was "actively concerned with ... the organisation of the Dundee University College" as the firm's role evidences. See Dundee *Obituaries Notices 1895-1909* 107.

[75] Quoted in Dundee University Archives ("DUA") Recs A/98, UCD Council Minutes April 1882-November 1889, Meeting of 1 October 1885. No equivalent entry can be identified in FPSD Index to Minutes 1846-87. While "upwards of 100" seems high, and the *Dundee Directory 1885-86* (like that of 1864-65) does not record law clerks and apprentices, as such, James Thain's letter of 1868 (see note 48 and associated text) asserted that there were 200.

[76] DUA Recs A/98, UCD Council Minute Book April 1882-November 1889, Meeting of 1 October 1885.

[77] John Campbell Smith (1828-1914), stone-mason, advocate 1856, Sheriff-Substitute of Forfarshire at Dundee 1885-1912: see Walker *Biographical Directory*, Grant *Faculty of Advocates*. Sheriff Campbell Smith gave a eulogy in the Sheriff Court on Thomas Thornton's death.

[78] Probably John Robertson of Elmslea (*alias* 325 Perth Road, *alias* University House, i.e. that acquired for the Principal, adjacent to West Park Hall), a member of the UCD Council: Southgate, *University Education* 89, 139, 143 & 287. See also DUA A/680/5 "*The College: the official publication of the Student Representative Council of University College, Dundee*", New Series vol IV, No 2 (December 1906) 21 "Editorial", which, in a brief obituary, records him as born at Craigton in 1831, coming to Dundee about fifteen years later into his uncle's business.

[79] DUA Recs A/98, UCD Council Minute Book April 1882-November 1889, Meeting of 16 October.

[80] *Dundee Courier and Argus* 22 October 1885 and *Dundee Courier and Argus and Northern Warder* 23 October 1885. No equivalent entry can be identified in FPSD Index to Minutes 1846-87.

[81] Henry A Pattullo (1858-1934), nephew of Thornton's former partner James Pattullo (I am grateful to Dennis Collins for this information), attended the High School of Dundee and Edinburgh University, and was apprenticed in Perth and Forfar, becoming a law agent in 1878, in practice with a cousin in J&H Pattullo. He was on the Dundee District Committee of Angus County Council and "road clerk" for the Dundee District of Forfar, also a member of Newport Burgh Committee, and a leading light of the Dundee Parliament "in its palmy days": Dundee City Library Family and Local History Centre *Obituaries Notices 1913-35*, 7.

[82] Alexander Agnew (1841-1910), native of Wigtownshire, took law classes in Edinburgh University, qualified in 1865, and worked for Shiell & Small, then on his own account from 1873, becoming Procurator-Fiscal for Dundee in 1887 (dealing with the Elliot Junction railway disaster, and subsequent prosecution of the train driver: see http://www.railwaysarchive.co.uk/eventsummary.php?eventID=75 last accessed 28 July 2018): Dundee Family and Local History Centre *Miscellaneous Press Cuttings 1910-12* (undated) 292.

[83] DUA Recs A/337/1/3 (folded foolscap m/s marked "Shiell & Small" and "Minute of Joint Committee ... to Consider the Institution of a Course of Lectures in Law 16 November 1885").

[84] DUA Recs A/337/1/1 (separate folded foolscap m/s marked "Shiell & Small" and "Minute of Joint Committee ... to consider the institution of a Course of Law Lectures 18 December 1885").

[85] Though given that the whole of Scots Law was to be covered in 80 lectures on the LLB (see Chapter 1), twelve for contract may not seem quite so perfunctory.

[86] Presumably John Ferguson MacLennan (jnr) (1855-1917), MA LLB, advocate 1881, KC 1905, Sheriff of Caithness, Orkney and Shetland 1905-17: see Walker *Biographical Directory*, Grant *Faculty of Advocates*.

[87] With Thomas Thornton (who was not, of course, on the Committee)?

[88] Thomas Shaw (1850-1937, dying as "father of the Bar"), advocate 1875, Advocate-Depute 1886, (Liberal) MP for Hawick Burghs 1892-1909, QC 1894, Solicitor-General 1894-5, Lord Advocate 1905-9, Lord of Appeal in Ordinary (i.e. House of Lords judge) 1909-29 (as Baron Shaw of Dunfermline), created Lord Craigmyle in 1929, one of the outstanding lawyers of his generation: see Walker *Biographical Directory,* Grant *Faculty of Advocates*.

[89] The handwriting is unclear. 60 students at 7/6 per student produces £22/5/-, less than half the lecturer's fee.

[90] DUA Recs A/337/1/47 (folded m/s marked "Excerpt From Minute of Meeting of [FPSD] held in Dundee on 23 December 1885"); Recs A/98, UCD Council Minute Book April 1882-November 1889, Meeting of 21 January 1896; also *Dundee Courier and Argus* 24 December 1885 and *Dundee Courier & Argus and Northern Warder* 15 December 1885.

[91] DUA Recs A/98, UCD Council Minute Book April 1882-November 1889, Meeting of 2 December 1885.

[92] Aberdeen was the obvious comparator because, at this time, it also offered law classes, but no law degrees, and, seemingly, had one chair and no lectureships at this time: Anon "Bill to Amend Law Agents (Scotland) Act" (1887) XXXI *JoJ* 386-388. It adopted the BL in 1895, and the LLB in 1908. The reference to the Faculty of Advocates and Court of Session was presumably deemed necessary, even though any Dundee students aspiring to the Bar would almost certainly attend Edinburgh University, because the 1886 removal of the requirement of attendance at university classes (discussed below) rendered the idea of recognition for law agents meaningless.

[93] AS 4 November 1886 repealing the relevant part of AS 20 December 1873. See Anon, "The New Act of Sederunt anent the Admission of Law Agents" (1886) XXX *JoJ* 644-648.

[94] That the Faculty of Advocates continued to require attendance is unlikely to have been a consideration, as few if any of students would be aiming at the Bar.

[95] DUA Recs A/814/5, UCD Calendar Fifth Session 1887-88, 158-159.

[96] HC Bill 1887 No 284.

[97] DUA Recs A/814/5, UCD Calendar Fifth Session 1887-88, 158-159. Another possible beneficiary would have been St Mungo's College, discussed in Chapter 1 and below, since, at least shortly after this time, it seemingly boasted ten chairs: see Anon, "St Mungo's College – Faculty of Law" (1889) 1 *JR* 390-392; Anon, "St Mungo's College" (1890) XXXIV *JoJ* 506-507.

[98] DUA Recs A/814/5, UCD Calendar Fifth Session 1887-88, 158-159. Since the Faculties of Canon Law and Civil Law had ceased operations centuries earlier, "at present" is beautifully modulated.

[99] It passed its Second Reading in the Commons, in effect on the nod (see *Hansard* HC Deb, Third Series, vol 316, cols 1015, 1121, 27 June 1887), but no further proceedings appear to be recorded.

[100] *Dundee Courier and Argus* 21 & 22 August 1888. This was a strongly disagreeing reply to an earlier letter, which has not been found, and suggested that a class could be got up to cover certain subjects at £1/1/- a quarter, as seemingly occurred in Edinburgh and Glasgow.

[101] *Dundee Courier and Argus* 20 December 1889.

[102] D S Littlejohn (1822-1903), "enthusiastic antiquary and naturalist" from Forfar, where his ancestors were "eminent burgesses", was a writer there, then in Edinburgh in 1842, and started business with Gershom Gourlay as Littlejohn and Gourlay (later D S & T Littlejohn and other manifestations) in Dundee, was Preses of FPSD and Honorary Sheriff-Substitute 1886. He started the Forfarshire Building Society and was Chairman of several companies, took a leading part in incorporation of Broughty Ferry as a burgh and was first Clerk to its Commissioners (till 1895), etc: Dundee *Obituaries Notices 1895-1909* 31; also Anon, "David Stewart Littlejohn, Esq, solicitor in Dundee" (1893-4) 1 *SLT* 81.

[103] *Dundee Courier and Argus* 13 March 1890. The "Order" was dated 21 March 1890.

[104] D S Littlejohn *A Popular Sketch of the Law of Scotland: being an address to the Dundee law apprentices* 1st ed (1890), 3rd ed (1893). Only copies of the third edition appear to have survived.

[105] *Dundee Courier and Argus* 13 March 1890.

[106] Anon, "David Stewart Littlejohn" (see note 102). The third edition itself carries half-a-dozen generally laudatory press comments and half-a-dozen more "Excerpts from Letters to the Author Containing Opinions of the Profession".

[107] FPSD Minutes 1887-1960, Meeting of 23 April 1890.

[108] Note Thornton's later reference to "secrecy", quoted below.

[109] Comprising W Hay (Preses), W Heron (Vice-Preses), W D J [*quaere* D S?] Littlejohn, W Smith & A Agnew (Secretary).

[110] Had he bounced the FPSD into action, or did their activities force his hand?

[111] Curiously, Thornton always spells the name "Petterson".

[112] DUA Recs A/99, UCD Council Minute Book, December 1889-February 1897, Meeting of 23 April 1890, also FPSD Minutes 1887-1960, Meeting of 23 April 1890. The original letter appears lost, but a copy, dated 23 April 1890, is at DUA RU/191/8 ("Faculty of Law Centenary: Miscellaneous Papers"), photocopy m/s headed "Folios 14, 15 & 16 Xerox copies of original entry in the Minute Book of the Faculty of Procurators and Solicitors, Dundee, currently held by Mr Donald Gordon, Secretary to the Procurators, c/o Gilruths, Solicitors, Dundee, 8 Nov 1990 J.J. R[obertson]".

[113] Upon which Edinburgh University may have just started giving lectures: Anon, "Bill to amend Law Agents (Scotland) Act" (1887) XXXI *JoJ* 386.

[114] DUA RU/191/8.

[115] Ibid. D S Littlejohn's Preface to the First Edition of his *Popular Sketch* dated 30 May 1890, just after his barely disguised disappointment that his fellow law agents' failure to follow his example in giving lectures, continued that "all doubt as to the success of the movement [to have law lectures in Dundee] will now be removed, and the object we had in views will be better accomplished, through the generosity of Mr Thornton, whose offer to establish a Law Lectureship

for three years in Dundee, at his own expense, is at present before the authorities of the College and the profession".

[116] No doubt one friend on the bench was Lord Trayner, considered below, who had been appointed judge in 1885.

[117] Occurring just a few weeks before. The second Tay Bridge had opened in 1887.

[118] DUA RU/191/8. Was this last location cocking a snook at the University? The burgh of St Andrews can have provided very few clerks or apprentices.

[119] The traditional university year then comprised two unequal sessions, i.e. October-April and April-May (though some subjects also used a "Summer Session", taught by assistants, as Professors exempted themselves): DUA Recs A/422, UStA Senatus Academicus Minutes 1905-08 Meetings of 19 January & 9 February 1907.

[120] An echo of John Austin's "command theory of law", very popular at the time, which seeks to define "law properly so-called", as opposed to laws of God, laws of nature, etc?

[121] By this time, as noted above, it is possible that Edinburgh was offering lectures of Forms of Process: Anon, "Bill to amend Law Agents (Scotland) Act" (1887) XXXI *JoJ* 386.

[122] DUA RU/191/8.

[123] DUA Recs A/99, UCD Council Minute Book December 1889-February 1897, Meeting of 23 April 1890. The Committee comprised Principal Peterson, Rev W J Cox, Mr J Martin White, Mr Robertson, and Mr Thornton.

[124] DUA Recs A/99, UCD Council Minute Book December 1889-February 1897, Meeting of 14 May 1890. At this meeting, Thornton also intimated his assent to his appointment as Council representative on the St Andrews University Court.

[125] No Committee Report is minuted.

[126] For biographical details, see below.

[127] DUA Recs A/99, UCD Council Minute Book December 1889-February 1897, Meeting of 11 June 1890.

[128] DUA Recs A/814/8, UCD Calendar Eighth Session 1890-91, 77.

[129] DUA Recs A/99, UCD Council Minute Book December 1889-February 1897, Meeting of 10 September 1890.

[130] A Bill to Amend the Law Agents Act 1873 (Bill No 69) was introduced on 26 November 1890 by Mr Caldwell (James Caldwell, Liberal MP for Glasgow St Rollox at the time), and others, becoming the Law Agents and Notaries Public (Scotland) Act 1891, s 5 of which gave the power.

[131] Discussed below.

[132] DUA RU/191/8 (emphasis in original).

[133] FPSD Minutes 1887-1960, Meeting of 7 August 1890 (starting half an hour late as Preses, Vice-Preses and Secretary were absent).

[134] FPSD Minutes 1887-1960, Meeting of 12 September, 1890 (also starting half an hour late for the same reason).

[135] *Dundee Courier and Argus* 8 August 1890.

[136] FPSD Minutes 1887-1960, Meeting of 12 September 1890, "Circular referred to in the preceding Minute".

[137] *Dundee Directory 1889-90* lists 61 Procurators and Notaries Public in Dundee but, as in earlier years, law clerks and apprentices are not listed, as such.

[138] *Dundee Courier and Argus,* 29 September 1890 reported that solicitors would be willing to pay for the clerks to attend.

[139] John Trayner (1834-1929, dying, like Shaw later, as "father of the Bar"), advocate 1858, counsel to the North British Railway Company in the Tay Bridge Enquiry in 1880 when Thornton was their solicitor (see David Swinfen *The Fall of the Tay Bridge* (1994) 57-59). Possibly this was how they met, though the nearness of their ages suggests that they might have been at university together. In any case, he was also one of the original Governors of UCD, *ex officio* as Sheriff of Forfar (DUA Recs A/95, Register of Governors, entry No 7). He was appointed Sheriff of Forfar 1881-85, elevated to the Court of Session as Lord Trayner in 1885 (in room of Lord Deas), and the High Court of Justiciary in 1887 (at this time, the former did not automatically involve the latter, as it now does), and was Railway Commissioner for Scotland 1889-1898. He was also editor of *Trayner's Latin Maxims* (1st ed 1861), for cautious praise of the 2nd ed. of which, as better than the 1st, see (1876) XX *JoJ* 587, and was awarded an LLD by Glasgow University in 1886. He had considered seeking election as a Liberal MP, but stood aside for the Law Officers. His daughter married the future Lord Salvesen (a noted judge of the next generation, who later gave law lectures in Dundee: see below): see Walker *Biographical Directory*, Grant *Faculty of Advocates*, Anon, "Appointments" (1885) XXIX *JoJ* 160; Anon. "Lord Trayner" (1893-4) 1 *SLT* 311, Anon, "The Hon Lord Trayner" (1904-05) 12 *SLT* 145-150; and Anon "The Late Lord Trayner" 1929 *SLT* (News) 21-22. His portrait, by George Reid, is owned by the University of Dundee and at the time of writing hangs in the Scrymgeour Building.

[140] Who described himself in Walker *Biographical Directory* as "Thornton Lecturer [*sic*] in Scots Law, Mercantile Law and Conveyancing" (though without reference to where).

[141] Discussed below. He was adopted as Liberal Unionist candidate on 9 December 1890, just before the inaugural lecture: see *Dundee Courier and Argus* 9 December 1890.

[142] DUA unclassified (Per 378.4133G) 208.

[143] *Dundee Courier and Argus* 3, 4 & 7 October 1890.

[144] *Dundee Courier and Argus* 13, 16, 19 & 23 December 1890. GW Alexander, born in Halifax NS, but early emigrated to Scotland, graduated at Edinburgh in 1883, also studying at Berlin and Erlangen, but was prevented from entering the ministry by a throat condition. He was Secretary of both UCD and the Dundee Technical Institute 1889-1892, before becoming Secretary to the Glasgow School Board (1892-1906) (while also acting as Clerk to the Burgh Committee on Secondary Education and Honorary Secretary to several other School Boards and the West of Scotland Technical College), then Clerk to the Edinburgh School Board, followed by appointment as Senior Assistant, and in 1922, Second Secretary, to the Scottish Education Department: *The Scotsman* 7 March 1922.

[145] *Dundee Courier and Argus* 30 December 1890.

[146] I.e. the Free Kirk of St John's building in Small's Wynd, demolished in 1904 for the "Old Medical School": see Southgate, *University Education* xiv, marked "I" on plan of "Major Building Developments North and West of the Original site, 1882-1967" (also Michael Shafe, *University Education in Dundee 1881-1981: a pictorial history* (1982) 53).

[147] *Dundee Courier and Argus* 6 January 1891; DUA Recs A/680/1, "*The College*" vol III, No 3 (February 1891) 289 "Notes".

[148] *Dundee Courier and Argus* 6 January 1891.

[149] In the light of the delayed start, one wonders if William Smith found his attendance at Court interfered.

[150] DUA Recs A/814/9, UCD Calendar Ninth Session 1891-92, 83: cf Recs A/680/1, "*The College*", vol III, No 3 (February 1891) 289 "Notes".

[151] DUA Recs A/680/1/, "*The College*" (see note 78) vol III, No 3 (February 1891) 289, & vol IV, No 4 (June 1891) 333 "Notes", respectively.

[152] DUA Recs A/814/9, UCD Calendar Ninth Session 1891-92, 83. The successful students are identified below.

[153] A late hour to allow William Smith to travel after the Courts adjourned for the day?

[154] DUA Recs A/814/9, UCD Calendar Ninth Session 1891-92, 48; Recs A/814/10, UCD, Calendar Tenth Session 1892-93, 66.

[155] DUA Recs A/814/10, UCD Calendar Tenth Session 1892-93, 66.

[156] Ibid. 82.

[157] The successful students are identified below. It seems very likely that Thomas Thornton funded the prizes.

[158] Though as noted above, Edinburgh University may have started doing so shortly before: Anon "Bill to amend Law Agents (Scotland) Act" (1887) XXXI *JoJ* 386.

[159] John Erskine, *An Institute of the Law of Scotland* (1st ed 1773, 8th ed 1871). (A number of major legal works from the 17th to the 19th centuries are known as the "Institutional Works" as several have the title "Institutions" or "Institutes", in imitation of the *Institutiones*, one of the four parts of the *Corpus juris civilis* (for which, see Chapter 1).

[160] George Joseph Bell, *Principles of the Law of Scotland*.(1st ed 1829, 10th ed 1899)

[161] David Hume, *Commentaries on the Law of Scotland, Respecting the Description and Punishment of Crimes*.(1st ed 1797, 4th ed 1844).

[162] John Erskine, *Principles of the Law of Scotland* (1st ed 1754, 21st ed 1911). The Preface to First Edition of Gloag & Henderson's *The Law of Scotland* (1927), which sought to replace it, records that "[s]ince its publication in 1754, Erskine's *Principles*, as revised and brought up to date by various editors, has held the leading place as a textbook in the classes of Scots Law in the Universities".

[163] The 18th edition, edited by Rankine, was published in 1890.

[164] FPSD Minutes 1887-1960, Meetings of 5 February & 27 February 1891.

[165] William Smith's political ambitions might suggest an inspiring speaker, and his obituary (though not necessarily to be relied on) described him as "a lucid pleader".

[166] See the sample questions in Begg, *Law Agents* 2nd ed Appendix (and c.f. Anon, "The Education of Scotch Lawyers" 177-187 ("Faculty of Procurators in Glasgow")).

[167] DUA Recs A/357/3/10.

[168] As argued above, it might have been important for the classes not to be evening classes if they were to be treated as "university classes", as and when the obligation to attend such classes was re-imposed.

[169] See note 130.

[170] Anon, "Incorporated Society of Law Agents" (1891) VII *ScLR* 256 & 291.

[171] 55 & 56 Vict c 30. Its chief purpose was the same as that of the 1887 Bill, that is, to create the offence of purporting to be, or acting as, a law agent, when unqualified: see ss 2-4.

[172] Section 5 (emphases added).

[173] Anon, "St Mungo's College – Faculty of Law"; Anon, "St Mungo's College"; see also David M Walker *A History of the School of Law, the University of Glasgow* (c.1990) 78-82, and David M Walker *A Legal History of Scotland* (1988-2004) vol vi *The nineteenth century* 269).

[174] Ordinances No 39 (General No 11) and 40 (General No 12) of 1893, reproduced in Alan E Clapperton (ed), *The Universities (Scotland) Act 1889 together with the Ordinances of the Commissioners under the Act* ... (1916) 129 & 131, and *General Report of the Commissioners under the Universities (Scotland) Act, 1889* ... (Cd 276: 1900) 69 & 70.

[175] See Anon (possibly William C Smith), "Law Graduation" 1894 *SLT* 456.

[176] As observed above, he was adopted as Parliamentary candidate just before the first lecture.

[177] DUA Recs A/99, UCD Council Minute Book December 1889-February 1897, Meeting of 9 May 1894.

[178] Possibly successors to the Law Clerks and Apprentices Society of the 1860s?

[179] FPSD Minutes 1887-1960, Meeting of 2 August 1894.

[180] Though, as noted above, Anon. "Bill to amend Law Agents (Scotland) Act" (1887) XXXI *JoJ* 386 suggested a lecturer in procedure existed in Edinburgh University by this time.

[181] Anon. "Law Lectures in Dundee" (1895-6) 3 *SLT* 254. The advocates were Mr Salvesen (later Lord Salvesen and John Trayner's son-in-law: see note 139) on Bills of Lading, Mr Alistair Donaldson on Formation of Companies and Allotment of Shares, Mr Chisholm on Extinction of Obligations, Mr W Lyon Mackenzie (given the similarity of names, possibly a relation of W Lyon Mackenzie (1997-1861), Dundonian, first mayor of Toronto, and controversial Canadian politician) on Cautionary Obligations, Mr Constable on Sale of Goods and Mr Craigie on Partnership (for details of whom, see Walker *Biographical Directory*, Grant *Faculty of Advocates*).

[182] DUA Recs A/100, UCD Council Minute February 1897-November 1905, Meeting of 14 April 1897.

[183] The following, including quotations, is culled from Anon, "Sir Thomas Thornton LLD, solicitor, Dundee" (1895-96) 3 *SLT* 89-90; Anon, "The late Sir Thomas Thornton, LLD, Dundee"

(1903-04) 11 *SLT* 9-10; *The Scotsman* (obituary) 22 April 1903; William Angus Knight *Biographical Sketch with Reminiscences of Thomas Thornton (including several estimates of him* (1905) (which includes several "Estimates by Citizens of Dundee" and five "Reminiscences" by important people); Dundee University Archives, and FPSD Minutes 1887-1960 (various entries). Some of Thomas Thornton's lecture notes, including lectures by "Mr [George Joseph] Bell" (i.e. the author of Bell's *Principles*) in the late 1840s and a diary of similar date, commencing " ... it would be interesting and a happy memento, to look back on in after life (D.V. ['Deo volenti', i.e. 'God willing'])", but towards the end noting that "[m]elancholy is indigenous to my system": DUA Recs MS 17/11/1 & 2. Other papers relating to him are held in Dundee City Archives, but are not presently relevant.

[184] I am grateful for this epithet to Alastair McDonald (*int. al.* formerly senior partner in Thorntons, successor to the firm founded by Thomas Thornton).

[185] Charles McKean & Patricia Whatley, with Kenneth Baxter, *Lost Dundee: Dundee's lost architectural heritage* (2008) 135 & 145.

[186] A H Millar (ed), *Roll of Eminent Burgesses of Dundee 1513-1886* (1887), available at http://www.fdca.org.uk/Burgess_List.htm (last accessed 28 July 2018).

[187] "[P]resented to him by his fellow citizens, in remembrance of his varied work in their behalf. Although not the best portrait of him which exists, it is a good likeness, and now hangs in the Albert Institute, to which he generously handed it over". On the presentation of this portrait, see Knight *Biographical Sketch* 82-83.

[188] In Thornton Castle, inhabited by his descendants. A reproduction hangs in the Scrymgeour Building at the time of writing.

[189] Who is strangely absent from most obituaries and memorials, but see obituary in *Dundee Year Book 1903-4*: I am grateful to Dennis Collins for this reference.

[190] James Pattullo (1818-1903), previously partner in Neish and Pattullo, later in J & H Pattullo, also uncle of Henry Pattullo, involved in the law lectures of the 1860s (see note 81 and associated text): Anon, "James Pattullo, Esq: Solicitor, Dundee" (1902-03) 10 *SLT* 105; and Anon, "The late James Pattullo, Esq, Solicitor Dundee" (1903-04) 11 *SLT* 159-160.

[191] FPSD Minutes 1887-1960, 2-5 (list of members).

[192] Most Acts today are "Public general" ones, introduced by an MP or peer, and typically on behalf of the Government, but (as "Private Members' Bills") not necessarily so, and change the general law. "Private Bills" (not to be confused with "Private Members' Bills") are introduced by interested parties outside Parliament, seeking an exception to the general law. In the 19th century, before the great municipal reform legislation (effected by Public general Acts) local authorities commonly did not have powers to provide various services, such as paving and sewerage, so had to seek Private Acts to acquire them. Consequently, expertise in private legislation procedure was invaluable to a municipality.

[193] I.e. the Court of Session which, together with the High Court of Justiciary, have long been termed "the Supreme Courts of Scotland".

[194] This firm continued until 1968-69 when it amalgamated with Dickie, Gray, McDonald and Fair to form Thorntons and Dickies, now simply Thorntons: I am grateful to Dennis Collins for this information.

[195] Now occupied by Boyles Solicitors. There is a well-known photograph (a copy of which is held by Dundee City Libraries Local and Family History Centre) of Thomas Thornton with Robert Fleming (who founded Robert Fleming & Co, a very successful bank until 2000, and was grandfather of Ian Fleming, the novelist), dated c.1890, crossing Albert Square, no doubt on his way there.

[196] Obituaries and appreciations tend to gloss over the fate of the first Tay Bridge (for the failure of which, of course, he can hardly be held responsible), and not to mention any involvement in the second.

[197] Southgate *University Education* 23 & 25.

[198] "[I]n recognition of his services to Education, to the Legal Profession, and to the University itself". He "rais[ed] money in Dundee to augment [existing] Bursaries [in the University]", "found[ed] (or advis[ed] his clients to found) new scholarships in the University" and "help[ed] to obtain funds to build a Hall of Residence for women students at St Andrews": Knight *Biographical Sketch* 37-38.

[199] DUA Recs A/95, Register of Governors, entry Nos. 21 & 46.

[200] Sir John Leng (1828-1906), a pioneer in journalism and newspaper production, was editor and later (through John Leng & Co), owner of the *Dundee Advertiser*, and founder of the *People's Journal*, *People's Friend*, and *Evening Telegraph*. John Leng & Co merged with the rival D C Thomson company, publishers of the *Dundee Courier*, in 1926 (DC Thomson having earlier obtained a controlling interest). Sir John Leng was involved in the setting up of UCD, and became a Governor and Council member, using the columns of the *Advertiser* to promote its interests, and was awarded an LLD in 1904. He was also (Liberal) MP for Dundee 1889-1905, a supporter of Home Rule, and knighted in 1893. The Sir John Leng Trust for the promotion of education, the arts, etc (the Governors of which are nominated, *int al*, by the University of Dundee Court and Senate), among other things still distributes the Leng Medal to pupils of Dundee schools for solo singing of Scots songs.

[201] DUA A/99 UCD Council Minute Book December 1899-February 1897, Meeting of 25 September 1895.

[202] Knight *Biographical Sketch* ch VII lists over twenty offices and honorary posts held, also including also Deputy Lieutenant of the County of City of Dundee, Justice of the Peace for Forfarshire and Dundee, and Honorary Sheriff-Substitute of Dundee.

[203] FPSD Minutes 1887-1960, Meetings of 28 May and 2 August 1894.

[204] FPSD Minutes 1887-1960, Meeting of 2 February 1895.

[205] Knight *Biographical Sketch* 44, records previous "autumn residences" at such places as Wemyss Hall in Fife and Middleton in Angus.

[206] Laurencekirk to Banchory, the relevant station, by the "Old Military Road" over the Cairn o' Mount (now the B974) is some 22 miles and rises to some 450m (1500 feet).

[207] See Anon, "William Guthrie, Esq, Sheriff-Substitute, Glasgow" (1893-4) 1 *SLT* 17 and Walker *Biographical Directory*, Grant *Faculty of Advocates*. There is a photograph of him, illustrating a pen-portrait in the *Scots Law Times* pen portrait.

[208] See obituaries in *Scotsman* 11 May 1915, 1915 *SLT* 42, and (1915) 31 *SLR* 135, also Walker, *Biographical Directory*, Grant, *Faculty of Advocates,* also images at https://www. scran.ac.uk/database/record.php?usi=000-000-519-986C&scache=1x8ou8eacp&searchdb=scran (last accessed 28 July 2018). There is a signed photograph of him, dated 1892, in Dundee Central Library (and a printed election manifesto), and another, reproduced from the illustration in a pen-portrait in the *Scots Law Times* ((1896-97) 4 *SLT* 137), hung in the Scrymgeour Building at the time of writing.

[209] Grant, *Faculty of Advocates* does not mention this office, and gives slightly different dates to those in Walker *Biographical Directory*.

[210] Anon, "The Chair of Law in Aberdeen University" (1907-08) 15 *SLT* 42, 50 (which lists all the candidates).

[211] I am grateful to Ross Macdonald for drawing my attention to this last.

[212] A notice advertising him speaking, and referring to the law lectures, appears in *Dundee Courier and Argus* 17 November 1890.

[213] DUA Recs A/814/9, UCD, Calendar, Ninth Session, 1891-92, 95. For biographical details of several, see below.

[214] James Grant, solicitor, 25 Barrack Street, is recorded in the *Dundee Directory 1904-05.*

[215] James Macarthur Souter, solicitor, 31 Reform Street, is recorded in *Dundee Year Book 1904-5.*

[216] Alfred Watson Carlisle (1868-1947): in practice in Commercial Street: Dundee City Library Family and Local History Centre *Obituaries Notices 1946-57*, 10.

[217] DUA Recs A/814/10, UCD Calendar Tenth Session, 1892-93, 99.

[218] DUA Recs A/814/11, UCD Calendar Eleventh Session, 1893-94, 95.

[219] See Dundee City Library Family and Local History Centre *Obituaries Notices 1957-66*, 171.

[220] See notes 81 & 190.

[221] See Dundee *Obituaries Notices 1957-66*, 103.

[222] See Dundee City Library Family and Local History Centre *Obituaries Notices 1913-35*, 202.

[223] See DUA MS 88/11/1/5. I am grateful to Kenneth Baxter for this information.

[224] See Dundee City Library Family and Local History Centre *Obituaries Notices 1935-46*, 220. I am also grateful to Dennis Collins for further information.

CHAPTER 3

1899-1938: CHALLENGING DECADES: LIMITED TEACHING AND FURTHER REFORM

Continuous law teaching in University College Dundee (UCD) finally commenced at the fourth attempt in 1899, and was specifically intended for the professional law agents' examinations, and with the barest minimum of staff. It commenced against a backdrop of newly harmonious relations between UCD and the rest of St Andrews University, and probably it was that harmony which at last permitted Thomas Thornton to achieve some of what he had been seeking for decades.

Despite initial high hopes, and an attempt to start a law degree, however, this law teaching remained very restricted for 40 years, with little change of staff, (though gradually rising student numbers from the 1920s), while relations between UCD and the rest of the University again soured. Nevertheless, there were other events of interest, such the Bachelor of Commerce saga. But perhaps the most important events in this period were changes in the requirements for professional qualification, which finally produced a law degree in Dundee at the end of the period.

In addition to narrating these events, this Chapter considers the people involved in law teaching over the period, including both the lecturers, their identities and careers (and their extraordinary continuity), and the students, their numbers, gender and achievements, so far as can be retrieved from the records.

1899-1939: Backdrop

The difficulties of the 1890s, involving affiliation, dis-affiliation, and re-affiliation, with concomitant disruption, were described in Chapter 2. In the following 40 years, from 1899 to 1938, relations between UCD and the rest of St Andrews University went through a number of phases[1].

An initial "happy decade"[2] saw sufficient government grants, Carnegie largesse[3] and private donations to allow expansion on both sides of the Tay. This expansion included UCD's acquisition of more two houses on the Perth Road (Union Mount and Ellenbank), to the west of the original acquisitions. The former[4] became the Library, and remained so until the Tower Building was completed in the 1960s. The latter[5] became the Students' Union, and remained so until current Union building in Airlie Place was built in the 1970s[6].

However, this decade was followed by a period of "temporary discord", because, in 1911, government funds intended for UCD were sent, by mistake, to St Andrews University centrally, and used by it for other purposes. This unhappy interlude was succeeded by a dozen years of "marking time", in which UCD still felt itself discriminated against in the distribution of university funds, and certainly little development occurred. Worse still, after that came a "decade of depression", during which time, an official enquiry twenty years later concluded, UCD "had not advanced or prospered either materially or culturally to the extent it might reasonably have expected"[7]. And Sir James Irvine, Principal of the University, thought by some to have "despised 'Dundee'"[8] (as possibly evidenced by depriving it, not only of Carnegie largesse, but also of any money from the Berry Bequest windfall of the 1890s[9], and the new funds from the Harkness foundation received in the 1920s[10], not to mention his presumed complicity in the diversion of the 1911 grant), became "Interim" Principal of UCD as well (though the "interim" lasted a decade). A showdown at the end of the 1930s, however, produced "life and hope in University College".

1899-1938: The "Law School" - an Overview and Recapitulation

Law teaching recommenced in UCD in 1899. It did so not as a preliminary to university classes, for general interest, as "continuous professional development", or some mixture of the three, but solely and specifically for professional purposes, but with high hopes of Professors, the institution of a degree and a new (or in St Andrews terms, possibly resuscitated) Law Faculty in the near future.

However, in the event, though suffering fits and starts, and punctuated by various events, the period from 1899 to 1938 was largely one of stasis. Small numbers of non-graduating students (declining to zero in one year of the First World War), eventually increasing (though including a proportion of accountancy students, who were required to take Scots Law, and who, in one year, constituted 100% of the class), were taught by a staff never exceeding two in number at any one time. Of these staff, one lasted the whole period and beyond, but another unilaterally declined to give classes in some years and left after a few more, a third essentially constituted privatised outsourcing, though a fourth turned out to be a mover and shaker. For some years, there were only Scots Law classes, and it would not have been surprising if this initiative had failed, like the previous ones.

But during this period, some occurrences gave it a little support. These included not only an ambitious attempt to institute a law degree, an interesting proposal for a Bachelor of Commerce degree, but also the curious "Railway Lectures". More importantly, despite an almost complete vacuum in academic thinking about what law teaching was for, cumulative changes in regulations for professional qualification (incidentally seeing the translation of "law agents" into "solicitors") required changes in law teaching in UCD. These, in the period covered by the following Chapter, produced a law degree, some half-century after UCD law teaching first started. Unexpectedly, it is possible to conclude that, though the recommencement of law classes in 1899 once more flowed from Thomas Thornton's efforts, backed by the UCD Principal Mackay, their later survival resulted from support by the University Principal Irvine.

It is useful to divide this period into two parts, 1899-1917, and 1918-1938. But before examining them, it is also useful, in the light of the importance of changes in regulations for professional qualification, to recapitulate what was required for professional qualification, and for a law degree (discussed in Chapter 1 and illustrated in Appendices 2 and 3 to this Chapter). The requirements for law agents in 1899 were those stipulated in the 1893 Act of Sederunt under the Law Agents (Scotland) Act 1873[11]. So far as law teaching was concerned, in addition to a five year apprenticeship, they involved a law examination covering what Chapter 1 called the "law agents' triad" of Scots Law (for which Erskine's *Principles*, Bell's *Principles* and Hume's *Commentaries* vol 1 were mentioned, implicitly defining the syllabus), Conveyancing, and Forms of Process, civil and criminal (in respect of both of which nothing was mentioned to further define the syllabus)[12]. They did not require attendance at university classes.

The requirements to become a Writer to the Signet or Solicitor to the Supreme Court (the two privileged Faculties or Societies in Edinburgh) were stipulated in their own regulations. The former involved much the same as for ordinary law agents by way of apprenticeship and law examinations[13]. The latter involved somewhat less[14]. Both, however, did require attendance at some university law classes[15]. The requirements for the Faculty of Advocates, stipulated in its regulations, included no apprenticeship, but a distinctly wider "private" law examination and attendance at the equivalent university classes (together with the mere ritual of the "public" law examination)[16].

Thus, no professional body required a law degree, and the great majority of law students across all the universities remained non-graduating[17]. However, law agent apprentices with a BL or LLB were exempted from the Scots Law and Conveyancing parts of the law agents' law examination, and intrant advocates with an LLB were exempted from the whole "private" law examination.

All the law schools, save St Andrews, offered one or both of the LLB and BL degrees, which were governed by the 1893 Ordinances[18]. The LLB (echoing Faculty of Advocates' concerns), required Civil Law, either Scots Law or English Law, Jurisprudence, Public International Law, Constitutional Law & History, one subject from a list of Conveyancing, Political Economy and Mercantile Law, and two subjects from a list of

Private International Law, Political Economy, Administrative Law and Forensic Medicine, totalling eight subjects in all. The BL required, roughly, Civil Law, Scots Law, Conveyancing and Forensic Medicine, but in part-substitution for Civil Law and Forensic Medicine, one or more subjects could be taken from a list of Jurisprudence, Public International Law, Constitutional Law & History, Private International Law and Administrative Law, totalling four to six subjects in all.

1899-1917: The "Law school" - Developments

Recapitulation of the professional requirements provides a perspective on two 1899 initiatives. The first was on the St Andrews "campus". In the late 19th century, there had been concern within the Scottish universities that civil service jobs, open to competitive entry since the Northcote/Trevelyan reforms, were snapped up by Oxbridge candidates at Scottish candidates' expense, in part because of their different age of graduation, in part because the civil service preferred the Oxbridge curricula[19].

In 1899, this remained a concern in St Andrews University, as Senate asked Boards of Studies to consider remedies. One suggested a "Lectureship in Public Law", linked to history[20]. The idea was taken no further, but illustrates an attitude to UCD, since the lectureship would clearly be in United College[21], and was discussed without reference to a simultaneous initiative in UCD.

The recapitulation also provides background for the simultaneous, and contrasting, initiative in 1899 on the Dundee "campus". This was the recommencement of law teaching, solely for professional examinations. The complexity which the recapitulation indicates also incidentally demonstrates that, usefully for UCD, a law school could chose its level of involvement, and start small and grow.

But an obvious question is why, after the false starts of the 1860s, 1880s and early 1890s, the turn of the century should produce yet another attempt at law classes. The answer must be the reawakening of the dormant ambitions of Thomas Thornton (and no doubt others) caused by the re-affiliation of UCD to St Andrews University in 1897, coupled with new government money for expansion specifically intended for UCD[22] (introducing the "happy decade"). The delay of a couple of years before recommencement probably requires no explanation, but it is worth observing that the Marquess of Bute, who had marshalled opposition to the "affiliation" of UCD (but "now a sick man, and more erratic than ever"[23], indeed dying in 1900) demitted office in 1898.

Intriguingly, however, there is no hint of this initiative in Minutes of UCD Council or its Education Board, nor in those of Court and Senate, in the period leading up to the summer of 1899. Thus, the first intimation appeared unheralded, probably in July 1899, in the Report in the College Calendar by John Yule Mackay, Principal of UCD, on the academic year just completed. He declared, with some exaggeration, and in a triumph of hope over experience, that:

> [t]he successful results of the temporary courses in law provided some years ago through the generosity of Sir Thomas Thornton make it clear that the institution of permanent teaching in this subject would prove of the greatest benefit, and that the opportunities afforded would be widely taken advantage of[24].

The rest of the University had clearly been squared, as he added that:

> [t]he establishment in the College of a Professorship of Scots Law and Conveyancing would be regarded with satisfaction at St Andrews, as it would mark the first step towards the formation of a University Faculty of Law[25].

Scots Law and Conveyancing were, of course, two of the three parts of the "law agents' triad" (and traditionally law schools did not offer classes on Forms of Process, the third). The matter also appeared urgent, for it was raised almost simultaneously in the UCD Council, in a report by Principal Mackay on "the proposed Law Class", and the matter was remitted to Dr Baxter[26] and himself, with plenipotentiary powers "to make any arrangements that they may see necessary, should it be found possible to hold Classes in the coming session [ie 1899-1900]"[27].

Acting with the required urgency, Dr Baxter reported back to the next Meeting that he was negotiating with the Faculty of Procurators and Solicitors in Dundee (FPSD), who had the matter under consideration[28].

Surely not coincidentally, Thornton had been elected FPSD Preses in February of that year[29] and, ostensibly at least, at the instance of a Mr Ogilvy[30] and in response to Dr Baxter's contact, it had set up a Committee in August including Thornton "to consider the desirability and practicability of having lectures on law in University College[31]".

This Committee (as might be expected of one containing Thornton) also acted with the required urgency and presented a report to the FPSD Annual General Meeting that month, indicating that there were 51 law apprentices and law clerks[32], and 24 accountancy apprentices, likely to attend lectures (a total of 75 which hindsight showed to be over-optimistic). The report was adopted and sent, with a recommendation for the lectures, to the College Council[33].

And in addition to all this activity, it was reported to College Council at its September meeting that (rehearsing their action of the 1860s and 1880s, discussed in Chapter 2) "[t]here was also a numerously signed petition from apprentices and accountants' offices in the city praying for the establishment of a qualifying course of lectures[34]". No copy of the petition appears to have survived, however, so its signatories are unknown.

Looking at these events in the round, we can observe that Thornton had been elected Preses; no discussions in the relevant bodies had been minuted before Mackay's announcement; the rest of the University had been squared; the FPSD was taking parallel action; and the clerks and apprentices had produced a petition at the same time. Even without Mackay's mention of him, this head of steam indicates Thornton's hand.

By 1899, he was entering his 70th year, and ill, so like John Boyd Baxter in the 1870s, an old man in a hurry. His doubts on the profligacy of UCD (mentioned in the previous Chapter) no doubt stilled (but possibly with fears, raised by the "Public Law lectureship", of being out-flanked by a St Andrews-based Law Faculty), he could be expected to get his ducks in a row to achieve the ambition first expressed in 1866.

Astonishingly, the College Council's September meeting went on actually to appoint a lecturer, with a view to lectures commencing the following month. But Thornton did not get all he hoped. Possibly Mackay had overstated matters (as his apparent suggestion that the chair would cover both Scots Law and Conveyancing suggests); possibly unrecorded financial arguments restricted funds; possibly a philanthropist unexpectedly failed to unbutton. In any event, what emerged in 1899 was a mere part-time lectureship in Scots Law, supplemented a few years later by a part-time lectureship in Conveyancing, an arrangement which continued for 40 years.

Nevertheless, it should be noted that, at this time, numbers of staff in all law schools were, by modern standards, tiny. Edinburgh (the giant among law schools) still only had seven, Glasgow had five, and Aberdeen three[35], and staff were normally part-time everywhere for another 60 years.

A lecturer, James Allison, MA (StA), LLB (Edin), a sole practitioner in his 30s[36], was appointed with continuing extraordinary rapidity. As further evidence that the whole matter had been arranged in advance by Thornton, there were no advertising of the position, no interviews, nor even a formal appointment process. Rather, at the same September meeting at which it received the FPSD recommendation and the apprentices' petition, UCD Council both fixed fees (3 guineas for matriculation and "either 10/- or 21/-" - unexplained alternatives - for the class), and made the appointment[37]. Within the week, Court had accepted the appointment[38], and Senate did so the following month[39] (by which time, the lectures might actually have started).

There is no contemporary record of the lecturer's salary, though a few years later, it was £25 plus class fees[40]. This compared with £100 plus class fees for full-time lecturers[41]. Whether it was worth Allison's while for the money was clearly for him to decide, but in 1910, he wrote a letter, both plaintive and angry, pointing out that he had then been teaching for over a decade without a rise[42]. In any event, in the following year, when the Treasury imposed the "Fee Fund" principle of pooling and redistributing fees (thereby benefitting lecturers of small classes such as Allison's) this was converted into £100 "inclusive of fees"[43].

Law teaching started again in October 1899, and continued (almost) unbroken to the present day. But what did Allison teach? It had long been accepted that the whole of Scots Law could hardly be covered in a single series of lectures. Thus, however ambitious the lecturer, he could not cover all the vague law agents' professional requirement of "The Law of Scotland, civil and criminal".

We cannot tell precisely what he covered for, no doubt because the rapidity of events, there was no formal approval of any syllabus, nor any published version of it, for the first year of lectures[44]. But we do know the doubtless identical syllabus for the following year, when (as in later years) it appeared in the College Calendar (and is reproduced in Appendix 1A to this Chapter). There were 100 lectures, held daily through the "Winter Session", ie October-April (though it is not known where[45]), covering "Domestic and Social Relations", "Obligations and Contracts", "Rights – heritable and moveable" and "Succession", though noticeably, not "Criminal Law".

The College Principal, in his retrospective Report in the College Calendar for 1900-01, recorded that:

> [a] large measure of success attended the qualifying classes of Scots Law, instituted last Session and conducted by Mr James Allison, LLB. Altogether twenty-one students attended, and the work done was of the highest standard. The class will continue next winter[46].

However, there is evidence some years later, that some of the students did not much enjoy the experience[47]. Minutes make no mention of any expenses, class grant or Library expenditure, so it is not clear that any law reports or legal texts were acquired for them. Possibly the FPSD Library was relied on again.

Twenty-one students looks like a very small number though, just as staff numbers were surprisingly small to modern eyes in all the law schools (as noted above), so were student numbers in some. While the giant Edinburgh had 365 law students in that year (implying an entry approaching 200, since the great majority would take Scots Law in one year and Conveyancing in the next, but seek no degree), and Glasgow had 204 (implying an entry in the order of 100), Aberdeen (centuries longer established than UCD) only had 38 (suggesting an entry of perhaps 20)[48]. Thus, no doubt, the self-congratulatory tone.

But 21 must have been a disappointing number for Thornton, who had approved, if not actually generated, the prediction of 75. Worse still, numbers declined thereafter. Possibly because of this, nowhere near matching the teaching (and research) of the scientific departments, the Principal did not discuss Law again in his annual Report until 1903-34, when he recorded only nine students, including accountancy apprentices[49]. The references to accountancy students are important, for they seem to have kept the classes going and, in 1910, were the only Scots Law students[50].

Various reasons for this decline were suggested in subsequent years, including "the inconvenience of a train journey and the want of necessary time" preventing the hoped-for students from Perth, Forfar and Arbroath (and St Andrews), in respect of whom it seems Thornton had been excessively optimistic[51].

Principal Mackay's 1899 announcement had referred to a "Professorship of Scots Law and Conveyancing" but initially, no Conveyancing lectures accompanied the Scots Law ones. No doubt the reason was financial, though nothing is minuted.

But at the end of the first Scots Law session, a deputation of students approached Principal Mackay requesting such lectures, and College Council remitted the matter to a Committee[52]. Its report appears to have been unminuted by College Council, but in his 1900 annual Report, after recording the "large measure of success attended the qualifying classes of Scots Law" noted above, the Principal went on, rather wordily, to say that "[i]t is a matter of regret that the Council is not in a position to undertake in the coming session the responsibility of maintaining a ... class in Conveyancing, very earnestly sought for by a number of students[53]".

Nevertheless, a new, plausible, argument for Conveyancing classes emerged, whether generated by the students[54], the Principal, or others. This was that investment in Conveyancing would produce more students for Scots Law, by removing any need for St Andrews students to transfer to Edinburgh or Glasgow for such classes (as they might readily do if in any case, to gain experience, their apprenticeships were spread over more than one firm). Although Thomas Thornton did not live to enjoy the moment, this argument was deployed in the Principal's Report in 1904 which concluded, once more with barely-justified optimism, that:

> [p]ast experience leads one to believe that there is a regular, though not large, supply of students for the [Scots Law] class, but it is thought that if additional [Conveyancing] classes were provided, the supply would be greater. One solitary Law Class occupies a difficult position[55].

Six months later, College Council agreed to Conveyancing lectures "to supplement the Course at present given in Scots Law"[56]. Conceivably because Thomas Thornton was not around to arrange matters, proper procedure was observed for the appointment of a lecturer, with the proposal going through Senate, various Committees and Court[57]. In the result, in March 1905, Principal Mackay reported that Mr John M Hendry[58], Solicitor, Dundee, a local practitioner (who, it is not surprising to learn, had been apprenticed to Thomas Thornton) had been appointed for a year, at the same salary as James Allison, that is, £25 a year plus fees[59]. His duties (given *in extenso* in Court Minutes) would start on 1 October 1905, and he could be "re-elected" [*sic*] as often as Court saw fit[60].

No syllabus appeared in the College Calendar until 1908-09 (repeating the Scots Law experience), but was no doubt the same in previous years (and is reproduced in Appendix 1B to this Chapter). The class met at 8.55 Monday to Friday[61] (though again, it is not known where in the College).

However, the course does not appear in every Calendar over the next few years[62], and is referred to only twice in the Principal's Reports[63], where it was noted on one occasion to have only five students (though their attendance was "exceedingly regular" and their achievements "creditable and in some cases excellent"). Such small numbers, incidentally, make it surprising that the course was regarded as financially viable.

In fact, it appears that Hendry only gave the course some five times over the decade of his appointment. This is, in itself, unremarkable given the student numbers, but it does appear that he was off on a frolic of his own, because this intermittent nature only became public in December 1912, when Court minuted that three students wanting to take Conveyancing said that they had been told by him that he was not giving the course that year, and was anyway thinking of resigning[64]. The University Secretary was asked to obtain an explanation.

The explanation given was that, when only two or three students wanted to take the course (clearly a not uncommon occurrence), he held it over till the following year (but he was nevertheless willing in the current year to lecture in his office at 4.30)[65]. Court took this remarkably calmly, especially since it concerned a lecturer on an annual contract. Possibly it did so because it needed him more than he needed the job, possibly because the practice must in fact have been widely known (whether or not he took the salary in the off-years[66]). Such knowledge might, incidentally, explain the intermittent appearance of the course in the Calendars. But perhaps more to the point, Hendry was probably ill, as noted below.

In any event, Court simply indicated that it was acceptable for him to restart the lectures in his office as he suggested, and replied to "an inquiry" he made (with some brass neck) about his salary, by telling him that when the Additional Treasury Grant was received, his salary would rise to £100 (despite the penny numbers of students). Perhaps as insurance, perhaps to retrieve goodwill, it also arranged for a Circular to be sent to local firms advertising the restarted lectures, and asking for names of applicants to be sent to the College Principal.

Nevertheless, Hendry did resign a year later (and, indeed, died in 1916, aged about 48[67]), so there may have been no Conveyancing students at all in 1913-14. In that year, it was decided that the lectures be "held in abeyance for a year or two"[68]. They were described, in marked contrast to the Principal's optimism when they started, as being an "experiment", with "meagre" attendance [69], and the argument that they supported Scots Law tacitly forgotten. In any case, the whole question was overtaken by the outbreak of War, which reduced numbers of students even further, so that in 1917, there were no law students at all[70].

(The lack of a Forms of Process class is the dog that didn't bark. This subject had been part of the law agents' "triad" since 1865, but since no other university had yet offered classes in it[71], perhaps Principal Mackay's silence on the subject is less surprising).

Four other events between 1899 and 1918 are worth recording, of which the last was of most importance. The first involved a Mr Robertson. In December 1904, the College Council agreed to the Principal's proposal "to accommodate Mr Robertson, barrister, London, with a room in College for the delivery of a short course of lectures on Constitutional Law & History[72]." What prompted this is unclear. Perhaps it was posthumous fulfilment of a promise made to Thomas Thornton, who had died the previous year, and with whom "Mr Robertson" had been good friends for decades (and of whom he wrote an appreciation in a memorial volume)[73].

For the intriguing thing is "Mr Robertson's" identity[74]. He must have been Edmund Robertson (1845-1911) a local lad made good, with several degrees[75], a considerable legal practice[76], academic appointments[77], and articles published[78], who was at that time Liberal MP for Dundee (1885-1908, when he was kicked upstairs to the House of Lords, as Baron Lochee of Gowrie, to make the seat available for Winston Churchill). He had also been one of the assessors for the appointment of the first Principal of UCD[79].

In 1904, he was between government jobs, having been Civil Lord of the Admiralty (1892-93), and shortly to be Parliamentary Secretary to the Admiralty (1905-08). Lectures by him would be a *coup*. But there seems no record of them taking place.

The second event involved a Dr Burden. In March 1906, College Council received a letter "from Dr Burden, LLB, Solicitor, Dundee, suggesting the establishment of a lectureship in Civil Law"[80]. The Principal consulted Messrs Allison and Hendry who, diplomatically but unsurprisingly, and with a touch of irony "were agreed that it would be desirable to have a course of Lectures on Civil Law[81] but did not feel able to testify that the Class would be taken advantage of to the same extent as the Scots Law or Conveyancing."

Dr Burden's identity is unclear, and less intriguing. He was probably Duncan McNab Burden, MA, LLB (Edinburgh), in practice in Whitehall Street at the time[82], though his name does not appear in the FPSD Minutes, and it is not clear whence his doctorate came.

The third event involved an H H Brown. In July 1912, Court received an offer to be Honorary Lecturer, again, in Roman (ie "Civil") Law, in return for travelling expenses, from H H Brown, County Buildings, Cupar[83]. His identity is clear and again intriguing, for he was Henry Hilton Brown[84], who had been Procurator-Fiscal in Fife since 1900 and, most famously, was co-Editor of Renton & Brown *Criminal Procedure according to the Law of Scotland*[85] which (updated) remains the Bible on the subject[86].

He had a well-worked out plan to give 60 lectures over three terms (two a week on Mondays and Fridays at 4.30), but in St Andrews. James Allison's rejoinder, very publicly recorded in the Principal's Report in the College Calendar (in the same report in which he pointed out that no law apprentices from outwith Dundee had ever attended the Scots Law Class), is instructively sour, relating that "[i]t is gratifying that ... lectures are about to be delivered on Civil Law under the auspices of the University of St Andrews, but a class in St Andrews will prove little use to men employed in offices in Dundee"[87].

Nevertheless, Court had accepted the offer and expected a large response, fixing a fee of £1 for those who were not matriculated students, and requiring those wishing to attend to apply to the Secretary. There is no record of attendance.

Cynically, one might suspect that Brown had an eye on an academic career since, as well as producing *Renton & Brown*, he had written on legal education[88], had (like William Smith, who gave the first law lectures in UCD in the 1890s) applied unsuccessfully for the Chair of Law at Aberdeen[89], and may have known that a BL and LLB in St Andrews University were under discussion at the time (as discussed below).

Certainly, his enthusiasm was so great that, although appointed Procurator-Fiscal of Midlothian within months of making his offer[90], in the following year, he offered to restart the class, provided there were six Honours Classics and Philosophy students, though he would conduct it by "reading and examination" (presumably "distance learning"). He offered encouragement by mentioning a three guinea prize from an anonymous "St Andrews man and ... well-wisher of the University" (possibly himself)[91]. There were insufficient takers, but his offer to run the course again in 1914-15 was accepted, and there was even talk of it counting towards a degree[92].

However, the outbreak of War caused its postponement to 1915-16, when it was offered and may or may not have run, and in 1916-17, the offer was conditionally withdrawn[93]. Nothing more is heard of the matter, and H H Brown achieved greater fame for editing *Renton & Brown* than he would have for teaching Civil Law.

The fourth event, or rather, series of events, of the period 1899-1917 were clearly of the most the most significance, and concerned degrees. The LLB degree had been created in 1862 (as discussed in Chapter 1), and hopes of offering a law degree had possibly been implicit in Sheriff Guthrie Smith's call in 1867 for a "permanent law school"; in the discussions in the 1870s and 1880s preceding the founding of UCD (after the BL degree had been created, as also discussed in Chapter 1); in Thomas Thornton's "founding declaration" of 1890 (discussed in Chapter 2); and in the new initiative which produced permanent law teaching in 1899 (discussed above). In 1911, further changes in the BL and LLB provided the occasion for reviving plans.

Changes in law degree requirements had been much talked about in the early years of the 20th century[94], the discussions culminating in a new Ordinance (now made by the University Courts, rather than the executive Commission under the Universities (Scotland) Act 1889)[95], though some doubted how much better it was than its predecessor[96]. (Appendix 2 to this Chapter compares BL and LLB under the 1862, 1874, 1893 and 1911 dispensations).

The LLB changed little under the new Ordinance. The subjects now required were, as before, Civil Law; English or Scots Law; Constitutional Law & History; one out of a list of Conveyancing, Political Economy or Mercantile Law; Jurisprudence; Public International Law, and two out of a list of International Private Law, Political Economy, Administrative Law and Forensic Medicine, to which were now added Evidence & Procedure (finally ensuring classes in "Forms of Process", and thus the possibility of taking all of the "law agents' triad"), and any other History or Law subject, totalling 480 hours lectures over three years.

The BL changed much more. The Arts precondition was reduced, the degree extended to three years, and the required and optional subjects altered. These subjects were listed in extraordinarily complicated fashion.

In brief, however, Civil Law and Scots Law were required, as were either Jurisprudence or Forensic Medicine, and one out of Conveyancing, Constitutional Law & History or Mercantile Law. Also any of those subjects not taken as one of the required subjects could be taken as an option, as could Public International Law, International Private Law, Evidence & Procedure, or any History or Law subject (provided at least one 80-lecture course, or two 40-lectures courses, were taken each of the three years), totalling 360 hours (compared with 280 hours over two years under the 1893 Ordinance). On the face of it, a good deal of choice was introduced, but in practice it was much less, as not all subjects were available in all the universities. There were also some minor changes, including specifying that the BL examinations were of the same standard as the LLB, and that the BL could be awarded with distinction.

How did this affect St Andrews University? The answer must be approached obliquely. In November 1907, the universities collectively sent a Memorial to the Prime Minister and the Chancellor of the Exchequer, setting out a reasoned argument that they were underfunded, particularly in comparison with university institutions in England and Wales[97]. A Departmental Committee was set up to consider the matter and, possibly in response to a request from this Committee for more detail, in March 1908, the St Andrews Senate (as no doubt did the other Senates) asked Departments to state their needs. In relation to Law, these were recorded as being an increase of the Scots Law and Conveyancing lecturers' salaries to £150 (presumably not inclusive of fees) and, more importantly, institution of lectureships in Civil Law, and Constitutional Law & History, specifically to permit "a full Graduating Class"[98]. This is slightly curious since, in the absence of Jurisprudence, it is not clear that these additions would be enough, even for a BL. Nevertheless, this revival of a plan for a law degree, following closely upon the appointment of a Conveyancing lecturer, must have raised possibly flagging hopes.

These needs were translated into "Statements" by each University, sent to the Committee[99]. But in the course of the translation, the St Andrews University law needs were edited. The Constitutional Law &

History lectureship was modified into a (non-urgent) Constitutional History one, seemingly for the St Andrews "campus", and only the Civil Law lectureship was sought for the Dundee "campus", though each of these lecturers was intended to be available for classes on the other. Presumably, this editing lowered somewhat the raised hopes. Nevertheless, the assertion was repeated that, thereby, "students of Law would be enabled to a complete course of studies qualifying for Graduation in Law", and the observation made that "[t]hese Lectureships are regarded as of great importance for the development of Teaching in Dundee". The total St Andrews "Statement" bid for annual expenditure on salaries, etc, was £9,727/3/-[100].

Much was made in the St Andrews "Statement" of the relationship of UCD to the rest of the University, including the insistence that the University Court was "the proper body to make representations on behalf of the Dundee College ... as it alone can take a joint view of the needs of the College and of the University as a whole"[101]. Nevertheless, there was a lengthy separate UCD "Statement" which did not re-iterate the bids for Civil Law, and Constitutional Law & History, lectureships, but did re-iterate the wish to raise the Scots Law and Conveyancing lecturers' salaries to total the £150 in the original wish-list for Senate[102].

The Departmental Committee reported in August 1909, and recommended £6,000 for St Andrews, specifically stipulating that the sums recommended should be distributed by Courts, but that a further £3,000 should be paid to UCD direct, in place of the grant hitherto made from the University Colleges (Great Britain) Grant, and to be distributed by the College Council[103]. It is not clear how much of the recommended sums were in fact paid, but it seems likely that not all was, if only because the law lecturers probably did not get their rise; no other development in law occurred, at least in the short term; and the money intended for the College which the University diverted to other purposes in 1911, two years after the Report (causing the "temporary discord", discussed above), seems to have been from the University Colleges (Great Britain) Grant, rather than anything put in place of it[104].

There was no further law development in the short term. However, in early 1912 (thus, surprisingly, in the middle of the "temporary discord"), James Thomson[105], solicitor and General Council Assessor on Court, took the intiative. Perhaps he was seeking to restore lost momentum, and certainly he acted shortly after the University Court noted the LLB and BL Ordinance changes[106] (discussed above). His initiative was to get a Court ("Sub")-Committee set up "to consider and report as to the appointment of additional Law Lecturers ... with a view to provide a Course to qualify for the Degrees of LLB and BL"[107]. This Committee, seemingly enthused, took its terms of reference seriously, and suggested "a new Law School" to teach both BL and LLB, and all the necessary lectureships for a real "full Graduating Class", that is, classes in Civil Law, Public and Private International Law, Jurisprudence and Constitutional Law & History[108].

The Principal of UCD, a member of the Committee, no doubt recalling both the disappointing take-up of the Scots Law and Conveyancing classes over the whole decade since their introduction, and the reactions to the offer of Civil Law lectures in 1906, moved to delay consideration of the report. His motion was unsuccessful, but only on the casting vote of the Chairman, and he asked for his dissent to be minuted[109]. The matter was remitted to Court's Business and Finance Committee, and to Senate, though no announcement of the intention to appoint Law lecturers was to be made[110].

Senate organised itself into a Committee of the Whole Senate to report[111], and though, strangely, no report is minuted, Syllabuses and Schemes of Courses were approved six months later[112]. It must have appeared that escape velocity had been achieved. (Incidentally, as the 500th Anniversary of the University was approaching, the resurrection of a Law Faculty and the first law degrees for centuries might have formed an important part of the celebrations, but there is no evidence that this argument was ever raised).

Yet by January 1914, nothing more had happened, and the General Council felt it necessary to urge progress towards degrees and, indeed, also diplomas in law for public servants[113]. But Senate, on the motion of the UCD Principal (having a second bite) resolved that "as circumstances are at present not favourable to the prospects of success of such a School as is suggested the whole matter be allowed to lie over for the present"[114].

What stopped the plan cannot have been the "temporary discord", as that was resolved by 1913. Nor can it have been a sudden realisation on the St Andrews "campus" that the degrees would be taught in Dundee, for it was the UCD Principal who moved the resolution. Nor yet can it plausibly have been the expense, as such, for that was clear from the start (and anyway it was not expensive compared to, say, BSc Engineering, which also had few students). And it certainly was not the War, which did not break out until a full six months afterwards, and to general surprise.

Most plausibly, it was belated realisation on the part of the promoters (chiefly James Thomson), who must have deceived themselves mightily on the matter, that there would probably have been simply too few students[115]. But it remains that St Andrews nearly offered a law degree in 1914, 25 years before it actually achieved that aim. (Of course, October 1914 would have been a singularly inauspicious time to start and, as we shall see, in that sense, history repeated itself in 1939).

1918-1938: The Law School – Further Developments

The year 1917 was the lowest point in the history of law teaching in UCD. Two decades after the first lectures specifically designed for professional qualification, but started with expectations of a Chair and Faculty, and a decade after hopes of a degree again rose, then dwindled. There were simply no entrant students.

This was certainly in part the result of the War, but it must have made it difficult to justify any further spending at all on law classes. Thereafter, there was rapid change in law agents' professional requirements, which requires attention[116], and incidentally coincided with the transformation of "law agents" into "solicitors". At the same time, there was curiously little published academic and professional thought on law teaching, which also requires consideration. Yet despite these difficulties, James Allison[117] (later joined by Hugh Carlton) plugged away at Scots Law (and Conveyancing), indeed participated in some other *démarches*, including the BCom proposal and the Railway Lectures. They were rewarded, 70 years after William Guthrie's lecture, and half a century after William Smith's, by the appearance of law degrees.

The change in law agents' professional requirements was constituted by four changes in remarkably quick succession, that is: an Act of Sederunt in 1926; the Solicitors (Scotland) Act 1933; the General Council Regulations of 1936; and the General Council Regulations of 1938. The cumulative effect was considerable, and incidentally converted "law agents" to "solicitors".

In 1926, a new Act of Sederunt governing the admission of law agents[118] (illustrated in Appendix 3 to this Chapter) replaced the 1893 one. So far as law teaching is concerned, it split the law examination into "First" and "Second Examinations in Law". Regulations under it stipulated that the First Law Examination (taken after two years of apprenticeship) should include three papers, covering "The Law of Scotland, civil and criminal, with the exception of the Law of Trusts and Succession", but including "general principles of Income Tax", and with one whole paper on Mercantile Law[119]. The Second (to be taken at the end of the apprenticeship, when petitioning for admission), involved six papers, covering "Conveyancing (including general principles of Death Duties)" (two papers); "Law of Trusts and Succession" (one paper); and "Court of Session and Sheriff Court Practice, including criminal procedure and the Principles of Evidence" (three papers). While clearly consistent with the laconically defined "law agents' triad", this is not only more closely specified, but also probably more extensive, than earlier interpretations.

For unknown reasons, the Act of Sederunt (in the sixth stage of the odd and complicated history of the obligation, described in Chapter 1 and mentioned again in Chapter 2) also re-imposed the requirement to attend university law classes in Scots Law and Conveyancing[120], 40 years after the original version had been struck down as *ultra vires*, and 35 after a clear power to impose it had been given.

All this raised significant challenges for UCD law teaching. On the one hand, an enormously wide coverage was required of whoever was teaching Scots Law. On the other, the renewed requirement for attendance at university classes might now increase the student numbers, and the advantages of offering a degree were increased.

The 1926 Act of Sederunt was not, however, in force for long, as the constitutional arrangements for "law agents" under the Law Agents (Scotland) Act 1873, were replaced by new arrangements for "solicitors" (a name introduced by a side-wind), under the Solicitors' (Scotland) Act 1933. The central part of this new regime was a General Council of Solicitors, forerunner of the Law Society of Scotland, elected by the thirty or so local Faculties (plus the WS and SSC Societies), and set up "for the purpose of regulating the admission and enrolment of solicitors". Thus, control of admission greater than had been allowed to the diverse local Faculties under either the Law Agents (Scotland) Act 1873, or the Procurators' (Scotland) Act 1865, was handed to a largely self-governing and integrated profession. The General Council was enabled:

> "[i]n order to test the suitability and qualifications of applicants for admission ... [to] hold examinations ... in accordance with regulations to be made by virtue of this section ... and [to] have [subject to the veto of the Court of Session] the entire management and control of all such examinations"[121].

Setting out the requirements in "Regulations" by the General Council, in place of Acts of Sederunt by the Court of Session, demonstrated the magnitude of the change. However, the first new Regulations, the General Council Regulations of 1936[122], show only detailed differences from the 1926 ones (as illustrated in Appendix 3 to this Chapter), so necessitated no changes for UCD.

But thereafter, the General Council launched (in consultation with the universities[123]) a comprehensive redraft of these Regulations[124] (as also illustrated in Appendix 3 to this Chapter).

So far as law teaching was concerned, the First and Second Law Examinations were replaced by three Professional Examinations, collectively amounting to more than a law degree. The First had two parts, i.e. Book-keeping (minus Income Tax) and Constitutional Law[125], and the Second had one, comprising both basic Civil Law[126] and "elementary" Jurisprudence[127]. Thus, for the first time, subjects clearly not within the "law agents' triad" were required. The Third also had two parts, which covered the whole of the traditional "triad", even including "Forms of Process"[128]. No total number of papers was specified but, clearly, overall coverage was further expanded and, even more clearly, some of the parts did not fit together very well.

The exemption regime also became more complicated. Exemption from Part 1 of the First Professional Examination was possible through membership of a relevant professional body, or holding an accounting degree, but no exemption was possible from Part 2. Nor was exemption possible from the Second and Third Professional Examinations, as such, but those with a BL or LLB received a like-for-like exemption for individual subjects.

But, in the sixth stage of the odd and complicated history of the obligation (described in Chapter 1 and mentioned again in Chapter 2), the requirement to attend university classes disappeared once more.

This redraft raised different significant challenges to UCD. On the one hand, removal of the attendance requirement reduced any competitive advantage of being able to offer university classes. Further, though a lack of teaching of Court of Session, Sheriff Court and Criminal Procedure and Evidence was traditional, apprentices would now seek teaching of Constitutional Law, Civil Law and Jurisprudence, available only elsewhere. On the other hand, the new exemption regime further increased the desirability of offering a degree.

The redraft obviously presented significant challenges to students, too. In the first year of operation, examination results for the whole of Scotland showed 89/124 passes (say, 72%) in the First Examination, 18/45 (40%) in the Second, and 20/36 (36%) in the Third (including one candidate with a BL, and one with an MA LLB). Four graduates (two BL, two MA LLB) were exempted[129].

Given the extent of these changes, extraordinarily little academic discussion of law teaching was published. One article in 1919 (noted above in relation to the inadequacies of the 1911 Ordinance) seems almost the total haul[130]. Written from a Glasgow LLB student point of view, by an academic who had experienced it, this article is attractively acerbic. It points out that the order in which degree courses were taken was "haphazard"; the session was too short; the teaching was "most obviously open to criticism"; but that the "worst blemish of all" was the degree examinations. In particular, 80 lectures would "not cover even thinly the whole field of Scots Law"; elementary textbooks were lacking[131]; Law Faculties were starved of funds; and "the greatest obstacle in the way of reform [was] indifference" (a conclusion supported by the very lack of literature).

And though outside this period, a second article from the same hand, published in 1943 (by which time the author was Regius Professor at Glasgow) is worth attention[132]. Much of it can be ignored, as critiquing individual subjects as taught in Glasgow, but the broader message reiterated the earlier one, in particular, lack of funding. Solutions offered were to abolish the BL and reduce the Arts prerequisite for the LLB to one year (making it a four-year degree), to improve teaching methods and literature, and (engaging an issue noted above) to split Scots Law into constituent parts and rethink what subjects were really necessary (suggesting promotion of Conflicts of Laws; demotion of Public International Law; teaching of Civil Law only for comparison with Scots Law; and simply excising Forensic Medicine).

By way of contrast with this dearth of academic comment, there was a small efflorescence of discussion by practitioners. It varies in insight and usefulness, and does not found a consistent, theoretically underpinned, critique. But, as end-users, the authors deserve respect. Familiar targets were the academic/practical distinction (including the interesting suggestion that, as men of business, solicitors needed a broader education than did advocates; that advocates' education was in any case neither broad nor practical, and that judges needed more education; that modes of lecture delivery and content required improvement; and other matters)[133].

One article worth remarking, as often quoted because of its author's identity, is at a high level of generality and written shortly after the re-imposition of the requirement to attend university classes, observes (with doubtful accuracy), that "the direction of legal education" fell principally upon the universities, and went on to suggest a "natural division" of legal education into General, Theoretical and Practical, with some critique of how it played out, at least in Edinburgh[134].

Meanwhile, James Allison continued to lecture in Scots Law, and we have a fascinating insight into his lectures from the lecture-notes for 1919-20 of one of his students, Edward R Simpson[135], of 157 Strathmartine Road, which have survived in five small hardback note-books[136]. However, as they precede the substantial changes in 1926-1938 outlined above, there is no clue how the expanded syllabus, specifically including Income Tax and Mercantile Law, were dealt with. Nor is there any clue from University Calendars for the period, for they are either lost, or do not contain syllabuses[137]. Nevertheless, since James Allison was one of the Examiners for the professional examinations, we can assume he kept abreast of the changes.

In 1920, in an echo of earlier events, seemingly out of the blue, in response to pressure from clerks and apprentices, an offer was made for Conveyancing classes, which had been in abeyance for half a dozen years. F B Graham[138], a local solicitor, wrote to the University Secretary in June that year recounting that "a number of Law Apprentices" had asked him to give such lectures, and requesting accreditation as a "Lecturer under the University Court", or at least a room in College[139].

Neither Council nor Court was prepared to appoint a lecturer (unsurprisingly, given that only small number of students might be expected), but allowed him a room, provided (with heavy emphasis) "that the class is not to be recognised as a University class or given under University auspices, or involving the Court or Council in any outlay or expenses"[140].

The lectures took place and two mementoes of them survive. One is a letter to College Council in November 1920 from five students (John R Bond[141], John A Moore[142], N D Simpson, James Russell and Edward R Simpson[143]) survive, asking for the "usual Certificate of Merit"[144] (as they thought Conveyancing likely to be made compulsory for the Final Examination[145]). The other is the actual Conveyancing lecture-notes of the same Edward R Simpson whose Scots Law notes survive[146]. The Calendar for 1920-21 is lost, so we do not know whether the five got the Certificate, but in October 1921, it was agreed to let F B Graham repeat the lectures[147], and they seem to have continued until 1927, when his renewed request was refused.

The circumstances of this refusal were complicated, but important. Some months before, the University Principal had received another letter, suggesting further law classes. Who it was from, and what classes were sought, are not recorded (though it was probably triggered by the requirement of the 1926 Act of Sederunt for attendance at university classes). In any event, the issue was remitted to the Joint Committee of St Andrews and Dundee, which recommended re-establishment of a Conveyancing lectureship[148]. College Council agreed, and suggested consultation with the FPSD which, having itself consulted James Allison, offered assistance[149].

However, College Council then dithered (possibly because of its agreement with F B Graham). In August the FPSD felt obliged to make enquiries, and in September, the University Principal reported to Court on the consultation, and sought to press the Council. But as no step had been taken, it was too late to institute the class that academic year[150].

F B Graham's class, for which he was about to request renewal, was not explicitly referred to, but it may be that his request finally caused the College Council, more than six months after approving the idea of a Conveyancing lectureship, tardily to set up a committee "to consider the possibility of revival [*sic*] of the Conveyancing Class at an early date", and to remit F B Graham's request to it[151]. The Committee reported that the lectureship should be re-established at £100 pa, and advertised but, hypocritically (or to save his feelings), that F B Graham should be told that "arrangements for the re-establishing of the Conveyancing Class in the College were so advanced that it did not seem possible to supply accommodation for another class of a similar type"[152].

The post was finally agreed for the following year[153]. Mr H J Carlton (from the firm of H Carlton, later H & H J Carlton[154]) and Mr L W Husband, both MA LLB (and specifically recorded as St Andrews graduates, no doubt for reassurance) were short-listed, and the former appointed with effect from 1 October 1928[155]. At the same time, presumably consequentially, a Board of Studies in Law was set up[156].

Thus, from 1928, Hugh Carlton gave Conveyancing lectures, and his name appeared in the College Calendar[157], though syllabuses were no longer printed there. No less important, he later became a pivotal figure in the development of law teaching in Dundee, starting the process of creating a BL, an LLB and a Faculty of Law, as discussed in the next Chapter.

James Allison was involved in two other roughly simultaneous *démarches* in this period. The first, which was important, but unsuccessful, concerned Bachelor of Commerce (BCom) degrees. Around 1900, these were seen as a means of "resolving the Scottish university crisis" of the 1890s, and meeting demand for commercial education[158]. St Andrews University had been uninterested, but in the early 20th century suffered falls in student numbers from a peak of 600 (40% in UCD) in 1910-11, to 400 (still 40% in UCD) in 1913-14, before a potentially catastrophic drop (clearly exacerbated by the War, though that also renewed interest in education for commerce and industrial management[159]) to 300 (30% in UCD) by 1916-17[160].

Unsurprisingly then, the General Council, thwarted in its desire for a law degree in 1913, proposed (again through James Thomson, looking forward to a post-war world) a BCom in 1917[161]. This was considered by the UCD Council and the University Court[162]. Presumably, it was intended to run in UCD, and certainly it would require a significant law component. No curricula were ever approved, but Allison later noted that it would contain "Mercantile and Industrial Law", and "International Law" (possibly both private and public)[163], so would require more law staff.

Court cautiously proposed a conference with Glasgow and Aberdeen Universities, only to find something it was surprising it did not already know, that is, that they had already started on their own BComs[164], and little was done until 1919. In that year, however, the University was offered £25,000 to provide courses for just such a degree[165]. The offer was made by the remarkable Dundee industrialist, George Bonar[166], who by then ran Baxter Bros[167] and had been an *ex officio* member of the College Council[168] as President of the Chamber of Commerce[169]. He was "enthusiastic about research and development, and long before it was established practice … appointed a graduate textile research scientist" at Baxter Bros and he also "had a high regard for the importance of education"[170].

Now galvanised, within weeks Court managed to produce a draft Ordinance[171], consult with Senate and UCD Council[172], and sign, seal and seemingly deliver the proposal[173]. But a sticking point emerged[174].

From the start, George Bonar insisted that the University accept the Certificate of the Dundee Chamber of Commerce as fulfilling its entrance requirements, in place of the University Preliminary Examination, because he thought it more practical. But the University, bound by the decision of the Scottish Universities Entrance Board, which saw no reason to make an exception, could not accept that. (At an early meeting, George

Bonar suggested, strangely naively, that the negotiating position with the Board would be "strengthened by a plea that a substantial endowment depended upon a favourable answer": the University representatives "did not share this view"[175]).

Various attempts at accommodation were made, but ultimately, in 1927, this sticking point scuppered the plan. Indeed, by then, George Bonar had concluded that similar schemes elsewhere had been unsuccessful, and put his money (by now £40,000) into facilities "under the administration of Dundee Education Authority"[176], who used it to found the Dundee School of Economics. This opened in 1931 in the purpose-built, and unsurprisingly named, Bonar House, in Bell Street, offering diplomas and teaching for London University external degrees. However, after entering a period of decline, in 1953, the School was finally (as described in Chapter 5) incorporated into Queen's College Dundee (as UCD was by then) and, as the wheel of fortune turned, Bonar House became the home of the Law Faculty in 1969[177].

The loss to UCD of this largesse was great. It would have provided a useful counterweight to the Berry and Harkness windfalls across the Tay (mentioned above) during the "decade of depression". Despite the orthodox conclusion that the University Principal disfavoured UCD, he does seem to have done all he could[178].

The second *démarche*, the Railway Lectures, was a very different proposition, unimportant but successful. In 1923, the London and North Eastern Railway Company approached the University Principal asking for university-accredited evening classes for its employees in the area, on the subjects of "Railway Law, Economics, Railway Administration and Geography"[179]. All financial obligations would be assumed by the Company, and the University Principal, perhaps scenting the start of a Dundee speciality in service teaching, was enthusiastic. College Council and Court approved[180], and Court set up a Committee which reported that James Allison was willing to undertake the Railway Law lectures at £80; that premises would be available; and that the lectures could start immediately[181]. Later Allison was asked to delay the start until January

1924[182], but he then gave 20 lectures to nearly 40 people[183]. There were also further meetings through the spring to set up a Joint Board of Railway Studies (*alias* "Universities Committee"), attended by Allison and then (surprisingly) by the Principal, to produce a Memorandum co-ordinating the teaching over the several subjects and, as it turned out, several universities, the other subjects being allotted to them[184].

The financial arrangements are fascinating, so deserve mention[185]. In brief, the plan was that students should pay 5/- each, and LNER another 5/- per student, for the course of lectures. However, LNER would guarantee a minimum of £110 for the course and, in addition, "for each examination", pay External Examiners four guineas; Internal Examiners two guineas plus 2/- per examination paper and 1/6 for each essay marked; and Invigilators, 3 guineas. Also Examiners would have free travel passes.

In the event, receipts from 31 LNER students at 5/- per student produced £7/15/-, and from six other students at 10/- per student another £3, totalling £10/15/-. Thus the LNER put up £99/5/- to fulfil the guarantee of £110[186].

Out of this sum came Allison's £80, plus another £5/16/- for setting and marking examinations. UCD was paid £4/8/6 for heating and lighting (but seemingly charged no rent, as such), and most of the rest of the money went on printing "Enrolment Cards, Class Cards and Certificate Forms" and advertising, leaving a credit balance of £5/7/6[187]. In addition, Allison received £5/16/- as examiner; H Willsher, the University Librarian, £1/10/- (rather than 3 guineas) as invigilator; and an unnamed printer, 12/6 for producing the examination papers[188].

Only Allison could say whether it was worth his while. It must have involved considerable extra work, but in effect it increased his University salary by more than 50%[189]. What the University got out of it is more difficult to say[190]. LNER clearly thought it worthwhile, however, as although there were considerable further negotiations through 1924, conducted at its expense at Kings Cross Station[191], the Railway Lectures continued until 1932, when they stopped through lack of demand, only to restart after the Second World War (as noted in Chapter 4). And again, despite the orthodox conclusion that the University Principal disfavoured UCD, once more, he seems to have done what he could.

1899-1938: People

Over these 40 years, only four people were involved in law teaching, only three actually on the staff, and only two at any given time. Unsurprisingly, all were men. What little is known about one of them, F B Graham, was discussed above[192]. About the other three, James Allison, John Hendry and Hugh Carlton, more is known, and they turn out to be individuals with substantially differing characteristics, but a common propensity to undertake a wide range of activities outside their strictly professional life.

James Allison, MA LLB CBE (1865-1951)[193], was son of a sailmaker and shipowner, graduated MA at St Andrews in 1884, and LLB (with distinction) at Edinburgh in 1888, qualifying as law agent and being admitted to the FPSD in the same year. Seemingly, he was a sole practitioner.

Frequent newspaper references indicate that his original office in the High Street burned down and he removed to other premises in the High Street, and later to South Tay Street, and that he took part in the usual range of law agents' activities, including property transactions and litigation in the Sheriff Court, and continued working until a week before his death.

He was also involved in other professional activities, including Searcher in the Burgh Register of Sasines from 1893 until local Registers were amalgamated into the national one in 1929, and Burgh Prosecutor in Newport for the even longer period of 1895 to 1949 (though it was perhaps not the most demanding of offices). From 1926, he was an Honorary Sheriff-Substitute (an accolade commonly given to law agents of standing). From 1929 to 1946, he was a member of the University of St

Andrews General Council Business Committee, and Convenor of its Ordinances, Draft Ordinances and Regulations Committee[194].

Though never Preses or Dean of the FPSD, he was a frequent attender at its meetings and he and Hugh Carlton (perhaps seen as the Faculty's two intellectuals), were in 1936 appointed by it as representatives on the proposed National Committee for Scotland in connection with the International Academy for Comparative Law.

Outside his strictly professional concerns, he was chairman of the Court of Referees for the Dundee District under the Unemployment Insurance Acts, Registration and Election Sub-Agent for Forfarshire, not to mention Clerk and Treasurer of the Forgan School Board, Secretary and Treasurer of the Gerard Cottage Hospital, Monifieth, as well as founding member of the Newport Boating Club, and an elder of St Fillan's Church, Newport. Most noteworthily, during the First World War he was Chairman of the Local Munitions Tribunal, clearly involving considerable work, as he was awarded a CBE for it in 1920.

In 1897, he married "a daughter of Dr Young of Broughty Ferry", but neither her name, nor any children, are recorded. He "delight[ed] in long tramps" and was genial with "broad views". But most importantly from the present point of view, he was appointed lecturer in Scots Law in 1899, when professional law teaching started, and held the post continuously for 46 years until 1945 (as discussed in Chapter 4), a record unlikely ever to be beaten, as well as being an examiner under the Law Agents (Scotland) Act 1873 and Solicitors (Scotland) Act 1933.

John M Hendry (1868-1916)[195], son of a law agent, was a Dundonian, educated at Craighall (presumably a private school) and Edinburgh University, but there is no evidence that he took a degree.

He was apprenticed to Thomas Thornton (no doubt of relevance to his UCD career) and then to Edinburgh and Leith firms, but worked thereafter in his father's firm, Andrew Hendry & Sons, at 39 Murraygate, (seemingly with his brother, Andrew Hendry, one of the lecturers of 1869-

70, discussed in Chapter 2) becoming partner in 1893 and head of the firm (later Hendry & Fenton) three years later, on his father's death.

Among non-professional activities, though he "took no active part in public life or party politics", he was Clerk and Factor to the Morgan Trust, Session Clerk of St Mary's Parish Church, Clerk to the Heritors of Mains and Strathmartine, and a Director of the Dundee Royal Infirmary. Though of a retiring disposition, he was genial, "fond of all sports", collected etchings and had a taste for poetry.

He appears never to have married, and to have been ill in his later years, dying at the age of about 48 after two appendicitis operations (shortly after his brother James, who had been awarded the Military Cross, was killed)[196]. But from the present point of view, Hendry's chief importance is that he was appointed the first lecturer in Conveyancing, from 1905 to 1914.

Hugh J Carlton MA LLB (1899-1979)[197], another son of a law agent, attended the Harris Academy and the High School of Dundee and obtained an MA (St Andrews) and LLB (Edinburgh). Joining the FPSD in 1923, he became a partner in his father's[198] firm (which then became H & H J Carlton) in the following year and was latterly senior partner in Carlton & Reid, at 94 Nethergate. He was appointed to the FPSD Council in 1932 (and, like Allison, as representative to the proposed National Committee in connection with the International Academy of Comparative Law in 1936), was on its Apprenticeships Committee, Dean in 1955 and 1967, and Honorary Member in 1979, when there was minuted "the great fun which he clearly got out of his professional life". In 1956, he was made an Honorary Sheriff-Substitute

In addition, he was an "Examiner in Law" for solicitors' examinations and took part in a variety of other activities including, for over 50 years, Secretaryships of the Master Printers' Association, the Dundee and District Licensed Grocers' Association, and the Wholesale Fruit Merchants' Association, and he was Deacon of the Bonnetmakers' Incorporation, and an elder of St Mark's Church and Session Clerk.

But most importantly from the present point of view, Hugh Carlton was appointed Lecturer in Conveyancing in 1928, and held the post for 25 years, until 1955 (as discussed in Chapter 5), during which time (to anticipate events discussed in Chapter 4) he was "responsible for the creation of the Faculty of Law at Dundee University". This, if anything, understates his contribution, since he was also responsible for the prior stages of introducing the BL, then LLB, degrees. He was, however, not appointed to the Chair of Conveyancing when it was created.

It is difficult to know how these three law agents experienced their role as part-time law lecturers in this period, while running solicitors' businesses and undertaking numerous other activities. They left no published recollections. However, we can infer that most of the working day was spent in the office but, typically for some twenty weeks between autumn and spring, at 9-10am or 4-5pm (to avoid eating into the firm's, and the students' firms', time), classes were given up the road in the College. There must also have been considerable preparation time required, not least coping with regulation changes, as well as changes in the law.

Given the teaching orthodoxy of the time, classes were presumably lectures (for which, see Edward R Simpson's notes) without benefit of tutorials (difficult to arrange with part-time lecturers), though possibly with occasional "quizzes", and regular examinations. Nevertheless, for the first half of the period, the small size of classes must have made a more interactive seminar style difficult to avoid. Much depends upon the lecturer's personality, and we can make guesses about those from the obituaries and other sources quoted above.

The number, gender and identities of staff, and some of their characteristics, are readily discoverable from university records, obituaries, etc. Equivalent information about students is much more difficult to find, because there were many more of them, and sources are much less unhelpful, and give unclear, varying and, indeed discrepant, methods of recording in Court and Senate Minutes and elsewhere. The Annex on Sources of Information on Students explains where the following information on law students' numbers and gender came from, and the difficulties those sources present, which render all numbers subject to possible error, and all conclusions tentative.

Subject to this *caveat*, it seems that, after commencing in 1899-1900 at 21, numbers of entrants varied, no doubt disappointingly, between 5 and 23 until 1914-15 (the upper figures possibly representing the years that the Conveyancing class was running). And in that year, there was a near-catastrophic decline (possibly partly because of withdrawal of Conveyancing, though clearly largely because of the War) reaching 0 in 1917. However, after the War, encouragingly, numbers rapidly increased to a higher average than before the War, varying between 17 and 34 in the 1920s, and between 25 and 45 in the 1930s. The total number of law entrants over these 40 years was thus the not unsatisfactory figure of about 750 (an average of, say, 19 a year, though perhaps more meaningful averages were, say, 11 a year before the War but, say, 29 a year after it).

Nevertheless, it is noticeable what a small proportion of them took Conveyancing in most of the years for which we have figures disaggregating it from Scots Law (probably paralleling the experience of the original Conveyancing lectures two decades earlier, again raising the question of financial viability). This suggests that, not only were accountancy students the total complement in one year (as noted above), but that a high proportion of them was typical, further suggesting the uncomfortable conclusion that accountancy students kept law teaching alive. On the other hand, it is at least possible that, insofar as law apprentices might still be undertaking part of their apprenticeships in Edinburgh or Glasgow (or elsewhere) to increase their experience, they might also have taken Conveyancing there, as the argument advanced in 1905 for starting Conveyancing classes in Dundee (noted above) depended upon precisely that assertion.

Given Mary Ann Baxter's insistence on "promoting the education of persons of both sexes"[199], it is worth asking how many law entrants were women. It appears that in only one of the 40 years from 1899 to 1938 were there as many as two women entrants, and in 31 of them, there were none at all. Indeed, of a total of approximately 750 law entrants over the entire period, there were only about ten women out (and probably only three in the first three decades), a barely perceptible percentage. (Hardly any of them took Conveyancing, suggesting that, like the larger cohort, many were accountancy students).

We can also note the identities of some sub-groups among the law entrants, that is, the women, the high achievers, those of later significance to the law school and otherwise, and also the distribution of addresses (which might give some idea of origins and post-qualifying destinations), but little else.

The first recorded woman law student in UCD, and possibly only the third in Scotland, was the clearly remarkable Mary Ferguson, entering as early as 1912. She was followed after a considerable gap by Phyllis Melville (1926), Isobel Bisset[200] (1929), Theora Robertson BSc (*alias* "Mrs Iain M McLean") (1930), Catherine Scrimgeour MA (1930), Catherine Meldrum (1931), Mary Cooper (1933), Betty Cochran (1934), Mary Fyffe (1936), and Mabel Crawford (1939)[201]. (There was also a Jean Kinmond, but her date of entry is unrecorded, and is probably later than this period).

High achievers, defined as those who obtained First or Second Class Certificates or other marks of merit, cannot be recorded for all years, but in the very first Scots Law class in 1899-1900 were as follows[202]:

First Class.

1. Thomas Scanlan (*1st Prize*)
2. George Nicolson (*2nd Prize*)
3. David E Mitchell]
   D W Patrick   ] Equal
5. James Wright

Second Class.

6. John C Mackay
7. J N Stewart
8. R Scott Chalmers[203]

(Other members of that very first class[204], high achievers simply by virtue of entering it, may have included Patrick Aitken, Marshall Anderson, Robert M Bates, David Blackadder, John H Boland, William A Leighton, John R Merry, James Morrison, George R Pirie, John B

Robertson, Robert C Smith, Douglas Taylor, George G Valentine, and James D Wighton[205]).

High achievers from the very first Conveyancing Class in 1905-06 were as follows[206]:

First Class.

1. D S Lamb (*Medal*)
2. A M Stewart, MA
3. W M M'Gill[208]
4. J M Fergusson[209]

Second Class.

5. H V Cuthbert
6. J M'Guckin[207]

Names of later significance to the law school include Christian Johnson Bisset, later Lecturer in Evidence & Procedure (and later still Mrs Tudhope, and much discussed in the next Chapter), who was awarded a First Class Certificate in Scots Law in 1927[210], and Harold How (whose widow endowed an extremely handsome sum of money, allowing, from 1990-91, the Harold How Prize of £2,500 each to the two best first year students) was awarded a Merit Certificate in Scots Law in 1929[211].

In addition, the names of several law students of the early years are recorded on the UCD War Memorial[212], i.e. Robert C Cunningham[213], Harvey S Steven[214], Sidney H Steven[215], Bernard S Sturrock[216], Frederick J Watson[217], Stanley L Watson[218] and Alexander L Watt[219]. Joseph McLaren[220] and W Phillip Rettie[221] are also known to have been killed, though not so recorded.

Distribution of addresses is discoverable to a limited extent. However, only 45 addresses of students upon leaving UCD appear to be recorded, representing some 6% of students in the period, too few from which to extrapolate. For what it is worth, the most exotic address is Dumfries. Addresses collected half a century later might indicate post-qualifying destinations. However, only 72 are recorded, representing some 10% of students in the period, again too few to draw many conclusions. But again, for what it is worth, fifteen are in Dundee; nine in Broughty Ferry and Barnhill; and most of the rest are Angus, Fife and Perthshire.

One or two are in Edinburgh, Glasgow or London; one is in Ceylon (address on graduation in Cupar); one is in Canada (no address on graduation); and one is "c/o Polish Forces" (no address on graduation, and an exoticism returned to in Chapter 4). Incidentally, over half those giving graduation addresses gave the same "Present address", suggesting they had not moved away. There is almost no information on subsequent careers, as such.

Little beyond this can be inferred. Clearly a number of the students were mature, or changing career direction, as they included 21 BLs (who had presumably graduated without Conveyancing, so returned to take it); eighteen MAs (including two MA LLBs who had also presumably also graduated without Conveyancing); one "MC" (possibly a mistyping for MA); two BScs; two MBChBs (a surprising career change, unless a medico-legal career was planned); and one CA.

Turning to the question of the student experience, we find that it is also more difficult to catch than the staff experience. The most obvious aspect is that, while like Arts and Science students, most lived at home and commuted, unlike them (though like the staff), law students were part-time, and worked in an office most of the time, as had their predecessors in the earlier law classes. The lectures may have been in the traditional form, as their predecessors had also experienced, though, as noted in relation to the staff experience, the small class size must have meant a seminar form might have been difficult to avoid. Just as the pressures of professional life must have made tutorials, as such, difficult to arrange for part-time lecturers, so too must the pressures of apprenticeships upon students, rendering this form of teaching impossible, even had it been desired.

Thus, law students' opportunities to participate in normal student activities, such as participation in the Student Representative Council or Student Union, sports clubs, or other societies, "Charities" or "Gaudie Night" and "Raisin Monday", and indeed in any of the relative freedoms of student life (even for those living at home) must therefore have been severely restricted.

One particular question of interest is how far law students used the UCD library. While there are many discussions of the Library in Minutes, and frequent references to specific acquisitions (often lengthy lists of scientific tomes), there does not seem to be a single reference in the entire period to any law books. Since any library with pretensions to being a law library would require at least, say, *Session Cases* and the *Scots Law Times*[???], both major subscriptions, it must be inferred that they were not stocked. Presumably, law students, as apprentices, employed the library stocks of their firms (which may, of course, have been haphazard collections), or (if permitted) the FPSD Library in the Sheriff Court.

APPENDIX 1

A – UCD Scots Law Syllabus 1900-01[223]

"A Course of 100 Lectures or thereby ... embrac[ing] the following branches of the Law: -

I. The Domestic and Social Relations, including the Law relating to Husband and Wife; Parent and Child; Guardian and Ward; Judicial Factors; Master and Servant

II. Obligations and Contracts – their Constitution and Extinction. In this connection the Law of Sale, Partnership, Companies, Agency, Cautioners, Insurance, Arbitration, Bankruptcy, Trust Deeds for Creditors, Bills and Factories and Commissions will be dealt with.

III. Rights – Heritable and Moveable. Under this head the Law relating to Superior and Vassal; Landlord and Tenant; Fee and Liferent; Patents, Copyright, and Trademarks; and Redeemable Rights will be considered.

IV. Succession – Heritable and Moveable; Testate and Intestate. This will include the Law of Testamentary Trusts".

B – UCD Conveyancing Syllabus 1905-06[224]

I. *General Requirements of all Deeds, including –*

  (1) Those as to external form, integrity of text, solemnities of execution and authentication, with remarks on the Testing clause.

  (2) Deeds privileged as to solemnities.

  (3) The Law of Stamp Duty on Deeds.

  (4) The subject of voluntary consent and assent in entering into of Deeds, and the result of Deeds induced through error, fraud, force or fear.

(5) The effect of homologation and *rei interventus*.

(6) Capacity of persons to contract, including married women, minors, insane persons, and persons under interdiction.

(7) Lawfulness of subject-matter.

(8) Rules relating to delivery and acceptance.

(9) General structure of Deeds, with remarks on the narrative Clause, Clause of Warrandice, and Registration Clause.

II. *Deeds relating to the Constitution, Transmission and Extinction of Moveable or Personal Rights, including –*

(1) Indentures.

(2) Powers of Attorney.

(3) Deeds relating to Arbitration.

(4) Partnership Contracts.

(5) Joint Stock companies.

(6) Personal bonds (including those granted by Cautioners), Inter Vivos Transmissions, and discharges thereof.

(7) Writs relating to Corporeal Moveables.

III. *Deeds relating to the Constitution, Transmission and Extinction of Heritable Rights, including –*

(1) Feudal System.

(2) Deeds constituting a Feudal Estate.

(3) Conveyances dealing with or relating to that Estate.

(4) The Examination of Title, and Searches for Incumbrances.

(5) Heritable Securities.

(6) Leases.

IV. *Family settlements and deeds relative thereto or of a similar nature, including –*

(1) Completion of Title by the Heir or successor to Heritable Estate.

(2) Contracts of Marriage.

(3) Wills and other Trust Deeds.

(4) Completion of title to the estate of a deceased person.

(5) Destinations.

(6) Entails.

APPENDIX 2

SIMPLIFIED COMPARISON OF LLB AND BL UNDER COMMISSIONERS' ORDINANCE No 75 (GENERAL NO 8) OF 1862, (COMMISSIONERS') NOTE OF ALTERATION OF 1874, COMMISSIONERS' ORDINANCES No 39 (GENERAL No 11) AND No 40 (GENERAL No 12) OF 1893 AND UNDER COURT ORDINANCE No XXXVII (GENERAL No 11) OF 1911

LLB	COMMISSIONERS' ORDINANCE No 75 (GENERAL NO 8) OF 1862	COMMISSIONERS' ORDINANCE No 39 (GENERAL No 11) OF 1893	COURT ORDINANCE No XXXVII (GENERAL No 11) OF 1911
	Prerequisite MA	Prerequisite MA	Prerequisite unchanged
	Subjects required (i) Civil Law (ii) The Law of Scotland (iii) Conveyancing (all 80 hours)	Subjects required (i) Civil law (ii) The Law of Scotland or the Law of England (iii) Constitutional Law & History	Subjects required unchanged, save that Evidence & Procedure and "such other subject included in the Department of

(iv) Public Law
(v) Constitutional Law
  & History
(vi) Medical
  Jurisprudence
 	
(all 40 hours)
	(iv) one out of:
	  Conveyancing,
	  Political Economy
	  Mercantile Law
	
	(all 80 hours)
	
	(v) Jurisprudence
	(vi) Public International
	  Law
	
	(all 40 hours)
	
	(vii) and (viii) two out of:
	  International Private
	  Law
	  Political Economy
	  Administrative Law
	  Forensic Medicine
	
	(all 40 hours)
		History and Law
		or in the Faculty of
		Law as the
		Senatus, with the
		approval of Court,
		may from time to
		time determine"
		added to (vii) and
		(viii).

Total lectures 360 hours over 3 years part-time	**Total lectures** 480 hours over 3 years part-time	**Total lectures** unchanged

BL	(COMMISSIONERS') NOTE OF ALTERATION OF 1874	COMMISSIONERS' ORDINANCE No 40 (GENERAL No 12) OF 1893	COURT ORDINANCE No XXXVII (GENERAL No 11) OF 1911
	Prerequisite MA, or: **in Edinburgh**, one Arts year, including: (i) Latin (ii) Greek, French or German (iii) and (iv) two out of: Logic Moral Philosophy Mathematics **in Glasgow**, two Arts years, including: (i) Latin (ii) Logic or Mathematics (iii) and (iv) any two out of: Greek, French or German Moral Philosophy Natural Philosophy English Literature	**Prerequisite** One Arts year, including: (i) Logic and Psychology, or Moral Philosophy (ii) Latin (iii) one additional Arts subject (not also taught in the Law Faculty)	**Prerequisite** Pass at Preliminary Examination in Arts or equivalent, including Latin on the higher standard

Subjects required	Subjects required	Subjects required

(i) Civil Law
(ii) Law of Scotland
(iii) Conveyancing
 	
(all 80 hours)
 	
(iv) one out of the three other LLB subjects (see above)
 	
(40 hours)
	(i) Civil Law (or "half course, plus one "extra subject")
	(ii) Scots Law
	(iii) Conveyancing
	
	(all above 80 hours)
	
	(iv) Forensic Medicine (or "extra subject")
	
	(above 40 hours)
	
	"Extra subjects"
	  (a) Jurisprudence
	  (b) Public International Law
	  (c) Constitutional Law & History
	  (d) International Private Law
	  (e) Mercantile Law
	  (f) Administrative Law
	
	(all above 40 hours)
		(i) Civil Law
		(ii) Scots Law
		(iii) one out of:
		  Conveyancing
		  Constitutional Law & History
		or
		  Mercantile Law
		
		(all 80 hours)
		
		(iv) one out of:
		  Jurisprudence or Forensic Medicine
		
		(both 40 hours)
		
		(v) **either** one (if not already taken) out of
		  Constitutional Law & History
		  Mercantile Law
		or
		  Political Economy
		
		(all 80 hours)
		
		or two (if not already taken) out of:
		  Jurisprudence

		Forensic Medicine Public International Law International Private Law Evidence and Procedure, or any other subject approved by Senate and Court
Total lectures 280 hours over 2 years part-time	**Total lectures** 280 hours over 2 years part-time	**Total Lectures** 360 hours over 3 years part-time

APPENDIX 3

SIMPLIFIED COMPARISON OF LAW AGENTS AND SOLICITORS LAW EXAMINATIONS UNDER 1893 & 1926 ACTS OF SEDERUNT AND 1936 & 1938 REGULATIONS

	Law Examination/First, Second & Third Professional Examinations	Book-keeping and Accounting Examination

1893 Act of Sederunt[225]	The Law of
	  Scotland, Civil
	  and Criminal
	Conveyancing
	Forms of Process,
	  Civil and Criminal
		Additional Book-keeping Examination (double and single entry book-keeping)

1926 Act of Sederunt[226]	**First Law Examination** The Law of Scotland, civil and criminal (except the Law of Trusts and Succession), but including general principles of Income Tax, and one paper on Mercantile Law **Second Law Examination** Conveyancing (including general principles of Death Duties): two papers the Law of Trusts and Succession: one paper Court of Session and Sheriff Court practice, including criminal procedure and the Principles of Evidence: three papers	Book-keeping, Preparation of profit and loss accounts and Balance-sheets and Statements of Affairs Framing Statements of Trusts and Executry Accounts and schemes of Division, Allocation between Capital and Income, and Interest States.

1936 Regulations [227]	**First Law Examination** As 1926, save that Principles of Income Tax transferred to Book-keeping and Accounting Examination **Second Law Examination** As 1926, save that general principles of Death Duties transferred to Law of Trusts and Succession	Essentially the same as 1926, save that Principles of Income Tax transferred from First Law Examination
1938 Regulations [228]	**First Professional Examination** Book-Keeping (minus Income Tax) Constitutional Law **Second Professional Examination** Outlines of Roman Law Elementary Jurisprudence **Third Professional Examination** Law of Scotland, Civil and Criminal (except the Law of Trusts and Succession) Conveyancing Law of Trusts and Succession, including the general principles of Death Duties Court of Session Procedure, Sheriff Court Practice, Criminal Procedure and the Principles of Evidence	Transferred to First Professional Examination

¹ This section summarises chapters 5 and 6 of Donald G Southgate *University Education in Dundee: a centenary history* (1982) (and see Michael Shafe *University Education in Dundee 1881-1981* (1982)). For other views, see Ronald Gordon Cant *The University of St Andrews: a short history* 3rd ed (1992) 147-168 and Norman H Reid *Ever to Excel: an illustrated history of the University of St Andrews* (2011) 160-161 (which records that "the title of [Principal] Irvine's file on the subject [was] "The Dundee problem").

² This description and related descriptions of parts of these 40 years, are Southgate's. On the difficulties of university finance at this time, however, see Report of the [Departmental] Committee on Scottish Universities Cd 5257 (1910), which considers the St Andrews/Dundee issues at paras 7-9. It was precipitated by a Memorial to the Prime Minister and the Chancellor of the Exchequer complaining of underfunding (reproduced in its Appendix I), discussed in note 98 *et seq*, and associated text.

³ The significance of the then newly-formed Carnegie Trust for the Universities of Scotland can hardly be exaggerated. It "was spending more than the state ... [and] ... became practically a ministry for Scottish universities": R D Anderson, *Education and Opportunity in Victorian Scotland* (1983) 288.

⁴ Containing Economic Studies at the time of writing.

⁵ Containing Accountancy and Finance at the time of writing.

⁶ Later generations of students may recall the wonderful Breughelesque murals in the bar which occupied most of the basement of both houses in the 1960s.

⁷ Southgate, *University Education* 171, quoting (without full citation) the Report of the Inquiry appointed in February 1949 to review and report on the organisation of University Education in Dundee and its relationship with St Andrews University (1949) (the "Cooper Inquiry"), discussed in Chapter 4.

⁸ Southgate, *University Education* 166. Reid *Ever to Excel* 162 observes that "Although Irvine sometimes seems to have had an ambivalent attitude to University College, he was certainly prepared to advance its interests as part of the overall institution. Notwithstanding, there remained a strong (and not entirely unjustified) feeling amongst staff in Dundee that the St Andrews establishment remained antagonistic towards developments north of the Tay ...". For a sympathetic view of Irvine's attitude to Dundee (and more than sympathetic view of the man himself), see Mabel V Irvine *The Avenue of Years: a memoir of Sir James Irvine ...*(1970) 116-118 which records that "[t]h shadow that lay across his thirty-two years as head of the University was his inability to make UCD happy, content and successful", that "[t]here was nothing personal in the college's discontent" and that "[h]is ideal for the college was that it should develop its natural advantages – Engineering and the allied sciences, the Law Faculty, and the Medical School – all of which needed a city for their furtherance, and he thought that chairs in St Andrews should not be duplicated in Dundee. This would have drawn the college closer to the old foundation": also 227-228 (*et passim*). However, see the Prologue by a later Principal, J Steven Watson. Nevertheless, and one cannot but feel sympathy for someone whose only son, in the RNVR, died during the Second World War, but in an accident, leaving a wife and baby.

⁹ Discussed in Chapter 1.

¹⁰ Edward Stephen Harkness, a "millionaire philanthropist" who admired Oxbridge, gave money to Harvard and Yale, and was persuaded by Principal Irvine to give some £100,000 or more to St

Andrews as well: Cant *University of St Andrews* 162-3, also Reid *Ever to Excel* 157, and Southgate, *University Education* 166.

[11] AS 18 March 1893, reproduced in contemporary editions of *Parliament House Book,* and summarised in *Green's Encyclopaedia of the Law of Scotland* 1st ed (1896-1904) *sub voc.* "law agent". C.f. the essentially similar (save for the university attendance requirement) AS 20 December 1873 reproduced in J Henderson Begg, *A Treatise on the Law of Scotland relating to Law Agents* ... 2nd ed (1883) 400.

[12] AS 18 March 1893 s 8.

[13] Examination in Heritable Rights; Moveable Rights; Conveyancing; Contracts; Summonses, Actions and Forms of Process; Diligence; and Criminal Law and Procedure: see WS *Regulations Respecting Apprentices and Intrants*, reproduced in contemporary editions of *Parliament House Book.*

[14] Seemingly no Law examination save in "the practice and forms of procedure before the supreme Courts": see SSC regulations, reproduced in contemporary editions of *Parliament House Book.*

[15] The former required attendance at Scots Law, Conveyancing and (although unexamined) Civil Law: the latter at Scots Law and Conveyancing.

[16] Examination in Civil Law, Scots Law and Conveyancing, Public or International Law, Constitutional Law and "Medical Jurisprudence,": see *Faculty of Advocates Regulations as to Intrants* of 21 November 1894, reproduced in contemporary editions of *Parliament House Book.*

[17] In 1956, it was asserted that "[p]rior to the 1914-18 War more than 50 per cent of practising solicitors entered the profession by serving five years' apprenticeship and passing Law Agents Examinations": Anon. [J Spencer Muirhead, as President of the Law Society of Scotland] "Legal Education" [part of the President's Report] (1956) 1 *JLSS* 95-97. However, this seems an underestimate when compared with the data produced in Alistair R Brownlie, "The Universities and Scottish Legal Education" 1955 *JR* 26-61 at 54 & 55 (Tables 1 & 3), discussed further below.

[18] Ordinances No 39 (General No 11) and No 40 (General No 12) of 1893, reproduced in *General Report of the Commissioners under the Universities (Scotland) Act, 1889* ...(Cd 276: 1900) and Alan E Clapperton (ed), *The Universities (Scotland) Act 1889 together with Ordinances of the Commissioners ... and University Court Ordinances* (1915) 139-131 & 131-133. See also Appendix 3 below.

[19] Anderson, *Education and Opportunity* 64.

[20] See Dundee University Archives ("DUA") Recs A/421, University of St Andrews ("UStA") Senatus Academicus Papers 1891-1905, especially (i) *Memorandum on the Civil Service Examinations as affecting the University of St Andrews*, undated (but marked in manuscript "March 1899"), and over the name "J Burnet" [Professor of Greek]; (ii) *Memorandum on "Preparation for the Civil Service: Home, Indian and Eastern Cadetships ..."*, dated July 1900, noting that optional subjects for the entrance examinations included English Law and Roman Law; and (iii) *Reports by the St Andrews Members of each of the Boards of Studies as to the Requirements of their Respective Faculties in St Andrews* of various dates, but seemingly for Senate in 1899. However, University of St Andrews Archives ("UStAA") UY 452/23, University of St Andrews Senatus Academicus Minutes 1899-1903 (New Series Vol V) (unfortunately handwritten and unindexed) appear to reveal no Minute relating to these documents. The matter may have been still live a decade later as in 1910, St Andrews University was seeking a lecturer in Constitutional History, but this was referred to by UCD as

"Constitutional Law and History" in relation to the then-proposed Law degree: see Report of the Committee on Scottish Universities, Appendix II, 20 ("Other Lectureships") and 12 ("Lecturer in Civil Law").

[21] As noted in Chapter 1, the St Andrews University's "campus" comprised United College (in effect co-terminous with the Arts Faculty) and St Mary's College (in effect co-terminous with the Divinity Faculty).

[22] Southgate, *University Education* 112 records that "alone of the twelve beneficiaries, [UCD] had its grant from the [Treasury's] University Colleges (Great Britain) Fund doubled".

[23] Ibid. It is impossible not to sympathise with Bute in his later years, however, given his medical condition: see Rosemary Hannah, *The Grand Designer: Third Marquess of Bute* (2012), chs 13-15 (and indeed, given his upbringing, in his early years: see Hannah *Grand Designer* chs 1-3, and *Marquess of Bute v Stuart* (1861) 2 Giffard 582, *Stuart v Marquis* [sic] *of Bute* (1861) 11 ER 799, *Marquis* [sic] *of Bute v Stuart* (1888) 8 R 191 and *In re Marquess of Bute* (1884) LR 27 Ch D 196; see also the well-known case on directors' duties, *In Re Cardiff Savings Bank (Marquis* [sic] *of Bute's Case)* [1892] 2 Ch 100, on which see also Hannah, *Grand Designer* 254-54).

[24] DUA Recs A/814/1/17, UCD Calendar, Seventeenth Session, 1899-1900, 74. No month is given, but other years' Calendars are dated July.

[25] Was one chair intended to cover both subjects, just as a Glasgow chair covered both Scots Law and Civil Law?

[26] George Washington Baxter (1853-1926), great-nephew of Mary Ann Baxter, a graduate of St Andrews, signatory of the Agreement between UCD and St Andrews University, much involved in the subsequent disputes, and other matters, as member of College Council 1895-1925, and President of UCD 1925-26, receiving an LLD from St Andrews University in February of that year. He fought two elections, unsuccessfully, as a Unionist (including against Winston Churchill in Dundee in 1908), and became Sir G Baxter, Bart, in 1918.

[27] DUA Recs A/100, UCD Council Minutes February 1897-November 1905, Meeting of 12 July 1899.

[28] Ibid, Meeting of 9 August 1899.

[29] FPSD Minutes 1887-1960, Meeting of 2 February 1899. Since he could probably have achieved that office at any time in the preceding 40 years, it seems likely that he did so then in order to facilitate his long-term dream of permanent law classes.

[30] Presumably not the Mr Ogilvie who attended the 1866 meeting which started the original law lectures, discussed in Chapter 2.

[31] FPSD Minutes 1887-1960, Meeting of 3 August 1899. It comprised the Preses, Vice-Preses, Robert Smith, George Ogilvy, J Thomson, W Nixon, F E Scott and W [not G W] Baxter.

[32] *Dundee Directory 1899-1900* lists 76 members of the FPSD, but law clerks and apprentices are not listed, as such.

[33] FPSD Minutes 1887-1960, General Meeting of 25 August 1899.

[34] DUA Recs A/100, UCD Council Minutes February 1897-November 1905, Meeting of 12 September 1899.

[35] Stephen D Girvin, "Nineteenth century Reforms in Scottish Legal Education" (1993) 14 *JLH* 127-140 at 131.

[36] Discussed at length below. It is not recorded with whom he was apprenticed, but it might have been Thomas Thornton.

[37] DUA Recs A/100, UCD Council Minutes February 1897-November 1905, Meeting of 12 September 1899.

[38] DUA Recs A/416, UStA Court Minutes, 1895-1901, Meetings of 16 September ("Lecturer in Scotch [*sic*] Law – Urgency having been voted, Principal Mackay reported that a Lecturer in Scotch Law had recently been appointed and asked Court to recognise the Lecturer for the coming session"), and 25 November 1899 ("Lecturer in Scotch Law – An excerpt from the Minutes of Senatus was submitted, bearing that they had agreed to recognise the Lecturer in Scotch Law"). The contract was annual: no nonsense about academic freedom.

[39] UStAA UY 452/23, UStA Senatus Academicus Minutes 1899-1903 (New Series Vol V), Meeting of 14 October 1899.

[40] DUA Recs A/100, UCD Council Minutes February 1897-November 1905, Meeting of 12 August 1903.

[41] DUA Recs A/415, UStA Court Minutes, 1891-95, Meeting of 9 July 1892 (French lecturer).

[42] DUA Recs A/337/3/5, letter dated 22 July 1910, and worth quoting, i.e. "... the necessity of always keeping the lecture hour free is confining ... involves loss of fees through refusing other work ... and .... absorbs not only a considerable amount of time, but also prevents me from striking out in other directions ... When I raised this question ... last year, the reply I got was, that there was no money available, but there always seems to be money for purposes which the University Court approve ...". Given that he was also Searcher of the Burgh Register of Sasines and Burgh Prosecutor for Newport at the time, it is unclear whether he was motivated by righteous anger, or limited profits from the firm. It is also possibly unfair, as there had just been attempts to increase his salary, connected to the attempt to start law degrees: see notes 99-104, and associated text.

[43] DUA Recs A/101, UCD Minutes, December 1905-July 1915, Meetings of 8 March, 14 April, 10 & 13 May 1911.

[44] Indeed, it does not seem to have been approved until 1906, when Professor Lawson successfully moved that, there being no Faculty of Law, the Faculty of Arts be empowered to receive law syllabuses and transmit them to Senatus: DUA Recs A/422, UStA Senatus Academicus Minutes 1905-08, Meeting of 10 February 1906. They were dealt with within the Faculty of Arts by the "Board of History and Law".

[45] UCD premises were at this time still confined to the four houses in the Nethergate, between Park Place and Small's Wynd (where the Tower Block now sits), acquired at its foundation, and connected by a corridor at the back, together with the Carnelley Building and "Old" Technical Institute: see plan in Southgate, *University Education* xiv. Within these premises most space was dedicated to the Science and Medical Departments, so presumably other classes were fitted in around them.

[46] DUA Recs A/814/1/18, UCD Calendar, Eighteenth Session, 1900-01, 85.

[47] DUA Recs A/680/2, *"The College: the official publication of the Student Representative Council of University College, Dundee"*, New Series vol 1, No 1 (December 1903) 22 "Notes", records "We are nine, and week in, week out, from five to six, the law of Scotland is meted out to us in all its legal dryness. The great drawback to the usefulness of the classes is its [*sic*] late hour, which makes one wish for some refreshment not quite so dry as the study of law; which may be *fortiter in re*, but hardly *suaviter in modo* [i.e., approximately, "*strong on fact*, but hardly *gentle in manner*"] ... ".

[48] Anderson, *Education and Opportunity* Appendix 1(C). It is instructive to calculate raw staff/student ratios from these figures and those given above for staff.

[49] DUA Recs A/814/1/22, UCD Calendar, Twenty-second Session, 1904-5, 95-6 (for the nine self-identified, see note 47 above).

[50] DUA Recs A/814/1/28, UCD Calendar, Twenty-eighth Session, 1910-11, 152.

[51] DUA Recs A/814/1/30, UCD Calendar, Thirtieth Session, 1912-13, 172-3.

[52] DUA Recs A/100, UCD Council Minutes February 1897-November 1905, Meeting of 11 April 1900.

[53] DUA Recs A/814/1/18, UCD Calendar, Eighteenth Session, 1900-01, 85.

[54] DUA Recs A/680/2, *"The College"* New Series, vol II, No 3 (January 1905) 151, carried an anonymous article making the same argument, noting that, with Conveyancing "[w]e would ... be in a position to offer systematic courses in the subjects necessary for the Final Law Examination, so Law Students would no longer require to betake themselves to other centres for assistance in their studies" and looking forward to what "we hope to see firmly established in the near future – a Faculty of Law".

[55] DUA Recs A/814/1/22, UCD Calendar, Twenty-second Session, 1904-5, 95-6.

[56] DUA Recs A/100, UCD Council Minutes February 1897-November 1905, Meeting of 11 January 1905.

[57] DUA Recs A/100, UCD Council Minutes February 1897-November 1905, Meeting of 8 February 1905; Recs A/416, UStA Court Minutes 1904-07, Meetings of Committees of 19 January, 28 January & 17 February 1905, and of Court 25 February 1905.

[58] Discussed below.

[59] DUA Recs A/100, UCD Council Minutes February 1897-November 1905, Meeting of 8 March 1905.

[60] DUA Recs A/418, UStA Court Minutes 1904-07, Meeting of 25 February 1905.

[61] DUA Recs A/814/1/23, UCD Calendar, Twenty-third Session, 1905-06.

[62] I.e., only in DUA Recs A/814/1/24, 26, 28 & 31, UCD Calendars, Twenty-fourth, -sixth, -eighth & Thirty-second Sessions, 1906-07, 08-09, 09-10 & 13-14.

[63] DUA Recs A/814/1/27 & 28, UCD Calendars, Twenty-seventh & -eighth Sessions, 1909-10 & 1910-11, 85 & 152, respectively.

[64] DUA Recs A/19, UStA Court Minutes 1912-13, Meeting of 7 December 1912.

[65] DUA Recs A/19, UStA Court Minutes 1912-13, Business and Finance Committee Meeting of 7 December 1912.

[66] UStAA UY 7 Secy 7 (which is curiously superscribed "mega biblion, mega kakon", that is, roughly, "big book, big evil", a saying attributed to Callimachus of Cyrene) (Secretary's Court and Senate Papers Etc – Session 1911-12) includes a bundle labelled "Dundee Problem 1911-12" containing UCD Accounts for the year ending 31 July 1911, in which, under the heading "XVI Law Lectures", expenditure includes £100/-/- to James Allison, but £0/-/- for John Hendry: the same is true for the Session 1912-13. However, in May 1918, James Allison asked for his salary despite having had no students (no doubt largely because of the War) and he was paid: DUA Recs A/102, UCD Council Minutes August 1915-September 1926, Meeting of 8 May 1918.

[67] Anon, "The Late Mr J M Hendry, solicitor, Dundee" 1916 *SLT (News and Statutes)* 81.

[68] DUA Recs A/115, UCD Education Board Minutes, Meeting of 24 January 1914.

[69] DUA Recs A/20, UStA Court Minutes 1913-14, Meeting of 16 February 1914.

[70] Student numbers are considered more extensively below.

[71] Although in 1887 Edinburgh may have had a lectureship in Procedure, the subject was not on the syllabus for either BL or LLB: Anon, "Bill to Amend Law Agents (Scotland) Act" (1887) XXXI *JoJ* 386-388.

[72] DUA Recs A/100, UCD Council Minutes February 1897-November 1905, Meeting of 14th December 1904.

[73] William Angus Knight, *Early Chapters in the History of the University of St Andrews and Dundee* (1905) Appendix A.

[74] See Southgate *University Education* 46 & 47, and http://en.wikipedia.org/wiki/ Edmund Robertson, 1st Baron Lochee#cite ref-thepeerage.com 1-0 (last accessed 29 July 2018) and http://thepeerage.com/ p23743.htm#i237426 (last accessed 29 July 2018).

[75] MA (St Andrews), BA, MA (Oxford).

[76] Barrister (1871, QC 1895).

[77] Fellow of Corpus Christi College (1872), Reader in Law to the Council of Legal Education, Public Examiner in Jurisprudence at Oxford University (1877-79) and Examiner in English Court History at London University (1877-82).

[78] Articles on law and constitution in *Encyclopaedia Britannica* (9th ed).

[79] Southgate, *University Education* 45.

[80] DUA Recs A/101, UCD Council Minutes December 1905-July 1915, 14 March 1906.

[81] On the nature and significance of "Civil Law", see Chapter 1.

[82] Residing at 2 Windsor Terrace, with a Mrs James Burden, wine and spirit merchant in Union Street (no doubt his mother): see *Dundee Directory 1905-6*.

[83] DUA Recs A/18, UStA Court Minutes 1911-12, Business and Finance Committee Meeting of 10 July 1912. A copy of the letter, dated 10 May 1912, is in UStAA UY 7 Secy 7 (Secretary's Court and Senate Papers, Etc – Session 1911-12).

[84] H H Brown (1856-1927), born in Elgin, attended Elgin Academy and Edinburgh University (obtaining 1st prize in Criminal Law and Mercantile Law), trained in the Edinburgh offices of Phillips, Laing & Co SSC, and Gibbon, Craig, Dalziel and Brodie WS, returning to Elgin in 1880

to join the firm of Alex. Morrison. He wrote a *Principles of Summary Criminal Justice* ("complete, accurate and lucid") and an *Elements of Practical Conveyancing* for law apprentices "in whose education he evinced a particular interest", as well as articles in the *Scots Law Times* (and "Renton & Brown", for which, see following two footnotes). He was devoted to music and entomology. See Anon, "The late Mr Henry Hilton Brown ..." 1927 *SLT* 19.

[85] 1st ed Edinburgh, W Green & Sons (1908).

[86] Currently, 6th ed (looseleaf) eds G H Gordon & C H W Gane.

[87] DUA Recs A/814/1/30, UCD Calendar, Thirtieth Session, 1912-13, 172.

[88] Henry H Brown "Legal Education of Apprentices" (1896-97) 4 *SLT* 106-107.

[89] Anon, "The Chair of Law in Aberdeen University" (1907-08) 15 *SLT* 42.

[90] DUA Recs A/19, UStA Court Minutes 1912-13, Meeting of 16 November 1912.

[91] DUA Recs A/19, UStA Court Minutes 1912-13, Meeting of 10 May 1913.

[92] DUA Recs A/20, UStA Court Minutes, Meeting of Business and Finance Committee of 25 May, and of Court of 21 February and 30 May 1914.

[93] DUA Recs A/21, UStA Court Minutes, Meetings of Business and Finance Committee, 19 October 1914 and 2 July 195, Recs A/24, UStA Court Minutes, Meeting of 17 November 1917.

[94] DUA Recs A/417, UStA Court Minutes 1901-4, Meetings of 7 November & 19 November 1903 and 2 April 1904; Recs A/418, UStA Court Minutes 1904-07, Meetings of 28 October 1904; Recs A/419 UStA Court Minutes 1907-10, Meetings of 15 November 1909, 6 June and 8 October 1910.

[95] (Court) Ordinance XXXVII (General No 11) of 1911 (reproduced in Clapperton, *Universities (Scotland) Act, 1889* 506-509). As noted in Chapter 1, Appendix 2, when the "executive Commission" under the Universities (Scotland) Act 1889 was wound up, its Ordinance-making powers were transferred to University Courts. By a convention (not always honoured), Ordinances were thereafter described as "Court Ordinances" (as opposed to "Commission Ordinances"), and their numbering changed from arabic to roman.

[96] For a highly critical account of the way the Ordinance worked, at least in Glasgow, see Anon [Andrew Dewar Gibb], "The Scots Law School in 1913" 1919 *JR* 267-272 (discussed in more detail below). Gibb (1888-1974) graduated from Glasgow in 1913, became an advocate, and after military service in the First World War became a barrister, then lecturer in English Law in Edinburgh and Scots Law in Cambridge, finally being appointed Regius Professor of Scots Law at Glasgow, also publishing numerous books. He was also a founder member of the SNP and, for a period, its leader: see Stephen P Walker, *The Faculty of Advocates: a Biographical Directory of Members Admitted from 1 January 1800 to 31 December 1986* (1987), and F J Grant, *The Faculty of Advocates in Scotland 1532-1943 ...* (1944).

[97] Report of the Committee on Scottish Universities, with Appendices (Cd 5257: 1910), Appendix I. Strangely, UStA Court Minutes do not appear to record agreement to construct or send it.

[98] DUA Recs A/422, UStA Senatus Academicus Minutes 1905-08, Meeting of 7 March 1908 and Annex ("Summary of Statements of Needs of Social Science Departments, February 1908") bound into Minutes.

[99] Report of the Committee on Scottish Universities, Appendix II.

[100] Ibid, 20, 21, 22.

[101] Ibid, 20-21.

[102] Ibid, 31-33.

[103] Ibid, 11. Also, £1,500 of the £6,000 should be spend on the joint Medical School. Oddly again, there appears to reference in UStA Court or Senatus Academicus Minutes, nor UCD Council Minutes.

[104] Southgate, *University Education* seems to make no mention of the Committee and Report, thus does not record whether any money was paid, but, at 147, refers to the Treasury allotting UCD from "the grant to English provincial university institutions [*scil.* the University Colleges (Great Britain) Grant] … its usual 1 per cent *but sen[ding] it to St Andrews*" [italics in original]. James Alison was paid £100 in 1910-11 (following his letter referred to above: see note 42), but this was inclusive of fees, following imposition of the "Fee Fund"

[105] James Thomson, MA LLB, minuted as "of St Andrews" till 1912, and "of Dundee" thereafter, and giving an address of 1 West Dell Street from 1923, was very active in the General Council for, as well as being elected one of its Assessors on Court from 1910 to 1923, he was elected to its Business Committee in 1908, its Ordinances, Draft Ordinances and Regulations Committee (of which he became Convenor) in 1910 (and subjected some Ordinances to considerable scrutiny), and its Committee upon the Future of the University (which he caused to be set up, and of which he was Convenor) in 1917, demitting office only in 1929 when he "removed to Durham" (possibly in retirement?). Interestingly, James Allison took over from him Convenorship of the Ordinances Committee: UStAA 615, UStA General Council Minutes, Meetings of 31 October 1908, 29 October 1910, 28 October 1911, 27 January 1917, 30 June 1923 and 26 January 1929. James Thomson also proposed Robert Macgregor Mitchell, later Lord Macgregor Mitchell, and Rector, whose importance is noted in the following Chapter, (and who had received an LLD in the previous year) as a General Council Assessor on Court: UStAA UY 615 UStA, General Council Minutes 28 January 1933, 4. Southgate, *University Education* does not mention these events.

[106] DUA Recs A/18, UStA Court Minutes 1911-12, Meeting of 18 November 1911. Undated copies of the Ordinances are in UStAA UY 7 Secy 7 (Secretary's Court and Senate Papers, Etc). The Ordinances [etc] Committee, under James Thomson's Convenorship, had approved the Draft General Ordinance on the BL in 1910, on the same occasion amending its own name by the addition of "and Regulations": UStAA UY 615, UStA General Council Minutes, Meeting of 29 October 1910, 5-6.

[107] DUA Recs A/18, UStA Court Minutes 1911-12, Meeting of 23 March 1912. (A letter anent the Sub-Committee, is in UStAA UYUY 7 Secy 7 (Secretary's Court and Senate Papers, Etc – Session 1911-12). Oddly, given James Thomson's position in the General Council, no discussion of this initiative is recorded in its Minutes.

[108] DUA Recs A/18, UStA Court Minutes 1911-12, Meeting of 20 July 1912. (A copy of the report, dated 21 June 1912, is in UStAA UY 7 Secy 7 (Secretary's Court and Senate Papers, Etc – Session 1911-12). The recommended salaries, from £50 (Jurisprudence) to £200 (Constitutional Law) showed all would be part-timers).

[109] Ibid.

[110] Ibid.

[111] DUA Recs A/424, UStA Senatus Academicus Minutes 1911-13, Meeting of 19 October 1912.

[112] DUA Recs A/424, UStA Senatus Academicus Minutes 1911-13, Meeting of 2 March 1913.

[113] UStAA UY 615, UStA General Council Minutes, Meeting of 31 January 1914, 7: motion by James Thomson "That this Council urges the Senatus to consider favourably the scheme which was passed by the University Court for the completion of the Law School in (UCD), and for the granting of the degrees of LLB and BL; and further, to formulate a scheme whereby a Diploma can be granted, after examination in the appropriate subjects, to persons desirous of entering public life, and of journalists". The penultimate clause recalls the proposals of those setting up law degrees in the nineteenth century noted in Chapter 1.

[114] DUA Recs A/425, UStA Senatus Academicus Minutes 1913-15, Meeting of 14 February 1914 (and see UStAA UY 615, UStA General Council Minutes, Meeting of 27 June 1914, 8)

[115] No figures appear available for this period but, as noted in Chapter 1, in the thirty-five years from 1918, in Edinburgh there was an average of only about 20 BLs and 20 LLBs a year, and in Glasgow of about 27 BLs and 17 LLBs: Brownlie, "The Universities and Scottish Legal Education" 1955 *JR* 26 at 55 (Table 2).

[116] Not least because, unlike earlier requirements, there is little literature on the subject.

[117] Incidentally, as noted above, replacing James Thomson in 1929 as Convenor of the UStA General Council Ordinances, Draft Ordinances and Regulations Committee, and as member of its Business Committee: UStAA UY/615, UStA General Council Minutes, Meeting of 26 January 1929.

[118] AS 18 March 1926, reproduced in contemporary editions of *Parliament House Book*, summarised in *Green's Encyclopaedia* 3rd ed *sub voc.* "law agent", and discussed in Anon, "Act of Sederunt Anent Admissions of Law Agents" 1926 *SLT (News and Statutes) (Statutes – Appendix)* 113.

[119] Mercantile Law became treated separately from Scots Law probably because, like Conveyancing (also treated separately), it could not claim a Civil Law inheritance, though the necessity of splitting Scots Law into several classes chiefly reflected the impossibility of teaching it all in one course.

[120] Section 9.

[121] Section 12.

[122] See "Summary of Regulations relating to Examinations and Admission ..." dated 1 October 1936 in contemporary editions of *Parliament House Book*.

[123] DUA Recs A/42, UStA Court Minutes 1934-5, Meeting of 15 May 1935.

[124] *Regulations for Examination and Admission of Solicitors ... 19th March 1937*', in force 1 January 1938, reproduced in contemporary editions of *Parliament House Book*. (The contemporary Regulations for the Society of Writers to the Signet appear in Anon. *The Society of Writers to HM Signet ....* (1936), Appendix II.

[125] "(a) National Government (including Parliament, The Cabinet, The Crown, Executive Government Departments, and the Judiciary); (b) Local Government; and Freedom of the Press, of Public Meetings, and of Speech".

[126] "Outlines of Roman Law". The significance of "Civil Law" was discussed in Chapter 1, where it was observed that despite its apparent centrality to Scots Law, it had never been required of the majority of Scots lawyers, that is, "law agents". Why it was now demanded begs explanation and, cynically, one wonders if it was intended to enhance the status of the new "solicitors" over that of the otherwise identical former "law agents".

[127] "(a) Nature and Sources of Law, (b) Rights, Persons and Things, (c) Possession and Ownership, (d) Liability for acts and omissions, (e) Obligations and Contracts, and (f) Evidence [sic]".

[128] "Law of Scotland, Civil and Criminal, with the exception of the Law of Trusts and Succession" and "(a) Conveyancing, (b) The Law of Trusts and Succession, including the general principles of Death Duties, and (c) Court of Session Procedure, Sheriff Court Practice, Criminal Procedure and the Principles of Evidence".

[129] Anon, "Solicitors' Examinations" 1938 *SLT (News)* 90.

[130] Anon. [Andrew Dewar Gibb], "The Scots Law School in 1913" 1919 *JR* 267. (TBS "Law and Lectures" 1922 *SLT (News and Statutes)* 39-40 cannot have been written by TB Smith, Professor of Scots Law at Edinburgh and Law Commissioner, as he was then only seven).

[131] And "nothing short of an examination on Bell and Erskine will induce [students] to wade through the works of Bell or Erskine".

[132] A D Gibb, "Reform in the Scottish Law School" 1943 *JR* 152-165.

[133] See e.g. John C Gardiner, "The Necessity for a Reformation of Legal Education in Scotland" 1928 *SLT (News)* 57, and "Suggestions for Strengthening the Position of the Legal Profession in Scotland" 1929 *SLT (News)* 163.

[134] TMC [presumably the future Lord President Cooper], "Legal Education in Scotland: a criticism" (1922) XXXVII *ScLR* 71-75.

[135] Edward Reginald Simpson (1896-1983), born in Oxfordshire, came to Dundee at the age of 11, attended Morgan Academy, was apprenticed with his brother, qualified in Edinburgh in 1921, thereafter was in Glasgow as an assistant, returning in 1928 to his brother's firm which became J & ER Simpson, carrying on after his brother's death in 1948 and assuming J M Boath as a partner, as Simpson, Boath & Co., also Honorary Sheriff-Substitute and Dean of the FPSD: Dundee City Library Family and Local History Centre *Obituaries Notices 1983-89*, 154.

[136] DUA Recs A/669/105.

[137] UCD Calendars for 1917-18 to 1922-23 are lost, and those thereafter contain no syllabuses.

[138] F B Graham (1873-1950), came to Dundee in 1906, and joined L Melville, the firm taking over that of D Stewart on his death, and assuming J W Coull as a partner at that time to form Melville, Graham & Stewart, of Reform Street, also Chairman of the Dundee Royal Infirmary, Dean of the FPSD, and Honorary Sheriff-Substitute, and political agent for several Parliamentary candidates, including W S Churchill: Dundee City Library Family and Local History Centre *Obituaries Notices 1946-57*, 47.

[139] DUA Recs A/337/3/11 (letter from F B Graham to W A Waterstone), and A/102 UCD Council Minutes August 1915-September 1926, Meeting of 14 June 1915.

[140] Ibid.

[141] John Richmond Bond MM (1898-1973), attended Morgan Academy, had his studies interrupted by the First World War, in which he was a bombardier in the Royal Artillery and was awarded the Military Medal in 1917 for holding a gun position against a "big push", and later, after a period working on his own account, in 1936, joined Rollo & Steven, ending up as senior partner, made Honorary Sheriff-Substitute in 1961, and was also a director of the Royal Insurance Co, and six other companies and Chairman of the Rents Tribunal: Dundee City Library Family and Local History Centre *Obituaries Notices 1966-74,* 232. He acted for Jessie Johnson, a Dundee hairdresser who was prosecuted under the Official Secrets Act for spying for Germany in the UK and acting as a post-box for spying in the USA: see *The Herald* 20 April 2000 and http://www.dundeewomenstrail.org.uk/jordan-jessie-spy/ (last accessed 29 July 2018)

[142] John Alexander Moore MBE (1896-1949), apprenticed to Shiel & Small, in practice in Wick, Town Clerk of Wick and procurator-fiscal for Caithness, and a civil defence official there during the Second World War, later in practice on his own account in Edinburgh: Dundee *Obituaries Notices 1946-57* 40.

[143] See note 135.

[144] DUA Recs A/337/3/4.

[145] This is obscure, as Conveyancing had been compulsory since 1865. Possibly it was intended to mean compulsory attendance at university Conveyancing classes, as there might have been early indications of the 1926 Act of Sederunt.

[146] DUA Recs A/669/6 & 7.

[147] DUA Recs A/102, UCD Council Minutes August 1915-September 1926, Meeting of 12 October 1921.

[148] DUA Recs A/33, UStA Court Minutes 1926-27, Meetings of 4 February and 18 March 1927.

[149] DUA Recs A/104, UCD Council Minutes October 1926-September 1928, Meetings of 21 March and 18 April 1927; FPSD Minutes 1887-1960, Meeting of 18 April 1927.

[150] FPSD Minutes 1887-1960, Meeting of 4 August 1927; DUA Recs A/104, UCD Council Minutes October 1926-September 1928, Meeting of 21 November.

[151] DUA Recs A/104, UCD Council Minutes October 1926-September 1928, Meeting of 21 November 1927.

[152] DUA Recs A/104, UCD Council Minutes October 1926-September 1928, Meeting of 19 December 1927.

[153] DUA Recs A/104, UCD Council Minutes October 1924-September 1928, Meeting of 18 January 1928, Recs A/34, UStA Court Minutes 1927-28, Meeting of 18 March 1928.

[154] I am grateful to Dennis Collins for information.

[155] DUA Recs A/34, UStA Court Minutes 1927-28, Meeting of 4 May (which records terms and conditions) and 22 June 1928.

[156] DUA Recs A/421, UStA Senatus Academicus Minutes 1927-29, Meeting of 25 May 1928.

[157] DUA Recs A/814/1/40, UCD Calendar, Forty-sixth Session, 1928-29.

[158] Anderson, *Education and Opportunity* 277-78.

[159] Southgate, *University Education* 206.

[160] DUA Recs A/420, UStA Court Minutes 1910-11, Meeting of 15 July 1911; Recs A/20, UStA Court Minutes 1913-14, Business and Finance Committee Meeting of 19 January 1914; Recs A/23, UStA Court Minutes 1916-17, Business and Finance Committee Meeting of 29 January 1917.

[161] UStAA UY 615, UStA General Council Minutes, Meeting of 30 June 1917, 8-9, recorded that its newly-formed Committee on the Future of the University (set up at James Thomson's instance, and convened by him) had considered "instituting a Commerce Degree or Diploma at St Andrews [*scil* University]", had referred to a plan drawn up "a number of years ago" by Dr W R Scott (now Professor of Economics at Glasgow University), had looked at the English experience and the Edinburgh University draft Ordinance, and had drawn up a tentative scheme, but decided to recommend the idea without specific content. (In the event, there was no discussion at the General Council's next Meeting and the Committee reports dropped off its agenda).

[162] DUA Recs A/102, UCD Council Minutes August 1915-September 1926, Meeting of 9 May 1917; Recs A/23, UStA Court Minutes 1916-17, Meetings of 7 July & 8 September 1917; Recs A/24, UStA Court Minutes 1917-18, Meeting of 6 October 1917.

[163] DUA Recs A/29, UStA Court Minutes 1922-23, Meeting of 20 October 1922.

[164] DUA Recs A/24, UStA Court Minutes 1917-18, Meetings of 6 October & 17 November 1917.

[165] DUA Recs A/25, UStA Court Minutes, 1918-19, Meeting of 4 February 1919.

[166] See obituary in the *Glasgow Herald* 8 April 1938. Southgate, *University Education* 206, not having mentioned James Thomson at all, simply says "the impetus came from Bonar". Were Thomson's and Bonar's initiatives linked, or did Thomson let his be overtaken by Bonar's munificence?

[167] At one time the biggest linen manufacturer in the world, and which had provided John Boyd Baxter and Mary Ann Baxter with the wealth to found UCD.

[168] Southgate, *University Education* 205.

[169] Ibid. 186.

[170] Ibid.

[171] (Court) Ordinance No LXXXII (St Andrews) No 127) Institution of a Degree in Commerce, and relative Regulations. Strangely, the General Council's Ordinances [etc] Committee does not appear to have discussed it.

[172] DUA Recs A/25, UStA Court Minutes 1918-19, Meetings of 4 & 15 February and 12 April 1919; Recs A/426, UStA Senatus Academicus Minutes 1918-21, Meetings of 8 February, 8 March & 13 December 1919 (when it even discussed the colour of the BCom hood); Recs A/102, UCD Council Minutes August 1915-September 1926, Meetings of 12 March & 9 April 1919.

[173] DUA Recs A/25, UStA Court Minutes 1918-19, Meeting of 19 June 1919.

[174] The history of the negotiations is given in Southgate, *University Education* 205-214 (Appendix to ch 6) and see also 178-179.

[175] DUA Recs A/28, UStA Court Minutes 1921-22, Meeting of 4 November 1921.

[176] DUA Recs A/34, UStA Court Minutes 1927-28, Meeting of 20 December 1927.

[177] For a brief history of the Dundee School of Economics, see Southgate, *University Education* 205-214 (Appendix to ch 6, and sources cited therein); S G E Lythe "The Dundee School of Economics: how it began and prospered" (feature) *The Scotsman* 1 July 1955; and D L Munby "The Dundee School of Economics: In Memoriam" (1957) 4 *Scottish Journal of Political Economy* 60-65. Ronald Coase, later of the University of Chicago, and world famous economist, taught there 1931-32.

[178] Southgate, *University Education* 206 quotes Sir Garnet Wilson's oral evidence to the Tedder Commission (curiously dated as "(1924)") asserting that George Bonar's cheque for £25,000 was "disappearing into the waste-paper basket" at Principal Irvine's insistence (adopting the metaphor himself, at 169), but this is too harsh. Irvine *The Avenue of Years* 118 records that "[Irvine] was touched by the handsome gesture [but the] academic conscience could not be lulled to sleep by a large sum of money if the standard of learning was to be lowered, and an offer that was generously intended had to be refused". As noted above, Reid *Ever to Excel* 162 concluded that the University Principal was "certainly prepared to advance [University College's] interests as part of the overall institution".

[179] DUA Recs A/102, UCD Council Minutes August 1915-September 1926, Meeting of 12 September 1923; Recs A/29, UStA Court Minutes 1922-23, Meeting of 24 September. There had been lectures on railway engineering in 1910 by the Chief Engineer of the North British Railway: see Recs A/115, UCD Education Board Minutes October 1906-November 1930, Meeting of 8 November 1910.

[180] DUA Recs A/102, UCD Council Minutes August 1915-September 1926, Meeting of 12 September 1923; Recs A/29, UStA Court Minutes 1922-23, Meeting of 24 September: also Recs A/429, UStA Senatus Academicus Minutes 1923-25, Meeting of 14 December 1924.

[181] DUA Recs A/30, UStA Court Minutes 1923-24, Meeting of 27 October 1923 (though Professor Steggall only consented to his lecture room being used "on condition that no Drawing Pins were stuck into his Blackboard"): Recs A/115, UCD Education Board Minutes October 1906-November 1930, Meeting of 12 December 1923).

[182] DUA Recs A/30, UStA Court Minutes 1923-24, Meeting of 26 November 1923.

[183] DUA Recs A/30, UStA Court Minutes 1923-24, Meetings of 7 December 1923 and 1 February 1924.

[184] DUA Recs A/30, UStA Court Minutes 1923-24, Meetings of 21 March, 2 May and 18 July 1924.

[185] DUA Recs A/30, UStA Court Minutes 1923-24, Meeting of 26 November 1923.

[186] DUA Recs A/30, UStA Court Minutes 1923-24, Meeting of 2 May 1924.

[187] DUA Recs A/30, UStA Court Minutes 1923-24, Meeting of 2 May 1924; Recs A/102, UCD Council Minutes August 1915-September 1926, Meeting of 9 April 1924.

[188] DUA Recs A/30, UStA Court Minutes 1923-24, Meeting of 18 June 1924.

[189] His wish in 1910 to increase his salary, and in 1918 to receive his salary despite there being no class, were noted above.

[190] For comparison, at this time, the University received £11/4/11 per annum rent on farm lands at Hallowhill (at £1/8/0 per acre); noted £52/17/0 election expenses (for the University

Parliamentary seats); agreed to pay Aberdeen University Press £123/9/0 for publication of *Pseudo-Aristotle de Mundo* by a member of staff; and was paying student bursaries in the region of £25-30: see DUA Recs A/30, UStA Court Minutes 1923-24, Meeting of 20 December 1924.

[191] DUA Recs A/30, UStA Court Minutes 1923-24, Meetings of 21 March, 2 May, 18 July, 29 September and 20 December 1924.

[192] What is known about F B Graham was recorded above (see note 138). What is known about the others comes from pen-portraits in the *Scots Law Times*, obituaries and other references in the press, the FPSD Minutes, and the recollections of Dennis Collins (himself discussed in Chapter 6).

[193] See in particular Anon, "James Allison, Esq, solicitor, Dundee" (1909) 17 *SLT (News and Statutes)* 161; *Dundee Courier* 28 March 1951; FPSD Minute 1887-1906, Meeting of 6 August 1936. A copy of a photograph of him accompanying this pen-portrait hangs in the Scrymgeour Building at the time of writing.

[194] As noted above and UStAA UY 615, UStA General Council Minutes, Meetings of 26 June 1929, 7 & 29 June 1946, 6 (read with list at 3).

[195] See Anon, "Appointment of Lecturer on Conveyancing in Dundee College" (1904-5) 12 *SLT* 190-191 (which includes a photograph of him); Anon, "The late Mr JM Hendry, solicitor, Dundee". Quotations in the text are taken from these.

[196] I am grateful to Kenneth Baxter for this information.

[197] See Dundee City Library Family and Local History Centre *Obituaries Notices 1974-80,* 142.

[198] Hubert Carlton died in 1959 "in his ninety-third year": Anon, "Obituary" 1959 *SLT* 52.

[199] Reproduced in General Report of the 1889 Commissioners 186, as a Schedule to the Commissioners' Order of 21 March 1890 (see next note); and is quoted in Southgate, *University Education* 74-76. Reproduced in General Report of the 1889 Commissioners 186, as a Schedule to the Commissioners' Order of 21 March 1890; and is quoted in Southgate, *University Education* 74-76.

[200] Possibly an erroneous reference to Christian Bisset, see next note, and discussed in the next Chapter, though her time in UCD appears to have been slightly earlier than this.

[201] Regrettably, none received an obituary in either *Dundee Courier* or *Scots Law Times*, at least under their *noms de jeune fille*, nor seem to appear as solicitors in the *Dundee Directories* for likely years (though most may have been accountancy apprentices), save for Isobel Bisset, if this was an error for Christian Bisset (1905-79 and see previous note), and Catherine ("Kitty") Scrimgeour (1909-90). The latter was described as one of the first women solicitors, born and brought up in Newport, attended the High School of Dundee, and entered practice in the family firm of J & J Scrimgeour, with her uncle and brother (both "John") in 1937 (presumably after apprenticeship elsewhere) and within three years was running the practice alone, as in 1940 John snr. died suddenly, and John jnr. was killed. She was joined by a nephew in 1957, and they jointly ran the firm until 1970: Dundee City Library Family and Local History Centre *Obituaries Notices 1990-95,* 172. On the first women lawyers, see Chapter 1, Appendix

[202] DUA Recs A/814/1/18, UCD Calendar, Eighteenth Session, 1900-01, 104.

[203] Again, none received an obituary in either *Dundee Courier* or *Scots Law Times*, nor seem to appear as solicitors in *Dundee Directories* for likely years (though again most may have been accountancy apprentices).

[204] The *Register of Law Students in UCD from 1897-1947* (DUA Recs A/665), discussed in the Annex on Sources of Information on Students) and College Calendars do not completely agree.

[205] Yet again, none received an obituary in the *Dundee Courier* or *Scots Law Times*, nor seem to appear as solicitors in *Dundee Directories* for likely years (though some may have been accountancy apprentices), save that, a few years later, Patrick Aitken was in practice as an accountant at 30 Meadowside, Marshall Anderson as a solicitor at 20 Reform Street and James Morrison at 30 Castle Street: *Dundee Directory 1909-10*. Also David Blackadder, then being senior partner in Blackadder, Gilchrist & Robertson, died in a street accident in 1964 and David Taylor, apprenticed with Moody, Stuart & Robertson, qualified in 1903, went into partnership with Fred. J Robertson as Robertson & Taylor, becoming upon amalgamation senior partner in Cram, Worsley, Robertson & Taylor, and dying 1906: Dundee City Library Family and Local History Centre *Obituaries Notices 1957-1966*, 207 and 90, respectively.

[206] DUA Recs A/814/1/24, UCD Calendar, Twenty-fourth Session, 1906-07, 110.

[207] Once more, none received an obituary in either *Dundee Courier* or *Scots Law Times*, nor seem to appear as solicitors in *Dundee Directories* for likely years (though none will have been accountancy apprentices), save that a few years later, H V Cuthbert was a solicitor with Henry Vaughan at 45 Commercial Street, and James Millar Fergusson (1882-1953), educated at Glasgow High School, apprenticed under W W Stephen, went to Edinburgh, qualified in 1908, was taken into partnership in his uncle's firm, becoming senior partner in Ferguson & Stephen: Dundee *Obituaries Notices 1946-57* 112.

[208] Third in Scots Law in 1904-5.

[209] Second in Scots Law in 1904-5.

[210] DUA Recs A/814/1/39, UCD Calendar, Forty-fifth Session 1927-28. There is an oddity about this, since she does not appear in the *Register of Law Students*. This is discussed in the next Chapter.

[211] DUA Recs A/814/1/41, UCD Calendar, Forty-seventh Session 1929-30. Harold How received no obituary in either *Dundee Courier* or *Scots Law Times*, but is recorded in the *Dundee Directories* as having a business address, seemingly as sole practitioner, in 10 Reform Street from 1938-39 to 1940-41, at 67 Murraygate from 1940-41 to 1948-49, and thereafter at 3 Hilltown (where he had a very untidy office: personal recollection).

[212] I am grateful to Kenneth Baxter for the information in this paragraph and its notes. Most were in the 4th Battalion, The Black Watch. Given the dates of their deaths, too soon for them to have been conscripted, all must have been volunteers. No doubt there were many other volunteers (and conscripts) who survived.

[213] Law student 1908-10, became an accountant, awarded Military Cross, and missing in action 1916.

[214] Law student 1907, son of R Steven, solicitor, became a solicitor in Stirling, killed in action 1915, a month after his brother, commanding the same company: see next note.

[215] Law student 1909, brother of the above, became an accountant, probably awarded the Military Cross in 1915, killed in action 1915.

[216] Law student 1912, son of J S Sturrock, solicitor, missing in action 1915.

[217] Law student 1908, became an accountant in Edinburgh, then emigrated to Canada, killed in action 1916: see next note.

[218] Law student 1913-14, became an accountant, killed in action 1915, brother of above: their parents gifted illuminated windows in their memory to St Fillan's Church, Newport.

[219] Law student 1902-03 (Arts 1899-01), son of Sheriff Clerk of Forfarshire, became a solicitor, then emigrated to Australia, killed in action 1915.

[220] Law student 1902-03, became a solicitor in Thos. Thornton & Co, then emigrated to Canada, killed in action 1915.

[221] Law student 1913-14, son of William Rettie, Governor of UCD, killed in action 1916: his parents "purchased, equipped and presented as a [Dental] Hospital, No 2 Park Place" in his memory (see Southgate, *University Education* 159-160).

[222] Which, incidentally, commenced in 1893, roughly co-incidentally with law teaching in Dundee.

[223] DUA Recs A/814/1/18, UCD Calendar, Eighteenth Session, 1900-01, 34-5.

[224] DUA Recs A/814/1/23, UCD Calendar, Twenty-third Session, 1905-06.

[225] AS 20 December 1873.

[226] AS 12 March 1926.

[227] Regulations dated 1 October 1936.

[228] Regulations dated 19 March 1937.

CHAPTER 4

1938-49: BLIGHTED SUCCESS:

A BL DEGREE AND A SCOTS LAW CHAIR, BUT WAR-TIME WOES

The end of the 1930s was a turning point in the fortunes of law teaching in University College Dundee (UCD). Despite a background of continuing disharmony between the College and the rest of the University, a BL degree was finally achieved, and the teaching staff tripled in number in consequence. But its start almost exactly coincided with the outbreak of the Second World War, and war-time exigencies immediately and severely limited its success (though these years also produced the Polish "soldier-students"). Nevertheless, it survived and, post-war, another turning point was the appointment of a Professor of Scots Law (the first full-time post), and the hope of an LLB degree. Almost simultaneously with this, there was a major Inquiry into relations between UCD and the rest of the University. However, though the consequential Cooper Report shed light on those relations, it was a failure, solving nothing, and having no effect upon law teaching.

This Chapter again, in addition to the narrative, considers the identities and careers of the lecturers (and new professor), and the numbers, gender, achievements and identities of the students, insofar as they can be retrieved from the records.

1938-49: Backdrop

The difficult relationship between UCD and the rest of St Andrews University continued in these years, Southgate proleptically describing the period as "The Penultimate Battle"[1]. Within it, what he termed the "Fulton Years 1939-46" were marked by A R Fulton, Professor of Engineering, replacing Sir James Irvine's "Interim" Principalship of UCD (though the latter remained Principal of the University as a whole). But whatever changes this might have produced were overshadowed by the consequences of the Second World War.

In any event, any lull in intra-University hostilities ended with post-war planning for the University, in which UCD once more felt disfavoured, since Principal Irvine saw St Andrews' future as a small liberal arts college, undertaking a little specialised science teaching, leaving no obvious role for UCD. What Southgate termed the "Wimberley's First Years 1946-48" opened with Fulton's replacement by Major-General Wimberley[2]. He instilled an *esprit de corps* but, despite increasing local pressure, both internal and external, did not seek independence for UCD, although conceding that the University sought to keep UCD "undeveloped, weak and divided"[3]. Evidence for this conclusion emerged in 1948, when it was found that (in something of a re-run of the events of 1911, discussed in Chapter 3) Government funds intended for UCD had been diverted to other parts of the University. The crisis that this produced generated the Cooper Inquiry in 1949. This was chaired, rather remarkably, by the Lord President of the Court of Session[4] (the most senior judge in Scotland), with two "assessors"[5]. Its terms of reference were "to review the organisation of university education in Dundee and its relationship with St Andrews University[6]."

Because of the significance of the unhappy history of this relationship, which cast its shadow over most of the life of UCD, and the presumed impartiality of the Inquiry, it is worth examining its conclusions, despite its failure to solve any problems.

Meeting in private, because of the "considerable delicacy" of the situation[7], in essence, it concluded that the "affiliation" might have worked if it had been accompanied by a genuine will to succeed. But the governance arrangements were inherently unsuitable. UCD's constitution resembled "the Memorandum and Articles of a joint stock company", and created an *imperium in imperio* – a state within a state – while the shadowy existence of United College and St Mary's College was also preserved. These features had produced a lack of long-term planning, with unequal

176

and haphazard division of teaching between the two sites. In turn, on the one hand, this had produced both a lack of self-sufficiency and duplication, and on the other, starved UCD of funds. Cooper's prescription was full amalgamation of UCD into the University, the former relying on the latter's goodwill to prevent further underdevelopment, but it was universally rejected. The Inquiry's observations upon Law, as such, are briefly discussed below.

1938-49: The Law School - an Overview

The continuing disharmony between UCD and the rest of the University was not all-pervasive, however, for this period provides an extraordinary contrast with the preceding 40 years in respect of law teaching, which moved from a small service operation to a small, but complete, law school.

As the process started under Sir James Irvine's "Interim" Principalship of UCD, despite his tendency to disfavour UCD, he can take some credit for the introduction of a BL degree; the consequential increase in staff from two to half a dozen or more; support during the War years; the appointment of the first Chair; and, despite continuing tiny BL numbers, allowing progress towards the introduction of an LLB degree in the period covered by the next chapter.

It is useful to divide the period into four (partly overlapping) sections, 1938-39, examining the introduction of the BL; 1939-1949, discussing the first few years of the BL; 1944-49, considering the commencement of the first Chair in Law; and other events 1946-49.

1938-39: The BL Introduced

In early 1938, Hugh Carlton, who taught Conveyancing, fired off a letter to the University Court (possibly in conscious imitation of James Allison's, in similar tones, 30 years before, noted in Chapter 3) intimating that he might not continue teaching because, after a decade, he still only received £100 per session[8]. This set the cat among the pigeons, and the matter was batted, with some recrimination and confusion, between Court and UCD Council[9].

But of greater significance is that, in the same letter, Carlton also complained that "no progress had been made towards enabling the University to confer the Degree of BL"[10]. But why should he have expected progress after 40 years of non-graduating classes? The answer lies in the 1938 Solicitors Regulations[11], discussed in Chapter 3. These required the expansion of the Scots Law and Conveyancing curricula, and possibly the teaching of Forms of Process (the third part of the traditional "law agents' triad"[12]) for the first time, but certainly made necessary the teaching of Constitutional Law, Civil Law and Jurisprudence (newly added to the "triad"). If all these subjects were not taught, there would be little reason for students to attend UCD: but if all were taught, a BL (though not, perhaps, an LLB) was almost possible[13]. Moreover, a decision was urgent, as the new Regulations had been in force from 1 January 1938 (so existing UCD students must have taken advantage of the fortunately generous transitional provisions).

Indeed, Carlton's letter was probably the latest item in a course of lobbying, because fifteen years later, the law lecturers' evidence, submitted over his name to another major investigation into intra-University relations[14] (dealt with in Chapter 5), recalled that to obtain introduction of the BL "much pressure was required, and it was obtained largely though the good offices of … Lord MacGregor Mitchell[15]."

This was Robert Macgregor Mitchell[16], an advocate who was now a judge, so might have been sympathetic to legal aspirations, and had been involved in university affairs for some years. Moreover, he was now Rector of the University, thus chairman of Court, so may have advised Carlton to raise the matter there.

In any event, a complicated train of events ensued over the following eighteen months. At the meeting which received Carlton's letter, Court invited Macgregor Mitchell to report on "the regulations for Solicitors ... and the question of providing additional instruction in Law"[17]. But in what must have seemed a catastrophe, Macgregor Mitchell (who had been ill) died suddenly, at the beginning of the very meeting of Court at which he was due to report[18]. Carlton, however, nothing daunted, then drafted a Memorandum himself (which might have been very similar to what Macgregor Mitchell intended to propose, since no doubt they consulted).

This Memorandum was sent to UCD Council, not Court. Perhaps it seemed the more appropriate *point d'appui* in the absence of Macgregor Mitchell, as UCD Council would have to organise the degree. In a manifesto comparable to Thomas Thornton's of 1890 (noted in Chapter 2), recorded in Council Minutes, it asserted:

> the desirability of a course for the Degree of Batchelor [*sic*] of Laws [*sic*] being instituted in the University of St Andrews in order that local students might be able to qualify as Solicitors without the necessity of proceeding to other Universities[19].

The reference to "the necessity of proceeding to other Universities" was misleading, insofar as the 1938 Regulations (discussed in Chapter 3) removed the requirement to attend university law classes, though did allow degree examination passes to exempt from some of the professional examinations. The word "Laws" introduces an ambiguity, implying an LLB[20] (requiring further subjects, and a prior MA). However, Carlton's original letter specifically referred to "the Degree of BL", and this Minute referred to "solicitors" (and not to "advocates", on whom possession of a BL conferred no advantage). So like "Batchelor", "Laws" was probably a slip of the minute-taker's pen. There were, however, ambitions.

The Minute also noted that Aberdeen University, offering both LLB and BL, had but one Professor, all other staff being part-time practitioners like Carlton and Allison. (It did not also mention that the BL might also fulfil the Baxters' aim in endowing UCD of allowing no-frills qualifications for the ambitious). Council favoured the plan, and forwarded it to Court (adding, in an abundance of caution, that "the courses ... would be held in Dundee").

Court deferred consideration of Carlton's plan[21]. But this was not a brush-off. It was to allow Irvine to get his ducks in a row, while he performed an apparent *volte-face*. With some reason, he was not regarded as a friend of UCD, and (though he had been helpful on the Railway Lectures, discussed in Chapter 3) "much pressure" had been needed to get the BL proposal taken up, with only Macgregor Mitchell's good offices achieving it. However, Irvine now seems belatedly to have recognised the opportunity and, coming to the end of his tenure as "Interim" Principal of UCD, may have wanted a Dundee legacy.

In any event, Irvine now took over the idea of a BL, and in November 1938 reported on consultations with Allison and Carlton, submitting his own Memorandum (no doubt similar to Carlton's and, for that matter, Macgregor Mitchell's), considered by Court in December[22]. It was brief, and skated over a central question, suggesting that he had taken his decision and was simply managing Court into approval. It started with his conclusion that:

> [a]lthough the scheme [for a law degree] is unlikely to grow large in dimensions there is a reasonable expectation that, in view of the new regulations governing Solicitors' Professional examinations, a steady recruitment of candidates will be forthcoming[23].

Assuming Court's acceptance, he put three consequential questions to it: (i) whether a new Ordinance was required (a technical issue which Court resolved by a fudge, as Edinburgh had done[24]); (ii) whether there should be a separate Law Faculty (and Court agreed with the Principal that a separate Faculty would have "obvious [though unspecified] disadvantages", and that there were precedents for Law within Arts, as Dentistry was within Medicine, and Engineering within Science; and (iii) whether Court or UCD should bear the financial responsibility (on which Court, in the tones of Uriah Heep, thought the Council should be "given the opportunity to provide for the remuneration of additional lecturers"), and keep class, but not matriculation or examination, fees.

The central question, skated over, was whether a BL could be delivered. The Principal must have satisfied himself, but Court could hardly ignore the question and, seemingly late in the discussion, concluded that "the subjects in which lectures are to be made available should be in Scots Law, Conveyancing, Civil Law, Constitutional Law & History, and Forensic Medicine[25]."

This list involved compromises. Court concluded that Constitutional Law & History would have to double up with the existing Constitutional History class in Arts (a device familiar from the abortive 1907 plan for a degree, discussed in Chapter 3), and Forensic Medicine with the existing course for medical students. Even so, the list is slightly odd. It would achieve a BL under the 1911 Ordinance but, perversely (unless there was a mistake in recording the Minute), the lack of Jurisprudence would prevent it from fulfilling the 1938 Regulations, which would be a fatal flaw (see Appendix 1 to this Chapter). Book-keeping and Evidence & Procedure, also omitted, were not generally taught, so their absence was a non-fatal flaw.

Court also considered timetabling, fixing lecture hours at 9-10am and 4-5pm (except for Forensic Medicine) over two terms (and with no reference to any other form of teaching), but not library expenditure, though this was dealt with later.

UCD Council considered Court's conclusions at length ten days later[26]. It is a tribute to Carlton's leg-work that it could note that syllabuses and schemes of courses were already drafted. Clearly eager, Council decided the BL should start in October 1939, the very next session.

It also decided, in a reverse-Bartleby[27], that it would "prefer to be responsible for the expansion", and agreed to Court's proposed division of class, matriculation and examination fees, hoping that the degree "might come within reach of being self-supporting". The number of lectures was fixed by Ordinance[28], but, strangely, UCD Council did not decide how many lecturers would be required, nor whether they would be part-time or full-time (though the assumption must have been one lecturer per subject, part-time).

Senate was apprised of the matter for the first time in January 1939[29]. It received a clearly supportive report from the Faculty of Arts (both Allison and Carlton attending the relevant meeting). This fleshed out the plan by deciding that the "proposed syllabus of study" would be:

First Year: Civil Law and Constitutional Law & History (both 80 lectures)

Second Year: Forensic Medicine (40 lectures) and Scots Law (80 lectures)

Third Year: Jurisprudence (40 lectures) and Conveyancing (80 lectures).

As this shows, it also expanded the "syllabus", by adding Jurisprudence, crucial for the 1938 Regulations, as explained above. Why this subject appeared so late in the proceedings is unexplained. However, the staying power of this "syllabus" was great. It reflected that of the original law degrees 75 years earlier, and was still visible, under a couple of accretions, 25 years later.

The Arts Faculty also made a long series of recommendations, some involving further expansion. There should be an Evidence & Procedure course in Second Year (clearly desirable for the 1938 Regulations, though Book-keeping was not mentioned). And, it observed, for the price of two more 40-lecture courses, say (Public) International Law and Economics (already taught), an LLB might be had. Was Carlton keeping up the pressure? Further, contrary to the conclusion of the Principal and Court, it thought that there should be a Law Faculty (as continued inclusion in Arts was an "anomaly", and graduates would suffer in comparison with those of other universities). But overall, it recommended that Senate should approve the plan.

Senate, while approving the Arts Faculty plan, ignored most of these recommendations and got down to the more exciting tasks of designing a degree certificate (remitted to Professor Rose: Greek) and a hood (remitted to Professors Allen: Natural Philosophy; Baxter: Ecclesiastical History; and Williams: History). Their reports were approved at Senate's next meeting[30]. The Hood Committee's report was very full, concluding by recommending scarlet cloth with a white silk edging three inches broad (and, in anticipation, an LLB to have a white fur edging)[31].

Other consequential issues were dealt with, including financing the extra lecturers, which UCD Council undertook to do, and sought to appoint them "with the minimum possible delay"[32].

In February 1939, at some length, and carefully minuting UCD Council's financial responsibility for all the lecturers, Court concurred with Senate and UCD Council on the extended plan including Jurisprudence and Evidence & Procedure (though not the other suggestions), and on the urgency (even though there was none for Second and Third Year subjects)[33]. It therefore asked the Board of Studies to draft advertisements for the posts, their terms and conditions, and to recommend external examiners, and asked UCD Council to recommend salaries.

On 2 May 1939 (which we shall see was a momentous day), Court approved the terms and conditions and advertisements which had been drafted, and noted that a leaflet informing students of the new degree had gone to proof[34]. It also approved the recommendations that the Scots Law lecturer's salary (and seemingly the Conveyancing lecturer's salary) be raised from £150 to £200, and that the new Civil Law lecturer should receive £150, the new Jurisprudence, and Evidence & Procedure, lecturers each £80, and the new Constitutional Law & History lecturer a figure not exceeding £150, all to be part-time, unsuperannuated, annually renewable[35], posts[36].

The relative sizes of these salaries broadly reflects the different numbers of lectures required, but the last lectureship deserves special mention. Firstly, as noted above, the original plan depended upon Constitutional Law & History doubling up with the MA Constitutional History. Seemingly, uncovenanted and unminuted, this plan had been dropped (which would have considerable, presumably unforeseen, adverse effect on progress, as explained below). Secondly, approval of it was therefore effectively retrospective and displayed other curious features (as also explained below).

On the same occasion, fees were fixed at 6 guineas for 80-lecture courses, 5 guineas for Forensic Medicine, and 4 guineas for the rest, with an Inclusive Tuition Fee for all classes of £31/10/- (thus giving a small discount), but also an additional £7/17/6 "fee for the Degree of BL" (seemingly for matriculation and examinations, and thus destined for University funds). External Examiners were to receive £5 "for each period of examination" and 5/- per candidate, plus first class travelling expenses[37]. (At about the same time, steps were taken to decide whether Law students were eligible for Arts Bursaries, though no decision is recorded[38]).

Also on that day in May, and presumably not coincidentally, Allison, though strangely absent from much of the discussion leading to the introduction of the BL, but after teaching Scots Law single-handed for forty years, was promoted to a Readership (and perhaps hoped for a Chair in the future)[39]. Carlton, the mover and shaker in the introduction of the BL, after teaching Conveyancing single-handed for ten (and perhaps with similar hopes) was not.

As to new posts, firstly, appointment of a Constitutional Law & History lecturer was effectively retrospective. Once more on that same 2 May 1939, Court actually appointed this lecturer at £120 a year, to give "not less [*sic*] than 80 Lectures qualifying for Graduation in Law". Seemingly, it did so on the strength of a "letter … submitted from the [College] Council recommending [him]" and an interview of him by a "Sub-Committee" of the Court Finance Sub-Committee[40]. The terms and conditions are set out *in extenso* in the Minute[41].

The rapidity and informality (reminiscent of the appointment of Allison, 40 years earlier) was no doubt in part due to the fact that the lecturer would teach in First Year, thus commencing within six months of appointment. But since the same consideration applied to the Civil Law lecturer, there was clearly another factor at work. That was that the appointee, Alan Simpson BA[42], was already "Lecturer in Modern History and in American and Colonial History at the United College, St Andrews". This curious title inaccurately suggests he already had two jobs[43], to which a third was now added. In any event, an existing full-time lecturer was being offered, not an honorarium, but an additional, potentially permanent, part-time lectureship, in order to undertake extra teaching. (This, incidentally, underlines the abandonment of the "doubling up" plan, discussed further below).

Secondly, and yet again on that same 2 May 1939, Court also set up a Joint Committee of Court and UCD Council to interview candidates for the other new posts. Both Allison and Carlton were suggested as members, but Court decided to exclude them, presumably on the ground that, as local practitioners, they might suffer insuperable conflicts of interest. UCD Council allowed Patrick Cumming to apply for the Civil Law lectureship, although he was the UCD Secretary, and thus an existing full-time member of staff (though not academic one), thereby raising seemingly superable conflicts of interest.

In mid-June, that appointing committee recommended Patrick Cumming MA LLB for Civil Law (seemingly on the same curious terms as Alan Simpson, though only for an initial three years); Bernard ("Ben") C Bowman[44] MA LLB (from Gray, Robertson & Wilkie) for Jurisprudence; and Christian J Bisset MA LLB (from the Town Clerk's Department, noted in the previous Chapter and discussed further below) for Evidence & Procedure[45]. Shortly thereafter, and in contrast to the arrangement with Alan Simpson, Court approved a mere honorarium to William Fyffe Dorward, Lecturer in Forensic Medicine (also police surgeon, and a GP[46]) for teaching BL students (who presumably simply went to the existing Medical students' classes)[47]. Though on one-year contracts, all the 1939 appointees except Alan Simpson continued in post for three or more decades.

At about the same time, Senate considered three other Arts Faculty recommendations. The first, that Allison and Carlton be members of the Faculty of Arts, was uncontroversial[48]. The second, that Civil Law and Constitutional Law & History count as MA subjects as well as BL ones in order "to evolve a five years' course for the combined Degrees of MA, BL", was odd[49]. This "five years' course" would depend on counting those subjects for both degrees. However, the MA was a precondition of the LLB, but not of the BL, so there seems no reason why any student should seek to take that combination. In any case, the terms of Simpson's appointment indicated a decision to run a Constitutional Law & History course separate from any existing Constitutional Law course for Arts students. And just a month later, the Arts Faculty decided that Constitutional Law & History was "too restricted and specialised" for the MA[50]. Not only did this decision reinforce the clearly already abandoned "doubling-up" plan, but more to the point, it scuppered a "five years' course".

Odder still, as difficult to reconcile with this rejection of doubling-counting, the third recommendation raised again the possibility of teaching Public International Law, explicitly in order to achieve an MA LLB, and thus give "students of this University precisely the same opportunities for graduation in Law as students in the sister universities"[51]. Clearly, hopes for an LLB remained, whether double-counting allowed it in five years, or not.

Nevertheless, while approving the appointment of the two law lecturers to the Arts Faculty, Senate blandly concluded that it was "not expedient, at the present time, to confer a Degree of LLB or to institute the necessary courses for that purpose".

1939-49: The BL Starts and Survives

Thus, by October 1939, shortly after Sir James Irvine resigned from the "Interim" Principalship of UCD, just eighteen months after Hugh Carlton's letter to Court, and despite Lord Macgregor Mitchell's demise, there were seven lecturers in post. And 40 years after continuous law teaching started, 65 years after the first law classes in UCD, and 75 years after the very first, extra-mural law classes, there was a law degree. The fly in the ointment was, of course, that the Second World War had broken out a month before (curiously paralleling the outbreak of the First World War just after the final attempt to institute a law degree 25 years before) . Hugh Carlton might reasonably have thought he was cursed.

As considered more fully below, 22 entrant law students (all male) matriculated in the first year of operation[52], including some 6 graduating students and 16 non-graduating[53]. This is fewer than the total of non-graduating students of previous years[54] though, in October 1939, the reason is easy to imagine.

There is no reason to think that teaching (which on the more limited scale had taken place for 40 years) did not get off to a good start, though only in October was money finally sought for unspecified "essential books for the teaching of Law"[55]. The University Calendar[56] rehearsed the 1938 Solicitors Regulations and BL Ordinance requirements, and gave some teaching arrangements for the BL (but explicitly not, "meantime", for an LLB), repeating the Senate "syllabus of courses" with slight changes and the addition of class times, as follows:

First Year:

> Civil Law: 9am in Martinmas and Candlemas Terms
>
> Constitutional Law & History: 5pm in Martinmas and Candlemas Terms

Second Year:

> Scots Law: 5pm in Martinmas and Candlemas Terms

Jurisprudence: 5pm in Whitsunday Term

Forensic Medicine: 3pm in Whitsunday Term

Third Year:

Conveyancing: 5pm in Martinmas and Candlemas Terms

Evidence & Procedure: 5pm in Whitsunday Term

Economics was also listed as an option, though it not taught in UCD.

Full syllabuses are not recorded (though reading is suggested for Scots Law[57] and Jurisprudence[58]), but outlines of some courses are given in later Calendars[59]. There is a small mystery as to which classes actually ran in this initial year. Clearly the First Year ones (Civil Law and Constitutional Law & History) did. Equally clearly, Scots Law (Second Year) and Conveyancing (Third Year) ran for non-graduating students (and presumably Forensic Medicine for medical students).

However, all the new appointments were made from 1 October 1939, all the appointees' names are in the Calendar, and with "Additional" (i.e. External) Examiners for all subjects[60]. So presumably Ben Bowman (Jurisprudence – Second Year) and Christian Bisset (Evidence & Procedure – Third Year) taught non-graduating students for the 1938 Solicitors' regulations examinations.

Over the summer of 1939, no doubt because of the start of the BL, Hugh Carlton had been appointed Adviser of Studies in Law, at £5 a year plus expenses, but without any job specification (though later events show that he was put in charge of law admissions)[61]. "Advisers of Studies" had been appointed in the University as a whole from December 1907[62], with no honorarium or list of duties, though their consent to subject selection was required from a couple of years later[63]. This requirement appeared in Calendars thereafter, but was of little moment to law students who had little or no choice of subject to make.

From 1939, University Calendars also "asked" that "[a]ll women students *matriculating for the first time*"[64] see the Adviser to Women students, Dr Edith Philip Smith, in Botany[65]. This was presumably elementary pastoral care, but no other form of it appears to have existed in UCD until the "Regent Scheme" was introduced in 1946[66], as discussed below.

War clearly had some direct effects, as hinted at above. Potential entrants were overwhelmingly in the age group likely to volunteer for, or be conscripted into, the armed forces[67] and, unsurprisingly, BL numbers remained small until well after the War ended. But those numbers were enhanced by the members of the Polish armed forces who came to Dundee after the German and Russian invasions of Poland in 1939, and German invasion of France in 1940, becoming students, indeed graduates, in a "Polish Law School" in Dundee, discussed further below.

Some members of the newly appointed staff were also within that age group, and any who were not, but principally employed in small organisations like law firms, with employees within that age group, might also be affected indirectly.

Ben Bowman was thought liable to conscription, but obtained deferment long enough to allow his teaching to be completed before his expected departure[68]. In the event, he was never called up, though he undertook war work (described below). Later the question of "de-reserving" staff was raised in connection with Patrick Cumming[69].

More seriously, as the 1940-41 session commenced, Alan Simpson was awaiting call-up though, in the event, it too was delayed long enough for him to at least start teaching[70]. He seems to have managed the Michaelmas Term, as Christian Bisset[71] was recommended for an honorarium of £40 for teaching the course in the Candlemas Term[72]. Indeed, though there were further toings-and-froings with called-up students, she was asked to undertake the class again in 1941-42 (chiefly for the Polish students), and in 1942-43, for which she was paid £80 per session, but thereafter she declined[73]. A Committee appointed to advise

Court reported that it would be "difficult, if not impossible" to recruit a replacement locally, given manpower shortages, so the syllabus was rearranged to put the class into Second Year in 1943-44, presumably in the hope that something would turn up[74]. Something did turn up, as six months later Ivan Chalmers[75] was appointed to a Temporary Lectureship to teach the subject on the same terms as Simpson had, unless the latter returned from HM Forces[76].

The problem continued post-war as, though Simpson returned in 1946 (at which point Chalmers was translated to Scots Law, as discussed below), he seems to have left shortly thereafter[77]. He was replaced in the History Department by Norman Gash, later Professor of Modern History and biographer of Peel so, on the face of it, ideal for teaching Constitutional Law & History. But seemingly he was not expected to do so, as the History Department found someone else. No doubt to his surprise, it lit upon an early-medievalist, Frederick Wainwright[78], who taught it for some years[79].

There were, of course, further staff changes over this period. Clearly the most important was the appointment in 1947 of a Professor of Scots Law. However, this is of sufficient importance to be dealt with separately below. One other staff change, seemingly not war-related, and very significant, was James Allison's retiral in 1945, ending a remarkable 46 years of teaching Scots Law[80] (through the three final editions of Erskine's *Principles* and the first three of Gloag and Henderson, the standard student text-books).

Why he resigned at that time is unclear. He was 80, but it was less than a year since his Readership had been renewed for five years (interestingly, subject to the condition that it would terminate "in the event of a Chair of Scots Law being established"), which suggests suddenness of departure. Possibly he was unwell, but the resignation followed Court's forceful rejection of a plan to start an LLB[81] (discussed below) which must have been a major disappointment to him. While the Faculty of Procurators and Solicitors in Dundee (FPSD) recorded an appreciation of him[82], rather extraordinarily, neither Court[83], nor Senate, nor UCD Council did, so perhaps his departure was stormy.

Replacement (like that for Constitutional Law & History) was difficult, for no applications were received by the closing date[84], and Principal Fulton was authorised to consult with Hugh Carlton. This consultation produced William Low Mitchell MA LLB[85]. But sadly, Allison's unequalled forty-six year tenure was followed by William Low Mitchell's equally unequalled tenure of little more than forty-six days. An Inaugural Lecture, in the Mathematics Room[86], open to the public, at 5pm on Friday 25 November 1945, had been advertised[87]. Possibly this was the actual first lecture of the session (though Mitchell had been appointed in September), possibly a conscious post-war relaunch of Scots Law teaching. But in any case, it is unlikely that it was actually delivered, for Mitchell's death (though after a "sudden illness") occurred on 9 December 1945, almost exactly three months after Court approved his appointment[88].

Hugh Carlton no doubt again rolled his eyes heavenward in despair, but T L Hird MA LLB WS[89] (seemingly well-qualified, then working in the same firm as Mitchell, so possibly under some pressure, but also about to embark upon practice on his own account) filled in the gap "in respect of conducting the course … during the Martinmas Term"[90]. Clearly this must have been brief service, as he was only paid £10 (compared with the £90 paid to Mitchell's executors). But Chalmers, having just been released from teaching Constitutional Law & History ("with much acceptance") by Simpson's return, was available, and he filled in for the rest of the year at £100[91].

After that, the post was presumably advertised, and in June 1946, a Committee (Sheriff Mackinnon[92], Dr Salmond and Principal Fulton) produced a short leet of Bowman, Chalmers, Hird and D K Adam[93]. The first two were not interviewed, as already members of staff. The latter two were, but it was unanimously decided to appoint Bowman, who had presumably had his fill of Jurisprudence[94]. Court further decided to appoint Ivan Chalmers, fresh from teaching Constitutional Law &

History, and even fresher from teaching Scots Law, to the vacated Jurisprudence post (for which he may have applied back in 1939), in which he remained until he died, just after this period, in 1950[95] (to be replaced by Bowman!). Hird, despite filling in at short notice when Mitchell died, got nothing.

However, in September 1946, awkwardly just before the start of session, Patrick Cumming, appointed in 1939, tendered his resignation from teaching Civil Law. Seemingly this was because of UCD Council's concerns about pressures of his day-job during post-war expansion, as it "waived its objection" to him continuing for one more session when there were difficulties in finding a replacement[96]. He in fact continued for only one term, because a replacement was found from the beginning of 1947[97]. And this was Hird, who had briefly filled in on Scots Law after Mitchell's demise, been turned down for the permanent Scots Law job, had just undertaken the "Railway Lectures" (discussed below), and was embarked upon practice on his own account (so may have been glad of the assured income). He held this post for some 25 years[98].

Hugh Carlton made a successful bid for a part-time Conveyancing Assistant in 1947-48, and Alexander James Waddell Robertson Coupar DFM BL[99] (from J & H Pattullo and Donald) was appointed at £75[100]. He may have taken tutorials, in which case, these would be the first recorded in the law school. Bowman changed jobs yet again when the Chair of Scots Law was appointed (as noted above and discussed below).

In addition to staff changes, in 1949, there were substantial salary rises, as follows[101]:

	Present salary (£)	Proposed increase (£)	Total (£)
Bowman (Scots Law)	220	20	240
Carlton (Conveyancing)	195	55	250

Wainwright (Constitutional Law & History)	100	30	130
Hird (Civil Law)	165	35	200
Chalmers (Jurisprudence)	90	30	120
Bisset (Evidence & Procedure)	90	30	120
Dorward (Forensic Medicine)	40	25	65

No record reveals the reasoning for these various increases, but two things are obvious. One is the difference in the sizes of increase, from less than 10% (Bowman) to more than 50% (Dorward). The other is that the resulting variation broadly reflected the difference between 80-lecture and 40-lecture classes (though Wainwright was already a full-timer in History, and Dorward had been teaching Forensic Medicine to Medical students since 1933).

1944-49: A Chair Created, but still no LLB

As noted above, the most important staff change was the appointment of a Professor of Scots Law, an issue closely tied to progress towards an LLB. The road was rocky (and seems to have resulted in Hugh Carlton over-reaching himself on a related matter).

In spring 1944, Principal Fulton produced a Memorandum for UCD Council to submit to the University Grants Committee (UGC)[102]. It noted that law teaching was long-established, though the BL had started only five years before and its development had been blighted by the War, and concluded that, in the light of experience and "the decided trend in legal[103] opinion", an LLB was necessary. This could be achieved by adding a single class, though a greater choice of subjects was also necessary. Moreover it was:

> highly expedient to raise the status of the Law School by the institution of a Chair in its most important subject – Scots Law [which would be] a full-time appointment if the Professor were also required to teach one or more of the smaller subjects required for the ... LLB[104].

This Memorandum fell foul of a Court (or Principal)/Council trial of strength, involving Council threats to approach the UGC separately, too complicated and tangential to record here[105]. In brief, in the result, it was almost entirely rejected by Court in short order. However, though the proposal for an LLB did not survive, seemingly rather inconsistently, that for a Chair did[106]. Principal Irvine's role is intriguingly ambivalent. On the one hand, surprisingly, he had given, and continued to give, his support to the BL, and the plan for a Chair amidst his general demolition of Fulton's plans. Nevertheless, as shown below, on the other hand, he now strongly set his face against an LLB.

In any event, a further Memorandum to Court, from law staff unhappy with this outcome, urged institution of an LLB but, surely with Irvine's approval, it was disdainfully rejected on the ground that it contained "no information or argument" not already considered[107].

Undaunted, the law staff then sent their Memorandum to UCD Council which remitted it to a Special Committee (Sheriffs Mackinnon and Gibb[108], and J Gordon Simpson). UCD Council accepted the Committee's obviously sympathetic report "as a statement of its desire that Court should consider the LLB again in the light of fresh circumstances which have arisen"[109]. It also raised the possibility of abbreviated degrees in the light of the concessions to servicemen under war-time legislation[110]. The unspecified "fresh circumstances", inferred from Court Minutes, were the discovery that Court had rejected the Memorandum without most of its members of Court having seen it.

If Court's original reaction was disdainful, its second, surely expressing Irvine's feelings, was black-affronted, finding the assertion that the decision was taken improperly "most objectionable", and thundering that it "might be presumed that the Court knows its own business best and … the fact that other Universities were prepared to grant War Emergency Concessions [was not] a relevant factor[111]."

This overblown response, seeming to show Irvine caught on the raw, presumably reflected the tensions between him and the Court on one hand, and Council on the other. But the Chair remained secure and, objectively, the moment was hardly propitious for expansion. In 1942-43 there had been only 2 BL entrants, and in 1941-2, 1943-44 and 1944-45, none at all (as noted below). It would have been justifiable to shut the degree down. And shortly after this, possibly because of the forceful rejection of the LLB plans, James Allison resigned (as discussed above).

These tensions were probably also behind a series of incidents with some consequences, in which Hugh Carlton, though a veteran of university politicking, seems to have over-reached himself. In the summer of 1945, he drew attention to the fact that, as an Adviser of Studies, he could not recommend students thinking of "a combined Arts-Law course" to come to UCD, as it would require six years, while elsewhere it required only five[112]. This was, of course, because in UCD, after the Arts' decision that there was a mismatch between its Constitutional Law class and law's Constitutional Law & History class, the subject could not count for both degrees. A year later, he reopened the issue[113]. Six months after that, it was decided that, although law admissions had hitherto been dealt with by him, in future, they would be dealt with by the Dean of Arts[114]. Possibly this was tidying up. Possibly it was a consequence of the Memorandum and his outspokenness on combined degrees.

This was not the end of the matter, however. Though the new admissions system was put into operation for 1947-48, in the course of later discussions on the accuracy and helpfulness of entrant student statistics, a report was sought on the method of admitting Arts students[115]. At this time, Carlton took objection to a note expressing the new policy in the "Law leaflet" (presumably a pamphlet summarising BL admissions procedure), because there had been no consultation, and threatened to resign his Advisership if it were not withdrawn[116].

Senate sought to call his bluff and he replied that the new policy was a change to a successful practice, flew in the face of Board of Studies feelings, reduced the "Head of the School of Law" (a self-conferred title) to a cipher, was not in the interests of the Law School, and was an insult to "a teacher of twenty year's service in the university"[117]. This was as overblown as Court's thunderings three years earlier, but one can sympathise. Carlton had actually got the BL going despite great setbacks, and would probably have got an LLB going had the War not intervened. But Senate simply appointed Bowman to the Advisership in his place. Relations between the two must have been strained for a while.

Although progress on an LLB was stalled, on the Chair it was rapid. In the summer of 1947, the Carnegie Trust granted £4,000 towards establishing a Chair of Scots Law (and the Civil Law lectureship)[118]. The FPSD offered its moral support, but carefully minuted that this did not commit them to financial support[119]. Wimberley (who had succeeded Fulton) unsuccessfully sought a Minute that the Chair be in the Arts Faculty only "until such time as the Faculty of Law is instituted"[120].

The Ordinance founding the Chair was approved in August 1948[121], though questions of salary, and, indeed, whether it was to be full-time or part-time, remained undecided[122] and were remitted to a Committee (Sir Garnet Wilson[123], Professor Copson and Sheriffs Cullen[124], Mackinnon, Middleton[125] and More[126]). They reported that the Chair should attract the same salary as an Arts Chair (seemingly £1,450) and (anticipating an advocate) that the appointee be "permitted to carry on a Chamber practice as a member of the Scottish Bar, insofar as it does not interfere with the discharge of his duties"[127].

Two candidates were interviewed in July 1949[128], Arthur Matheson (discussed below) and J J Gow[129]. The former was appointed, at a salary of (in the event) £1,900[130], and inducted in October 1949[131] (and immediately put on the Library Committee)[132]. He was the first Professor of Law in UCD and the first in the University of St Andrews for centuries[133]. Again manifesting its moral support, the FPSD set up two book prizes, one each for Scots Law and Conveyancing[134] (which continue to the present day).

One wonders what undertakings Matheson was given on plans for an LLB and a Law Faculty, given Irvine's apparent ambivalence. Without some undertakings, the job would have seemed a dead-end to a young advocate of high scholarly achievements. Obviously, he not only knew of the Cooper Inquiry when he applied (and incidentally, it appears that he was recommended for the Chair by Cooper[135]), but also of its conclusions by the time of his interview[136], and must have learned how marginal law teaching was at that interview, if he did not already know. However, presumably, Irvine's plan for a Faculty of Law and Commerce, unveiled six months later (and discussed in Chapter 5) was not revealed, as it seems to have been a bomb-shell to all.

Creation of the Chair in Scots Law displaced Bowman from the Lectureship in Scots Law. No doubt on account of his stalwart service since 1939, and the clear foreseeability of the displacement, money was found to appoint him to an unspecified Lectureship in Law in 1949[137]. (Ivan Chalmers' death in 1950 then allowed him to revert to his recently-vacated Jurisprudence lectureship, having, indeed, to set and mark papers for the preceding year[138]).

1946-49: Other Events

There were, of course, a variety of other events over this time. One was that, in May 1946, the London and North Eastern Railway sought to resume the Railway Lectures (discussed in Chapter 3), in broadly the same form as before, to start immediately, and for a fee of £150, plus further fees for examining. A Committee (the Chairman of Council, Principal Fulton and Hugh Carlton) clearly considered this worthwhile, and T L Hird (much noted above) was appointed. He received a handsome £115 (more than half his later Civil Law lectureship salary), with the UCD Council retaining the rest for accommodation and printing[139].

This arrangement continued until 1950-51 (just after the present period), when the Railway Executive, successor to LNER, terminated the relationship on the ground of lack of demand[140].

Also among these events was the Cooper Inquiry. As noted above, in 1949, because relations between UCD and the rest of St Andrews University were so bad, Lord Cooper was asked to chair an inquiry into the matter. Hugh Carlton (as non-professorial Head of Department) had made representations to it (as did Christian Bisset as Depute Town Clerk, and Patrick Cumming as College Secretary), largely on constitutional matters.

But what did it say about Law? As it was chaired by the Lord President of the Court of Session, it might have been expected that his Report would consider Law's position. However, his Report said little on the subject, save to note numbers of staff and graduates; that some UCD departments required "concurrent training in Arts subjects, typical instances [including] the Department of Law, which now aims at the LLB Degree"; and that UCD should concentrate on "Law, Engineering, Social Studies and the like"[141]. In any case, as noted above and in Chapter 5, the Report as a whole was a failure, and overtaken by the Tedder Report.

And finally among these events, while Senate was considering the draft Ordinance for the Scots Law Chair, it agreed to take part in a Conference of Scottish Universities on Law Degrees, appointing Carlton (shortly to embark upon his dispute about admissions) and the College and University Secretaries to attend. It approved their Report in February 1949[142].

Matters discussed by the Conference included the automatic recognition of *pro tanto* passes[143] (rejected), the creation of higher degrees (deferred), and a new draft BL and LLB Ordinance prepared by Glasgow (a useful basis for discussion, and considered in next Chapter). This

Ordinance also sought to tighten up limitation of studies[144] regulations, and make Conveyancing compulsory again for both degrees. Further, for the LLB, Private International Law, probably as part of an extended Scots Law class, should be substituted for Public International Law. For the BL, a full-time year of Arts prerequisite should be reimposed. This last seems bizarre, and ought to have raised again the question of why there were two law degrees, and how far law graduates needed a liberal education. However, so far as St Andrews University was concerned, the proposal was not taken forward.

1938-49: People

At the beginning of this period, in addition to the two staff in post at the end of the period covered by the previous Chapter, a further five were appointed for the BL (though one was called up shortly thereafter). They were replaced or supplemented by several more over the years, including the first professor, so the effective strength was between six and eight, varying with the comings and goings and changing of jobs described above[145]. One was a woman.

Despite the twists and turns of staff history, a pattern emerges of continuity, rather than change. This is shown in recruitment. Existing reliance upon solicitors in private practice, which meant reliance on part-time staff, was reinforced in 1939 and 1944-47. Admittedly, one 1939 recruit was a solicitor in public practice; another was, among other things, in private practice as a GP; some were not solicitors; and two were career academics. Further, three such recruits were part-timers only in a special sense, being already employed full-time by the University, but were nevertheless part-time so far as law was concerned. But these exceptions did not alter the general picture. What did, albeit to a limited extent, was the appointment in 1949, at the end of the period, of a full-time professor who was an advocate, and became a career academic.

Continuity is again shown in length of service. Of the pre-1939 members of staff, one retired in this period after forty-six years, while the other, and three of the 1939 recruits, remained in post for the whole of it and, indeed, in those three cases, well beyond. Three others recruited in 1944-47, and 1949, also remained for the whole of this period and beyond, or even well beyond. Moreover, those departing did so chiefly through retirement or death, rather than employment elsewhere, though two are, for different reasons, exceptions.

But, there was change, paradoxically chiefly shown in the ability of most staff, although part-timers, teaching their classes on top of their day-jobs, and in some cases, other duties, too, to turn their hands to anything, moving from Jurisprudence to Scots Law (and back to Jurisprudence just after this period); from Constitutional Law to Scots Law (at short notice) and then to Jurisprudence; from Scots Law (very briefly, but at short notice) to Civil Law (after a brief gap, and having also taken on the Railway Lectures), and even from early medieval history to Constitutional Law & History. Also one undertook Constitutional Law on top of Evidence & Procedure for several years.

Of these various members of staff, two, Allison and Carlton, were discussed in the last Chapter. About some others, what little is known is recorded in endnotes, but the three most prominent remaining staff deserve fuller treatment.[146].

Bernard Clifford Bowman OBE (1908-1993)[147], a Forfar man like Thomas Thornton, and universally known as "Ben", took a St Andrews MA and an Edinburgh LLB. He joined Gray, Robertson & Wilkie (today, significantly, simply Bowmans) in Dundee in 1932, was made partner in 1936, senior partner in 1971, and consultant from 1984. An obituary (not a statement on oath, but probably true) described him as "one of the most senior and respected figures in the legal profession in Dundee", and he was awarded an OBE for services to the legal profession in 1988.

As a prominent member of the profession, he undertook a number of associated roles, including Clerk to the Guildry Incorporation of Dundee, and was for a time a director of the local board of the

Commercial Union Insurance Company, Secretary of the Blyth's Benevolent Trust, and an Honorary Sheriff from 1971 (recognised twenty years later as, apparently, the longest serving in such a role). He was prominent in the FPSD[148], elected Dean 1968-71, and was an honorary member from 1987.

But in addition, he had been appointed lecturer in Jurisprudence in the great recruitment of 1939 in anticipation of the BL degree. He was transferred to Scots Law, then back to Jurisprudence, as well as being Adviser of Studies in 1948, sitting on numerous committees, and becoming Dean of the Law Faculty 1969-71. Indeed, he was continuously on the staff, albeit part-time, until 1974, and was an honorary lecturer for a decade after that. His relationship with students was avuncular and, at least in later years, his teaching was observed to stick closely to the recommended book.

His academic duties must have taken up a considerable proportion of his working time since, until 1949, there was no full-time member of staff. After that, there was one, Arthur Matheson, but in 1958 he became Master of Queen's College Dundee (QCD), and therefore unavailable for many Faculty duties. And through the war years, Bowman was simultaneously partner in a firm, lecturer in the Law School and a civil servant in the Ministry of Food. Also, after that, he was simultaneously Senior Lecturer, Dean of the Faculty of Law and Dean of the FPSD. Thus, he was thus something of a Grand Old Man of the Law Faculty for a generation or more.

He was also much involved in music (becoming president of the Dundee Music Club) and sport, in later years recounting to students that in his own student days, he could leave home in Forfar to go to St Andrews to attend lectures by train (changing at Dundee and Leuchars), and return to Forfar by the same means, in time to play professional football for Forfar Athletic.

One of his sons, Neil, was a law student in QCD from 1964-67, and later a partner in the firm, but has since moved on.

Christian Bisset (later Tudhope) OBE (1905-1997)[149] (daughter of C J Bisset OBE, noted in Chapter 2) was Grand Old Lady of the Faculty to Ben Bowman's Grand Old Man, among other things living to the age of 92.

A pioneer in numerous ways, she was one of the earliest UCD woman law students, though in slightly curious circumstances[150]. She graduated MA (Hons) in St Andrews University in 1926[151]: she then appears to have taken Scots Law as a non-graduating student, as she received a First Class Certificate in the subject in 1927[152] (continuing a family tradition[153]): she then entered Edinburgh University, graduating LLB in 1929, relying on the non-graduating pass in Scots Law to obtain a *pro tanto* pass in that subject[154]. Why this path was pursued is unclear. Did she take Scots Law in UCD to discover if her talents lay in that direction? Did she intend to qualify without a law degree, but change her mind in the light of the Scots Law result? In any event, her obituary, no doubt accurately, described her as "the first woman in [Dundee] to obtain the degree of Bachelor of Laws".

Her pioneering continued, in that, in 1930, she qualified as a solicitor, becoming possibly the first woman law agent in Dundee, and she was certainly the first woman member of the FPSD in 1933. Her career continued in local authority practice, in the Town Clerk's Office, where she became the first woman Depute Town Clerk[155]. This led to her sitting on a number of committees on reform of Scots Law, including the Mackintosh Committee, which resulted in the Succession (Scotland) Act 1964. She also became the first woman president of the Scottish Association of National Health Service Executive Councils. In 1965, she was awarded an OBE for public service. Yet further, she was a founder member of the Soroptimist Club of Dundee.

From the present point of view, her pioneering is most interesting in that, in 1939, she was one of those recruited to the new BL degree, teaching Evidence & Procedure (but also Constitutional Law & History in the war years), which she continued to do until 1972. She thus became not only the first woman on the law staff in Dundee, but the first woman legal academic in Scotland[156]. (She also became Warden of Macintosh Hall, a women's residence in St Andrews in the 1960s, continuing after the Dundee/St Andrews split, until 1970). Christian Bisset changed her name in 1949, upon marriage to George Tudhope, lecturer in pathology[157].

Arthur Alexander Mathcson (1919-1981)[158] (whose father, Charles Matheson, was a school master[159]) went to Daniel Stewart's College in Edinburgh where he was Dux and Gold Medallist, and then first to Balliol College, Oxford (traditional destination of many a Scottish student), followed by Edinburgh University, where he received a First in his MA (specialising in classics), and a distinction in the LLB, also obtaining a Guthrie Fellowship in Classics and a Vans Dunlop Scholarship in Public Law[160].

These distinctions clearly suggest a considerable scholar, though he published nothing during his academic career, no doubt in part because little was published in law in those days; in part, perhaps, because he took advantage of his job description permitting opinion work; in part because of the burdens of administration noted below; and in part because, at least in later years, he suffered chronic ill-health and died at a relatively early age.

He does not appear to have undergone national service, and was admitted advocate in 1944, devilling to Sir J Randall Phillip, who paints an attractive picture of him (involving a surprising talent for light verse)[161]. He appeared to commence pursuit of a normal path for an ambitious advocate, being Junior Counsel to the Ministry of Trade (Scotland) from 1947 to 1949. However, his academic interests rapidly came to the fore, insofar as in 1949, five years after call, he was appointed Professor of Scots Law (Phillip claiming "a share in securing his appointment"). He was appointed QC in 1956 (at the same time as T B Smith)[162]. At the time of writing, the writ conferring the status hangs in the Scrymgeour Building, as does his grant of arms.

He chiefly taught Scots law, but initially also Public International Law. However, at least after the first few years, he did not give many

Scots Law classes, no doubt in part at least because of his administrative duties, and illness. Unsurprisingly, as the first, and for a time only, full-time member of the law staff, he was Dean of the Faculty of Law from 1955-1958, and again 1963-1964. In addition, he was also Master of QCD from 1958-66, thus during the negotiations preceding the separation from St Andrews, in which his contribution was "outstanding"[163].

In 1950, he was appointed Honorary Sheriff-Substitute, was Deputy Chairman of the Dundee Valuations Appeal Committee from 1957 to 1966, and Chancellor of the Diocese of Brechin from 1957 till his death, and of that of Aberdeen and Orkney from 1968 to 1972.

Turning from individuals to generalities, as most of the law staff remained part-timers, they spent most of their time, for most of the year, in the office, working as solicitors in private practice (or local government), though necessarily also spending time preparing lectures, and examining, as in the preceding forty years (though for the first time, some tutorials, while still not required by the governing Ordinance, and difficult to arrange with part-time staff, may also have been provided). However, two or three factors must have made their experience somewhat different from that of that period covered by the previous Chapter.

Firstly, there were now several of them, and all must already have known each other, and have been already interacting in professional and social settings. However, it is doubtful whether they enjoyed a corporate life as lecturers, precisely because they were part-timers[164]. Secondly, there was now a BL, and some staff, notably Carlton and then Bowman, were deeply involved in creating and then running the law school. But thirdly, most of the period was war-time, which must have made teaching a much more difficult task, in particular for part-timers in short-staffed firms, in addition to all the other exigencies. And as noted above, several showed considerable flexibility in the subjects they taught.

We have some idea of the lecturing style of some of them, insofar as memory stretches to their later years. For example, as described above, Bowman is probably remembered by those he taught as avuncular and given to anecdote, though heavily reliant upon the textbook. Hird, as described above, is probably remembered by those he taught as unapproachable and seemingly "on automatic pilot"[165]. Matheson is probably remembered as distant and precise, though well-disposed towards students (but also latterly somewhat disorganised).

So far as students are concerned, as noted in the previous Chapter, the sources for information on the number, gender and characteristics, the difficulties they present, and the consequent tentativeness of conclusions, are discussed in the Annex on Sources of Information on Student Sources.

Entrant numbers are of increased interest in this period because, while non-graduating entrants continued, BL students appear for the first time, although for the usual reasons, numbers can only be very approximate. Subject to this, we can say that BL entrant numbers, disappointingly but unsurprisingly, appear to have been low during the War years, seemingly varying between six and none, save conceivably in 1940-41 (for which we have no information), and certainly in 1942-43 (when they were inflated to twelve by the presence of Polish "soldier-students", discussed above and below). In the immediate post-War years they seem to have been consistently somewhat higher, but still probably disappointing, varying between six and twelve. Overall, there were at least 60 BL entrants over these years. (The lack of information for 1940-41 and the addition of Polish "soldier-students" in 1942-43, make any estimate of an average for the War years meaningless, but more meaningfully, the probable total of 32 entrants in the immediate post-War years gives an average of, say eight a year).

Women BL entrants were relatively rare (indeed seemingly rarer than women non-graduating entrants before the War), with none in some half of the years, and two in the other half (ignoring 1940-41, for which we have no information), thus totalling perhaps ten (say, 17%).

Non-graduating entrant numbers while, unsurprisingly, perhaps halving on the outbreak of War, seem to have shown a roughly similar trajectory to that of BL entrants, albeit at a higher level, during the War years, apparently varying between sixteen and four (though for 1940-41 we have no information, and for 1941-42 the number is particularly uncertain). Immediately post-War, non-graduating entrant numbers picked up rapidly, probably rising from eight a year to 45 a year, thus matching pre-War entrant numbers. As in the period covered by the previous Chapter, few seem to have taken Conveyancing, however, suggesting that many were accountancy students (though law students might have taken the subject elsewhere, while undertaking part of their apprenticeship there). Overall, there were at least 150 non-graduating law entrants (an average of, say, fifteen a year), including over a hundred in the post-War years (an average of, say, 25 a year).

Women non-graduating entrant numbers seemingly varied between none and three, giving an overall number of some fourteen (say, 10%). As in the period covered by the previous Chapter, few took Conveyancing, so many were probably accountancy students.

Total entrant numbers are, of course, the sum of these two cohorts, so overall there were well over 200 law entrants, of whom perhaps 25 were women (say, 13%). For what it is worth, these numbers (presumably a matter of moment to the University) show a steady dip from 22 in 1939-40, down to four in 1944-45 (when, incidentally, James Allison resigned), then up to 51 in 1949-50. There is little evidence of progress towards any greater representation of women among law students implicit in Mary Ann Baxter's desire to "promot[e] ... the education of persons of both sexes[166]. But the most important conclusion is that the BL remained marginal, and law teaching was again possibly preserved by accountancy.

And as to identities, as in the previous Chapter, we can again note some sub-groups. Different records[167] produce different sets of names, but women who are recorded in this period are, chronologically, Eve Laburn (entered 1940), Elizabeth Malcolm[168] (1942), Jess M Page[169] (1942), Margaret Walker (1942), Anne Yule (1943), Marjory Munro (1944), Isobel Ross[170] (1944), Agnes Duncan (1945), Anne McKerchar[171] (1945), Kathleen Husband (1945), Agnes McCracken (1946), Moira Morgan (1946), Vivien Scott (1946), Pamela Halley (probably 1948[172]), Helen

Johnston (probably 1949[173]), and Jean Kinmond (undated, and conceivably in the previous period).

Of these, the graduates were Jess M Page and Margaret Walker in 1945[174] (thus joint first graduating women), Anne McKerchar[175] and Agnes Duncan[176] in 1948, Moira Morgan and Vivien Scott in 1949[177], Pamela Halley in 1951[178], and Helen Johnston in 1952[179] (the last-mentioned pair graduating in the next period, so mentioned again in Chapter 5).

High achievers include the first two BL graduates, in 1942, Alan Salt Brand[180] and William Scott McCulloch[181], and the winners of the FPSD Scots Law and Conveyancing prizes, Robert S Swinton[182] and Alexander Wanless, respectively[183] in 1948-49 (the first year of operation), and I D Stuart and (again) R S Swinton, respectively[184] in 1949-50.

Names of those of significance to the law school, and familiar to later generations, include A J W R Coupar (noted above) and I M S Robertson (noted in Chapter 6)[185], who later became Conveyancing Assistant and part-time lecturer in Mercantile Law, respectively.

The numbers of graduates being so small, no attempt has been made to draw conclusions on origins and destinations, or on any other information, save in respect of the Polish "soldier-students" (considered below).

Also as with the previous period, it is difficult to catch the student experience. There were now, of course, BL students in addition to non-graduating ones. Nevertheless, apart from the fact that they were students for three years, rather than one or two, their experience must have been essentially similar. All were still part-timers, living at home and commuting, while working in a law office most of the time[186], and the fact that most of the period was in war-time must have affected students as it had staff, including the possibility, if not volunteering, of conscription into the armed forces[187].

Teaching may have remained largely tied to the traditional lecture though, as noted above, for the first time tutorials (while not required by the governing Ordinance, and difficult to arrange with part-time staff and students) may have been provided, and the small numbers may have allowed departures[188]. There are references to Library acquisitions, but no clue as to what was acquired, save that subscriptions are not mentioned, so it does not seem likely that there were *Session Cases*, the *Scots Law Times*, or any other series of reports. Thus, it seems unlikely that there was much of a Law Library. Alastair McDonald recalled, when he arrived in 1955, "a small room at the west end of the western front building facing Perth Road, which housed the Law Library, and was furnished with a desk and two or three chairs"[189]. However, law apprentices presumably still had access to their firm's libraries and to the FPSD library in the Sheriff Court[190].

Students' ability to participate in clubs and societies, the Student Representative Council, the Student Union, Charities or Gaudie Night and Raisin Monday, or indeed (of some interest in war-time) the Officer Training Corps (from an unknown date) and University Air Squadron (from 1941), all remained much less than that of their Arts and Science contemporaries.

Senate Minutes continue to contain references to disciplinary matters, though most referred to the St Andrews "campus". However, one reference specifically related to a law student in UCD, who was observed by an invigilator to be using notes during an examination. On being challenged, the culprit confessed. The Faculty of Arts recommended that this person's examinations be cancelled and s/he not be allowed back until Senate gave permission, but Senate decided upon expulsion[191]. We do not know his or her name.

In addition to these "standard" students, and clearly displaying very different characteristics and undergoing a very different experience, there were the Polish "soldier-students", who deserve special mention. As noted above, they came to Dundee after the invasions of Poland and France. In 1940, the Polish Embassy asked the University for facilities for Polish refugees (not necessarily soldiers), and one or two seem to have been accepted in UCD, though none in law[192]. Relations with these displaced Poles were clearly good, as in 1941, General Sikorski, Commander-in-Chief of Polish Forces and nominal Prime Minister-in-exile, was given an honorary degree[193]. And later in 1941, "as a result of proposals put forward by the Regional Committee for Adult Education, acting in conjunction with the Polish Headquarters, a number of Polish Students were desirous of taking the [Constitutional Law & History] class"[194].

Arrangements were made for them to be admitted at the lecturer's discretion[195]. Christian Bisset's offer, noted above, to run that class in 1941-42 "on a voluntary basis for the benefit of the Polish students", in the absence of local students, shows that some were admitted to it, and there is a note after Court's "Entrant Students" table for that year recording that four Polish and three Czechoslovak students were admitted without fees[196]. They may not have actually been included in the table (and thus constitute a concealed minor increase in numbers of law students), but may have included those taking Constitutional Law & History. Also, in 1942, one Polish soldier-student was recommended for a pass in Scots Law to count towards the BL, which must have been taken in 1941-42 as a non-graduating, possibly non-matriculated, student[197].

Further, in 1942-43, numerous Polish soldier-students, including several in law, were expected, and remarkably (though clearly with the assistance of *pro tantos* from Polish examination passes and possibly of wartime emergency regulations), it was thought that "a certain number might be able to complete a degree by the end of the current Session"[198]. The numbers from the various sources cannot be completely reconciled, but it appears that, in that year and the next, there were some thirty such "soldier-students", including at least eight or ten in law[199]. Without them, some law classes would again have been very depleted. In addition, in that year, nine soldier-students in law sought *pro tanto* passes for Civil Law and Economics examinations passed in various Polish universities, including Cracow, Lvov, Warsaw and Wilno[200]. There is no reference to entrant Polish students in the "Entrant Student" tables for 1943-44 or 1944-45, and the actual numbers of entrant students recorded seem too small to conceal any[201]. Some Poles entered the university in 1946-47, though probably none for Law[202].

Ben Bowman, many years later, at the Faculty of Law Centenary Dinner in 1990, recalled the "unexpected but welcome influx of Polish students", and "remember[ed] them well"[203]. He listed "Slerzynski, Bieszczad, Pietrowski, Skorobohoty, Roll, Sobieraz [all *sic*] and so on" (which, unsurprisingly after nearly 50 years, does not precisely accord with the names recorded). He went on recall that most "had an excellent command of the English language and many of them passed the degree examinations with considerable merit".

Of these "soldier-students", probably six graduated with a BL, ie Jozef Bieszczad and Ryszard Wrobel (1943); Edgar Franciszek Tadeusz Roll and Wladyslaw J Chlebowski (*in absentia*) (1944); Bronislaw Piotrowski (1945, on the day after the VE Day celebrations); and Czeslaw Sercukzewski (1948)[204]. Thus, not only did they increase the size of some small classes significantly, they increased the number of BL graduates as well.

In UCD as a whole, between 1941 and 1950, some ninety Poles (including seven women) graduated[205], about a quarter returning to Poland, with mixed outcomes, but many emigrated to other parts of the Commonwealth, and the USA, as well as going to England & Wales[206]. A list of those whose names are known is given in Appendix 3.

APPENDIX 1

SIMPLIFIED COMPARISON OF SUBJECTS REQUIRED FOR BL UNDER 1911 ORDINANCE, FOR PROFESSIONAL QUALIFICATION UNDER 1938 REGULATIONS, AND PROVIDED BY 1938 BL PLAN

1911 Ordinance	1938 Regulations	1938 BL Plan
(i) Civil law (80 lectures) (ii) Scots law (80 lectures) (iii) one out of: Conveyancing, Constitutional Law or Mercantile Law (all 80 lectures) (iv) one out of: Jurisprudence Forensic Medicine (each 40 lectures) Conveyancing, Constitutional Law or Mercantile Law (if not already taken) (all 80 lectures), or two out of: Public International Law Private International Law Evidence and Procedure another approved History or Law subject (all 40 lectures)	**First Professional Examination** (i) Book-keeping (ii) Constitutional Law **Second Professional Examination** (iii) Roman Law (iv) Elementary Jurisprudence **Third Professional Examination** (v) Scots law (except Trusts and Succession) (vi) Conveyancing (vii) Trusts and Succession (viii) Evidence and Procedure	**First Year** (i) Civil law (ii) Constitutional Law & History **Second Year** (iii) Forensic Medicine (iv) Scots law **Third Year** (v) Jurisprudence (vi) Conveyancing

At least one course of 80 lectures, or two of 40, per year		

APPENDIX 2

ACADEMIC DRESS AND DEPORTMENT

The effort put into choosing a BL hood was remarked upon above. At the risk of the enormous condescension of posterity, the following extracts from Senate and UCD Council Minutes draw attention to themselves:

From 1906[207]: "Graduation Ceremonial – Academic Costume – The Meeting considered questions which had been raised regarding Academic Costume, and the following conclusions were arrived at: - That, although instances may have occurred of the LLD hood having been worn with the full-dress robe of the LLD Degree, the robe, by itself, fully indicates the Degree, and the hood is superfluous when the robe is worn. The same is applicable to all Degrees. The insignia of only one Degree should be worn. As a matter of convenience a Graduand might wear the full-dress robe of any other Degree he holds, and have a new hood put on over such robe at a Graduation Ceremonial. But not more than one hood should be worn, except where at the same graduation Ceremonial a Graduand received two or more Degrees".

From 1934[208]: Senate received recommendations by the Student Representative Council that the wearing of gowns in class, and going to and from classes should be encouraged (though wearing them on bicycles should be "interdicted"); that the growing practice of women not to wear "trenchers" should be discouraged (though they should not made compulsory, as the requirement would not apply to men) and their shape should not be "distorted"; that pipe smoking in academic dress should be forbidden (cigarettes not being mentioned); and also that staff should wear academic dress in class and going to and from them.

From 1951 (possibly displaying some of the more obvious differences of outlook between St Andrews and Dundee): A "Committee on Undergraduate Gowns", convened by Arthur Matheson, was set up[209]. Senate wished to bring individual College Regulations into line, preferring the United College version, which was as follows: "Students shall wear their Gowns not only in attending College classes, but on all academic occasions."

The UCD version, however, was: "Students are expected to wear academic costume during College hours[210]."

The Report took into account that, firstly, accountancy students attended Scots Law classes not for the purpose of graduation, but simply to obtain a certificate of due performance; secondly, the pool of gowns for hire was "quite inadequate", and new gowns cost about £10, so "it would be neither reasonable nor practicable to exclude from classes a student who is unable or unwilling to pay that sum"; and thirdly, that gowns were impractical in practicals in science and medicine.

Matheson's masterly compromise (with no interpretation section, but a lengthy *explication de texte*) was: "Students attending classes for the purpose of graduation are expected to wear the appropriate gown not only at lectures but on all academic occasions." As a result, a reformed gown pool was provided, supported by a £400 fund, with gowns borrowable for £1 a year subject to a £3 deposit, though this was later found underfunded[211], but as late as 1967, there was discussion of the enforceability of the system[212].

APPENDIX 3

Polish "soldier-students" in law recorded in A Frankiewicz (ed) *Polish Students at the University of St Andrews: lives and times of Graduates 1941-1950* (1994) are:

Jozef Bieszczad

Wladyslaw J Chlebowski

Bronislaw Piotrowski

Edgar FT Roll

Czeslaw Sercukzewski

Stanislaw Sobieraj

Ryszard Wrobel

Others not mentioned in Frankiewicz, but recorded in a *Register of Law Students in UCD from 1897-1947*, include Stanislaw Cinoniak (1942), Kazimerz Janigar (1942), Wladyslaw Kosiewicz (1942), Casmir Weker (1942), Mieczyslaw Zawilski (1945), and Jan Zolna (1942).

In addition, Messrs Kosiewicz, Cuiz Niak, Szyz-Szyzieski, Radwanski and Zelan, neither mentioned in Frankiewicz, nor recorded in the *Register of Law Students*, must have attended, as their names appear in Senate Minutes as obtaining *pro tanto* passes.

---

[1] This section summarises chapter 7 of Donald G Southgate, *University Education in Dundee: a centenary history* (1982). This term, and related descriptions, are Southgate's. See also Ronald Gordon Cant, *The University of St Andrews: a short history* 3rd ed (1992) 168-169, which, however, deals with the whole period in less than two pages (and the Cooper Report in one sentence).

Norman H Reid *Ever to Excel: an illustrated history of the University of St Andrews* (2011) does not mention these years in relation to Dundee.

[2] Major-General Douglas Neil Wimberley, CB DSO MC (1896-1983), a career soldier who fought in the First World War, between the Wars served in Ireland, the North West Frontier and the War Office, later commanding the 51st Highland Division at the Battle of El Alamein before retiring from the Army as Director of Infantry.

[3] Southgate, *University Education* 245, quoting Wimberley (without citation).

[4] Thomas Mackay Cooper, PC KC (1892-1955), advocate 1915, MP for Edinburgh West 1935-41, Solicitor General for Scotland, then Lord Advocate, 1935, Lord Justice-Clerk 1941-47, Lord President 1947-54, and author of various works (including TMC "Legal Education in Scotland: a criticism" (1922) XXXVII *SLR* 71-75), on retiral, created 1st Baron Cooper of Culross: see Stephen P Walker, *The Faculty of Advocates: a Biographical Directory of Members Admitted from 1 January 1800 to 31 December 1986* (1987), and F J Grant, *The Faculty of Advocates in Scotland 1532-1943 ...* (1944).

[5] Professor F S Noble, Regius Professor of Humanity at Aberdeen, and Professor A M Tyndall, Chairman of the Executive Committee of the National Physical Laboratory, and formerly Vice-Chancellor of Bristol University.

[6] Report of the Inquiry Appointed in February 1949 to Review and Report on the Organisation of University Education in Dundee and its Relationship with St Andrews University (1949) 1.

[7] Southgate, *University Education* 273, records that, nevertheless: (i) Court was represented by John Cameron, Dean of the Faculty of Advocates, and later Lord Cameron (and father of Lord Cameron of Lochbroom); (ii) UCD Council by J Randall Phillip KC, later Sheriff of Angus (who had known Lord Trayner - "an intimate friend of my father's", became "a dear friend" of General Wimberley - "we decided to call each other by our Christian names", and discussed further below, and see also Fiona Craddock (ed) *The Journal of Sir J Randall Phillip OBE QC: public and private life in Scotland 1947-1957* (1998) 101-103, 245, 374, 500 & 502); and (iii) the Separatist Governors by Hector McKechnie, KC, later Sheriff McKechnie.

[8] Dundee University Archives ("DUA") Recs A/44, University of St Andrews ("UStA") Court Minutes 1937-38, Meeting of 23 March 1938. Full-time lecturers (under the control of a Professor) had had in the previous year a rise to £400, and Senor Lecturers ("in independent charge of Departments") to £500 (both with annual increments): Recs A/107, UCD Council Minutes October 1936-September 1939, Finance Committee Meeting of 15 March 1937.

[9] DUA Recs A/107, UCD Council Minutes October 1936-September 1939, Finance Committee Meetings of 18 April and 19 September 1938; Recs A/44 UStA Court Minutes 1937-38, Meeting of 25 April 1938.

[10] An oddity is that it was not Allison, as senior of the two lecturers, who raised this issue. However, he was by then over 70 and might also have wished, as Convenor of the Ordinances, Draft Ordinances and Regulations Committee of University's General Council (see Chapter 3), to

216

keep his powder dry (though, in the event, this Committee did not comment on the resulting BL or, later, LLB). Also, he had proposed Robert Macgregor Mitchell, as he then was, as General Council Assessor on Court (see Chapter 3) which, in the light of Mitchell's role (discussed below), might also have suggested keeping a low profile.

[11] Regulations for Examination and Admission of Solicitors ... 19 March 1937, reproduced in annual editions of the *Parliament House Book*. See also Chapter 3, Appendix 4.

[12] I.e. Scots Law, Conveyancing and Forms of Process.

[13] See Chapter 3, Appendix 3.

[14] The Royal Commission on University Education in Dundee (Cmnd 8514: 1952) (the "Tedder Commission").

[15] Ibid., Written Evidence, vol II, Paper 13.

[16] Robert Macgregor Mitchell (1875-1938), MA LLB LLD (St Andrews), after being a solicitor in Perth, became advocate in 1914, briefly becoming Liberal MP for Perth (1923-24), took silk in 1924, and was appointed Chairman of the Scottish Land Court with the courtesy title of Lord Macgregor Mitchell in 1934. He had been elected General Council Assessor on Court in 1933 (see Chapter 3), and Rector in 1937: see Walker, *Biographical Directory* and Grant, *Faculty of Advocates*.

[17] DUA Recs A/44, UStA Court Minutes 1937-38, Meeting of 23 March 1937.

[18] *Glasgow Herald* 26 April 1938, 18, recorded that he was the first Rector to preside at Court for many years, that he had not even been officially installed, and that he died just before the meeting commenced. (University of St Andrews Archives ("UStAA") UY 615, University of St Andrews General Council Minutes 25 June 1938 renders this as him dying "as he moved to take his place at the head of the table"). There is a Court Minute for that meeting which, strangely, is silent on the matter: DUA Recs A/44, UStA Court Minutes 1937-38, Meeting of 25 April 1938. (The incident is inaccurately rendered as "died presiding at Senatus" by Grant, *Faculty of Advocates*.

[19] DUA Recs A/107, UCD Council Minutes October 1936-September 1939, Meeting of 27 June 1938. There is a correction in the Minute, oddly headed "Facilities available for Students in Law at St Andrews".

[20] As noted in Chapter 1, LLB is technically an abbreviation of "Baccalaureus Legum" (Bachelor of *Laws* - plural), and BL of "Baccalaureus Legis" (Bachelor of *Law* - singular).

[21] DUA Recs A/44, UStA Court Minutes 1937-38, Meeting of 6 July 1938.

[22] DUA Recs A/45, UStA Court Minutes 1938-39, Meetings of 23 November (the Minute containing the Memorandum) and 14 December 1938.

[23] In that year, the number of students taking Scots Law was twenty-one, and the number taking Conveyancing eleven, much the same overall total (though with a larger Conveyancing contingent) as for every year since their numbers were first recorded in Court Minutes in 1927: see Annex on Sources of Information on Students. Clearly, he expected most to take a BL if available.

[24] It concerned a mismatch between the requirements for Latin in the 1938 Solicitors' Regulations and the 1911 BL Ordinance.

[25] DUA Recs A/45, UStA Court Minutes 1938-39, Meeting of 14 December 1938.

[26] DUA Recs A/107, UCD Council Minutes October 1936- September 1939, Meeting of 19 December 1938.

[27] See Herman Melville, *Bartleby the scrivener: a story of Wall Street* (1853).

[28] I.e. (Court) Ordinance XXXVII (General No 11) of 1911 (reproduced in Alan E Clapperton (ed), *The Universities (Scotland) Act 1889 together with Ordinances of the Commissioners … and University Court Ordinances* (1915) 506-509, and discussed in Chapter 3.

[29] DUA Recs A/436, UStA Senatus Academicus Minutes 1937-39, Meeting of 20 January 1939.

[30] DUA Recs A/436, UStA Senatus Academicus Minutes 1937-39, Meeting of 10 February 1939.

[31] It included comparisons with Paris, as well as Aberdeen, Edinburgh and Glasgow, and is evidence for the inverse relationship in academic discussions between significance and time spent. The same Minute further records the Principal wishing to emphasise to staff that they should wear gowns in the street: see also Appendix 2.

[32] DUA Recs A/107, UCD Council Minutes October 1936-September 1939, Meeting of 20 February 1939.

[33] DUA Recs A/45, UStA Court Minutes 1938-39, Meeting of 27 February 1939. Although Allison was Convenor of the Ordinances, Draft Ordinances and Regulations Committee of the University's General Council, as noted above, there is no record of the introduction of the BL being discussed there (or indeed of the amendment to the 1893 Ordinance which introduced the BL, or the 1911 Ordinance which amended it, even though the Committee was then convened by James Thomson, also General Council Assessor on Court, who promoted idea of a St Andrews law degree in Court at that time, as discussed in the previous Chapter).

[34] DUA Recs A/45, UStA Court Minutes 1938-39, Meeting of 2 May 1939.

[35] As with Allison's original appointment (see Chapter 3), no nonsense about academic freedom.

[36] These recommendations do not appear in UCD Council Minutes: see DUA Recs A/107, UCD Council, Minutes October 1936-September 1939, Meetings of 20 February & 17 April 1939.

[37] DUA Recs A/45, UStA Court Minutes 1938-39, Meeting of 2 May 1939. These fees are presumably those recommended by UCD Council at Court's invitation, although there is no relevant reference in Recs A/107, UCD Council Minutes October 1936-September 1939, Meetings of 20 February and 17 April 1939.

[38] DUA Recs A/116, UCD Education Board Minutes October 1930-June1940, Meeting of 4 April 1939.

[39] DUA Recs A/45, UStA Court Minutes 1938-39, Meeting of 2 May 1939. Not only was Allison the first Reader in Law, for over 70 years he was the last, the next being Andrea Ross, appointed Reader in 2011 (professor in 2012), followed by Elizabeth Kirk appointed Reader in 2014 (professor at Nottingham Trent University 2016).

[40] DUA Recs A/45, UStA Court Minutes 1938-39, Meeting of 2 May 1939.

[41] Condition 3, that the class fees should be "applied in such manner as the University Court shall from time to time appoint", is an odd one to find in a contract of employment, and inconsistent with the agreement that UCD receive the class fees, and while Condition 1 declares that the lecturer is employed by the Court, Condition 6 specifies that UCD Council is responsible for paying the salary.

[42] Thus graduate of an English (or American) University.

[43] The post was created in 1930 as lecturer in "American and Colonial History", though the Court Meeting appointing him renders this as "Lecturer in Modern and Constitutional History": DUA Recs A/432, UStA Senatus Academicus Minutes 1929-30, Meeting of 23 May 1930.

[44] Much discussed further below.

[45] DUA Recs A/107, UCD Council Minutes 1936-39, Meeting of 19 June 1939. Unsuccessful candidates were Ronald S Aitken, Robert L Dick and Ivan Chalmers (discussed further below), but it is not known who applied for which job.

[46] I am grateful to Dennis Collins for this information.

[47] DUA Recs A/45, UStA Court Minutes 1938-39, Meeting of 26 June 1939.

[48] UStAA UY 452/41, UStA Senatus Academicus Minutes 1938-39, Meeting of 26 May 1939. The oddity is that there they were not already, though possibly "member of Faculty" meant what "member of Faculty Board" meant later (i.e. member of an elected representative body).

[49] A matter remitted, slightly surprisingly, to W L Lorimer, Reader in Humanity (i.e. Latin) in UCD and later Professor of Greek in St Andrews, and W J Nesbit, later Professor of Political Economy.

[50] UStAA UY 452/41, UStA Senatus Academicus Minutes 1938-39, Meeting of 29 June 1939.

[51] Ibid.

[52] DUA Recs A/46, UStA Court Minutes 1939-40, Meeting of 27 November 1939 (when Law students are first recorded other than as an addendum to statistics of attendance).

[53] DUA Recs A/108, UCD Council Minutes October 1939-September 1940, Finance Committee Meeting of 16 October 1939 records seventeen: seemingly there was a drop-out.

[54] See Chapter 3.

[55] DUA Recs A/108, UCD Council Minutes October 1939-September 1943, Meeting of 16 October 1939. A couple of years later, the Librarian managed to acquire £274/9/6 worth of

(unspecified) books from the late Sheriff Malcolm's library for £68: Recs A/108, UCD Council Minutes October 1939-September 1943, Meeting of 20 October 1941.

[56] DUA Recs A/814/2/2, St Andrews University Calendar for the Year 1939-40, at 505 *et seq.,* curiously including (probably standard) specific references to "Admission of Foreign Students" and "Indian Students", but also listing the Teaching Staff and Adviser of Studies for Law Students (Hugh Carlton). At 22, it also recorded a Board of Studies in Law, comprising (mentioned by name) James Allison as Convenor, and (anonymously) "the Lecturers in Conveyancing, Civil Law, Constitutional Law & History, Jurisprudence, Evidence & Procedure, Forensic Medicine, the Professor of History, the Professor of Moral Philosophy, the Lecturer in Economics, the Reader in Latin at Dundee". At 30-32, it records "Examiners for Degrees" but, presumably by oversight, without including any law examiners.

[57] I.e. W M Gloag & R C Henderson, *Introduction to the Law of Scotland.*

[58] I.e. Sir J Salmond, *Jurisprudence,* Sir T E Holland, *Elements of Jurisprudence* and H Maine, *Ancient Law.*

[59] E.g., DUA Recs A/814/2/11, St Andrews University Calendar for the Year 1948-49, 514: Scots law (1) Sources, Courts and Jurisdiction, (2) Obligations and Contract (Sale of Goods, Partnership, Company Law, Agency, Insurance, Cautionary Obligations), (3) Bankruptcy (Trust Deeds for Creditors, Negotiable Instruments, Rights in Security, Diligence), (4) Reparation, (5) Landlord and Tenant, Ownership of Moveables, Patents & Trademarks, Hiring Loan and Deposit, Carriage by Land, Sea and Air, (6) Master and Servant, (7) Husband and Wife, Parent and Child, Succession, (8) Criminal law.

[60] DUA Recs A/46, UStA Court Minutes 1939-40, Meetings of 11 March and 6 May 1940. They included J Randall Phillip, advocate for Constitutional Law & History; RP Masson, lecturer in Aberdeen, for Civil Law and Jurisprudence; and Hugh W Eaton, lecturer in Edinburgh, for Evidence & Procedure. Their duties were heavy, including assisting in setting papers, marking all of them in time for oral examinations, presence at oral examinations, and personal responsibility for making the Pass/Fail returns and Pass Lists, for all of which they received only £5 and first-class rail fare up to 7 guineas.

[61] DUA Recs A/1 107, UCD Council Minutes October 1936-September 1939, Meeting of 17 July 1939: Recs A/814/2, St Andrews University Calendar for the Year 1939-40, 829.

[62] DUA Recs A/422, UStA Senatus Academicus Minutes 1905-08, Meeting of 4 December 1908 (with Professor Steggall, though professor of Natural Philosophy and Mathematics, as Adviser "for Arts in Dundee").

[63] DUA Recs A/423, UStA Senatus Academicus Minutes 1908-11, Meetings of 14 November, 12 December 1910 and 24 March 1911.

[64] Emphasis in original.

[65] DUA Recs A/814/2, St Andrews University Calendar for the Year 1939-40, 829.

[66] UStA UY 452/48 UStA Senatus Academcus Minutes 1945-46, Meeting of 27 June 1947.

[67] UStAA UY 452/43, UStA Senatus Academicus Mintues 1940-41, Meeting of 8 November 1941 records a report on those likely to be conscripted and seeking early examinations. The National Service Act 1939, requiring all men aged 18-41 to register for military service, passed all its Parliamentary stages, including Royal Assent, on 3 September 1939.

[68] DUA Recs A/108, UCD Council Minutes October 1939-September 1943, Meeting of 27 November 1940.

[69] DUA Recs A/48, UStA Court Minutes 1941-42, Meeting of 22 December 1941.

[70] DUA Recs A/108, UCD Council Minutes October 1939-September 1943, Meetings of 16 September and 27 November 1940.

[71] As Depute Town Clerk, her job was arguably somewhat closer to the subject matter of Constitutional Law than was that of a solicitor in private practice. Perhaps more to the point, as a woman over thirty, she was not liable to conscription.

[72] DUA Recs A/108, UCD Council Minutes October 1939-September 1943, Meeting of 20 October 1941.

[73] DUA Recs A/108, UCD Council Minutes October 1939-September 1943, Meetings of Finance Committee, 20 October 1941, and 12 January and 21 September 1942.

[74] DUA Recs A/108, UCD Council Minutes October 1939-September 1943, Meetings of 19 July 1942 and 20 September 1943 (also Recs A/49, UStA Court Minutes 1942-43, Meeting of 17 September 1943). The Committee comprised W H Valentine (Chairman), R A Fulton (Principal) and H J Carlton (Adviser of Studies).

[75] Ivan Chalmers (1908-50), an Aberdonian, attended Robert Gordon's College, MA LLB (Aberdeen), moved to Dundee in 1934 to J & H Pattullo and later in practice on his own account, was Burgh Prosecutor in the Dundee Police Court 1947, also Honorary Secretary of the Abertay Historical Society: Dundee City Library Family and Local History Centre, *Obituaries Notices 1946-57*, 46. He was also *proxime accessit* in 1939 for one or more of the lectureships.

[76] DUA Recs A/109, UCD Council Minutes October 1943-September 1946, Meeting of 17 January 1944.

[77] DUA Recs A/109, UCD Council Minutes October 1943-September 1946, Meetings of 21 January, 18 March and 24 September 1946.

[78] Frederick Wainwright BA PhD (Reading), later "a thorn in the flesh" of Court, as he railed against the limitations upon History teaching imposed upon UCD, was only persuaded to take on Constitutional Law & History ("a galling fate for one pre-occupied with the pre-history of the Picts") if given the assistance of Geoffrey Seed: Southgate, *University Education* 233, 248-49. Praise for his teaching style is recorded below. Presumably he taught it in 1946-47 and 1947-48, although the University Calendars for those years show the post as "vacant" in the former, and has no

name in the latter, his name only appearing in the 1948-49 Calendar: DUA Recs A/418/2/76 to A/418/2/78, St Andrews University Calendars 1946-47 to 1948-49. He certainly taught it later, as discussed in Chapter 5.

[79] DUA Recs A/110, UCD Council Minutes October 1946-September 1948, Finance Committee Meetings, 26 May and 29 September 1947, and 21 June 1948; Recs A/111, UCD Council Minutes October 1948-September 1950, Meetings of 21 June 1948, and 18 July and 26 September 1949.

[80] DUA Recs A/51, UStA Court Minutes 1944-45, Meeting of 25 May 1945.

[81] Minuted at the same meeting of Court which decided that Readerships were awarded on personal merit for "outstanding ability either in research or in teaching", and not on the importance of the subject.

[82] FPSD Minutes 1887-1960, Meeting of 2 August 1945.

[83] Which merely noted that the post was personal, and that a replacement should be advertised at £200. Shortly after, all staff received increases, ranging from £10 to £20: Recs A/109, UCD Council Minutes October 1943-September 1946, Meeting of 17 September 1945.

[84] DUA Recs A/51, UStA Court Minutes 1944-45, Meeting of 5 July 1945.

[85] DUA Recs A/51, UStA Court Minutes 1944-45, Meeting of 11 September 1945. William Low Mitchell (1886-1945), a Glasgwegian, removing to Dundee at the age of one (his father becoming Editor of the *Courier*), attended the High School of Dundee, MA (St Andrews), apprenticed to Reid Johnston & Co, called to the Bar 1910, practised until 1914 when he joined the Black Watch, achieving the rank of Captain, transferred to Divisional Signals and commanded 1st Army Signals School 1917, then in Rhineland Army of Occupation, returned as solicitor with W B Dickie & Co (later part of Thorntons, and thus successor to Thomas Thornton's original firm: see Chapter 2), in the General Strike was "secretary of the organisation for maintaining supplies", also [presumably before joining the Black Watch] vice-chairman of St Andrews Ambulance Association (Dundee Branch) responsible for ambulance trains to Dundee, and "last month ... was appointed to the Readership [*sic*] in Scots Law" at UCD: Dundee *Obituaries Notices 1946-57* 242.

[86] A tiered lecture room, with semi-circular benches, holding perhaps a hundred people, and situated where the Tower Building is now. I am grateful to Dennis Collins for this information.

[87] DUA Recs A/109, UCD Council Minutes October 1943-September 1946, Meeting of 28 November 1945.

[88] Dundee *Obituaries Notices 1946-57* 242; DUA Recs A/109, UCD Council Minutes October 1943-September 1946, Meeting of 17 December 1945.

[89] Thomas Leonard Hird (1909-75) MA LLB (distinction) (Edinburgh) and LLB (London) [External?], WS, son of an Arbroath draper, apprenticed to David Maxwell, then Maxwell, Gill & Pringle (Edinburgh), then Clerk, Oliver, Dewar & Webster (Arbroath), assistant then junior

partner in WB Dickie & Co (William Low Mitchell's firm) 1941, admitted to the FPSD 1942 (and took an active part in its activities), in practice on his own account 1946-50, legal assistant in Town Clerk's Department 1950-? (confusingly, an AT Herd had become Town Clerk in 1948: see Anon, ("General News") 1948 *SLT* 32), Commissioner of the Society of Writers to the Signet 1950, and elected member of the Law Society of Scotland 1950 (presumably one of the first elected, since the Society only came into existence in 1949), appointed by the Law Society to Dundee Local Committee on Legal Aid, and sometime Secretary of the Dundee and District Housing Association: see FPSD Minutes 1887-1960, 6 August 1942 and 31 May 1950; Dundee City Library Family and Local History Centre *Obituaries Obituaries Notices 1974-80,* 50; Anon., *Register of the Society of Writers to Her Majesty's Signet* (1983), and I am grateful to Dennis Collins for further information. TL Hird also undertook the renewed "Railway Lectures" (see below) and from an unknown date was teaching in the Dundee School of Economics (see Chapter 6).

[90] DUA Recs A/109, UCD Council Minutes October 1943-September 1946, Finance Committee Meeting of 18 March 1946.

[91] DUA Recs A/109, UCD Council Minutes October 1943-September 1946, Meeting of 18 March 1946.

[92] James Alexander Rudolf MacKinnon (1888-1955), MA LLB, advocate 1915, examiner to Aberdeen and Edinburgh Universities and Police Examination Board, lecturer in Jurisprudence Edinburgh University 1927-32, Extra Advocate-Depute (Glasgow Circuit) 1929-32, Sheriff-Substitute of Forfarshire at Forfar 1932, and of Perthshire and Angus at Dundee 1946-55, author: see Walker, *Biographical Directory* and Grant, *Faculty of Advocates.*

[93] DUA Recs A/321/1 7(9), UCD, Principal Fulton files 1935-47. David Kinmond Adam (1911-1965) attended the High School of Dundee, Edinburgh University MA (1930) LLB (1933), was apprenticed to Morton, Smart, McDonald and Prosser (Edinburgh), partner in Reid, Johnston, Bell & Henderson 1935, and was a Lieutenant in the Fife and Forfar Yeomanry during the Second World War: Dundee Local and Family History Centre *Obituaries Notices 1957-66,* 245.

[94] DUA Recs A/52, UStA Court Minutes 1945-46, Meeting of 9 July 1946.

[95] DUA Recs A/56, UStA Court Minutes 1949-50, Meeting of 29 September 1950.

[96] DUA Recs A/52, UStA Court Minutes 1945-46, Meeting of 30 July 1946.

[97] DUA Recs A/53, UStA Court Minutes 1946-47, Meeting of 4 December 1946.

[98] It appears initially to have been Carnegie funded in addition to the £4000 for a Scots Law Chair (see below): DUA Recs A/48, UStA Court Minutes 1941-42, Meeting of 9 July 1942. Sadly, by the end of his career, he was clearly seriously ill, and his lectures did not vary over the years, and were illuminated by a particular trope. Several concepts of the Civil Law end in "-io", such as "specificatio" and "confusio". These were identified by the mantra "'specificatio', that is 'specification' minus the final 'n'", "'confusio', that is, 'confusion' minus the final 'n'", and so on: personal direct and vicarious recollection.

[99] DUA Recs A/437, UStA Senate Minutes 1946-48, Meeting of 27 July 1947. A J W R Coupar (later "Robertson-Coupar" - I am grateful to Dennis Collins for this information - under which

names his obituary is indexed in Dundee *Obituaries Notices*) attended the Grove Academy, Broughty Ferry, and obtained a BL at <u>UCD</u>, was apprenticed to Johnstone, Simpson and Thomson, volunteered for the RAF, and awarded a DFM (for "an act or acts of valour, courage or devotion to duty whilst flying in active operations against the enemy") as a sergeant-pilot who successfully crash-landed a badly damaged aircraft after bombing Essen, became a partner in J & H Pattullo (successor to Thomas Thornton's original firm), then worked on his own account as Robertson-Coupar & Co, was also Secretary of the Flax Spinners Association: Dundee City Library Family and Local History Centre *Obituaries Notices,* 14 March 1998.

[100] DUA Recs A/110, UCD Council Minutes October 1946-September 1948, Meetings of 17 December 1947 and 2 August 1948.

[101] DUA Recs A/111, UCD Council Minutes October 1948-September 1950), Meeting of 26 September 1949.

[102] DUA Recs A/231/6, "Memorandum to University Grants Committee", which contains a longer draft, undated but referring to a Council Meeting of 20 December 1943, and a shorter one, seemingly of January 1944, and drafts of a counter-Memorandum (one in corrected galley-proofs), plus related correspondence. The UGC was the means for distribution of Government funding from 1919 to 1989, principally by quinquennial grants.

[103] The longer draft says "local" but this is corrected m/s to "legal".

[104] The shorter draft specifically mentions International Private Law and Mercantile Law, but also suggests as an alternative, converting a "major Lectureship" (clearly Hugh Carlton's) into a part-time Conveyancing Chair.

[105] See Southgate, *University Education* 227 *et seq.*

[106] DUA Recs A/109, UCD Council Minutes October 1943-September 1946, Meeting of 27 March 1944.

[107] DUA Recs A/51, UStA Court Minutes 1944-45, Meeting of 24 November 1944.

[108] James Rattray Gibb (1884-1946), advocate 1915, lecturer on Veterinary Jurisprudence (Royal Dick Veterinary College Edinburgh), Editor *Scots Law Times (Sheriff Court)*, Sheriff-Substitute of Ross and Cromarty and Sutherland at Lerwick 1935-41, also Tain from 1937, of Perthshire and Angus at Dundee 1941-46: see Walker *Biographical Directory* and Grant *Faculty of Advocates*.

[109] DUA Recs A/109, UCD Council Minutes October 1943-September 1946, Meeting of 9 February 1945.

[110] I.e. Emergency Ordinance (St Andrews No 2) (Regulations for Degrees, Diplomas, Certificates, Examinations and Examiners) of 1940, and/or the Emergency Ordinance (St Andrews No 6) (Regulations for Degrees, Diplomas and Certificates), both sub-delegated legislation under the Scottish Universities (Temporary Provisions) Order 1940, No 319, itself delegated legislation under ss 3(1) & 7 of the Chartered and Other Bodies (Temporary Provisions) Act 1939, Part II, 252 and 256-67: collected in W A Fleming (ed), *University Court Ordinances from*

1st January 1925 to 31st July 1947 with … Emergency Ordinances (1948). These allowed Senates, where courses had been interrupted by "war service" or "conditions arising from the war", *int. al.*, to waive requirements in respect of courses of study, periods of attendance and examinations: see DUA Recs A/51, UStA Court Minutes 1944-45, 6 March 1945.

[111] DUA Recs A/51, UStA Court Minutes 1944-45, Meeting of 6 March 1945.

[112] DUA Recs A/109, UCD Council Minutes October 1943-September 1946, Meeting of 22 July 1945.

[113] DUA Recs A/110, UCD Council Minutes October 1946-September 1948, Meeting of 21 July 1947.

[114] DUA Recs A/437, UStA Senatus Academicus Minutes 1946-48, Meeting of 8 November 1946.

[115] DUA Recs A/437, UStA Senatus Academicus Minutes 1946-48, Meeting of 5 March 1948.

[116] DUA Recs A/437, UStA Senatus Academicus Minutes 1946-48, Meeting of 7 May 1948.

[117] DUA Recs A/437, UStA Senatus Academicus Minutes 1946-48, Meeting of 24 June 1948.

[118] DUA Recs A/110, UCD Council Minutes October 1946-September 1948, Meeting of 23 June 1947.

[119] FPSD Minutes 1887-1960, Meeting of 7 August 1947.

[120] DUA Recs A/54, UStA Court Minutes 1947-48, Meeting of 14 October 1947.

[121] (Court) Ordinance No 249 (St Andrews No 45) (Foundation of Chair of Scots Law). The recital rehearsed that the Carnegie Trust had granted £4,000 to endow the Chair which, with interest, had grown to £4,140; that a total of £8,140 was thus available; and that "the importance of the … subject … requires that the Lectureship in Scots Law should be converted into a Chair …" (this last indicating both the probable source of the other £4,000 of the endowment). Once more, the Ordinances, Draft Ordinances and Regulations Committee of the General Council, was silent.

[122] DUA Recs A/54, UStA Court Minutes 1947-48, Meeting of 23 September 1948.

[123] Garnet Wilson (1885-1975), of the Wilson's Corner (the junction of Murraygate and Commercial Street) department store family, local politician and businessman, Lord Provost 1940-46, President of UCD 1946-52, credited with facilitating Dundee's post-war industrial revival.

[124] Kenneth Douglas Cullen (1889-1956), MA LLB, advocate 1919, law reporter 1927-37, editor of *Faculty Digest of Decisions* 1929-36, junior counsel to the Post Office (Sc) 1934, Honorary Sheriff-Substitute of Fife and Kinross 1936, Sheriff-Substitute at Roxburgh, Berwick and Peebles 1937-41, of Argyll and Bute at Dunoon 1942-5, of Perth and Angus at Dundee 1945-46 (also son of Lord (William James) Cullen, Senator of the College of Justice 1909-29 and father of Lord (William Douglas) Cullen, Senator of the College of Justice 1986-2005, Lord Justice Clerk 1997-2001, Lord President 2001-2005): see Walker, *Biographical Directory* and Grant, *Faculty of Advocates.*

[125] Kenneth William Bruce Middleton (1905-1995), MA LLB, advocate 1931, Military Department Judge Advocate-General's Department 1941-45, Sheriff-Substitute (later Sheriff) of Perth and Angus at Forfar 1946-50, Sheriff of Lothian and Borders at Edinburgh and Haddington 1950-86, member of Departmental Committee on Criminal Procedure 1970, author: see Walker, *Biographical Directory* and Grant, *Faculty of Advocates*.

[126] John William More (1879-1959), MA, BA, advocate 1905, Sheriff-Substitute of Aberdeenshire, Kincardine and Banff at Banff 1919-39, of Fife and Kinross at Cupar 1939-50: see Walker, *Biographical Directory* and Grant, *Faculty of Advocates*.

[127] DUA Recs A/55, UStA Court Minutes 1948-49, Meeting of 14 December 1948: full terms and conditions are in the Minutes of 2 July 1949. J Randall Phillip (noted above), observed shortly before this time, in relation to the recently vacated Edinburgh Chair of Scots Law (then in the gift of the Faculty of Advocates, and for which he had been encouraged to apply), that it had become more lucrative, but full-time, as "the Professor [was] only … entitled to produce opinions, apart from the work of the Chair. But what are opinions worth anything unless the author of them has to defend them in Court? The new system of appointment is calculated to exclude the most ambitious and enterprising Counsel from competing". Seemingly, he nevertheless recommended the successful candidate: see Craddock, *Journal of Sir Randall Philip* 16 & 41.

[128] DUA Recs A/55, UStA Court Minutes 1948-49, Meeting of 2 July 1949. The appointing committee was Sir G Wilson, Principal Wimberley, Professor Copson, Sheriff Cullen, with P Cumming (by then no longer teaching Civil Law) in attendance, but not Principal Irvine.

[129] James John (Hamish) Gow, 1918-2009, author of numerous articles from the 1950s in the *Juridical Review* and elsewhere, of *The Law of Hire Purchase in Scotland* (1961) and of *The Mercantile and Industrial Law of Scotland* (1964), an Aberdeen BL graduate, appointed to a lectureship there in 1951, obtaining a PhD in 1952, leaving for a post in Tasmania in 1954, and by 1964 was professor at McGill University, but was unsuccessful in an application for the new Lord President Reid Chair in Edinburgh in 1972 (when W A (Bill) Wilson was appointed). However, he was appointed judge of the County Court in Vancouver, and of the Supreme Court of British Columbia, and on retiral from that, returned to practice see http://www.sln.law.ed.ac.uk/2010/02/25/j-j-hamish-gow-1918-23-february-2009/ (last accessed 29 July 2018): I am grateful to Ross Macdonald for drawing my attention to this.

[130] DUA Recs A/111, UCD Council Minutes October 1948-September 1950, Meeting of 18 July 1949.

[131] DUA Recs A/74, UStA Senatus Academicus Minutes 1948-50, Meetings of 13 & 14 October 1949.

[132] DUA Recs A/74, UStA Senatus Academicus Minutes 1948-50, Meeting of 13 October 1949.

[133] Indeed, arguably, the first ever, as the "professorial" style of teaching, with one expert per subject, was only introduced in St Andrews in 1747: see Cant, *University of St Andrews* 38, 63, 108-09.

[134] FPSD Minutes 1887-1960, 4 August 1949.

[135] Southgate, *University Education* 287. Despite doubts, noted above, as to the desirability of an ambitious advocate taking a Chair, but possibly taking account of "that tender sensitive nature which makes his mind so distinctive", a "share in securing his appointment" was claimed by J Randall Phillip, who was his devil-master (i.e. equivalent of an apprentice-master: on "devilling", see Chapter 1) and, as son of the manse of Invergowrie and FP of the High School of Dundee, had a Dundee connection and was acquainted with Hugh Carlton: see Craddock, *Journal of Sir J Randall Phillip* 63, 115, 192, 372-373 & 451.

[136] The timing of the appointment process to the Chair of Scots Law curiously closely paralleled that of the Cooper Inquiry. The Inquiry was set up in February 1949, shortly after Court had decided on the terms and conditions for the Chair; the post was presumably advertised thereafter, possibly co-inciding with the Inquiry's visit to Dundee in April, which Southgate, *University Education* records at 274; and its Report published on 24 June 1949 33, just a week before interviews were held.

[137] DUA Recs A/111, UCD Council Minutes October 1948-September 1950, Meeting of 26 September 1949.

[138] DUA Recs A/56, UStA Court Minutes 1949-50, Meeting of 29 September 1950.

[139] DUA Recs A/109. UCD Council Minutes October 1943-September 1946, Meeting of 20 May 1946.

[140] DUA Recs A/56, UStA Court Minutes, 1944-45, Meeting of 6 July 1950; Recs A/58, UStA Court Minutes 1951-52, Meeting of 6 November 1951: see also miscellaneous correspondence and Minutes of Law and LNER Education Lectureships (including a syllabus and account of preceding discussions) in Recs A/321/4, UCD , Principal Fulton files 1935-47. "Solatium" of £50 was offered to the Economics lecturer to compensate for non-continuance.

[141] *Cooper Inquiry* Appendices A & B.

[142] DUA Recs A/437, UStA Senatus Academicus Minutes 1946-48, Meeting of 6 February 1948.

[143] I.e. credit for passes obtained elsewhere.

[144] I.e. "progress".

[145] Economics, as taken by very few BL students, is ignored.

[146] The information given here is largely taken from the *Courier* news stories and obituaries, but also personal recollection, including that of Dennis Collins.

[147] See obituary *Dundee Courier* 26 January 1993: I am grateful to Dennis Collins for providing me with a copy.

[148] E.g. on the Apprenticeships Committee (with, *int. al.* Hugh Carlton): FPSD Minutes 1887-1960, Meetings of 6 August 1953, 5 August 1954, 7 February 1957 and 6 August 1959.

[149] See obituary *Dundee Courier* 4 September 1997. I am grateful to Dennis Collins for providing me with a copy, and to Peter Robson for additional information..

[150] I am grateful to Peter Robson, and Scott Docking of the Edinburgh University Library Centre for Research Collections for helping unravel the curiosity.

[151] DUA Recs A/430 UStA Senate Minutes 1925-27, Meeting of 8 October 1926.

[152] DUA Recs A/814/1/39 UCD Calendar Forty-fifth Session 1927-28.

[153] In Chapter 3, her father, Christopher Johnston Bisset, was noted as a prize-winner in one of the first cohorts in UCD.

[154] I am grateful to Scott Docking for this information.

[155] See Anon, ("General News") 1948 *SLT* 32.

[156] I am grateful to Peter Robson for this information.

[157] She did not suffer the indignity later visited upon Miss Brown, Director of Physical Education for Women in Queen's College who, fifteen years later was required to resign upon marriage "in accordance with the conditions of her contract": DUA Recs A/70, UCD Council Minutes 1963-64, Meeting of 6 January 1964.

[158] See Walker, *Biographical Directory* and Grant, *Faculty of Advocates,* and *Dundee Courier* 10 April 1956 and 20 May 1958 24 December 1981. I am grateful to Dennis Collins for providing me with copies.

[159] I am grateful to Dennis Collins for this information.

[160] Currently "[a] scholarship, to the value of £1,000 maximum, … awarded to a student who has passed within three years immediately prior to the date of the award the last exams necessary for graduation in Law. The holder must pursue a course of advanced study in law approved by the School during his or her tenure, and must not undertake any other employment or course of study except with the consent of the School": see http://www.ed.ac.uk/schools-departments/student-funding/current-students/university-prizes-awards/ humanities/law (last accessed 29 July 2018).

[161] See Craddock, *Journal of Sir J Randall Phillip* index.

[162] Anon, "New Queen's Counsel" 1956 *SLT* 84. Sir Thomas Smith was Professor of Scots Law at Aberdeen at the time, was later Professor of Civil Law at Edinburgh University, a Law Commissioner and General Editor of the *Stair Memorial Encyclopaedia of the Laws of Scotland.*

[163] Southgate, *University Education* 325.

[164] In the late 1940s and 1950s, there was a Staff Club on the ground Floor of the Old Technical Institute: I am grateful to Dennis Collins for this information.

[165] It is regrettable that some students gave insufficient respect to an ill man.

[166] Reproduced in General Report of the 1889 Commissioners 186, as a Schedule to the Commissioners' Order of 21 March 1890 (see next note); and is quoted in Southgate, *University Education* 74-76.

[167] I.e. principally, University of St Andrews Students of University College (DUA 378.413 3 U 58), Dundee and Medical School 1897-1947 and Register of Law Students in UCD from 1897-1947 (DUA Recs A/665), (discussed in the Annex on Sources of Information on Students) and UStA Senate Minutes.

[168] A related record refers to "Guthrie L Malcolm", but no address is given.

[169] Later, *int. al.,* author of a Dundee-based children's book *The Three Elizabeths* (1950), and Town Clerk of Wick: see DUA KLoc/157: I am grateful to Kenneth Baxter for drawing this to my attention.

[170] An accountancy student, sister of the future Lord Justice Clerk Ross: I am grateful to Dennis Collins for this information.

[171] A related entry is "Duncan W McKerchar", at the same address, who was Anne McKerchar's brother, their father being partner in J&H Pattullo & Donald: I am grateful to Dennis Collins for this information.

[172] Not in *Register*, but Senate Minutes show graduated in 1951.

[173] Not in *Register*, but Senate Minutes show graduated in 1952.

[174] UStAA UY 452/47, UStA Senatus Academicus Minutes 1944-45, Meeting of 29 June 1945.

[175] DUA Recs A/437, UStA Senatus Academicus Minutes 1946-48, Meeting of 25 June 1948

[176] DUA Recs A/74, UStA Senatus Academicus Minutes 1948-50, Meeting of 8 October 1948.

[177] DUA Recs A/74, UStA Senatus Academicus Minutes 1948-50, Meeting 30 June 1949.

[178] DUA Recs A/75, UStA Senatus Academicus Minutes 1950-52, Meeting 29 June 1951: the other 1948 women entrant appears not to have graduated.

[179] DUA Recs A/75, UStA Senatus Academicus Minutes 1950-52, Meeting 4 July 1952: the other 1949 women entrant appears not to have graduated.

[180] Whose sons David and Steven graduated from Dundee Law School in 1972 and 1976, respectively, and became partners in Thorntons. The former also became a Senior Lecturer in the Law School in 1997, and Director of the Diploma in Legal Practice 2000-2010, when he retired.

[181] UStAA UY 452/44, UStA Senatus Academicus Minutes 1941-42, Meeting of 26 June 1942.

[182] Whose son, Ken Swinton graduated from the Dundee Law School in 1976, at the time of writing had recently retired from being Subject Leader of Law, and Senior Lecturer in Law, in the University of Abertay, Dundee, and a Council Member of the Law Society of Scotland and was past President and Council Member of the Scottish Law Agents Society.

[182] DUA Recs A/111, UCD Council Minutes October 1948-September 1950, Meeting of 17 October 1949.

[183] Ibid.

[184] DUA Recs A/111, UCD Council Minutes October 1948-September 1950, Meeting of 17th July 1950.

[185] DUA Recs A/437, UStA Senatus Academicus Minutes 1946-48, Meeting of 27 July 1947

[186] A curious article of this time compares the part-time experience of law students with the full-time experience of others: HLM "The Faculty [sic] of Law looks on", "*The College: the official publication of the Student Representative Council of University College, Dundee*" (1940-41) vol XX [sic] No 4 (February 1941).

[187] The National Service (Armed Forces) Act 1939 (which passed all its Parliamentary stages on 3 September 1939, required all men aged 18-41 to register for military service (later extended to men aged up to fifty if unmarried, and women 18-30 if childless) but students were exempted from actual conscription.

[188] Lecturing was not necessarily inadequate, but any inadequate lecturing was not solely a St Andrews problem. In Edinburgh, Professor Montgomery (Scots Law) copied out Gloag and Henderson *Introduction to the Law of Scotland* in his own hand, then read it out, with the result that, on an occasion in 1948, mistaking his own handwriting, he read out "fencing" for "feuing". I am grateful to Alastair McDonald for this recollection. See also John W Cairns & Hector L MacQueen *Learning and the Law: a short history of Edinburgh Law School* (2011) 22 & 24. In any case, at least in the 1950s, "although meant to be by lectures [teaching] was frequently done much more on a tutorial or seminar basis ... [and Frederick Wainwright, for instance] ... rather deplored the formal teaching in a classroom, and much of [his] teaching was done in the Oglivie Bookshop [then within the Queen's Hotel] in the basement of [which] was a very fine coffee room and there the classes of Constitutional Law & History were held ... [and] others used this as an unofficial seminar room": J J Robertson "Random Reflections" (1981) vol. 6 no 4 *Contact* 289.

[189] I am grateful to Alastair McDonald for this information: see next Chapter. Even a few years later "one visiting Law professor, when we showed him the library, commented that he had more books in his own private collection ... [but it] ... was adequate for our purposes ... [though] ... we spent much more money on buying books [than did later generations of students]: Robertson "Random Reflections" (see previous note).

[190] I am grateful to Dennis Collins for some of the above observations.

[191] UStAA UY 452/44, UStA Senate Minutes 1941-42, Meeting of 25 June 1942.

[192] DUA Recs A/46 and A/47, UStA Court Minutes 1939-40 and 1940-41, Meetings of 11 March, 6 & 8 May, 10 July, 28 October and 27 November 1940: see also Anna Frankiewicz (ed), *Polish Students at the University of St Andrews: lives and times of Graduates 1941-1950* (1994) Introduction,

which contains a looseleaf Addendum by Professor Peacock asserting that the initial, informal, arrangements actually commenced in Dundee.

[193] UStAA UY 452/43, UStA Senatus Academicus Minutes 1940-41, Meeting of 28 February 1941.

[194] DUA Recs A/108, UCD Council Minutes October 1939-September 1943, Finance Committee Meeting 20 October 1941: Frankiewicz, *Polish Students* Introduction, refers to an Agreement "minuted" on 22 December 1941, notes "concessions" allowed to those with passes in Polish Universities, and includes Principal Irvine's 1943 graduation address which implies early informal arrangements, but credits General Kukiel with the scheme for seconding students for a year, extended to allow graduation.

[195] DUA Recs A/108, UCD Council Minutes October 1939-September 1943, Finance Committee Meeting 20 October 1941.

[196] DUA Recs A/48, UStA Court Minutes 1941-42, Meeting of 22 December 1941.

[197] UStAA UY 452/45, UStA Senatus Academicus Minutes 1942-43, Meeting of [date missing] October 1942.

[198] DUA Recs A/108, UCD Council Minutes October 1939-September 1943, Meeting of 19 October 1942.

[199] UStAA UY 452/44 to 452/43, UStA Senatus Academicus Minutes, 1941-42 to 1942-43, Meetings of 25 June & 11 December 1942 and 24 June 1943 (showing some 30 enrolled in each year, including eight in law entering in 1942); Recs A/108, UCD Council Minutes October 1939-September 1943, Meetings of 19 October and 21 December 1942 (showing 38 enrolled, including ten in law); Recs A/665, *Register of Law Students* ... , under "Date and Year of Entry" records thirteen enrolled, including nine entering in 1942; Frankiewicz, *Polish Students* Introduction, declares that 82 Poles matriculated in the whole university in 1942-43, including a few civilians.

[200] UStAA UY 452/45, UStA Senatus Academicus Minutes 1942-43, Meetings of 9 October, 13 November 1942 and 28 May 1943.

[201] Frankiewicz, *Polish Students* Introduction, records that most of the Polish soldiers were withdrawn in 1944 in preparation for D-Day.

[202] Frankiewicz, *Polish Students* Introduction.

[203] DUA Recs RU/191, "University of Dundee, Faculty of Law Centenary Dinner ...".

[204] UStAA UY 452/45 to 47 and DUA Recs A/47, UStA Senatus Academicus Minutes, 1942-43 to 1944-45 and 1948-50, Meetings of 25 June 1943, 30 June and 13 October 1944, 29 June 1945 and 8 October 1948. DUA Recs A/437, UStA Senatus Academicus Minutes 1946-48, 11 October 1946 records nine Polish students as "discontinued", but none appear to be law students.

[205] Frankiewicz, *Polish Students* Introduction.

[206] Ibid.

[207] DUA Recs A/422, UStA Senatus Academicus Minutes 1905-08, Meeting of 29 June 1906.

[208] DUA Recs A/435, UStA Senatus Academicus Minutes 1935-37, Meeting of 18 January 1934.

[209] DUA Recs A/112, UCD Council Minutes, October 1950-September 1952, Meeting of 17 September 1951.

[210] It appears that this was only found by combing the Calendar for 1938-39, a dozen years earlier.

[211] DUA Recs A/62, UCD Council Minutes 1955-56, Meetings of 14 November 1955 and 16 April 1956.

[212] DUA Recs A/83 UStA Senatus Academicus Minutes 1966-67, Meeting of 10 March 1967.

1 – Mary Ann Baxter of Balgavies (1801-1884) by Edward Hughes: Co-founder of University College Dundee and generous charitable donor.

2 – John Boyd Baxter LLD (1796-1882) by Daniel Macnee: Co-founder of University College Dundee, solicitor and procurator-fiscal.

4 – 3rd Marquess of Bute (1847-1900): Rector of St Andrews University 1892-1898, who sought to invalidate the affiliation of University College Dundee (probably wearing a self-designed gown and hood for his installation as Rector).

3 – Sir William Peterson KCMG (1856-1921): First Principal of University College Dundee (1882-1895) and supporter of attempts to start law lectures in the 1880s.

5 – David S Littlejohn (1822-1903):
Solicitor. Delivered law lectures in 1890,
and author of *A Popular Sketch of the Law of
Scotland for the use of Students.*

6 – William C Smith (1849-1915):
Advocate, delivered the first law lectures
in University College Dundee 1891-1893.

7 – James Allison CBE (1865-1951):
Solicitor, part-time lecturer, then Reader,
in Scots Law 1899-1945.

8 – Hugh Carlton (1899-1979): Solicitor,
part-time lecturer in Conveyancing 1928-
1955, moving spirit behind BL and LLB
degrees.

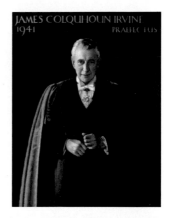

9 – Lord Trayner LLD (1834-1929) by George Reid: Senator of the College of Justice, formerly Sheriff of Forfarshire, Governor of University College Dundee and chaired the inaugural law lecture in 1891.

10 – Sir James Irvine KBE, FRS, FRSE, FEIS (1877-1952) by Keith Henderson: Principal of St Andrews University 1921-1952, 'Interim' Principal of University College Dundee 1930-1939, but not regarded as supportive of UCD, though supporting of developments in law teaching there.

11 – Thomas Mackay Cooper, 1st Baron Cooper of Culross PC, KC, FRSE (1892-1956): Lord President of the Court of Session 1947-1954, chair of the unsuccessful inquiry into relations between University College Dundee and the rest of St Andrews University in 1949.

12 – Arthur William Tedder, 1st Baron Tedder of Glenguin GCB (1890-1967): Marshal of the Royal Air Force, Chancellor of the University of Cambridge, chair of the more successful inquiry into relations between University College Dundee and the rest of St Andrews University in 1952.

13 – Arthur Alexander Matheson QC (1919-1981) by J McIntosh Patrick: Advocate, Professor of Scots Law 1949-1981 (and first full-time member of the law staff), Dean of the Law Faculty 1955-1958 and 1963-1964, Master of Queen's College Dundee 1958-1966, largely responsible for the smooth transition from Queen's College to the University of Dundee.

14 – Alexander ("Alastair") John McDonald (1919-2018): Solicitor, Professor of Conveyancing 1955-1979 (and thereafter), Dean of the Law Faculty 1958-1963 and 1965-1966, negotiator of property transactions creating the Dundee 'campus', author of standard works on Conveyancing, initiator of the modern LLB in Dundee, invaluable supplier of information for this book.

15 – Bernard ("Ben") Clifford Bowman OBE (1908-1993): Solicitor, part-time lecturer in Jurisprudence and Scots Law 1949-1974, Dean of the Law Faculty 1969-1971, Dean of the Faculty of Procurators & Solicitors in Dundee 1968-1971.

16 – Ian Douglas Willock (1930-2013): Advocate, Professor of Jurisprudence 1965-1997, Dean of the Faculty of Law 1965-1966 and 1967-1970, founder of the Dundee Legal Advice Centre, co-founder of the Scottish Legal Action Group and editor of *Scloag*, and encourager of talent.

17 – James Joseph Robertson (1933-2011): LLB graduate of 1956, solicitor, full-time lecturer in Conveyancing, Comparative Law, Conflicts of Law and Civil Law 1964-1998, inspiring lecturer, enthusiast of all things Roman and organiser of student entertainment.

18 – Dennis Ferguson Collins (1930-2017): LLB graduate of 1956, solicitor, part-time lecturer in Scots Law and Conveyancing 1960-1979, Dean of the Faculty of Procurators & Solicitors in Dundee 1987, invaluable supplier of information for this book.

19 – Sir Neil MacCormick QC, FBA, FRSE (1941-2009): Full-time lecturer in Jurisprudence and English Law 1965-1967, later Professor of Public Law and the Law of Nations at Edinburgh University, MEP, and foremost exponent of Jurisprudence of his generation in the United Kingdom.

SOCIETY OF PROCURATORS. — A meeting of the Dundee Society of Procurators was held yesterday in the Sheriff Court Buildings—Mr W. Reid, the President of the Society, in the chair. Mr J. W. Thomson was appointed to represent the Society at the General Council, which meets in Edinburgh on the 30th October next. A committee was also appointed to consider the various duties imposed upon the Society, and the powers conferred upon it by the Procurators' Act, and to report. The same committee was instructed to meet with Sheriff Ogilvy to consider as to the course of law lectures proposed to be instituted in Dundee. After the transaction of of some private business, the meeting adjourned.

20 – Report in *Dundee Courier & Argus* 4 August 1865 of the first plan for law lectures in Dundee.

UNIVERSITY COLLEGE, DUNDEE.

LAW LECTURES.

The FIRST of the COURSE of LECTURES on SCOTS LAW, previously Advertised, will be Delivered by W. C. SMITH, Esq., Advocate, on MONDAY, 5th January, 1891, at 6.30 P.M.

The Lectures will be Continued on MONDAYS, WEDNESDAYS, and FRIDAYS at the same Hour.

Fee (including College Registration), 10s 6d.

G. W. ALEXANDER, M.A., Secretary.

21 – Advertisement in *Dundee Courier & Argus* 13 December 1890 for first law lectures under the auspices of University College Dundee (and Thomas Thornton).

22 – Dundee Sheriff Court (completed 1863), site of inaugural meeting of Law Clerks & Apprentices Society in 1866, site of first law lectures in 1867.

23 – Dundee Sheriff Court interior in the 19th century.

24 – The houses acquired for University College Dundee in 1881, later referred to as 'Front Buildings'.

25 – 'Front Buildings' in the mid-20th century (before demolition to make way for the Tower Building and Extension).

26 – Free Kirk of St John's, Small's Wynd: original College Hall and probable site of the first law lectures under the auspices of University College Dundee (demolished in 1902 to make way for the Medical School).

27 – Union Mount and Ellenbank, acquired 1904 (and later linked) for the Library and Students' Union (now containing Economic Studies and Accountancy & Finance, respectively).

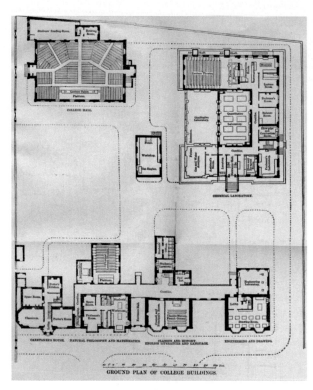

28 – Plan of University College Dundee buildings in c.1892: law lectures were probably given in the westernmost rooms, marked "Classrooms".

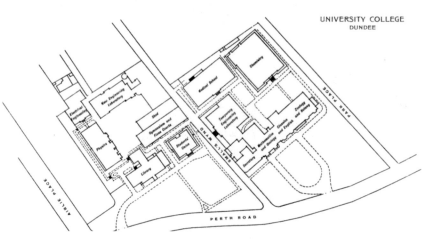

29 – Plan of University College Dundee buildings in 1911.

30 – Nethergate frontage in the 1950s before the Tower was built.

31 – The Master's Room in the Front Buildings in 1966.

32 – The Princess Cinema in (Old) Hawkhill, acquired for additional (but unheated) lecture accommodation (and used for some law lectures).

33 – St Mary Magdalene church and hall, off (Old) Hawkhill, acquired for use as the (also unheated) Well Road Examination Halls.

34 – The Tower Building, opened 1961, housing the Library in the East Wing, the University Administration on the fourth floor, and the Law Faculty on the seventh floor (until 1966).

35 – Bonar House, home of the Dundee School of Economics, then the Faculty of Social Sciences, and finally, the Faculty of Law 1969-1978 (now part of the High School of Dundee).

36 – Interior of the old Library in Union Mount (with the timbers presumably supporting the weight of books on the floor above).

37 – Interior of the new Library in the Tower.

ELIZABETH THE SECOND by the Grace of God of the United Kingdom of Great Britain and Northern Ireland and of Our other Realms and Territories Queen, Head of the Commonwealth, Defender of the Faith:

TO ALL TO WHOM THESE PRESENTS SHALL COME, GREETING!

38 – The Charter of Incorporation of the University of Dundee, 28 June 1967.

FACULTY OF LAW

39 – The entrance to the 'Terrapins', housing the Law Faculty from 1966 to 1969, situated near what is now the north entrance to the Students' Union (with the author on his graduation day).

40 – The Scrymgeour Building, home of the Law School since 1978.

CHAPTER 5

1950-55: A FAIR BREEZE:

AN LLB DEGREE, A CHAIR IN CONVEYANCING, AND A LAW FACULTY

The previous period, the decade from 1938 to 1949, had seen, at last, the introduction of a law degree, though one the development of which had been stultified by the effects of the Second World War, and unassisted by the "Cooper Inquiry". However, at the end of that period, a quickening had occurred with the appointment of a Professor of Scots Law, the first full-time post.

In the present period, the half-dozen years from 1950 to 1955, saw a rapid increase in the rate of change, with the institution of an LLB, the creation of a Faculty of Law and the appointment of a second (if part-time) professor of Conveyancing. Remarkably, this rapidity occurred against the disruption caused by the failure of the Cooper Inquiry, followed by a critical Royal Commission Report and, at last, consequential reform. This reform constituted the biggest constitutional change in the University of St Andrews as a whole since the affiliation, dis-affiliation and re-affiliation of University College, Dundee (UCD) in the 1890s.

As with previous Chapters, this narrative is followed by a consideration the identities and careers of the new staff, chiefly the new professor, and the numbers, gender, achievements and identities of the students, insofar as they can be retrieved from the records.

1950-55: Backdrop

The period 1950-55 was, for St Andrews University as a whole, again dominated by continued attempts to resolve the tension between its two parts (and in particular how far Arts teaching might continue in UCD)[1].

The report of the Cooper Inquiry into the problem, discussed in the last Chapter, though speedily accomplished, was a failure. Rejection of its conclusions produced some years of stagnation with undiminished dissension, numerous proposed solutions, continued lack of academic planning and increasing isolation for Principal Irvine. The University Grants Committee (UGC) therefore, in effect, forced St Andrews University towards a resolution[2].

Resolution was provided by the Report of a Royal Commission, the "Tedder Report"[3], and its consequential legislation[4] and internal reorganisation (which incidentally renamed UCD as Queen's College, Dundee (QCD)). But far from making the College independent (which was widely called for), the reorganisation more fully incorporated it into the University. Also at this time, Principal Irvine, not widely regarded as a friend of Dundee, died, and Professor Thomas Malcolm Knox became Acting Principal.

Because of the importance of its consequences, as well as the light it shines on University/College relations, the Royal Commission requires some discussion. It was set up in 1951 with terms of reference (echoing those of the Cooper Inquiry) to:

> inquire into the organisation of University education in Dundee, and the relationship with St Andrews University, and to recommend what changes should be made in the constitution, functions, and powers of the University of St Andrews, of University College, Dundee, or of any other body or institution concerned.

It was conducted by Marshal of the Royal Air Force, Lord Tedder[5], with eight other members[6]. The Commission took written and oral submissions, was completed as rapidly as the Cooper Inquiry, and produced much the same analysis. The constitutional structure, in particular the relationship of Court and College Council, was incompatible with that laid down for universities generally in the Universities (Scotland) Act 1889 (discussed in Chapter 1), inevitably producing conflict, and with the college structure splitting loyalties. One manifestation of this was the disputes over teaching of Arts on both sites, and "[t]he controversy which surrounds Arts also involves Law"[7].

The remedy was more radical than Cooper's, however. Separation was rejected, in part because it would damage the St Andrews Colleges (United and St Mary's), but in part because of projections of student numbers[8]. The later significance of this second reason is discussed in Chapter 6. Instead, the Report concluded greater adherence to the 1889 Act constitution was required, that is, a straightforward split between Court (in overall charge and responsible for property and revenue), and Senate (responsible for academic matters and discipline), though subject to several modifications.

The modifications were, in brief, as follows. The three Colleges (University, United and St Mary's) should be abolished as corporations, and replaced by two "unincorporated societies" (a Dundee College and a St Andrews College) as subordinate administrative units, one on each "campus", and each with a "Provost" and a consultative Council (one of which would thus replace the UCD Council[9]). The University Principal, as chief administrative officer of the University, should be attached to neither of the new Colleges. Court should no longer be chaired by the Rector, and should include three Assessors appointed by the Privy Council ("Crown Assessors"), who might be local people, but who would be independent of university interests, and there to bang heads together. Also, the Dundee School of Economics (noted in Chapter 3) should be incorporated into the Dundee College[10], which might, incidentally be given "a name indicative of Royal Favour"[11].

Finally, there were proposals (in effect directions), as to how the reformed University ought to proceed academically. One was that Arts should continue to straddle both "campuses", but that the St Andrews College might concentrate on traditional Arts, while the Dundee College might develop the Social Sciences, with new Chairs. The implications of this for Law are considered below.

The passage of the Bill to effect these changes was not easy, with some wrecking amendments introduced[12]. However, the only successful amendment of substance was retention of the Rector as chair of Court (something which was to cause considerable difficulty later), and the Bill became the University of St Andrews Act on its date of enactment, 31 July 1953, though most provisions were brought into force by a series of Commencement Orders over the following eighteen months[13].

In addition to imposing the new constitution, and in order to ensure Tedder's further proposals were carried out, the Act also revived the device, used by the Universities (Scotland) Acts of 1858 and 1889 (and discussed in Chapter 1), of an "executive Commission". These "University of St Andrews Commissioners" (*alias* "Crown Commissioners", so as not to be confused with the "Crown Assessors" on Court) had transferred to them Court's power to pass Ordinances, including the power to enact any other Ordinance "as may appear to them necessary or desirable" to effect the Act and, "subject to any modifications which may appear to them to be expedient", the Tedder recommendations[14].

The Commissioners were appointed for a three year term, which might be extended (and was, for a further two[15]). They included, most notably, Sir J Spencer Muirhead[16] (a member of the Tedder Commission and first President of the Law Society of Scotland), J Bennett Miller (a legal academic[17]) as Secretary, and four others[18]. They made 21 Ordinances in all[19], on a wide range of topics, including creating Engineering degrees[20], laying down the method of election of College Councils[21], and founding new Chairs (including the Chair of Conveyancing, considered below)[22]. One Ordinance which caused much discussion substituted "Master" for Tedder's "Provost", as the title for the Heads of Colleges (there being no traditional term, but numerous suggestions)[23]. Another naming issue was that of the Dundee College. The Act imposed no name, but gave the power to name it to the Secretary of State for Scotland, which he exercised it some months later (fulfilling

Tedder's recommendation of a name "indicative of Royal Favour"), with the title "Queen's College, Dundee"[24].

However, all this activity did not produce peace. The Tedder Report had envisaged appointing an outside figure as Principal, but retention of the Rectorial chairmanship of Court probably torpedoed the possibility of attracting a suitable figure[25]. Therefore Professor TM Knox, Acting Principal under the *ancien régime*, was appointed Principal under the *nouveau*. And against near unanimity in UCD (albeit with the assent of the Crown Commissioners), he ousted General Wimberley by imposing the requirement that the office of Master of QCD be held by an academic. This was justified on the ground that, despite the constitutional changes, General Wimberley would continue to try to run the Dundee College as an *imperium in imperio*. This decision revitalised separatism.

1950-55: The Law School - an Overview

Although the years between Cooper and Tedder were ones of stagnation for UCD as a whole, they were not for the Law School for, in those years, the long-hoped-for LLB was introduced, in addition to the BL. The Tedder Report itself included conclusions of importance about law, though ultimately of little effect, as at just about the same time, there were new General Ordinances on BL and LLB degrees, and changes in professional requirements. But the consequences of the Tedder Report introduced even bigger changes, including a Faculty of Law and a Chair in Conveyancing. All this makes it useful to divide consideration of events in this period into three parts, 1950-51, 1951-53 and 1954-55.

1950-51: The LLB is introduced and a "fully-equipped School of Law" planned

In the first part of the period 1950-55, the two most important events were the introduction of an LLB, and planning for expansion into what was termed a "fully-equipped School of Law"

As the last Chapter noted, despite Irvine savaging Fulton's 1944 plans for UCD post-war in general, he allowed that part of them concerning a Scots Law Chair to survive, and Arthur Matheson was appointed (with, presumably, some undertaking as to the LLB).

Since being appointed, Matheson had made his presence felt. At the December 1949 Court Meeting, clearly with a view to an LLB and, one might have thought, with Irvine's blessing, he had sought a full-time lecturer in Public International Law, a part-time lecturer in Accountancy, and increased salaries for existing staff[26]. This last is particularly interesting. Although (in the wake of full-time staff pay increases) the part-time law staff had just received substantial increases, typically 25%-30%[27], nevertheless Matheson had at the same time notified College Council that these salaries were "quite inadequate", producing a chart to show how much more was paid elsewhere, and suggesting increases of at least 50%[28].

No action was taken on any of Matheson's proposals, because Professor Wright, Dean of Arts, intimated his intention of bringing up the whole question of a law school in the Faculty of Arts[29]. However, this initiative was overtaken by Irvine's response to the Cooper Report, revealed at the January 1950 Court meeting[30]. For Cooper, the Dundee School of Economics had been a side-issue. It was a non-university body, teaching a narrow range of subjects, mostly in evening classes to sub-degree standard, although it also taught for the External London BScEcon degree, and it was in deficit.

However, for Irvine (anticipating Tedder's conclusions), it was an opportunity. Displaying his customary ambivalence on the matter by reversing his views of 1944-45 (discussed in Chapter 4), he outlined to Court a plan, not only to institute an LLB, but also to revive the Bachelor of Commerce degree (discussed in Chapter 3). Both would be taught in a Faculty of Law & Commerce based on the Dundee School of Economics, rather than in UCD, which might also develop languages and Economic History, and continue sub-degree work[31]. The plan may have been an attempt to support law by invoking economies of scale, and even to assist UCD more generally by finally accessing what remained of George

Bonar's money. But seems to have come as a bomb-shell to all, including Matheson and, as we shall shortly see, it was roundly rejected by the legal establishment.

But Wright's initiative was not de-railed, and it assisted Matheson. In the following summer, the Arts Faculty reported to Senate the conclusions of the Board of Studies in Law, produced by a Committee comprising Professors Wright, Knox and Matheson, with Hugh Carlton as convenor[32]. The conclusions echoed Carlton's Memorandum of 1938 (discussed in Chapter 4). They rehearsed the existing position, and described the BL as a "secondary degree", but one only requiring the addition of Public International Law to generate an LLB, which the University already had the right to confer (presumably in that it could use the existing LLB Ordinance). In a nicely pitched argument, having referred to St Andrews as the first university to teach Law, the report asserted that the LLB would "continue to grow in popularity and public esteem at the expense of the [BL]", and so without it, St Andrews University would "always lose to other universities the most able and ambitious… potential law students."

The aim should be a five-year combined MA LLB degree (as elsewhere), and an ambitious 1950-51 start was recommended. Matheson would teach Public International Law meantime (as had been anticipated in the original discussions on the Chair in 1944, as noted in Chapter 4). In 1952-53, a part-time Chair of Conveyancing should be appointed. So should full-time Grade 1 lecturers[33] in Civil Law and Constitutional Law & History (and, later, in Jurisprudence), and those teaching 80-lecture courses should be paid £350 pa, those teaching 40-lecture courses, £250 pa, as their existing salaries were "quite inadequate, and out of keeping with the salaries paid … in other universities". Also, as was necessary for a five-year combined degree (and reversing the view of the Arts Faculty on Constitutional Law & History in 1939, discussed in Chapter 3), Civil Law Constitutional Law & History and Jurisprudence should all be made common to MA and LLB (failing which, students should be advised to go elsewhere).

Senate agreed with the recommendations and regarded the matter as urgent (which it clearly was, if the first students were to be received in three months' time)[34]. Court bit on the financial bullet, presumably with Irvine's approval, which was possibly grudging in the light of the reception of his Faculty of Law & Commerce plan, and agreed[35]. The *quietus* on this plan was delivered six months later, when Senate, in lengthy discussions on the Cooper Report, noted that the entire law staff, and legal profession generally, considered the idea "inadvisable" and recommended Law stay in the Arts Faculty until a Law Faculty was "considered appropriate"[36].

Court agreed, and fixed fees just in time for the 1950-51 session[37], and the same moment as College Council was recording, for a UGC visitation, that its plans included "The establishment of a Faculty of Law in Dundee"[38].

Thus, a decade after the BL was instituted, 50 years after continuous law teaching started, 60 years after the first law classes in UCD, and 85 years after the very first, extra-mural, law classes were held, an LLB (the "1950 LLB") commenced (albeit, as in the other universities, in tandem with the BL, with the same staff and common classes). The structures of the BL and LLB under the regime in force are set out in Chapter 3, Appendix 2 and, although no sequence of subjects for the LLB was explicitly required, in practice it must have followed that of the BL for the common subjects[39], as follows:

First Year:

> Civil Law
> Constitutional Law & History
> Public International Law

Second Year:

> Scots law
> Jurisprudence
> Forensic Medicine

Third Year:

> Conveyancing
> Evidence & Procedure

It is important, incidentally, to note that double-counting of Civil Law, Constitutional Law & History and Jurisprudence for MA and LLB, to allow a five-year "combined degree" (as done elsewhere), was not in fact achieved in this plan (nor, in fact, ever in St Andrews).

How many students entered in the first cohort is no easier to tell than it was for the BL, but the best bet is 2 (compared with 4 for the BL that year). The question is examined in more detail below.

Meanwhile, laurels were not rested upon. Before the year was out, a Committee comprising Matheson, Carlton, Cumming, Bowman and Wainwright had listed, for the Quinquennial Report on Arts to Senate, the requirements for a "fully equipped School of Law", as follows:

- a part-time Chair in Conveyancing (replacing an existing appointment, and imperative - £900)
- full-time Grade 1 lectureships in Civil Law and Constitutional Law & History (replacing an existing appointment, and imperative - £1,100)
- a part-time lecturer in Scots Law (replacing an existing appointment, and imperative - £250-300)
- a part-time lecturer in Administrative Law (imperative - £500)
- a part-time lecturer in Accountancy (£500)
- a part time lecturer in Private International Law (£250)
- two part-time Tutors, in Scots Law and Conveyancing respectively (£200)
- a full-time Chair of Jurisprudence (replacing an existing appointment)[40].

Given their ambition, and the mixture of Chairs and lectureships, and part-time and full-time posts, but absence of Public International Law, it is worth trying to infer the reasoning behind the proposals. Probably, it reflects the tension between the desire to employ practitioners who had up-to-date, practical knowledge of their subjects (who were necessarily part-time); the requirement to employ someone to teach subjects rather distant from private practice (probably necessarily full-time); and the need to give the prestige of a Chair to certain subjects (whether part- or full-time); all at a time when the universities collectively lacked an established legal academic community.

The upgrading of the three core subjects of Civil Law, Scots Law and Conveyancing[41] demonstrates this. A part-time Chair of Conveyancing, supported by a tutor, reconciled the tensions by ensuring a practitioner in a central area of practice, but with the prestige necessary for a core subject. The part-time tutorship in Scots Law achieved a similar reconciliation by ensuring a practitioner in a central area of practice, where the prestige was already provided by an existing full-time Professor of Scots Law, whose contract nevertheless enjoined undertaking opinion work, and who was also burdened with teaching Public International Law. The full-time Civil Law lectureship did so where there was little need for up-to-date, practical, knowledge, in an area distant from private practice (a difficulty hitherto masked by the lengthy tenure of Patrick Cumming, and not upset by T L Hird's more recent incumbency), with prestige provided vicariously by the possible Chair in Jurisprudence (which might also reflect a hope of extending teaching to MA students not on combined degrees). Similar considerations no doubt applied to the other new posts.

The Arts Faculty, to all intents and purposes, unanimously agreed to recommend it. Flatteringly, Senate decided that this was the only part of the Arts Quinquennial Report which was up to scratch and, to all intents and purposes, unanimously approved it. Thus, an LLB had been obtained cheaply by the Professor of Scots Law volunteering to teach Public International Law as well (as had been anticipated in the original discussions on the Chair in 1944, as noted in Chapter 4), but fulfilment of this wish-list would more than double the number of existing staff.

This was a quinquennial plan, so immediate implementation could not be expected, but it is noticeable that only one of the "imperative" items was fulfilled in the next three years, by which time the priorities had changed, as discussed below.

In the same month as Senate's approval of the plan, several other relevant things happened[42]. Firstly, Court ignored or deferred the requests by Matheson for a full-time lecturer in Public International Law and a part-time lecturer in Accountancy, which pre-dated the plan for a "fully-equipped school of law". Secondly, it also deferred again, to the end of the quinquennium, his request for increases of salary for law staff. But thirdly, Matheson himself had become ill, requiring temporary replacement[43], provided by the advocate[44] (presumably commuting from Edinburgh) who was a tutor in Scots Law in Edinburgh, but also External Examiner in Public International Law in UCD[45].

And, in the following month, Court approved the appointment of a part-time Lecturer in Law[46]. The speciality was unmentioned, but presumably this was the third imperative from the quinquennial plan, and Archibald Wedderburn Gillan BL (from Kinnear, Carlisle & Gillan[47]) was appointed[48] and certainly a year later was teaching Scots Law[49].

All this was achieved, it should be noted, before the Tedder Report was published, though simultaneously with its deliberations.

1951-53: New General Ordinances, continuing professional requirements, Tedder Report conclusions on law, salaries, a "fully-equipped School of Law" revisited, and research

In the second part of the period 1950-55, we must note both external events, including the introduction of new General Ordinances for the LLB and BL and the most important Tedder Report conclusions on Law, and internal events, including the related matters of salary rises, the revisiting of the planned "fully-equipped School of Law, and the first inklings of a research culture.

While the Tedder Commission was deliberating, co-incidentally, a Conference on General Law Ordinances (presumably carrying on from the 1948 Conference, noted in the last Chapter) was held to discuss draft Ordinances produced by Glasgow, with Matheson as the St Andrews representative[50]. These would replace the BL and LLB Ordinances of 1893 and 1911[51], and introduce an advanced Doctor of Jurisprudence (DJur) degree[52]. St Andrews did not object, and made a few suggestions in relation to the DJur, but most importantly, sought to delay introduction of any new Ordinances, in order to have time to absorb the Tedder Report recommendations[53].

However, Aberdeen, Edinburgh and Glasgow agreed on a new common LLB Ordinance, and Edinburgh and Glasgow on a common BL one. So St Andrews continued on the 1893 and 1911 Ordinances for both BL and LLB (as did Aberdeen in respect of the BL). Nevertheless, these "1954 Ordinances" [54] (from this point, no longer common, as will be seen) although not applying to St Andrews, deserve passing mention.

Under these Ordinances, for the LLB, the MA remained a prerequisite, but two subjects (differing as between the different universities) could double-count, in order to reduce the LLB to two years. Civil Law, Scots Law and Conveyancing remained compulsory, save that the list of subjects was modified such that Public International Law could substitute for Conveyancing (though English law as a substitute for Scots was completely dropped, there having been no demand for years). Jurisprudence and Constitutional Law & History (but no longer Public International Law) also remained compulsory, but the list of options was extended to include, for instance, Accountancy, Comparative Law and the History of Scots Law (available in one or other of the participants). Subjects might still be taken in any order but the requirement of 80 (or 40) lectures per course was dropped. No less importantly, broad powers to amend were delegated to Senates.

For the BL, the first year was made full-time (the first time this had happened on any law degree), but comprising Arts subjects, and Civil Law. Thereafter, the standard range of subjects, somewhat narrower than for the LLB, was available (the list varying as between the participants). And more surprisingly, two part-time years were required in Edinburgh, but three in Glasgow.

Overall, these provisions now look somewhat unimaginative. They show a late flowering of the argument that Law required a grounding in Arts; a half-hearted attempt to introduce full-time study; and a continuance of the BL/LLB distinction. The Tedder Commission (the conclusions of which are considered fully below) had already implicitly passed some comment on the last of these features in a draft statement early in its deliberations, which observed that there were unlikely to be more than a handful of BL students in the future because its "standing... has become so low that [it] was losing its attraction for students[55]."

Given that the BL had been as popular as the LLB before the Second World War, this conclusion seems surprising. However, it probably flows from some reasoning, expressed in slightly confusing fashion, but seeming to refer to the introduction of grants for students, which meant that they might just as well take an MA LLB as a BL with a compulsory Arts year (even though it still took longer).

But as discussed below, these reforms would shortly be overtaken by the biggest reforms in the 20th century, and meanwhile, a majority of students were still non-graduating.

Turning from degree regulations to professional requirements, we must note that the comprehensive redraft of the Regulations by the new General Council of Solicitors in 1938[56] was superseded by regulations in 1951[57], following its supersession by the Law Society of Scotland under the Solicitors (Scotland) Act 1949[58], but in very similar terms (simplifying the work of the Conference on General Ordinances). Nor did the Faculty of Advocates regulations change significantly[59].

But from the point of view of St Andrews University as a whole, but also from that of the Law School, by far the most important event of these years was the Tedder Commission. As noted above, it took written and oral evidence. This came from the Senate[60], but also separately from some

Professors and other Heads of Department in the Arts Faculty[61] (surprisingly, in the case of law, Carlton). In addition, it came from certain Arts lecturers[62] and certain Law lecturers[63], i.e. Carlton (again), Bowman, Tudhope and Wainwright.

The law lecturers' written evidence outlined what law teaching was done, and the chief factors "inimical to the growth of legal education", which boiled down to being treated as a mere off-shoot of Arts. However, their most interesting assertion was (as noted in Chapter 4) that for UCD to obtain even:

> the lesser degree of BL ... much pressure was required, and it was obtained largely through the good offices of the late Lord MacGregor Mitchell, [and though] the higher [sic] degree of LLB ... is now to be conferred, ... [it was achieved] again only after much pressure and considerable expenditure of energy[64].

Their oral evidence also expressed unease about the future. Carlton asserted that "if the University succeeds in terminating Arts within University College[65], it will shortly proceed to the gradual elimination of law[66]." The tone is harsh and seems to give insufficient credit to Irvine, who had not sought to eliminate law during the war years when he had every excuse; had appointed the first professor of Scots law only a couple of years before; and had encouraged the LLB even more recently. Nevertheless, disaffection is clear (and one wonders whether Matheson was embarrassed by the outburst or regarded the lecturers as stalking horses).

In any event, some of the law lecturers' evidence was accepted. The Report noted that law teaching had been envisaged in 1878 [sic][67], but that degree teaching had not started till 1939, and that though there was now a Chair and an LLB, law was still largely taught by part-timers (though admittedly this was general in all law schools). Most importantly, it concluded that the "facilities for Law student are still... markedly inferior to those of the other Scottish universities. Law is still, in fact, treated as a department within the Faculty of Arts[68]."

In its recommendations, the Report encouraged those seeking the combined degree, and taking their MA on the St Andrews "campus", to take the LLB on the Dundee "campus"[69]. More importantly, however, the urgent need was:

> [not] a nice adjustment of the arrangements linking the study of Law to the Faculty of Arts, but the establishment at the earliest possible opportunity of a Faculty of Law separate from the Faculty of Arts … A new Law Faculty will greatly strengthen the social science departments in the new College in Dundee, and will itself receive much help from these departments. This development will require the establishment of a number of part-time chairs, in particular, a part-time chair of Conveyancing[70].

The consequences of this conclusion are returned to below, but it is worth noticing that in a very useful further boost to law teaching, the "Crown Commissioners" made agreement on these matters a condition precedent of any Ordinances[71].

Meanwhile, Arthur Matheson's 1949 and 1951 attempts to increase substantially law staff salaries had, as discussed above, been kicked into touch.[72]. However, in 1952, a new salary scale for full-time staff was agreed, giving Junior Lecturers £550, Lecturers £650-£1,100 (including annual increases), and Senior Lecturers £1,200-£1,300 (including annual increases)[73]. No doubt it was this that caused Hugh Carlton, on this occasion, to raise the matter yet again in relation to part-timers[74]. After it had been batted back and forward between an *ad hoc* Council Committee and its Finance Committee, he achieved what Matheson had not, as follows[75]:

		Present salary (£)	Suggested increment (£)	Suggested new salary 1952/53
Conveyancing	Carlton	250	250	500
	Coupar (tutor)	75	45	120
Civil Law	Hird	200	200	400

Scots Law	Gillan	~~100~~ 120	~~100~~ 50[76]	200
Evidence & Procedure	Tudhope[77]	120	130	250
Jurisprudence	Bowman	120	130	250
Forensic Medicine	Dorward	65	60	125

The "present salary" figures differ slightly from those given at the last substantial rise, partly because of personnel changes, and Constitutional Law & History is completely omitted. However, clearly, most people's salaries doubled. There must have been rejoicing.

It is worth noting, incidentally, that, without prejudice to whether these sums were deserved, there were, at the time, probably just 6 LLB, 14 BL and 30 non-graduating law students (the last probably being largely accountancy students taking Scots Law)[78]. However calculated, expenditure per head was high, largely because numbers remained small despite admirable ambition and the support from the Tedder Commission, and viability continued to depend very heavily upon the non-graduating students. But this indicates the great achievement of the law teaching staff through this period in keeping both BL and LLB degrees going, albeit on the minimum of subjects.

The issue of salaries was clearly linked to the 1951 quinquennial plan for a "fully-equipped school of law", the hesitant initial implementation of which was discussed above. Its list of priorities was, however, changed comprehensively in 1954[79]. The Chair in Conveyancing (a subject still taught by Carlton, a part-time local practitioner) remained top priority. The part-time Lectureship in Accountancy (not "imperative" on the original list, unsuccessfully sought in 1951, and not taught at all) was now second priority. A part-time Administrative Law lectureship ("imperative" on the original list, but with the subject still not taught at all) was third. And a Mercantile Law lectureship (not even on the original list, and probably only taught as a small part of Scots Law) was fourth.

On the other hand, the full-time Civil Law lectureship ("imperative" on the original list, and still taught by Hird, a part-time local practitioner), was dropped to fifth place though, somewhat implausibly[80], transformed into a part-time Chair. The full-time Constitutional Law & History lectureship (also "imperative" in the original list and still taught by Wainwright, a medievalist, in effect part-time) was simply dropped. The full-time Jurisprudence Chair (less than "imperative" in the original list, and still taught by Bowman, a part-time local practitioner) was also dropped. The part-time Private International Law lectureship (less than "imperative" on the original list, and another subject not taught at all) was dropped as well.

Presumably this was all at Matheson's instance, but no explicit reasoning is recorded, and changes in professional requirements offer no clue. However, it is clear that, apart from the Conveyancing Chair, the change of priorities was to increase the range of subjects taught, at the expense of upgrading existing subjects. In any case, only one item, the top priority, was in fact achieved (as discussed below).

A final matter to consider at this point is research. To modern eyes, research is something very obviously absent from all discussions. This absence is unsurprising, since little that could be called research was done in any law school, largely, no doubt, because of the reliance upon part-time local practitioner staff[81]. However, as early as 1953, when Matheson was still the only full-time member of staff, and no Faculty of Law existed, the first further degree student was admitted to the law school[82].

He was Ahmed Tehrani LLB (Tehran), pgDipLaw (LSE), wishing to offer a thesis on the subject of "Parliamentary Government and the Crown in Great Britain and Persia". This was then fascinatingly topical[83], but why he sought to pursue it in UCD is a mystery. The thesis was in fact supervised by Matheson (although the topic was not obviously within the area of Scots Law) and Wainwright (although, *a fortiori*, not within Dark Age studies, although he did at least lecture on Constitutional Law & History). The Examining Committee included Professor D F Macdonald (History) and the Dean as internal examiners (as well as the supervisors), and A K Lambton and Dr Joan Smith as external examiners[84]. Tehrani was successful[85].

Another research degree commenced in 1954. Alexander Couratos LLB (Salonika) intended a thesis on "Some Aspects of the Law of Salvage"[86]. This was a little more easily comprehended within Scots Law, and Matheson again supervised, but Mr Courtadis withdrew after six months, for unknown reasons[87].

No doubt it was these events which caused the Board of Studies in 1954, with similar ambition to that which had produced the BL and the LLB, and would produce the Faculty of Law, to insert in the Faculty Handbook, the phrase "[t]he Teachers in the School of Law will supervise the work of students undertaking legal research in appropriate areas"[88].

1954-55: A Faculty of Law and a Chair in Conveyancing - Tedder Report consequences

In the third part of the period 1950-55, the recommendations of the Tedder Commission for a Faculty of Law and a Chair of Conveyancing were effected, the "Crown Commissioners" regarding them as a priority, and introducing relevant Ordinances.

A Commissioners' Ordinance brought the Faculty of Law into existence on 10 February 1955[89]. One observer of the October 1955 Graduation reported that "the Dundee Faculty of Law was inaugurated" then[90], but the event was simply fulfilment of the Principal's suggestion in the previous year that it might be "appropriate to mark in some way the [predicted] institution of the Law Faculty" at that Graduation[91].

The new Faculty's first report to Senate recorded that Matheson was elected Dean, with Professor Nisbet (Economics) as the other professorial member, and all others teaching law as non-professorial members[92]. At the same meeting, Senate also decided that, "in future, the Dean of the Faculty of Law should present Honorary Graduates in Law". This sounds sensible until it is recalled that (apart from divines, who were awarded

DDs), all honorary graduates were LLDs, but might have nothing to do with law[93]. However, in celebration of the creation of the Law Faculty, the 1955 LLDs included Lord President Clyde[94] (two years after Lord President Cooper had received one) and Lord Hill Watson[95]. That year also saw the first undergraduate Graduation Ceremony in the Caird Hall, with three BL and six LLB graduates (including the first woman LLB graduate)[96].

On the other hand, the Law Faculty had no accommodation, as such, only an office for Matheson in the 'Front Buildings' on Nethergate[97]. Nor was it well supported administratively for, as Dean of Law, Matheson, sought a Departmental Secretary to be "available for work on behalf of the Dean and [perhaps in anticipation of the appointment of a Professor of Conveyancing] other Law Departments [sic]", though the recommended rate of pay, £345 pa, was reduced by Court to £253[98]. On the same occasion, he also obtained an increase in departmental expenses from £60-£80, with an additional £80-£100 for a typewriter.

Another Commissioners' Ordinance instituted the Conveyancing Chair on the same day as the Law Faculty was brought into existence[99]. Even before then, an appointing Committee had been set up, comprising the Principal, the first Master of QCD[100] (Professor D R Dow) and the ubiquitous Sir J Spencer Muirhead[101].

Any tension between the desire to employ practitioners who had up-to-date, practical, knowledge of their subject, and the need to give the prestige of a Chair to certain subjects, had been clearly resolved by deciding upon a part-time Chair when the post had been the determined as the highest priority for a "fully equipped School of Law" listed in 1951 (as discussed above)[102]. Therefore, it was surprising that it was now left open whether or not it should be part-time, for fear of narrowing the field of applicants[103]. Also it was not decided whether the post should be superannuated or, indeed, what the salary should be[104]. Ultimately, it was decided it should be superannuated and the salary £1500 (thus, comparable to that of the full-time Professor of Scots Law, and several times higher than that of the holder of any non-professorial post, such as Carlton, then teaching Conveyancing), with a retirement age of 70[105].

The post was filled, with effect from October 1955, by A J McDonald BA LLB WS[106]. He would become an enormously important member of staff in a variety of ways noted below, which make paradoxical his initial lack of accommodation[107]. As a part-timer, his contract allowed him to practise, as long as that did not interfere with the discharge of his duties to the University[108]. One might have expected it to require him to practise.

But this was the end of an era for, in consequence, Carlton (who might have expected to be appointed) left at the same time, at the age of 56[109]. Very surprisingly, his departure was not recorded in Senate Minutes, despite his service of more than 25 years, through the period which saw expansion in law teaching from two part-timers undertaking service teaching for professional examinations, to a full-time professor, a part-time professor and half-a-dozen part-time lecturers teaching on two degrees, expansion which he had largely engineered.

College Council Minutes, however, recorded that the Master drew attention to his impending departure and, underwhelmingly "referred to Mr Carlton's long and valued service to the University and, in particular, to the part played by him, as former Convenor of the Board of Studies in Law, for developing the School of Law. It was agreed that this tribute to Mr Carlton be recorded in the Minutes[110]." Nevertheless, this seems a shamefully half-hearted way to mark the end of his career.

At the same time as the first priority in the modified wish-list for a "fully-equipped school of law", the Chair of Conveyancing, was fulfilled by the appointment of McDonald, so was the second, a Lectureship in Accountancy, by the appointment of Gordon Lowden, a Chartered Accountant who had been (alphabetically) the very first LLB graduate, just two years earlier[111].

One other event of this period deserves mention. Shortly after the Law Faculty was brought into existence and the Conveyancing Chair instituted, the Dundee School of Economics was brought into QCD (as Tedder had recommended), but clearly without forming part of a Faculty of Law & Commerce. Quite how this was effected is not clear. There was no legislation, and Court Minutes simply record 1 July 1955 as the date of "transfer"[112], with occasional references thereafter relating to consequences[113].

1950-55: People

Much happened in the period 1950-55, with the general turbulence within the University, but introduction of the LLB and appointment of another professor, though staff numbers increased little, to 9 or 10, and still with only one woman and one full-timer, so if anything, this period was more marked by continuity, and less by change, than the last.

This is shown in that the only staffing changes were one departure, in 1950, through death; one part-time appointment of a solicitor in private practice in 1951; another, in 1955, to a second Chair (and also one part-time accountant in private practice in 1955). By far the most important change was the addition of the second Chair, though it underlined the fact that the backbone of the staff remained local practitioners and there was only one full-time, career academic.

It is also shown in length of service. The remaining pre-1939 member of staff continued in post for the whole of this period, though leaving at the end, with some 27 years' service. The remaining three 1939 recruits also continued in post for the whole of it, thus with 15 years' service by 1955 (further continued well beyond this). The four recruits of the late 1940s again continued in post for all of it, thus with 8 to 10 years' service each by 1955 (and the last two further continued well beyond this). One recruit of this period, continued for the rest of it, with 5 years' service, and would leave after only another three. The two other recruits of this period remained for the rest of it (and well beyond).

The identities of all the above were noted or discussed in Chapter 4, or earlier in this Chapter, save for the most important (jointly with Matheson, at least), that is, A J McDonald, who would also have an enormous effect on the LLB and Faculty of Law, and is therefore necessary to consider in further depth.

Alexander John McDonald (1919-2018)[114], almost invariably called "Alastair"[115], went to Fettes College as an Open Scholar, then to Christ's College, Cambridge on an open classics scholarship. At the end of his second year, he was called up and finally graduated only after six years' service in the Army in India, Burma and Germany, with a "war emergency" BA.

He then took an LLB at Edinburgh University, obtaining the first prize in Conveyancing, the Thow Scholarship and John Robertson Prize, graduating with distinction in 1949. In that year, he also qualified as a solicitor, was admitted to the WS Society, and became a partner in the Edinburgh firm of Allan, Dawson, Simpson & Hampton WS. He lectured part-time in Edinburgh University before his appointment to Dundee in 1955, becoming a partner in W B Dickie & Sons there in 1956. (After later amalgamations[116], this firm became part of Thorntons, regarded as the successor to Thomas Thornton's original firm of Pattullo & Thornton, formed in 1857, thus completing a circle).

Though part-time, he was Dean of the Law Faculty in 1958-63, when Matheson became Master, and again 1965-66, when Matheson was ill, all in addition to his responsibilities for the Chair, and his firm. He became a member of Court (as well as Senate, *ex officio* as a professor), and was deeply involved on behalf of QCD in the numerous property transactions involved in extending the College site on the Nethergate into a campus extending from the Perth Road to the (New) Hawkhill, and from Park Place to Miller's Wynd, thus fulfilling Principal Knox's vision.

It is fair to say that his Conveyancing lectures and, more particularly, tutorials (which, though there may have been earlier examples, he probably largely introduced to law teaching in QCD), were viewed by students with apprehension, on account of their rigour[117]. His *Conveyancing Manual* (though now edited by others, including David Brand, noted later) is at the time of writing, in its 7th edition, and has been the recommended text for Conveyancing on the Diploma in Professional Legal Practice in all universities from its commencement. His lecture notes were later published for Diploma students as *Conveyancing Notes* (2nd ed 1984), and his opinions compiled and published as *Professor McDonald's Conveyancing Opinions* (1998).

In 1979, after 30 years' service, he retired, but only nominally, in order to reduce Law Faculty expenditure, and continued teaching for some years thereafter, unpaid, with much the same workload.

For most staff, as for him, the experience of the years 1950-55 must again have been similar to that of the previous dozen years, still spending most of their time, for most of the year, in the office, but for a few hours over 20 or 30 weeks of the year, going up the road to lecture, though also, of course, spending time preparing, and examining. However, there might be other pedagogical events and innovations. In 1952, Christian Bisset took the Evidence & Procedure class to Parliament House and Register House[118]. More significantly, in 1953, upon his appointment, and despite the part-time status of both himself and the students, as noted above, McDonald introduced frequent formal practical tutorials in groups of up to a dozen, taught by a Conveyancing Tutor, based on a progress of titles to heritable property, and requiring students to draft a series of writs based thereupon[119].

Three factors were discussed in Chapter 4 as markedly differentiating the period 1938-49 from the period 1899-1938, covered by Chapter 3. Two of them continued, that is, the existence of several law teachers rather than two, and a BL as well as non-graduating students. Only the third, the Second World War, did not (the Korean War having much less effect).

And the four factors discussed in this Chapter as markedly differentiating the period 1950-55, from the period 1938-49, covered by

Chapter 4, that is, change of name to Queen's College, commencement of the LLB, the creation of the Faculty of Law, and the institution of the Chair of Conveyancing, however significant in themselves, cannot have made much difference to the experience of most staff.

But for three people, these some of these changes made a considerable difference. Carlton departed; Matheson acquired large, though presumably not unexpected, responsibilities by becoming Dean of the new Law Faculty, but also larger, and presumably entirely unexpected, ones by becoming Master of QCD; and McDonald moved from practice with some part-time lecturing, to a Chair combined with practice, discovering a good deal less administrative support than he might have expected, and thereafter also acquiring further large and unexpected responsibilities.

As for students, the sources of information, and the difficulties that they present (very considerable in this period), are considered in the Annex on Sources of Information on Students, but numbers are of even greater interest as, in this period, the LLB joined the BL, while non-graduating students continued.

The BL, it will be recalled, seemed to have settled down at a steady six to eight entrants a year post-War. However, in the 1950s, it commenced a decline, probably varying from six to zero a year. The total BL entry for this period is thus only some 23 (an average of, say, four per year). Strikingly, while the number of women BL entrants probably varied from four to zero a year, totalling some eight overall (say, 35%), thus a much higher proportion then heretofore.

The LLB seems to have started quietly. Though no numbers are obtainable for 1954-55, entrant numbers were seemingly between two and five, save for a peak of possibly thirteen in 1952-53 (unexplained, for nothing in the history of the law school seems to explain a sudden quadrupling). Thus numbers were generally lower than those for the BL, save in the peak year, but unlike the BL, showed an increase over the period. The total number of LLB entrants is probably thus 32 (with an average of, say, five a year), though much assisted by the peak number. The number of women LLB entrants is less striking than with the BL, probably varying between zero and two, and totalling some four (say, 12%).

There were thus a total of some 55 graduating entrants in this period (averaging, say, nine a year), including some fifteen women (say, 27%). Though this was a time of turbulence within the University, such numbers must have been disappointing, especially in the light of the quinquennial plans for expansion to a "fully-equipped law school" (thereby incidentally underlining the level of support that Principal Irvine seems to have given). Hugh Carlton's fears that the failure to double-count some MA and LLB subjects constituted a disincentive may have been borne out[120], but we cannot be sure, as we do not know how many St Andrews MAs went to another university for an LLB.

Non-graduating law entrant numbers seem to have broadly continued the healthy level found at the end of the previous period, though without quite matching the highest numbers, seemingly varying between 23 and 51 a year (ignoring the year 1954-55, for which we have no numbers). The total number of non-graduating entrants was probably well over 160 (averaging over 27 a year). Strikingly, and unlike the situation with the BL and to some extent, with the LLB, there were hardly any women non-graduating entrants, possibly only three in the entire period. No information is available as to the proportion of non-graduating entrants who were accountancy students, but it seems safe to assume that it was a considerable proportion, so law teaching's reliance on them continued.

Total law entrant numbers is simply the sum of the three categories, but it is worth recording that there appear to have been well over 200 in this period (an average of, perhaps, 40 a year), though only including some fifteen women. There is little to suggest much advance in the promotion of the education of both sexes.

In respect to identities, there is little or nothing recorded in relation to non-graduating students. So far as graduating students are concerned, however, the women we can identify are, chronologically, Pamela Halley (BL 1951) (already noted in Chapter 4, having entered in the previous period), Helen Johnston (BL 1952) (also already noted in Chapter 4), Inez Ferguson (BL 1953), Kathleen Jolly and Patricia Scott (both BL 1954), Janet Hurst MA (LLB 1955, and the first woman LLB), and Joyce Stewart and Frances Donaldson (both BL 1955), which accords well with the recorded numbers of female entrant graduating students.

No less important, we can identify the first LLB graduates who were, alphabetically, Gordon Stewart Lowden MA, Charles Andrew Richmond Menzies MA, James Pearce Parker Smith MA and Ian David Stuart MA, all graduating (just after the Coronation) in 1953[121]. Two of those names, Lowden and Parker Smith, are memorable as they later became members of staff.

Other such memorable names include another, later, member of staff, David Hamilton Tweedie (BL 1955) [122] and, most widely known, Kenneth J Pritchard (BL 1954) [123], a local solicitor, later Secretary of the Law Society of Scotland.

In addition, high achievers include Harry Robert Scrymgeour (LLB 1954)[124] the first graduate to obtain the degree With Distinction, and Hector James Gibson (BL 1951), who was already MBChB[125]. The FPSD prizes for Scots Law & Conveyancing continued, and among prize-winners were Austin Lafferty (Scots Law 1950-51, whose identically named son was President of the Law Society of Scotland in 2012-13)[126], J P Parker Smith (Scots Law 1951-52, noted above)[127], and D H Tweedie (Scots Law 1953-54, also noted above)[128].

In 1953, Lord Dundee donated a £10 prize for Public International Law, to be called the "Henry Scrymgeour Prize"[129]. The Lord Dundee in question was Henry Scrymgeour-Wedderburn, 11th Earl of Dundee[130], and the eponym for this prize was Henry Scrymgeour (or Scrimgeour), the sixteenth century Dundonian. Among other things, he published a new edition of the *Novellae Constitutiones* (one of the four parts, along with the *Codex*, *Digest* and *Institutiones*, of the *Corpus juris civilis*, that is, the "Civil law", long the basis of university law teaching) taught philosophy and civil law (though possibly not well) in Geneva, and witnessed Calvin's will[131]. (The Scrymgeour Building, to which the Law Faculty moved in the 1970s, was also called after him). The first recipient of the prize was James Malcom Paton[132].

Also particularly worth noting was Evelyn E Gavin, an MA from Aberdeen who, having seemingly been admitted in October 1954, enjoyed an interesting First Year. At the end of it, firstly, as an exceptional case, she was allowed to take the LLB in two years[133]; secondly, at the same time, she was awarded the FPSD Scots Law Prize and Henry Scrymgeour Prize[134]; and thirdly, a little later, the condition that she fulfil the prerequisite for taking Civil Law of passing a concurrent Latin exam was waived, seemingly because she failed it but nevertheless passed Civil Law[135]. She graduated With Distinction (the second person to do so) in October 1956[136].

Addresses of graduates are also briefly indicated in the Senate minutes[137]. Unsurprisingly Dundee and district addresses continued to predominate. The rest constitute a scattering from a little further afield, such as Arbroath and Kirriemuir, with the occasional exotic specimen from Glasgow and Stirling, though also one from Nairobi.

In this period, the student experience (like the staff experience) again must have been similar in general to that in the previous period[138] (including the possibility of conscription[139]). The change of name to QCD, and the creation of a Faculty of Law, can have affected most students no more than they affected the staff. Even the introduction of the LLB can have had but a limited effect on BL and non-graduating students though, given McDonald's later reputation for rigour in tutorials, it may be that all Conveyancing students noticed a difference after his appointment.

Thus, law students all still generally lived at home and commuted from the surrounding burghs of Angus and Fife (those from further afield, such as Dumfries, Thurso and Wick, being in digs), while working in the office most of the time[140]. If straight from school, it may have seemed to them a simple continuation of school days and timetables. If straight from national service, it may have seemed a simple continuation of barrack life. They had little time to themselves, with a weekday running from a 9-10am lecture to a 5-6pm one, with the intervening time in the office, plus 9-1 on Saturdays, on top of any commuting. And as part-time students, they received no grant, only apprenticeship pay, in the order of £30, £40 and £60 for each successive year for the law apprentices[141]. Classes remained strictly lecture-based, with no handouts, and might be invariable year-on-year in some cases, or completely up-to-date in others. An address to students by the President of the Law Society of England and Wales, thought worthy of reprinting in the *Scots Law Times*, noted that, though much had changed in the preceding 50 years, students still should dress smartly, have good handwriting and not be diverted by the opposite sex[142].

To an extent, this experience was the same for the new LLB students. However, all LLB students had been full-time MA students (probably in QCD). But there was one way in which all law students' experience in this period differed markedly from that of the previous. In October 1955 the Students' Law Society was set up. Its first President was Jim Robertson (noted in the next Chapter) and its first Secretary was Alistair Clark (LLB 1957, and President of the Law Society of Scotland 1989-90). A facetious suggestion made at the time was that it be named the Lunatic Society, after Peter de Luna, the Antipope Benedict XIV who granted the Bull founding St Andrews University. Though the idea was rejected, the gules and argent (scarlet and silver) from his coat of arms nevertheless appeared in the thin stripes of the Law Society tie and the thick ones of the Faculty "college scarf" (then popular items of student clothing).

The Society was active with, for instance, Dinner Dances, the first being held in February 1956, in Nicoll & Smibert's function room in the basement of their shop and tearooms at 4 Nethergate. It featured a four-man orchestra wearing wigs and gowns (and the toilets were labelled "Forum Conveniens"[143]). More seriously, it organised a trip to Edinburgh (funded by the University) to visit the Court of Session and Register House. And most seriously, it invited prominent speakers, including Lord Hill Watson (Senator of the College of Justice and honorary graduate of 1955) on "Some Aspects of Scots Law and the Scottish Court"), R B Laurie (Secretary of the Law Society of Scotland) on "Apprenticeships", A J McDonald (a week or two after his installation) on "Property in Joint Names", and Viscount Kilmuir (David Maxwell-Fyffe) one of the Nuremburg prosecutors, a drafter of the European Convention on Human Rights, successively Solicitor General, Attorney General, Home Secretary and, in 1954, Lord Chancellor, elected Rector of St Andrews University in 1955.

---

[1] This section summarises chapter 8 of Donald G Southgate, *University Education in Dundee: a centenary history* (1982), but gives more detail on the Tedder Commission and the legislation. See also Ronald Gordon Cant, *The University of St Andrews: a short history* 3rd ed (1992) 169-174 and Norman H Reid *Ever to Excel: an illustrated history of the University of St Andrews* (2011) 162-163.

[2] Southgate, *University Education* 285 *et seq.* gives considerable detail on the Cooper Inquiry and consequential pressure for a Royal Commission. Mabel Irvine *The Avenue of Years: a memoir of Sir James Irvine …* (1970) 226-228 records, seemingly in relation to contemporaneous lobbying for independence, that it was one of two matters "which made an irreparable mark on [Irvine] and … shadowed his last years" (the other being the death of his son), that "University College, the bone of contention, remained silent and dignified, and [Irvine's] confidence in Dundee never wavered", that "[h]e believed that the ancient foundation in St Andrews was the fountainhead of the University" and that he declared that "'The part cannot be greater than the whole … and that is the vain ambition of the city of Dundee".

[3] Report of the Royal Commission on University Education in Dundee 1951-52 (Cmnd 8514: 1952). Paras 11-20 provide an unsurpassed brief history of the origins of UCD, its "affiliation" to St Andrew University, and the consequential problems.

[4] University of St Andrews Act 1953, and Orders in Council and more Ordinances thereunder, discussed below.

[5] Arthur William Tedder, 1st Baron Tedder of Glenguin, GCB (1890–1967), then recently appointed Chancellor of Cambridge University. Presumably it was a sign of Government concern that an unsuccessful inquiry headed by the Lord President of the Court of Session was replaced by one headed by the former Deputy Supreme Commander of Allied Forces on D-Day. Incidentally,

Tedder's son John (1926-94) became first holder of the Roscoe Chair of Chemistry in Dundee (1964-69), then Purdie Professor of Chemistry in St Andrews (1969-89).

[6] Ernest, Baron Grenhill (a Glasgow politician), Sir D Lindsay (Master of Balliol College), Dugald Baird (Professor of Midwifery, University of Aberdeen), David Emrys Evans (Vice-Chancellor, University of Wales), Isabel Finlayson MA BEd ("wife of Rev James Finlayson" [sic]), Harry Melville (Mason Professor of Chemistry, University of Birmingham), Andrew Robertson, DSc FRS and, of most interest to the law teachers, John (later Sir John) Spencer Muirhead, DSO, MC, TD, DL, LLB, LLD, President of the Law Society of Scotland (of whom more later).

[7] Tedder Report para 40.

[8] Tedder Report paras 60-63, contains a fascinating chart showing the university destinations of school leavers of 1950 from Dundee, Angus, Perth & Kinross, Fife and Clackmannanshire, disaggregated into local authority schools and fee-paying ones. Dundee local authority schools sent 35 students to UCD, twelve to United College, two to other universities and nine to external London degree courses taught at the Dundee School of Economics (of which more, later, while the High School of Dundee sent seventeen, seven, four and nine, respectively.

[9] When this was effected, confusingly, the new Dundee College Council overlapped with the old one for part of 1954. The Minutes of the original Council (1882-1954) are in Dundee University Archives ("DUA") Recs A/98 to A/113: the Minutes of its replacement (1954-1967) are in DUA Recs A/60 to A/73 (i.e. bound in with Court Minutes, as are those of its counterpart College on the St Andrews site).

[10] Tedder Report paras 128-33.

[11] Tedder Report para 81. This was, perhaps, a sop offered to ease the pain of the destruction of the original UCD. Southgate, *University Education* 313, records that "Queen's College, Dundee", the name chosen, "was envisaged by the Royal Commission before the [unexpected] death of George VI [on 6 February 1952], in view of the local connections of his wife [i.e. Queen Elizabeth, latterly the Queen Mother], born Lady Elizabeth Bowes-Lyon, daughter of 14th Earl of Strathmore and Kinghorne, of Glamis Castle". Presumably the accession of her daughter, as Elizabeth II, on that date, and coronation in 1953, underlined the argument.

[12] For a detailed account, see Southgate, *University Education* 304-12. A confusing oddity (not the result of amendment) was that, although Tedder recommended two new Colleges, s 1 of the Act declared that the University should comprise three "unincorporated societies of teachers and students, namely the United College of St Salvator and St Leonard, St Mary's College and a College to be known by such name as the Secretary of State shall determine and in this Act referred to as 'the College in Dundee'". Only when s 6 came into force, a year later, were the "common law foundations" of United and St Mary's Colleges abolished, and the UCD deed of endowment and trust simultaneously "ceas[ed] to have effect". Section 15(4) shows that s 1 was a device to permit the old Colleges to be used *ad interim* for elections to the new College councils.

[13] Southgate, *University Education* understandably fudges this. Commencement Orders are delegated legislation, in statutory instrument form (see Glossary), exercising the power delegated to Government to decide when to bring legislation into force. Sections 1 (in part) 2, 9-13 and 15 came into force on the date of enactment; ss 3 & 4 were brought into force on 30 September 1953; s 1 (in part) on 22 December 1953; ss 1 (remainder), 5, 6, 8 (in part) and 14 on 30 July 1954; and ss 7 & 8 (remainder) on 24 November 1954: by, respectively, University of St Andrews Act 1953 (Commencement) Orders No 1 (SI 1953/1451), No 2 (SI 1953/1898), No 3 (SI 1953/1031) and

No 4 (SI 1953/1564). See also DUA Recs A/60, University of St Andrews ("UStA") Court Minutes 1953-54, Meeting of 20 October 1953.

[14] Ss 9, 10, 11(1), 12(1): effected by The University of St Andrews (Appointment of Commissioners) Order 1953, SI 1953 No. 1562 (another piece of delegated legislation in statutory instrument form).

[15] The University of St Andrews (Extension of Duration of Commissioners' Powers) Order 1956, SI 1956 No. 1585 (a further piece of delegated legislation in statutory instrument form). When extension of their term was being discussed, Sir J Spencer Muirhead (observed above to be one of the Tedder Commissioners, and discussed further in the next note) pointed out that the idea of Ordinances dated from the time when a "National University" appeared possible, and (surprisingly ignoring the chronic St Andrews/Dundee problem) suggested that they were now "humiliating" for universities, and others hoped their use would be confined or major matters: DUA Recs A/62, UStA Court Minutes 1955-56, Meeting of 24 January 1956.

[16] Sir John Spencer Muirhead MC DSO TD DL (1889–1972), Lecturer in Civil Law in Glasgow 1920-54?, partner in Baird Smith, Barclay and Muirhead; Clerk, Treasurer, Fiscal and Dean of the Faculty of Procurators in Glasgow; first President of the Law Society of Scotland (seemingly suggesting its motto *Humani Nihil Alienum*, a quotation from the Roman playwright Terence); and author of the one-time standard *An Outline of Roman Law* 2nd ed (1947). He was also (among an extraordinary range of employments) a director of George Outram (publishing the *Glasgow Herald*) and Clerk to Glasgow University. Also, seemingly, he was author of an entry in D H S Nicholson and A H E Lee (eds), *The Oxford Book of Mystical Verse* (1917), presumably written during the First World War, in which he received an MC (1916) and DSO (1917), so must have been something of a hero. In addition, he was a Brigadier in Egypt during the Second World War. He had been knighted in the Coronation Honours List in 1953, and made Honorary Fellow of Oriel College, Oxford. See Anon "J Spencer Muirhead, DSO, MC, TD, DL, BA, LLB" 1951 *SLT* 1; Anon, "Sir J Spencer Muirhead" 1953 *SLT* 111, 180 & 204; and David M Walker, *A History of the School of Law, University of Glasgow* (c.1990) 67-68 (which records that he regarded himself as "really a classical scholar and treated the practice of law as a slightly tedious diversion of his time", and that his attitude post-war to ex-servicemen students was "kindly", resulting in him asking Walker two questions only for his Civil Law oral examination, *viz*, "Were you in the desert? What Division were you with?").

[17] J Bennet Miller, TD, Lecturer in Administrative Law in Glasgow University 1949, Professor of Mercantile Law 1963, and author of *An Outline of Administrative and Local Government Law in Scotland* (1961) and *The Law of Partnership in Scotland*, 1st ed (1973) 2nd ed, G H Brough (ed), (1994) and subsequently Professor of Law at Strathclyde University.

[18] Dr Alexander Greig Anderson CVO LLD (1885-1961, physician in Aberdeen Royal Infirmary, Honorary Physician to H.M. Household in Scotland and member of Aberdeen University Court); Sir Peter David Innes, CBE LLD (probably the Chief Education Officer, City of Birmingham); Mr Ronald Buchanan McCallum, MA (1885-1961, formerly lecturer in history at Glasgow University, Master of Pembroke College, Oxford); and Sir James Irvine Orme Masson, MBE FRC LLD (1887-1962, chemist and Vice-Chancellor of the University of Sheffield): DUA Recs A/60, UStA Court Minutes 1953-54, 17 November 1953.

[19] University of St Andrews Commissioners (Ordinance No 1) Order 1954 (SI 1954/1032), to University of St Andrews Commissioners (Ordinance No 21) Order 1959 (SI 1959/299) (yet

again, delegated legislation in statutory instrument form). To avoid confusion with earlier Commissioners' Ordinances, they are usually cited as "Ordinance No 1 (SAC)", etc. These Commissioners' Ordinances, and subsequent Court Ordinances (not cited "SAC") are reprinted in Anon, *University of St Andrews Ordinances* (c1964) which also contains the earlier Commissioners' and Court Ordinances under the Universities (Scotland) Acts 1858 and 1889 still in force at that time.

[20] Ordinance No 3 (SAC) (SI 1954/1034).

[21] Ordinance No 4 (SAC) (SI 1954/1368).

[22] Ordinance No 10 (SAC) (SI 1955/247).

[23] Ordinance No 5 (SAC) (SI 1954/1474).

[24] Edinburgh Gazette, 6 April 1954, 1 (s 1 of the Act having been brought into force on 23 December 1953 "insofar as it enables the Secretary of State to determine the name by which the College in Dundee is to be known" by the University of St Andrews Act 1953 (Commencement) (No 2) Order 1953 (SI 1953/1898). The first recorded usage within the University, though unremarked at the time, seems to have been a week later: see DUA Recs A/60, UStA Court Minutes 1953-54, Meetings of 13 April 1954; and Recs A/60, UCD Council Minutes, Meeting, 14 April 1954 (bound in with Court Minutes).

[25] Southgate, *University Education* 313, quotes Sir John Spencer Muirhead as referring to "the lunatic retention of the Rectorial chairmanship" making the Principalship even less attractive than the revelations of the proceedings of the Royal Commission had left it, and that the Scottish Office were "scraping the bottom of the barrel" when he was approached himself. Sir J Randall Philip (noted in the previous Chapter, and below, who attended T M Knox's installation at which Lord President Cooper, author of the previous failed Report, received an LLD) recorded that, in July 1953, Lord Cooper told him that "the number of those who had been invited, and had declined, the Principalship of St Andrews University would, laid head to toe, stretch from St Andrews to Dundee": see Fiona Craddock (ed), *The Journal of Sir J Randall Philip OBE QC: public and private life in Scotland 1947-1957* (1998) 359, 371-372.

[26] DUA Recs A/56, UStA Court Minutes 1949-50, Meeting of 13 December 1949.

[27] DUA Recs A/111, UCD Council Minutes October 1948-September 1949, Meeting of 26 September 1949.

[28] DUA Recs A/111, UCD Council Minutes October 1948-September 1950, Meeting of 19 December 1949. Hugh Carlton's salary, for instance, would increase from £250 to £500, T L Hird's from £200 to £500.

[29] DUA Recs A/56, UStA Court Minutes 1949-50, Meeting of 13 December 1949. Southgate, *University Education* 287, records that the salary suggestion had put Arthur Matheson "at odds with ... the University Secretary ... and the Dean of Arts".

[30] DUA Recs A/56, UStA Court Minutes 1949-50, Meeting of 17 January 1951.

[31] The significance of the Dundee School of Economics should not be underestimated. Though by then in decline, in 1950-51 it had 43 students taking first degrees (probably all external London BSc(Econ)) and two undertaking post-graduate study, as well as fourteen taking Diplomas, 30 accountancy students and ten others: see Tedder Report paras 128-133 (figures given therein repeated in Southgate, *University Education* 322 n 4, which gives useful background discussion).

[32] DUA Recs A/74, UStA Senatus Academicus Minutes 1948-50, Meeting of 29 June 1950.

[33] Grade 1 lecturers included non-professorial Heads of Department and Heads of "branches of Departments where the lectures cover a course qualifying for graduation", and full-timers could expect to be paid £600-700: DUA Recs A/51, UStA Court Minutes 1944-45, Meeting of 6 March 1945.

[34] DUA Recs A/74, UStA Senatus Academicus Minutes 1948-50, Meeting of 29 June 1950.

[35] DUA Recs A/56 UStA Court Minutes 1949-50, Meeting of 6 July 1950.

[36] DUA Recs A/75, UStA Senatus Academicus Minutes 1950-52, Meeting of 2 February 1951.

[37] DUA Recs A/56, UStA Court Minutes 1949-50, Meetings of 6 July and 20 September 1950.

[38] DUA Recs A/111, UCD Council Minutes October 1948-September 1950, Meeting 18 September 1950.

[39] Since Scots law and Conveyancing, and Jurisprudence and Evidence & Procedure, were timetabled against each other, they cannot have been taken in the same year: see e.g. DUA Recs A/814/2/13, St Andrews University Calendar 1950-51, 512.

[40] DUA Recs A/75, UStA Senatus Academicus Minutes 1950-52, Meeting of 9 March 1951.

[41] The "pattern of legal [university] education" identified in Stephen D Girvin "Nineteenth century reforms in Scottish legal education: the universities and the bar" (1993) 14 JLH 127-140, at 131, and distinguished from the "law agents' triad" in Chapter 1.

[42] DUA Recs A/57, UStA Court Minutes 1950-51, Meeting of 12 March 1951.

[43] Also described as an "Assistant".

[44] R R Kerr BA (Oxon), LLB (Glasgow), advocate, later Sheriff-Substitute at Fort William (1952-61) and at Banff (1961-69), and Sheriff at Falkirk (1969-83): see Stephen P Walker The Faculty of Advocates: a Biographical Directory of Members Admitted from 1 January 1800 to 31 December 1986 (1987).

[45] Did he therefore teach Public International Law class in Arthur Matheson's absence, then act as External Examiner for it?

[46] DUA Recs A/57, UStA Court Minutes 1950-51, Meetings of 12 March and 23 April 1951; Recs A/112, UCD Council Minutes, October 1950-September 1952, Meeting of 19 March 1951.

[47] I am grateful to Dennis Collins for this information.

[48] DUA Recs A/57, UStA Court Minutes 1950-51, Meeting of 25 September 1951.

[49] DUA Recs A/112, UCD Council Minutes October 1950-September 1952, Meeting of 20 October 1952. Arthur Matheson taught Criminal law, Bankruptcy, and Husband & Wife, while Archibald Gillan taught Sale of Goods, Company Law, Insurance, Bills of Exchange, etc. I am grateful to Dennis Collins for this information.

[50] DUA Recs A/75, UStA Senatus Academicus Minutes 1950-52, Meeting of 25 September 1951.

[51] I.e. Commissioners' Ordinance No 9 (General No 39) of 1893 and Court Ordinance No XXXVII of 1911 (summarised in Chapter 3, Appendix 3).

[52] DUA Recs A/75 & A/76, UStA Senatus Academicus Minutes 1950-52 & 1952-54, Meetings of 3 July 1952 and 9 January 1953; Recs A/58 & 59, UStA Court Minutes 1951-52 & 1952-53, Meetings of 18 November 1952 and 20 January, 17 February and 20 September 1953. See also David M Walker "Legal Studies in the Scottish Universities" 1957 *JR* 21-41, at 25.

[53] DUA Recs A/75 & A/76, UStA Senatus Academicus Minutes, 1950-52 & 1952-54, Meetings of 3 July 1952 and 9 January 1953; Recs A/58 & 59, UStA Court Minutes 1951-52 & 1952-53, Meetings of 10 June 1952 and 20 January, 17 February and 20 September 1953.

[54] Walker "Legal Studies" 25-37.

[55] DUA Recs A/57 UStA Court Minutes 1950-51, Meeting of 13 July 1951, Appendix.

[56] *Regulations for Examination and Admission of Solicitors … 19ᵗʰ March 1937.*

[57] *Examination and Admission of Solicitors (Scotland) Regulations 1951* (as amended) reproduced in contemporary editions of *Parliament House Book.*

[58] 12, 13 & 14 Geo 6 c 63.

[59] Reproduced in contemporary editions of *Parliament House Book.*

[60] Tedder Report, Written Evidence, Paper 2. This largely comprises the earlier Report of its Committee on the Cooper Report (for which, see Chapter 4), para 10 of which accepted that, as feeling was against a Faculty of Law and Commerce, Law should stay in Arts "until it is considered appropriate to form an independent Faculty of Law", and anyway should be strengthened.

[61] *Ibid*, Written Evidence, Paper 11, Oral Evidence paras 188-357; DUA Recs A/112, Special UCD Council Minutes, 16 July 1951.

[62] *Ibid*, Written Evidence, Paper 12, Oral Evidence paras 1-111.

[63] *Ibid,* Written Evidence, Paper 13, Oral Evidence paras 112-187. Frederick Wainwright also submitted his own memo.

[64] *Ibid*, Written Evidence, Paper 13.

[65] A continuing issue for much of this period.

[66] Tedder Report, Oral Evidence para 115. There was pointed questioning by Sir J Spencer Muirhead on student numbers and (also by Sir D Lindsay Keir) on professional expansion and the tension expressed in admission procedures on the two St Andrews University sites.

[67] A misprint for 1883 (i.e. the opening of UCD)?

[68] Tedder Report para 40.

[69] *Ibid,* para 126. It seems significant that this required to be said.

[70] *Ibid,* para 127.

[71] DUA Recs A/75, UStA Senatus Academicus Minutes 1950-52, Meeting of 17 November 1951.

[72] DUA Recs A/57, UStA Court Minutes 1950-51, Meeting of 12 March 1951; Recs A/112, UCD Council Minutes October 1950-September 1952, Meeting of 19 March 1951.

[73] DUA Recs A/58, UStA Court Minutes 1951-52, Meeting of 10 June 1952; Recs A/112, UCD Council Minutes October 1950-September 1952, Meeting of 21 July 1952. Eighteen months later, further substantial increases were agreed: DUA Recs A/61 UStA Court Minutes 1954-55, 23 November 1954.

[74] DUA Recs A/112, UCD Council Minutes October 1950-September 1952, Meeting of 21 July 1952.

[75] DUA Recs A/113, UCD Council Minutes October 1952-September 1954, Meeting of 20 October 1952, Appendix B.

[76] These amendments, and the inaccurate arithmetic, appear without explanation in the original, casting doubt as to how much A W Gillan received.

[77] Formerly Miss Bisset (see previous Chapter).

[78] DUA Recs A/113, UCD Council Minutes October 1952-September 1954, Meeting of 15 December 1952.

[79] DUA Recs A/60, 1954 UCD Council Minutes October 1953-September 1954, Meeting of 14 April 1954 (bound in with Court Minutes); Recs UStA Court Minutes 1953-54, Meeting of 11 May.

[80] As the Principal noted: see DUA Recs A/60, UStA Court Minutes 1953-54, Meeting of 8 June 1955, Appendix.

[81] In 1952, there was discussion was to whether (full-time) lecturers' conditions of appointment ought to change in order to reflect that they "engage in advanced study or research": DUA Recs A/58, UStA Court Minutes 1951-52, Meeting of 10 March 1952.

[82] DUA Recs A/76, UStA Senatus Academicus Minutes 1952-54, Meeting of 6 November 1953.

[83] Persia, *alias* Iran, was then under the regime of Reza Shah Pahlavi ("the Crown"), an army officer who had seized power in 1925 and sought to modernise the country, which was heavily reliant upon the British-owned Anglo-Iranian Oil Company ("AIOC"). The Majlis ("the Parliament") had elected Mohammad Mossadegh as Prime Minister, who in 1951 nationalised the AIOC, as a result of which (after a complicated series of events) a UK/US *coup* removed him in 1953, just a few months before Tehrani signed up for the PhD. The following year, AIOC became BP. A copy of the thesis is in the University of Dundee Library. It is strangely silent on these events just described, despite their apparent centrality to the topic.

[84] DUA Recs A/77, UStA Senatus Academicus Minutes 1954-56, Meeting of 11 November 1955.

[85] DUA Recs A/77, UStA Senatus Academicus Minutes 1954-56, Meeting of 13 January 1956.

[86] DUA Recs A/76, UStA Senatus Academicus Minutes 1952-54, Meeting of 7 May 1954.

[87] DUA Recs A/77, UStA Senatus Academicus Minutes 1954-56, Meeting of 12 November 1954.

[88] DUA Recs A/77, UStA Senatus Academicus Minutes 1954-56, Meeting of 10 December 1954.

[89] University of St Andrews Commissioners Ordinance No 9 (SAC) (Constitution and Composition of Faculties) (SI 1955/246). It provided that there be Faculties of Divinity, Arts, Medicine, Science and Law. See also DUA Recs A/77, UStA Senatus Acadmicus Minutes 1954-56, Meeting of 11 March 1955; Recs A/61 & A/65, UStA Court Minutes 1954-55 & 1958-59, Meetings of 22 March 1955 and 19 May 1959.

[90] I.e. Sir J Randall Philip: see Craddock *Journal of Sir J Randall Philip* 594. A J McDonald (discussed below) was installed, with some five other professors, at this ceremony, leading to an outbreak of singing of "Six Green Bottles". I am grateful to Dennis Collins for this recollection.

[91] DUA Recs A/76, UStA Senatus Academicus Minutes 1952-54, Meeting of 28 June 1954. In a report from the Principal, along with an injunction not to use embossed notepaper, it had been suggested that the old Faculty of Canon Law mace be used by the Faculties of Divinity and ("when instituted") Law: DUA Recs A/60, UStA Court Minutes 1953-54, Meeting of 20 October 1953.

[92] DUA Recs A/77, UStA Senatus Academicus Minutes 1954-56, Meeting of 13 May 1955.

[93] This practice continued for decades, into the period of Dundee independence. The late Professor ID Willock recalled having to perform the office many years later: personal communication. There is, incidentally, research to be done on who is offered, and who accepts, honorary degrees.

[94] James Latham McDiarmid Clyde, Lord Clyde (1898–1975), Lord President of the Court of Session 1954-1972, son of Lord Clyde (Lord President 1920-35) and father of Lord Clyde (Senator of the College of Justice 1986-96 and Lord of Appeal in Ordinary [i.e. House of Lords judge] 1996-2001): see Walker *Biographical Directory*.

[95] DUA Recs A/77, UStA Senatatus Academicus Minutes, 1954-56, Meeting of 13 May 1955. Lord Hill Watson (Lawrence Hill Watson, QC, 1895-1952) had been Sheriff (in modern terms, Sheriff-Principal) of Forfarshire, but was by then a Senator of the College of Justice of three years standing (see *Glasgow Herald* 21 June 1952), though he died only two years later (see *Glasgow Herald* 2 October 1957). Paradoxically, because of the desire for "a special emphasis on Law in recognition of the new Faculty" (fulfilled by these degrees), Sir J Randall Philip seems to have been denied a DD in recognition of his work as Procurator of the General Assembly of the Church of Scotland: Craddock *Journal of Sir J Randall Philip* 496.

[96] DUA Recs A/77, UStA Senatatus Academicus Minutes, 1954-56, Meeting of 5 July 1955.

[97] I am grateful to Alastair McDonald for this recollection.

[98] DUA Recs A/61, QCD Council Minutes 1953-54, Meetings of 16 May and 18 July 1955. The appointee, Mrs Massie, remained for many years. I am grateful to Alastair McDonald for this information.

[99] University of St Andrews Commissions Ordinance No 10 (SAC) (Foundation of the Chair in Conveyancing) (SI 1955/247).

[100] Under the new constitutional arrangements following the Tedder Report and effected by the University of St Andrews Commissioners (Ordinance No 5) Order 1954 (Ordinance No 5 (SAC) (SI 1954/1474)).

[101] DUA Recs A/60, UStA Court Minutes, Meeting of 21 September 1954.

[102] DUA Recs A/75, UStA Senatatus Academicus Minutes 1950-52, Meeting of 9 March 1951.

[103] DUA Recs A/61, UStA Court Minutes 1954-55, Meeting of 26 October 1954.

[104] *Ibid*. Meeting of 22 February 1955

[105] *Ibid*. Meeting of 22 March 1955.

[106] DUA Recs A/77, UStA Senatus Academicus Minutes 1954-56, Meeting of 11 October 1955. Some correspondence on the appointment is at Recs A/759/2.

[107] On arrival, he asked Dow, as Master, for accommodation in the Front Buildings or elsewhere, but was offered only "the glass enclosed telephone booth in the entrance to the front building", which he declined. In consequence, until he took up a partnership with W B Dickie & Sons in Whitehall Street six months later, he had no office and had to work "in a small room at the west end of the western front building which housed the Law Library and had a desk and two or three chairs" (as described in Chapter 3). Only when he became Dean did he get an office, but this was "limited accommodation in the Ewing Building for myself and Mrs Massie [the Secretary]". I am grateful to Alastair McDonald for this recollection.

[108] DUA Recs A/61, UStA Court Minutes 1954-55, Meeting of 12 July 1955.

[109] As the Professor's salary greatly exceeded the Treasury Grant for it, there was no money to pay a lecturer even had the will existed, so Hugh Carlton's annual appointment was not renewed: DUA Recs A/61, UStA Court Minutes 1954-55, Meeting of 25 July 1955.

[110] DUA Recs A/61, QCD Council Minutes 1954-55, Meeting of 21 September 1954 (bound in with Court Minutes).

[111] DUA Recs A/63, UStA Court Minutes 1955-56, Meeting of 4 October 1955.

[112] DUA Recs A/61 UStA Court Minutes 1954-55, Meeting of 23 November 1954.

[113] E.g. *ibid.*, Meeting of 21 June 1955. One consequence discussed in Chapter 6, was the transfer of some staff to the University.

[114] The information here is largely culled from the *Dundee Courier* 16 July 1955 and Anon, "St Andrews University: Chair of Conveyancing" 1955 *SLT* 135. A draft was also read by Alastair McDonald himself, but he bears no responsibility for what appears here.

[115] Though also "Supermac" (in imitation of a cartoonist's nickname for Harold Macmillan when Prime Minister) by some of his colleagues, and "the Prof" by some of his students (some later also colleagues): personal recollection. Seemingly, for unclear reasons, he was known in the Army as "Crazy Mac": personal communication from Alastair McDonald.

[116] W B Dickie & Sons became Dickie, Gray, McDonald and Fair, then Thorntons and Dickies, before becoming simply Thorntons: I am grateful to Dennis Collins for this information.

[117] Personal recollection of the accounts of others.

[118] DUA Recs A/112, QCD College Council Minutes October 1950-September 1952, Meeting of 18 February 1952, and personal communication from Alastair McDonald.

[119] I am grateful to Alastair McDonald for this information. They were later carried out by Dennis Collins and Jim Robertson.

[120] He drew attention to the problem in DUA Recs A/113, UCD [*sic*] Council Minutes October 1952-September 1954, Meeting of 15 December 1952.

[121] DUA Recs A/76, UStA Senatus Academicus Minutes 1952-54, Meeting of 30 June 1953.

[122] DUA Recs A/77, UStA Senatus Academicus Minutes 1954-56, Meeting of 5 July 1955.

[123] *Ibid.*, Meeting of 13 October 1954.

[124] DUA Recs A/76, UStA Senatus Academicus Minutes 1952-54, Meeting of 29 June 1954. (There was no Honours then).

[125] DUA Recs A/75, UStA Senatus Academicus Minutes 1950-52, Meeting of 12 October 1951.

[126] DUA Recs A/112, UCD Council Minutes October 1950-September 1952, Meeting of 17 September 1951.

[127] DUA Recs A/112, UCD Council Minutes October 1950-September 1952, Meeting of 21 July 1952.

[128] DUA Recs A/113, UCD Council Minutes October 1952-September 1954, Meeting of 19 July 1954.

[129] DUA Recs A/113, UCD Council Minutes October 1952-September 1954, Meeting of 15 June 1953; Recs A/76, UStA Senatus Academicus Minutes 1952-54, Meeting of 8 October 1953.

[130] Formerly an MP and Under-Secretary of State for Scotland. His claim to the Earldom was only accepted in 1953 but, as a Scottish peerage, this only entitled him to stand as one of the sixteen representative Scottish peers in the House of Lords, and he was given an additional UK title (Baron Glassary), which enabled him to sit unelected and thereby be eligible at all times to take further Government office.

[131] See H C G Matthew & Brian Harrison *Oxford Dictionary of National Biography* (2004).

[132] DUA Recs A/113, UCD Council Minutes October 1952-September 1954, Meeting of 19 July 1954.

[133] DUA Recs A/77, UStA Senate Minutes 1954-56, Meeting of 4 July 1955.

[134] DUA Recs A/77, UStA Senate Minutes 1954-56, Meeting of 5 July 1955.

[135] DUA Recs A/77, UStA Senate Minutes 1954-56, Meeting of 11 November 1955: as noted in Chapter 1, it is an interesting question as to when a knowledge of Civil Law ceased, in practice, to be a pre-requisite for learning Scots Law (and when Latin ceased, in practice, to be regarded as a pre-requisite for studying Civil Law): see Robin Evans-Jones, "Reception of Law, Mixed Legal Systems and the Myth of the Genius of Scots Private Law" (1998) 114 *LQR* 228-249 and David L Carey Miller "A Scottish Celebration of the European Legal Tradition", William M Gordon "A Comparison of the Influence of Roman Law in England and Scotland", John W Cairns "The Civil Law Tradition in Scottish Legal Thought" and Alan Rodger "The Use of the Civil Law in Scottish Courts", all in David L Carey Miller & Reinhard Zimmerman (eds) *The Civilian Tradition and Scots Law* (1997).

[136] DUA Recs A/78, UStA Senate Minutes 1956-58, Meeting of 10 October 1956,

[137] DUA Recs A/75 to A/78 UStA Senatus Academicus Minutes 1950-52 to 1956-58, July and October Meetings.

[138] For a useful brief account, see J J Robertson "Random Reflections" (1981) vol. 6 no 4 *Contact* 289. For an instructive comparison, see Callum G Brown, Arthur J McIvor & Neil Rafeek *The University Experience 1945-1975: an oral history of the University of Strathclyde* (2004) ch 3.

[139] The last cohort of national servicemen was conscripted in 1960, but from 1947, it was possible to defer service in order to complete one's education, and most of those with university places did so: Richard Vinen *National Service: a generation in uniform 1945-1963* (2014) xxvi, xxx & 49.

[140] I am grateful to Dennis Collins (who remembers one student's health breaking down under the "harsh and demanding regime"), for the information in this and the succeeding paragraphs, but he bears no responsibility for the words written.

[141] Though one later recalled that "apprentices generally received the lordly sum of four to five pounds per week", for which some four pounds went on board and lodging for those in a residence: Robertson "Random Reflections".

[142] F H Jessop "An Address to Students" 1955 *SLT* 65.

[143] "Forum Non Conveniens" is a legal principle justifying a court ("forum") in declining jurisdiction over a dispute, because it is not the appropriate court ("non conveniens").

CHAPTER 6

1956-67: A MODERN LAW SCHOOL ACHIEVED:

FULL-TIME STAFF, A CHAIR IN JURISPRUDENCE, AND AN HONOURS DEGREE

Our final period, from 1956 to 1967, saw changes in law teaching in Queen's College, Dundee (QCD) even greater than those of the previous period, indeed, arguably revolutionary ones. They were chiefly manifested in five interwoven strands: reform of the LLB (twice); abandonment of the BL; growth of student numbers, now full-time; growth of staff numbers, also generally full-time; and the emphasis on synergy with Social Science, and promotion of Jurisprudence and English Law as USPs[1]. In addition, a variety of other events impinged on these developments, such as changes in accountancy professional requirements and the elevation of Arthur Matheson to the Mastership of the College.

These developments took place, not only against the background of the Tedder Royal Commission proposals and their implementation, and more general university expansion, but also within the context of new academic thinking about, and a more general revolution in, law teaching. And yet once more, this Chapter also adds to the narrative some consideration of the identities and careers of staff, including another new professor and new lecturers and, insofar as they can be retrieved from the records, the numbers, gender, achievements and identities of the students.

1956-67: Backdrop

The settlement contained in the University of St Andrews Act 1953[2], based on the Tedder Report[3], and discussed in the previous Chapter, stuck, at least in the medium term[4]. All was not all plain sailing, however. At the University's initiative, and despite Scottish Office concerns, the "Crown Commissioners" (temporary legislators for the University like the earlier "executive Commissions") had their tenure extended (indeed twice) to 1959[5]. This was, initially at least, because "in many quarters", it was thought necessary in order to preserve equality between the "Colleges" (that is, the St Andrews and Dundee 'campuses'), but also because the Tedder conclusions were already becoming outdated (and because the creation of a Faculty of Social Sciences would be more easily achieved by a Commissioners' Ordinance[6]). The Commissioners' final report listed their Ordinances and concluded that the problems had at last been overcome[7]. The "Crown Assessors" on Court (intended to bang heads together) also had their tenure extended, to 1960[8]. Their final report, reiterating the Tedder plan requirement for concentration of "applied" subjects in QCD, and "pure" in the St Andrews College, nevertheless concluded that, although the new QCD Council had misconceived its role, which was as a committee of Court, the plan had succeeded[9].

With hindsight, these reports seem excessively optimistic, not least because of ill-feeling in Dundee caused by the ousting of College Principal Wimberley by University Principal Knox. Yet peace did break out, which Southgate attributes to the efforts of Principal Knox (also giving him credit for development of the still-recognisable Dundee campus, including the Tower Building) and to Professors Dow and Matheson, successive Masters (the role replacing the College Principal), working within Tedder's prescriptions.

Nevertheless, separation of QCD from the rest of St Andrews, eschewed by the Tedder Report, occurred in 1967, a little over a dozen years later. It did so largely as a result of a new factor, largely unseen in the 1950s, and specifically discounted by Tedder. This was the Government policy of the 1960s to expand universities enormously, carrying into effect the "Robbins Principle" that university places "should be available to all who were qualified for them by ability and attainment" and especially that there should be the "immediate foundation of six new universities, of which at least one should be in Scotland"[10]. The unprecedented consequential rise in student numbers across the UK was thus catered for by both expansion of existing universities, and creation of new ones.

This policy played out in unique fashion in St Andrews University. Firstly, the expansion (disliked by Knox) occurred largely in QCD. This meant that, for the first time, there were more students on the Dundee campus than on the St Andrews one. And as this expansion was principally of non-local students (at some point making the student population of Dundee, for the first time, largely non-local, as that of St Andrews had always been), it required expansion of student residences, and radically altered the student experience.

But secondly, taken with the strategy of confining QCD to "applied" subjects, expansion made separation unavoidable, leading to the creation of a new University of Dundee out of it. The separation was achieved by a combination of amendment of the University of St Andrews Act 1953[11] (clearing the path and dealing with consequential issues), and a Royal Charter[12] (actually instituting the University of Dundee). Paradoxically, however, this peaceable separation was only possible because of the relative harmony of the preceding period.

One other aspect of these events requires mention. One of Tedder's principal proposals was expansion of the social sciences[13], including incorporation of the Dundee School of Economics into the University, which took place in 1955 (as noted in Chapter 5). In 1960, this expansion produced the Faculty of Social Sciences, unique in Scotland, but possibly did so at the price of expansion in Law. Incidentally, the social science departments initially occupied the Dundee School of Economics Building in Bell Street, named "Bonar House" to recognise the legacy of George Bonar (discussed in Chapter 3), which later became the home of the Law Faculty[14].

1956-67: The Law School - Overview

Because of the hectic pace of change, it is useful to break the overall period into three parts.

1956-59: External and Internal Events

As noted above, in the first part of this period, a number of external and internal events require to be considered.

As to the external events, Chapter 3 remarked on the extraordinary dearth of published discussion on law degrees by law teachers through the first half of the twentieth century, probably on account of their small number[15] and generally part-time status.

With the influx of full-time law teachers, accompanying the expansion of student numbers, from the late 1950s, a literature began to emerge[16], surprisingly infrequently in "academic" journals, though nevertheless part of the remarkable upwelling of legal scholarship at that time, evidenced in the creation of the Scottish Universities Law Institute in 1960. A large proportion was attributable to one person, David Walker[17].

This literature provided a background for the revolutionary changes of the 1960s. Much of it was a critique of degree structures under the contemporary Ordinances, but from this flowed more general and principled concerns, chiefly laid out in two articles (both also containing useful brief histories of law teaching).

One[18] lengthily summarised arguments on whether law, as a practical subject, ought ever to be taught in universities. It concluded that it should, because of the need to synthesise theory and practice, and that the MA prerequisite for the LLB was essential (its absence from the BL mitigated by the presence of Jurisprudence). It also noted the lack of suitable textbooks, especially at introductory level; unimaginative teaching methods, which left much scope for tutorials, court attendance, "dispensary work" and the like; examinations that, on the one hand, encouraged mere repetition of lecture notes and, on the other (rather inconsistently), tended to be tests of fitness to practise rather than of academic excellence; and curricula that were inappropriate, largely on the grounds adumbrated as long ago as 1919, and repeated in 1943[19] (as discussed in Chapter 3).

The other[20] (even more lengthily, but more tightly, argued, and as a rejoinder to the first), concluded that, at root, the problem was part-time apprentice/students taught by part-time practitioner/staff to suit a Law Society which saw law degrees as vocational training. In consequence, students had little time to study, or teachers to write, producing the reliance on lectures. In any case, the value of apprenticeships was "enormously overrated". What was required was removal of the MA prerequisite (the function of which was essentially to differentiate BL and LLB) and merger of the two degrees (simple, as they were distinguishable only by length and the MA prerequisite). However, an all-graduate profession was not desirable, as it would exacerbate existing ills and confirm Law Society hegemony over law teaching. A "new approach" (following English precedent) required apprenticeship to follow degree, allowing a wider "liberal" element in the latter. More specific recommendations included introduction of a Scottish Legal System course[21]; recognition that Scots Law courses had not been able to cover the whole of Scots Law for a couple of centuries; the desirability of Honours degrees, LLMs and other advanced courses; and the setting up of a "professional School of Law" for vocational subjects.

A third article from a member of the profession[22] (largely a reply to the second article) also interestingly observed that the relationship between Law Society and the universities was "the confrontation of two interdependent monopolies", and explored the consequences.

Some arguments in these articles were familiar, others more novel, but much of what was recommended came to pass. Indeed, they underpinned the Report of a Conference of the four universities in 1959, which provided the manifesto for the revolution in law teaching which occurred in the 1960s, and is best examined later.

If this new thinking provided the rationale for reform of law degrees, what of professional requirements? Chapter 5 mentioned the replacement of the 1937 solicitors' admission regulations by the effectively identical 1951 regulations after the creation of the Law Society. These regulations were, in turn, replaced by the 1957 ones[23], but again, in effectively identical terms in regard to required subjects. Thus, they required no re-ordering of law teaching. However, the revolution in law teaching of the 1960s necessarily involved a revolution in professional requirements, and these also are best examined later.

At the same time, the Institute of Chartered Accountants in Scotland, stepping towards an all-graduate profession, was considering whether its apprentices should take not only Political Economy (i.e. Economics), but also more law subjects, to a degree standard[24]. Again, this is best examined later.

Turning to the internal events in the years 1956-59, we can note that, in 1956, after a hiccup[25], Donald Southgate, BA DPhil, replaced Frederick Wainwright[26] on the Constitutional Law & History course, and later I M S Robertson (a BL graduate of 1947 from Petrie, Allan & Robertson, noted in Chapter 5) was appointed to replace A W Gillan, teaching Scots Law[27].

But there were other staffing issues. One consequence of the incorporation of the Dundee School of Economics into QCD in 1955 (noted in Chapter 5) had been the transfer of some School staff to the University. Two of the people affected were T L Hird[28], who taught English Law and Industrial & Commercial Law, and J P Parker Smith[29], who taught Commercial Law (both mentioned in Chapter 5). Upon the incorporation, their rates of pay were much enhanced, to £100 and £80 respectively. Hird, however, "generously declined to accept a doubling of his honorarium"[30].

Another consequence of the incorporation was the need to preserve the position of the students taking the London University External BSc (Econ) degree, by continuing teaching the necessary subjects. This difficulty was exacerbated by a change of syllabus, requiring a course on the Law of Labour and National Insurance, which Parker Smith was asked to undertake, at £80 for twenty lectures and (surprisingly) five tutorials[31]. He and Hird continued with their subjects until BSc (Econ) teaching ceased in 1957, at which point when they were made redundant from those posts[32].

Parker Smith, clearly a safe pair of hands, was later appointed to teach Social and Industrial Law within QCD, in the School of Social Administration[33] and, shortly thereafter, became lecturer in Scots Law in the School of Law. Hird continued to teach Civil Law in the Law Faculty, as he had since 1947.

However, the university took the view[34] that, *prima facie*, both lecturers were entitled upon redundancy to compensation under the University of St Andrews Act 1953, s 14[35]. Actuarial assessment was thought unnecessary, and one year's salary appropriate. This was accepted by Parker Smith, but Hird, though he had declined the higher rate salary upon transfer, rejected the offer and sought compensation actuarially calculated, or at twenty years' purchase, which the University thought excessive. Court considered a compromise of £300, failing which arbitration, but in the event simply renewed the £100 offer. This was re-rejected, and Hird elected for arbitration. At this point, the university belatedly realised that an unfavourable arbitration would create a moral obligation to Parker Smith and others, and decided to call Hird's bluff. The ploy worked, as Hird sent a letter (dated 19 December 1957), intimating that he would not pursue his claim, and was paid nothing.

But in 1961, he revived the claim[36]. The University's legal advice suggested that any claim was, by then, extinguished by negative prescription, and that anyway, the 19 December 1957 letter, though not witnessed, nor specifically abandoning the claim, was formal in style and asked for acknowledgement, so would bar the claim. Should this be inaccurate, it would be best to offer £100 again and, if an unreasonable counter-offer was received, take the matter to arbitration. Ungenerously, it was suggested that if Hird was in financial straits, a sum well below £300 might settle the claim. The £100 was re-offered. It is not clear if it was accepted, but there the matter ended. Extraordinarily, Hird was continuing to give the LLB Civil Law lectures all the while, as he had been doing since 1946, and would continue until 1975.

Another staffing issue of a different kind was the appointment of an Adviser of Studies in Law in 1939, and the introduction of "Regents", a sort of moral tutor, into UCD in 1946. But it was noted that the former had no pastoral functions, and the latter had only vague obligations, unlikely to be of interest to law students who generally lived at home and worked as apprentices in offices.

Turning from staffing to other issues, the wish-list for the 1952-57 quinquennium, substantially modified in 1954 (as discussed in Chapter 5), had ambitiously sought staff for a "fully-equipped law school". The first and second of its priorities, a part-time Chair in Conveyancing and Lectureship in Accountancy, had come to pass in 1955 (as also discussed in Chapter 5). But in 1956, priorities were again re-ordered, restoring a full-time Jurisprudence post (but as a Lectureship, not a Chair) in place of the implausible part-time Civil Law Chair, but with a view to a full-time Chair in the following quinquennium, principally responsible for Jurisprudence, but also other things[37].

The reasoning for the re-ordering of priorities expressed three desiderata. Firstly, the period for the combined MA LLB should be aligned with that elsewhere at five years (a long-running saga recounted in Chapters 3 and 4)[38]. Secondly, Administrative Law and Mercantile Law (both still on the wish-list), and possible further options, should widen opportunities for Social Science students (as Tedder had expected). But thirdly, and more importantly, the re-ordering showed the first evidence of Jurisprudence as a USP. While accepting a third Chair to be still too heavy a burden for so small a law school, the law teachers looked forward to a future Public Law Chair, principally responsible for Jurisprudence (requiring 80 lectures if available for the MA) but also for Public or Private International Law or Comparative Law. The de-prioritisation of Civil Law was not discussed.

All this recognised that, though Senate certainly said it favoured the development of law, the Faculty of Law still offered only the bare minimum of subjects, and less than anywhere else[39]. Law was marginal in another way. Until this time, there were no premises that law teachers and students could call home. Lectures were given in the originally-acquired houses on Nethergate ('Front Buildings')[40]. However, 1957-62 quinquennial plans included capital expenditure to replace these houses with what became the Tower Building, and Law was allocated a whole floor, as befitted a Faculty[41].

But expansion raises questions of quality as well as quantity, and also at this time, questions were being asked about standards and reputation[42]. QCD, in particular, was pressed to raise entrance standards. Some English universities were understood to require 60% in each of three A-levels, a Headmaster's Report, and an interview. One English local authority had enquired if St Andrews really intended to admit a student (to an unnamed subject) with only two A-levels, at 40% and 50% respectively, since s/he would not get into its (unnamed) local university. And Glasgow ignored Higher passes below 60%.

In the end, no fundamental change took place[43]. There was to be standardisation of entrance forms, with a Head Teacher's reference and, more interestingly, no fee for application. Most interestingly, there were to be no preference lists (save in Medicine) and no special examinations. Nevertheless, among qualified applicants, those who made St Andrews their first choice were to be made offers, while others were to be told that they would be considered only when they indicated that they were not going elsewhere. The question of a Scottish preference was deferred. A little later, the Faculty of Law disapproved a plan to require a minimum of two A-levels at 50%[44].

While all this was going on, the question of the effects of professional changes, noted above among the external changes, was raised. The Law Society's 1957 admission regulations, being effectively identical to their predecessors, provided no reason for change. The Institute of Chartered Accountants in Scotland's proposed requirement that apprentices take more law subjects, and to degree standard, presented opportunities, however. It was therefore welcomed (not least, no doubt, because of the existing high proportion of accountancy students taking Scots Law). But more teaching would require more staff, and Senate, though also welcoming the opportunity, would not countenance unfunded staff increases[45].

Court also welcomed the opportunity[46]. Arthur Matheson reported the Institute's plan was to change from a requirement of part-time university study for several years (like law), to one of full-time university study for a single year. The demand could be supplied by two terms of law teaching, containing Mercantile Law and Trusts & Succession, plus a three-term Accountancy course. The law subjects were already taught, of course, and were in any case already squeezing out the rest of Scots Law, so that course could be increased from 120 lectures to 200, with a separate Mercantile Law course, which would fit well with the Institute's proposal.

One additional Scots Law lecturer and a part-time Accountancy Assistant (as well as an Economics Lecturer or Assistant) were necessary. The quinquennial budget already included £600 for the first of these posts[47]; the second would require £250; and the third £500-£600 (but was less urgent), giving an overall requirement of £1,400-£1,500 per year. Against this, the income from accountancy students would be £1,800 per year, if there were 30 students at £63 a head (which was likely). Moreover, 75% of existing accountancy students were already of university standard, and some were doing law already. Equally to the point, if Dundee did not take these students, Edinburgh would, and the Law Society was also considering changing admission requirements and the structure of the apprenticeship.

Matheson was persuasive, for the proposals went ahead, with a suggested fee of £50 for the year, to start in 1960, and on the assumption that within five years all students would fulfil university admission requirements[48]. He stressed that this was not service teaching, as the students would only be able to sit their professional examinations if they had satisfactorily taken the courses and passed a university examination.

One final, most important, internal event in 1958, with considerable consequences for the Law Faculty, was Matheson's elevation to the Mastership (in the event holding the post until 1966, when QCD was on the brink of obtaining independence again).

This cannot have been something he anticipated on appointment. The office did not exist then, and the idea of an academic as College Principal, part-time (the preceding equivalent), had been rejected with Wimberley's appointment in 1946. But more to the point, while of a strong academic cast of mind, he had no administrative experience, save the few years since appointment as Dean of a tiny law school[49]. It was only the failure of the Cooper Inquiry and Knox's decision to go against the Tedder recommendations and squeeze Wimberley out, that returned the Master to being an academic, part-time, office.

In any case, the first holder of the Mastership, Professor Dow, held it for only four years and Matheson, when prevailed upon, might have expected a similar term. However, the unanticipated university expansion, re-igniting pressure for QCD to become independent again, caused his tenure to be doubled, and gave him the chief responsibility in QCD for the smooth transition to independence (his contribution to which later described as "outstanding"[50]). It seems likely that all this contributed to his illness[51] and relatively early death.

Certainly, from the Law Faculty's point of view any advantage of a friend at the top must have been outweighed by the loss of much of the time of the only full-time member of staff (and professor), for some eight years, even though it was mitigated by the appointment (in addition to I M S Robertson) of J P Parker Smith (much mentioned above), and later

Dennis Collins (noted below, *et passim*), to teach Scots Law "in order to assist Professor Matheson ... in the light of his appointment as Master"[52].

Incidentally, the office accommodation for the Master, along with that of the Secretary, the Quaestor, the Cashier and the three or four secretaries who constituted the whole central administration of QCD, was in one of the old houses forming the 'Front Buildings'[53] until moving to the fourth floor of the Tower in 1961.

1960-63: The February Revolution (and other matters)

The events of 1956-59 shaped the environment of law teaching in QCD, and affected the path of its development. The years 1960-63 saw a 'February Revolution' in the structure and functioning of its LLB, and a simultaneous attempt to develop its own style.

It is useful to begin by pausing and considering the state of the Law Faculty on the eve of this February revolution. In 1960, College Council's projected expansion of law student numbers was comparatively modest, projected to be less than 25% (from 92 to 115 students) for 1959-68, while for the same period, Social Science was to be 3000% (from 10 to 300), and even the enormously more expensive Applied Science and Pure Science were both to be in the order of 250% (from 178 to 420, and from 299 to 700, respectively)[54].

Nevertheless, further expansion of numbers in law was sought and, in extensive discussions on academic development at the same time, Court reiterated that they would continue to rise in the light of an expected Law Society change of regulation (discussed below) and of the expansion of choice, which would be especially attractive to those not intending to practise law, who were treating the degree as a more general training[55]. Also, it thought Administrative Law to be of interest to Political Science, assisting the synergy with Social Science.

Expansion of numbers made it "vital to strengthen existing staff", and expansion of choice required appointment of a full-time Lecturer in

Public[56] and Private International Law, and a part-time one in Administrative Law (again re-ordering quinquennial plans after the 1956 re-ordering, discussed above)[57]. Comparative Law was added as an option to the LLB, and Comparative Law and Administrative Law to the BL[58].

In pursuance of all this, two lecturers were appointed. One was Gordon Cowie MA LLB (fresh from national service in the Army[59], and later Professor of Public Law at Glasgow, then Minister of the Church of Scotland), remarkable as the second full-time appointment to the Faculty, and appointed to teach Comparative Law as well as Public[60] and Private International Law, at £1050[61]. The other was Robert Moore BL[62] (Secretary of the Eastern Regional Health Board), appointed to teach Administrative Law, initially at £500[63].

At the same time, in a domino sequence, I M S Robertson (who had succeeded A W Gillan as Lecturer in Scots Law in 1959) was appointed to teach Mercantile Law (in anticipation of the expansion of accountancy students, discussed above) at £600[64]; Parker Smith, presently "supernumerary lecturer" while Matheson was Master, was appointed as his replacement[65]; and Dennis Collins (an LLB graduate of 1956, from Gilruth, Pollock & Smith) in the first of several manifestations, was appointed to the "supernumerary" lectureship[66], initially teaching accountancy apprentices in their new academic year[67]. (A little later, he also undertook the Conveyancing tutorship upon A J W R Coupar's retiral[68]). On the same occasion, Lindsay Sim (from Johnstone, Logie & Millar) was appointed Tutor in Accountancy.

A handy picture of the resulting Law Faculty was given in 1961 in the Quinquennial Estimates for 1962-67[69]. This showed that ten graduating subjects were taught, four of them "half courses"; three courses, Constitutional Law & History, Economics and Forensic Medicine were taught across departmental boundaries; and this constituted a bare minimum of courses, with few options on either degree (and no Honours). It revealed that there were one full-time and one part-time Professor, together with one full-time and seven part-time Lecturers, four in specified subjects (Accountancy, Civil Law, Evidence & Procedure, and

Jurisprudence) and three in "the Department of Scots Law"[70], plus one part-time Tutor in Conveyancing and one part-time Assistant in Accountancy. Finally, it recorded that the degrees comprised what until recently had been a common curriculum with the other Law Schools (although they had offered more options), designed primarily for practitioners (with the Law Society giving major concessions to encourage graduate entry), and was pursued part-time, concurrently with an apprenticeship. Qualification as an advocate was not mentioned.

On the other hand, the Tower foundation stone had been laid in 1959 by Principal Knox (in the absence of the first choice, the Chairman of NCR[71], who was unable to attend)[72] and the building, then the tallest in Dundee, was opened two years later, in 1961, by the Queen Mother. This gave the Law Faculty its own home for the first time, on the seventh floor. It was deemed sufficient[73] and, given the small number of students, as well as the (still minimally required) staff accommodation[74], it is likely that all classes were given there[75] and the Law Library (by now seemingly more substantial) certainly was[76]. (The central administration, including the office of the Master, was on the fourth floor)

Having considered the state of the Law Faculty on the eve of the February Revolution, we must turn to that Revolution itself (and will find that it largely happened elsewhere). As noted above, by the end of the 1950s, novel critical thinking in the universities about law degrees was bearing fruit. The "1954 Ordinances" adopted in the other Law Faculties (discussed in Chapter 5) had made some difference. But these Faculties sought more radical change. In initial discussions of possible change, however, the St Andrews Law Faculty, though not pressing its objections, had deplored both the overall radical nature, and the detail, of a Draft Ordinance proposed by Aberdeen and Glasgow[77].

As also noted above, the Report of a Conference of the four Universities in 1959, building upon the renewed academic and professional thinking of the 1950s, had provided the manifesto for a revolution[78]. There were significant differences between the proposals of Aberdeen, Edinburgh and Glasgow[79] but, in essence, a revolution was

302

intended, involving three fundamental changes which, taken together, would allow a wholly new sort of law degree, no longer essentially a vocational qualification.

Firstly, the elephant in the room, illuminated by the BL (in existence for nearly a century), was finally acknowledged. An MA was not really needed for any law degree. One prolific commentator, much involved in these events, pointed out that arguments for retention "ignored the fact that until 1858 or thereabouts [thus, shortly before the LLB was instituted] the Arts degree was taken by youths of fifteen to eighteen and was of the level of modern sixth-form [*sic*] studies[80].

Further, the prerequisite was already "pretty bogus" as MA-equivalents were accepted, so it "could be, and frequently was, satisfied by an Oxford BA in Jurisprudence or a Cambridge BA in the Law Tripos and could have been by a BA in Engineering Science![81]." Such a change, of course, would carry implications for the (previously more popular) BL which did not have the MA prerequisite.

Secondly, it was accepted that, whatever advantages might exist in principle for simultaneous part-time formal teaching and apprenticeship, in practice there was no advantage and possible disadvantage. The same commentator observed that he had "worked on conveyancing in the office when he was studying Constitutional Law and Scots Law, and worked on court process when he was studying Conveyancing![82]." Indeed, elsewhere, he considered that, under the old Ordinances, there "had grown up a system in which the requirements of the Law Society of Scotland for a professional qualification largely control the study of law in universities[83]." The principal implication was, of course, that law degrees might become full-time with the apprenticeship undergone afterwards. Taken with removal of the MA pre-requisite, this implied that law students would, for the first time, enter a law degree with neither prior university study, nor work experience.

Thirdly, it was acknowledged that, at least in the light of the first two issues, Honours was appropriate in law degrees, and that advanced courses, and others of no immediate benefit to practising lawyers, could be permitted, which might attract the new breed of full-time law staff which was emerging[84].

The result would be essentially, in the view of that same commentator, merger of BL and LLB[85], and the new 1960 Glasgow Ordinance (and by extension, as applied in Aberdeen and Edinburgh[86]) would constitute "the biggest revolution in legal studies since the creation of the LLB by the 1858 Act [sic][87]."

Perhaps the most powerful argument for a stand-alone law degree, however, was another one. Student grants, now an important feature of the landscape, were only available for one degree, so a powerful disincentive to a combined MA LLB.

The St Andrews Law Faculty continued to be unenthusiastic, however[88]. It made no objection to the other Universities' draft Ordinances, and agreed with them to abolish the BL[89], but laid out a reasoned response to the revolution[90].

This response objected to removal of the MA prerequisite on the grounds that it was a century-old tradition. It did not object to a new law degree without that prerequisite, but thought it should be distinguished from the LLB and called, perhaps, a Bachelor of Jurisprudence (BJur), presumably to enjoy status somewhere between the BL and the LLB, further crowding an already over-crowded law degree landscape. Also, it thought that even if not a prerequisite, a prior MA ought to be encouraged, though conceding that any loss in "greater maturity and intellectual capacity" might be compensated for by creation of Honours.

It did not object to full-time law degrees, (but possibly because it was aware that its hand might be forced as the Law Society was planning to abolish apprenticeships concurrent with university study anyway, as discussed below), and it could hardly hold out if all other Faculties were offering them. But (somewhat inconsistently with its views on the MA prerequisite) it strongly objected to the introduction of Honours, on the grounds of the tradition that this involved specialised study at advanced level, which it doubted could be reached.

Other areas of discord included the lack of Arts options. This incidentally underlined the significance of removal of the MA prerequisite. If Law was enough for a degree in itself, why should there be any Arts input at all? There was also talk of compulsory vacation work as a full-time degree followed by an apprenticeship produced, for the first time (in a minor revolution in itself), a summer vacation for law students[91].

In the result, the objections evaporated and, accepting that a new Ordinance for St Andrews alone was not on the cards, the Law Faculty recommended a neat trick to cope with the new proposals, while maintaining the 1893 Ordinance. Firstly, the provision of the 1893 LLB Ordinance imposing the MA prerequisite could be removed by an amending Ordinance, leaving the rest of it unchanged. Secondly, by simple *fiat,* the LLB could be treated as full-time (no part of the Ordinance actually requiring it to be part-time), and the BL could be simply "suspended".

The introduction of Honours, with its implication of greater choice, more advanced study, and thereby greater freedom from professional requirement constraints, was not possible in this minimalist response, but that was soon instituted, as we shall see.

The neat trick was effected. Firstly, te *fiat* treating the LLB as full-time, and suspending the BL, was promulgated in May 1960[92]. The amendment removing Section 1 of the 1893 Ordinance[93] which imposed the MA prerequisite (also incidentally removing Section 4, requiring at least one pass at every sitting) came into force just in time for the 1961-62 intake[94]. Together, they created the '1961 LLB'.

Secondly, draft Regulations for this LLB were approved meanwhile[95]. These still required Lower or O-level Latin, and allowed some subjects to double-count for MA and LLB (which was, of course, no longer necessary, though presumably constituted encouragement to take both degrees). They provided a new "progress"[96] provision, replacing the 1893 Ordinance's requirement of a pass at every sitting with one requiring at least one pass after one year, at least three passes after two years, and passes in all subjects after four years (or three years in the case of MA LLBs). Thus, the LLB became full-time by a side-wind.

And thirdly, transitional provisions simply prevented anybody entering the BL after 1961, but allowed those on course to continue or, with the Dean's consent, transfer to the LLB. As noted above, Honours still had to wait. (Appendix 1 to this Chapter shows the structure in practice, and some details of syllabus and examinations).

Clearly, this effected the biggest change in law teaching in St Andrews since the introduction of the BL degree in 1939, more than twenty years before. But it had been a February Revolution, because the content of the degree remained almost exactly the same as before. It was neither fish nor fowl and, surprisingly, no discussion is recorded of the interesting work-load implications of a degree designed to be taken part-time over three years now being taken full-time over the same length of time, or that the new "progress" provision was now lower for full-timers than it had been for part-timers, together making life remarkably easy for the lucky 1961, and some subsequent, cohorts[97].

The revolution was incomplete, but the opportunities it offered were seized by introducing some St Andrews Law Faculty USPs. The Quinquennial Estimates for 1962-67, adumbrated above, not only gave the handy picture of the Law Faculty at that time, they also looked forward. Planning under Alastair McDonald, as Dean, had commenced, just as the Law Faculty took up residence in the Tower[98].

The Estimates noted that Aberdeen taught fifteen subjects, and had two full-time Professors, four full-time Lecturers and three part-time ones, plus one full-time and four part-time Assistants. Edinburgh and Glasgow were even better supplied, and none of them was taking its maximum possible number of students. Moreover, in an important insight, abolition of concurrent apprenticeships meant local students would no longer be tied to Dundee. Thus, implicitly recognising the desirability of USPs to cope with a small hinterland compared with those of other universities, three linked themes crystallised. The imagination they evidence displays a marked contrast to the half-hearted reaction to the revolution described above.

Firstly and explicitly, in conjunction with Social Science (a rapidly-growing success in attracting students, also located in the Tower), and in accordance with Tedder's precepts, a law degree should be provided which (echoing thinking of a century before) not only equipped for practice, but was an end in itself.

This would require extra staff including a full-time Chair to enlarge "the Department of Jurisprudence" [99], a full-time Lecturer in English Law (seemingly the first recorded Minute on this speciality, of which more later), two full-time Lecturers in Scots Law "to widen the scope of this subject" by including subjects useful for Social Science (such as Criminology, Industrial Law, Company Law and also Scottish Legal History), one part-time Lecturer in Conveyancing, and one part-time Tutor in Accountancy. And tacitly reversing the 1960 distaste for Honours, it was concluded that all these appointments would allow Honours "at least in Jurisprudence", and possibly joint honours in combination with a Social Science subject such as Economics, History, Philosophy, Political Science or Psychology.

While this USP no doubt attracted some students, the exigencies of the Law Society professional requirements meant that few were able to take social science subjects at any level, and joint Honours was always rare[100]. Much more significant were the two other USPs, which became so marked a feature of the Dundee Law School.

Thus, secondly, and clearly linked, Jurisprudence was asserted to be

a vital subject in the Faculty ... taught by a professor in every other Law Faculty. The institution of a chair will also help the Faculty of Social Science. It will also enable the Faculty to make its contribution to the research in Law which is so imperatively necessary in Scotland[101].

Early fruit of this plan was acceptance of the need for a Chair in Jurisprudence[102], and the subject became a Dundee speciality to the extent that, after the October Revolution (discussed below), there was a compulsory Jurisprudence course in all three years of the Ordinary LLB, and a range of Honours options under the Jurisprudence flag.

This emphasis came from Alastair McDonald (albeit in consultation with Ben Bowman)[103]. He saw it as providing two benefits. It would supply the academic quality hitherto provided by the MA. And he wished to remove the degree entry requirement of Lower Latin, in order to facilitate the entry of those with no intention of practising in Scotland, and specialisation in Jurisprudence would provide an academic counter-argument against those likely to resist that removal (by whom he was regarded as something of a maverick, being a newcomer, and a part-timer and practitioner[104]). Whether, in itself, it did attract students is unclear[105].

And thirdly, and also clearly linked, was English law teaching. This had been available, in principle, as an alternative to Scots Law on the LLB under the 1893 Ordinance[106], but may never have been taught anywhere[107]. (In fact, it became available in the last days of the 1893 Ordinance in curious circumstances, as discussed below). However, students "are now being attracted into the Faculty, some from England, who have no intention of becoming legal practitioners. The Faculty is thus anxious to be able to provide a broad general law degree and not merely a narrow professionalised one[108]." Indeed, English Law teaching might positively encourage students considering qualification in England to apply to St Andrews (though that would depend upon the attitude of the English professional bodies).

To leap ahead, in the long run, the teaching of English Law was a much more important USP than either of the other two. Over the following decades, under the Ordinance which introduced the '1965 LLB' (discussed below) and later amendments, as many exemptions from

English (and Northern Ireland) professional bodies were obtained as from Scottish ones; a full Honours degree in English Law was permitted; and even (albeit half a century later) a dual-qualifying degree was achieved. (All of this produced, of course, a proportionately large number of students from England and Northern Ireland).

Moreover, the availability of English Law facilitated the development of Oil & Gas Law, and thus the Centre for Energy, Petroleum, Mineral Law & Policy, and its off-shoot, the Centre for Water Law, Policy & Science, two further Dundee specialities.

But the vehicle for these three linked themes was a most radical plan, completely redrafting the LLB, changing the "1961 LLB" to the "1965 LLB". But before considering this redrafting, it is necessary to look at the professional changes which were going on. The universities were now making the running but, clearly, the revolutionary changes described above implied radically different Law Society admission regulations[109]. Indeed, for that reason, discussions on these regulations must have proceeded in parallel with those on full-time degrees, though the most prolific of commentators on these matters recorded that the Law Society had not published what became its new regulations at the time when Glasgow Law Faculty was discussing its 1960 LLB Ordinance[110]. Nevertheless, he generously observed that "academic pressure for full-time degrees and better teaching was not met by stubborn opposition from the leaders of the profession[111]."

And in fact, these admission regulations were more revolutionary than were the new LLB Ordinances, laying the foundations for the admission requirements for solicitors which applied until the Diploma in Professional Legal Practice, a one-year post-graduate qualification, required for professional qualification, was introduced twenty years later.

They recast the examination requirements by replacing the three Professional Examinations dating back to 1938 (and discussed in Chapter 3), with a simple requirement to pass six subjects in any order[112]. These subjects were: Law of Scotland I and II, Evidence & Procedure, Book-keeping & Accountancy, Conveyancing, Taxation and Death Duties.

This looks like a simplification. Certainly all traces of Civil Law[113] were removed. However, Constitutional Law[114] was put into Law of Scotland I (alongside domestic relations, reparation, heritable property, leases, agricultural law, wills and succession, trusts, criminal law and other things) as was Elements of Jurisprudence[115]. Law of Scotland II included obligations, contract, sale of goods, master and servant, agency, partnership, bills of exchange, company law, carriage by land, insurance, patents, bankruptcy and professional conduct among other things.

But this slightly terrifying prospect for any examinee was entirely avoidable (and the ability to pass the subjects in any order explained), in that either BL or LLB exempted from everything, provided all the "Law Society subjects" had been taken in it. Nevertheless, the requirement to attend university classes imposed in 1873 but removed in 1886, re-imposed in 1926 and re-removed in 1938, in the odd and complicated history described in Chapter 1, was not re-re-imposed, so a person could still qualify "without systematic instruction", and "serve [his/her] apprenticeship in a country town, or completely free without interruption by classes or examinations"[116].

By far the most radical change, of course, related to apprenticeships. The period of five years, reduced to three for law graduates and some others, remained, though a "post-qualifying year" (that is, a year spent with a restricted practising certificate) was added[117]. However, much more significant, and overturning the practice prevailing ever since formal instruction had been introduced for law agents, and meshing with the introduction of full-time degrees, the apprenticeship became full-time.

No wonder that while "the attitude of the leaders of the profession [to the changes of the 1960s] was favourable to reform, and very helpful to the universities, there were many in the profession who were wholly obstructive[118]".

The revolutionary changes equally implied radically different advocates' admission requirements. Firstly, when the LLB was automatically preceded by an MA, this latter exempted from the general scholarship requirement. But now, intrants would either have to take an MA anyway (and thus exhaust any entitlement to a grant before taking the LLB), or the Faculty's own examinations (without tuition). Secondly, when the LLB was part-time, though it was not compulsory, intrants could work in solicitors' offices alongside apprentices, and even undertake informal 'devilling'. But now both were difficult. Nevertheless, the advocates' regulations were not changed until 1968, and thus after the period in question here[119].

1964-67: The October Revolution (and other matters)

The years 1960-63 had seen the 'February Revolution'. During the years 1964-67, the pace of change accelerated rather than decelerated; the 'October Revolution' took place, involving the complete redrafting of the LLB, changing it from the "1961 LLB" to the "1965 LLB"; and expansion continued. The Dundee Law School had arrived.

But not everything that occurred in these years was revolutionary, and we must look first at the recurring issue of accommodation. As noted above, the law school had finally got its own home on the seventh floor of the Tower Building, when it was completed in 1961. In 1964, McDonald (on both Works and General Planning Committees and, at that meeting, elected Council Assessor on Senate) reported on university properties. He recorded (as part of a box-and-cox attempt to use the Tower efficiently to accommodate the increase in Social Science students) that the Law Faculty then occupied five small (100 sq ft) "retiring rooms" and three large (250 sq ft) "seminar rooms or large offices", and would require an extra "retiring room" in 1965-66[120].

Occupancy of the Tower was relatively brief, however, as a few months later, Law was to move "as soon as possible"[121]. Sites at 2-16 and 21-25 Perth Road were considered[122]. They would be ready by October

1965, and the Faculty could choose which it preferred. However, over the summer of 1965, it actually moved elsewhere. The reasons for this move, and the change of destination, are unknown, and resulted from a "special report" (now lost) by McDonald, wearing his Dean of Law hat[123] (having been re-elected for 1965, though resigning shortly thereafter on account of temporary indisposition, catapulting Ian Willock, of whom more shortly, into the office[124]).

The new home of the Law Faculty was the 'Terrapins', in effect Portakabins, situated approximately where there is now a lawn between the north entrance of the Students' Union, and the Queen Mother Building. They were delivered as shells, fitted out on-site, costing £8,000 and were selected as economical and easy to extend. They provided a 1,150 sq ft Library Reading Room with 50 places, two seminar rooms for twelve, an office, a room for the Faculty Secretary, four Professors' rooms[125] (one reduced to "retiring room" size), and a room for part-time staff, with an "interview cubicle" [126].

They were, however, noisy and cold[127]. Problems with the small rooms were reported in 1966, shortly after which an additional bay was added for research and extra seminar use[128], though the Law Faculty only remained there for a few more years before once more removing, this time to Bonar House.

Arrangements for the law book collection to be transferred to the Terrapins referred to two sets of *Session Cases*[129] in each of the two seminar rooms (but also the return to the Main Library of some older books "presented by Mrs Badenoch Nicholson", save for a copy of Morison's *Dictionary*). This gives some idea of what the Law Library then contained, useful because of almost complete silence on the subject in Council, Senate and Court Minutes.

Nevertheless, and more importantly, there were revolutionary occurrences. The "1961 LLB", a modified version of that under the 1893 Ordinance, was a 'February Revolution'. In 1963 Alastair McDonald's planning (discussed above) came to fruition in the much more thoroughgoing changes of the Draft LLB Ordinance submitted to Senate, with Draft Regulations and an Explanatory Memorandum[130]. This was radically different from what went before in structure, and in being a vehicle for the three linked USPs of synergy with Social Science, Jurisprudence and English Law. Court approved the changes, subject to the views of the General Council[131] (which had no views). Senate also approved[132]. All were agreed that what became the 1964 Ordinance[133] should commence on the earliest possible date, that is, 1 October 1965. This "1965 LLB" constituted the 'October Revolution'.

Though significantly longer than the 1893 Ordinance, even as amended, the 1964 Ordinance was still brief. It did not specify either of the first two fundamental changes (discussed above) from the 1959 Report of a Conference of the four Universities (that is, that an MA was no longer a prerequisite, and that the degree was full-time, and not pursued simultaneously with an apprenticeship), as this was unnecessary. It did specify the third (and for St Andrews, novel) one, however, that is, that both Ordinary (after three years) and Honours (after four) LLB degrees were available, the latter being divided into First, Second or Third grades (making the Upper and Lower Second distinction an interpolation unbacked by Ordinance)[134]. It also specified that there should be 25 teaching weeks over three terms[135]. And it revoked the remaining earlier Ordinances, insofar as not saved to permit those already on course to continue (subject to one exception mentioned below)[136].

Such brevity was possible because (unlike the 19th century Ordinances) this Ordinance delegated almost everything else (including courses of study and the number and nature of examinations[137]) to Senate (subject to approval by Court and comment by General Council), to be expressed in separate Regulations, Syllabuses of Courses and Tables of Class Hours[138].

These delegated matters show how very different the new degree was from its predecessor. Clearly a programme of closely integrated study was intended, rather than a series of separate subjects taken (at least in principle) in any order. However, this resulted in some complicated drafting. The complexity was boiled down in the "General Information" section of the University Calendar[139] to a summary, which nevertheless remained Byzantine (and does not accord precisely with the Regulations[140]). A tabular version appears as Appendix 2 to this Chapter.

The Ordinary Degree comprised four Parts. Part I took place in the first two terms of First Year and comprised a compulsory "composite" Introduction to Law (160 lectures, including Jurisprudence I[141], Constitutional Law & History, Administrative Law, Public International Law and Scottish Legal System). Part II took place in the second (thus overlapping Part I) and third terms of First Year and the whole of Second Year (200 lectures, including 75 Jurisprudence II[142] lectures and 125 Scots Law ones).

Part III occupied the whole of Third Year (135 lectures, including 40 Jurisprudence III[143] lectures and 95 lectures on one out of a list of Conveyancing I, Commercial Law or English Law[144]). Part IV took place partly in Second Year and partly in Third Year (some 200 lectures, selected from a list of nine 40-lecture "single" courses, and eleven 75-lecture "double" courses, including Conveyancing I and II, Commercial Law, English Law, Comparative Law, Conflict of Laws, Civil Law and some Arts subjects). Thus some subjects were in both Part III and Part IV, allowing greater choice (for instance, Conveyancing I and Commercial Law could be taken in either Part III or Part IV), some advanced subjects (for instance, Conveyancing II built on Conveyancing I), and some new subjects (for instance, Conflict of Laws and Arts subjects).

Honours was entered at the beginning of Third Year, thus avoiding Part III and part of Part IV (though the need to take some such subjects for professional purposes produced some extraordinarily complicated pathways to Honours, and required some subjects to be both Ordinary and Honours, the latter version involving extra work and a separate examination)[145]. The Honours degree was either single Honours Private Law (with four Scots Law papers and four Conveyancing) or joint (though not so described, with four Jurisprudence papers and four Private Law ones, or either four or five Jurisprudence papers and four or three

Philosophy, Economics, Political Science or Modern History ones). Entry to Honours was selective[146]. All of Parts I and II, and three subjects from Part IV (ie those taken in Second Year) must have been passed, an application made, and a decision taken that the applicant was "academically fit to enter upon the proposed Honours study".

One feature easy to overlook in all this complexity is that the relative size of courses was still expressed in the traditional fashion of lecture hours. Tutorials were not mentioned at all, and were extremely rare (save in Conveyancing), at least in the early days[147], though the small size of Honours classes necessitated something other than the traditional lecture. But the most remarkable aspect of this structure, reflecting the reasoning discussed above on USPs, were the provisions for Jurisprudence (present in all three years of the Ordinary degree) and English Law (including Contract, Tort and Criminal Law, and returned to below).

The "General Information" section of the University Calendar also summarised the contemporary Admission as Solicitor (Scotland) Regulations (discussed above) and advocates' admission regulations, and those of the Law Society of England and Wales, which promised one-for-one exemptions from Part I of its Qualifying Examination (and "[r]ecent experience" indicated that passes in Constitutional Law & History, Administrative Law and Scots Law could expect to obtain exemption from its Constitutional Law, Administrative Law and Contract and Tort examinations)[148].

The final part of the October Revolution concerned the BL. Entry to it had been "suspended" in 1961. The 1964 Ordinance, by repealing the 1893 Ordinance, abolished the unfairly unloved degree after 90 years. Were tears shed?

The 1965 LLB implied staff expansion, in particular, in Jurisprudence and English Law. A third, full-time, Chair had been sought, with varying priority and specialisation, since 1951. As synergy with Social Science (doing so well) and Jurisprudence (foregrounded) were identified as USPs, the Quinquennial Estimates for 1962-67 sought a full-time Chair in order to enlarge "the Department of Jurisprudence" [149]. Thus, a dozen years after first proposed, an Ordinance providing for such a Chair was promulgated in 1963[150], and presumably the post was advertised and applications received.

An appointing Committee (including Professor A H Campbell, Dean of the Edinburgh University Law School, and leading exponent of the subject in Scotland, as External Assessor) was set up and recommended unanimously that Alan Watson, MA DPhil, of Oriel College, Oxford be appointed. (The External Assessor's concerns that his interest was in Roman Law rather than Jurisprudence[151] was over-ridden by "the sheer brilliance of Dr Watson")[152].

However, Alan Watson declined the offer[153] and, "in accordance with the External Assessor's advice", Ian Willock, then Senior Lecturer in Aberdeen[154] was invited to apply, interviewed, and appointed[155] and was inducted in January 1965[156].

Expansion also meant that there were appointments to other new full-time posts. From 1 January 1964, J J Robertson (an LLB graduate of 1956, considered extensively below, from private practice[157]) was appointed to teach Conveyancing, and from 1 October 1964 of J W R Gray MA LLB (formerly Resident Magistrate in Uganda), to teach Criminal Law[158], both roughly as anticipated in the Quinquennial Estimates 1962-67[159]. (Also Louise Houston was appointed in 1965 to replace Robert Moore[160], and William Fyffe Dorward, who had taught Forensic Medicine, died in 1965, and was replaced by Donald Rushton).

But of even greater significance, Neil MacCormick (from Balliol College, Oxford, also discussed below) and C D Baker, BA BCL (from an unknown but, given his degrees, clearly English, source), were appointed in April 1965[161] for Jurisprudence and English Law, respectively, and in May 1966, Robin L C Hunter (from Aberdeen University) to a further Jurisprudence Lectureship and R B Stewart to a Research Assistantship "under the direction of the Professor of Jurisprudence"[162].

Some of these appointments seem curiously far in advance of the need for them. Jurisprudence for the 1961 LLB had to be taught for a couple more years until those students taking it had all graduated (or, at least, passed the subject), and Jurisprudence I for the 1965 LLB would be required from October, but Bowman (just promoted to Senior Lecturer[163]) had taught the former for years[164], and Willock was already in post to teach the latter. Jurisprudence II would be required only from April 1966, and Jurisprudence III and Honours Jurisprudence only from October 1967. Was MacCormick known to be seeking employment and too good a catch to miss?

Similarly, the new English Law Part III course would not start until October 1967, a full two years after Baker's appointment. Was there a plan to teach English Law in the intervening years for the last 1961 LLB two cohorts, as a gentle run-in for the new regime[165]? In any event, Baker changed his mind shortly after appointment and never arrived[166]. Norman A P Methven MA, Barrister, was appointed to replace him in the autumn of 1965[167], and the first English Law syllabus appeared in the University Calendar for 1966-67 with his name[168], but he resigned with effect from December 1966[169] and possibly never taught the subject[170]. McDonald and the Law Faculty (like Carlton, a generation earlier) must have thought themselves cursed, and any plan for teaching English Law to the last two cohorts of the 1961 LLB was apparently evaporating.

However, in 1966, while Methven was at least nominally on the strength, English Law was added to the curriculum[171] as a 40-lecture option[172] (in addition to the never-used 80-lecture option [173]), for the last cohort of the 1961 LLB. But it was only taught in 1966-67, probably after Methven's actual departure, by MacCormick (for an honorarium of £100)[174]. Thus, paradoxically, English Law was first taught in Scotland, at least in modern times, by that Scottish nationalist *extraordinaire*. However, he, too, resigned shortly thereafter, returning to Balliol College[175].

Other staff changes and additions occurred in 1967 including appointment of Colin Campbell[176] (from Aberdeen University) to teach Jurisprudence after MacCormick's departure, and Nigel F Matthews[177] (from an unknown source) to teach Public International Law after Cowie's elevation to a Glasgow Chair[178].

The revolution had taken place, but the future still had to be considered. In 1966, with the 1965 LLB and its USPs firmly in place, yet further modified quinquennial proposals were made[179]. The three important aims identified for the Law Faculty were growth in student numbers, improvement of the staff-student ratio, and (once more) new courses.

Student numbers would be held at the current rate of 60[180] until 1970-71, rising then to 80, but selection techniques would be improved[181], and increased demand from intending accountants was noted. Local law students could easily be absorbed, but lack of residence places constrained expansion, and about a third of entrants were from England, which was acceptable.

The staff student ratio was 1:13, likely to deteriorate to 1:17 by the end of the quinquennium, as against a University Grants Committee recommendation of 1:7. This ratio should be reduced to 1:10, requiring 9.5 more staff, thereby increasing staff numbers from 13 to 23.5. Within that, a Chair in Accountancy & Tax, and a Lectureship in Constitutional Law, were sought in 1967-68; a Senior Lectureship in International Law and a Lectureship in Comparative Law in 1968-69; a Chair of Public Law and a Lectureship in Commercial Law in 1969-70; Lectureships in Accountancy and Conveyancing in 1970-71; and Lectureships in Jurisprudence, Administrative Law and Scots Law in 1971-72.

New courses would include the Land Law of England and Wales towards the end of the quinquennium, to give an adequate range of English Law in the Ordinary degree. The main expansion would be in Honours, however, achieving parity with Arts and Science, with growing demand expected, including from the strong minority of English students. (The norm in England was a three-year Honours degree, and an "Ordinary" degree, if indeed recognised there, probably signified a compensatory pass[182]). Two thirds of any cohort might be expected to seek to enter Honours, but high entrance standards would restrict entry to one third. Expansion was possible in Public Law and in Accountancy & Tax (as the plans for expanded staff numbers indicated), and Honours in both was possible, as also in combinations with Politics and Economics. But it was not yet possible in English Law, even though English students would expect it.

This, though bearing some resemblance to the 1951 wish-list for a "fully-equipped school of law", is clearly a remarkable and ambitious shopping-list. Jurisprudence and English Law secured, the next *démarches* were to be Accountancy and Public Law. But most interesting is that almost all the new posts would be full-time.

In an intriguing aside, in 1965, there was discussion of Jurisprudence, Civil Law and Comparative Law being taught on the St Andrews 'campus' (though not as part of a degree)[183]. Of greater relevance, in 1967, Strathclyde University started a BA Law as an off-shoot of the BA in the School of Business & Administration, with an entry of 50 students and Law Society recognition as equivalent to an LLB[184]. But, although it had no direct effect on law teaching, the most significant event of the years 1964-67 was clearly the translation of QCD into the University of Dundee.

1956-67: People

The rapid sequence of events over this period saw staff numbers creep up to about the dozen, until the big recruitment of the mid-1960s raised it to the mid-teens, with the number of women doubled. It thus provides a marked contrast with earlier periods.

Change was now as evident as continuity in recruitment. Unlike in previous periods, only three of the recruits of this period were solicitors in private practice, though two others were solicitors no longer in private practice, or in public service. Four more were advocates or barristers, but none of them was in private practice and, the other recruits were not professionally qualified (save for the doctor teaching Forensic Medicine).

Change was equally evident in that only those three solicitors in private practice were really part-time, though two more were part-time in a special sense, being employed full-time by the University. All the others were unequivocally full-time.

Change was again reflected in length of service. The three (professionally-qualified, part-time) survivors from 1939 continued in post for almost the whole period, or the whole period and well beyond. Of the (professionally-qualified, part-time) recruits of the late 1940s, and mid-1950s, two also continued for the whole period and well beyond. Other such recruits continued for much of it. Yet further, of the (professionally-qualified, part-timer) recruits of the present period, several remained for many more years thereafter. Moreover, most of these professionally-qualified, part-timers simply retired from the job, though often continuing in practice.

On the other hand, among the full-timers, while those professionally-qualified exhibited the same traits, those not professionally qualified did not, indeed left after very short periods in some cases, for employment elsewhere.

Thus an interesting and paradoxical contrast, harbinger of the future, grew up. On the one hand, there were part-time local practitioners, often alumni, serving for lengthy periods, though on annual contracts. On the other, there were full-time, non- professionally-qualified, academics, rarely alumni, sometimes serving for remarkably brief periods, though on permanent contracts. The paradox is resolved by recalling that many local solicitors had attended their local university, could only teach part-time as they were tied to local firms, but by the same token, were available for decades: while career academics might have come from a variety of other universities, intended to teach full-time and were not tied to any firm, and might seek promotion elsewhere.

This is another aspect of the revolution in law teaching at this time, encouraged by the introduction of full-time degrees, enhanced by the enormous growth in universities as a whole, and re-enforced by the consequential increasing professionalisation of university teachers with, perhaps, a new emphasis on research. We might also note that, while the drawbacks of part-time teachers of law had been aired in the literature for half a century or more, the drawbacks of full-time legal academics (such as possible lack of practical, or up-to-date, experience, and a tendency to flit) had not.

A related matter, important to mention, was the appointment from 1962, initially part-time and shared with Social Science, of a Faculty Secretary[185]. The first holder of the office was David Connelly[186], followed from 1964 by Jim Ryan (from the colonial civil service) "with certain duties in the Secretary's office" (in fact, servicing Senate)[187], until promoted to Assistant Secretary in 1966[188], then Douglas Wilson (also from the colonial civil service)[189].

The identities of several of the new staff were touched on above, but four figures who require greater examination are Ian Willock, Jim Robertson, Dennis Collins and Neil MacCormick.

Ian Douglas Willock (1930-2013)[190] graduated MA (1951) LLB (1954) from Aberdeen University, then undertook National Service in the Intelligence Corps. He lectured in Jurisprudence at Glasgow University from 1956 to 1960, incidentally passing advocate in 1957 (though it seems unlikely that he ever intended to practise), and spending 1958-59 as Senior Research Fellow at the University of Michigan. He then moved back to Aberdeen as Senior Lecturer, obtaining a PhD from Glasgow in 1963, published in 1966 by the Stair Society as *The Origins and Development of the Jury in Scotland.*

In 1965, clearly a bright young man, he was appointed at the early age of 34 as the first (and as things fell out, only) Professor of Jurisprudence at QCD (also second full-time Professor, the other being Master of the College, however, so busy with other things), and remained until retirement and elevation to Professor emeritus in 1997.

Shortly after his arrival, he was thrust into the Deanship (1965-66 and 1967-70) at a time when much was going on, principally both the introduction of the 'modern' LLB with Honours, and the split of Dundee from St Andrews. (Incidentally, because in practice the only honorary degree was an LLD, in his role as Dean he was required to deliver laureation addresses to all honorary graduands – probably over 40 – of whatever discipline or none, in St Andrews, and thereafter, Dundee, University).

He was also heavily occupied as Head of the Department of Jurisprudence, an onerous task in subject not a popular one with most students, though a Dundee speciality. Never closely tied to any school of Jurisprudence, he responded to this challenge by treating the subject not as a narrow study of theoretical issues, but as a device to explore a wide range of topical legal issues. Thus, he was ideal for organising the courses under the name "Jurisprudence" in all three years of the Ordinary Degree, which sought to do more than run through the natural law, positivist, realist, etc schools, and under his regime, Jurisprudence formed the basis of several Honours options, including criminal responsibility, industrial relations and race relations (the latter two very unusual for their time). He also gathered around him in the Department a heterogeneous (and occasionally difficult) group of academics, including a future Regius Professor and MEP (Neil MacCormick), two future Vice-Chancellors (Colin Campbell[191] and, after our period, Walter Kamba[192]), but also, again after our period, Abe Harari[193], Alan Norrie[194] and others.

With those students who found Jurisprudence stimulating, he was very popular, and a number of whom went on to achieve considerable academic success (including Zenon Bankowski, noted below), or high judicial office (including Lynda Clark, also noted below), who acknowledged his support and encouragement. His popularity was admittedly enhanced by his youthful appearance, mildly flamboyant style of dress, and propensity to own exotic cars. For some generations of students, long after he demitted that office, he was known simply as "the Dean". His desire to use his talents to teach students, and make law

322

accessible to ordinary people, put him somewhat at odds with the growing pressure towards funded research and publication, and his best-known publication is *Scottish Legal System*, a student text written with a colleague, first published in 1993, the fifth edition posthumously in 2013. As a testimony to his popularity, at the instance of students, the University Library now has a Willock Room, opened in 2014 by Lynda Clark, now then Lady Clark of Calton PC (and noted further below).

His view of Jurisprudence as simply a means of understanding how law could be employed for useful purposes manifested itself membership of the Stewart Committee on Alternatives to Prosecution (which produced the idea of fiscal fines), but also in two important linked developments he initiated or assisted in. One was the original Dundee Legal Advice Centre of the 1970s, in which free legal advice was delivered by students under supervision, something very unusual for the time (though much later re-emerging as Dundee University Student Law Clinic). The other was the Scottish Legal Action Group, and its journal *Scolag*, in its 40th year of publication at the time of writing, of which he was Editor for several years.

James ("Jim") Joseph Robertson (1933-2011)[195] was one of the first MA LLBs of St Andrews University, graduating in 1956, and first President of the Students' Law Society. After national service in the Navy (seemingly without ever seeing the sea), qualifying as a solicitor, and spending five years in practice in Edinburgh, he returned to QCD as Lecturer in Conveyancing in 1964, though he also later taught a number of other subjects. These included parts of both Comparative Law and Conflicts of Law with Gordon Cowie[196], parts of Scots Law, and the first year Western Legal Tradition course which existed for several years after our period. In addition, he was very active in University affairs, serving on Senate and Court.

But his name is more closely linked with Civil Law, which he continued to teach part of, even after nominal retirement. He spent many vacations visiting the Vatican archives (often in the company of Alastair McDonald), researching medieval appeals from Scotland to the *Sacra*

Romana Rota, the papal court for matters of canon law (on which subject he gave the Annual Lecture of the Stair Society in 1987). He also organised numerous very popular trips to Rome through the then Extra-Mural Studies Department.

Indeed, he had numerous archaeological and antiquarian interests, participating in, and expounding upon, Roman digs in Tayside, and for many years was Chairman of the Friends of Dundee City Archives. He also organised and stage-managed the celebrations in 1990 for the centenary of law teaching in the entity which became the University of Dundee.

However, what was most memorable about him was his extraordinary enthusiasm as a teacher, and willingness to engage in debate, in class and elsewhere (including student parties). But his *pièce de resistance* was the organisation, for many years, of a final year student trip, between the end of examinations and graduation, to Loch Tay for the purposes of fishing, pony-trekking (also encouraging several members of staff to learn to ride when he did so himself) and other outdoor pursuits during the day, followed by dinner at the Weem Hotel in the evening, and a coach back to Dundee as dawn was breaking. He was also for many years Warden of Peterson House, a new style of student accommodation comprising self-catering flats, opened in 1967.

Dennis Ferguson Collins (1930-2017)[197] was another of the first MA LLBs of St Andrews. A Dundonian born and bred, he attended the High School of Dundee, winning prizes every year, and often being dux, and later proudly declaring his grandchildren to be the fifth consecutive generation of alumni.

However, while still young, he was struck down by serious illness twice, both occasions resulting in a year's hospitalisation. He nevertheless graduated MA in 1952, and LLB in 1956, having been apprenticed to Gray, Robertson & Wilkie (now Bowmans). After that, he was assistant, later partner, in Pollock & Smith (later Gilruth, Pollock & Smith, then Carlton Gilruth, and now Blackadders), becoming both an SSC and a WS, and retiring after eighteen years as senior partner in 1993. In 1987, he was elected Dean of the Faculty of Procurators and Solicitors in Dundee, and in 1988, appointed Honorary Sheriff.

He was very active in a variety of other fields, including the Incorporation of the Guildry of Dundee (Guild Brother, Assessor, Guildry Clerk and Archivist), Lord Armitstead's Dundee Trust which, among other things, funds the Armitstead Lectures (Joint Chairman), the Dundee Society for the Prevention of Cruelty to Children (Honorary Secretary) and, not least, the Dundee Congregational Church, where his family worshipped (Treasurer for over 50 years).

As well as being a strong family man, keen golfer, angler and gardener, he was a Francophile (Honorary Consul for France for twenty years, with a Silver Medal of Honour from the French Government), a keen philatelist (President for some years of the Dundee & District Philatelic Society and of the Association of Scottish Philatelic Societies, and Esteemed Fellow of the Royal Philatelic Society of London, with a Victorian pillar box in his garden), a keen local historian (member of the Abertay Historical Society and others), publishing in 2016 *A Gentleman's Residence: the demesne and manor farm of Craigie: a monograph on the Estate of Craigie*), and a keen amateur of heraldry (with his own coat of arms).

But of most immediate interest, he was a part-time lecturer from 1960 to 1979, teaching Scots Law to generations of students, with a dedication to factual accuracy combined with a quiet joviality, and was an invaluable source of information in the writing of this book.

Sir Donald Neil MacCormick QC, FBA, FRSE (1941-2009), ultimately Professor of Public Law and the Law of Nations at Edinburgh University, holder of many academic honours, sometime MEP, and foremost legal philosopher of his generation in the UK (as well as scion of Scottish nationalism), received numerous obituaries, and it would be otiose to summarise them here[198].

It is worth recalling his popularity among students, however[199]. His style of lecturing was distinctive, involving 2½" x 5" record cards with notes about the relevant cases thereupon, removed one by one from the left side-pocket of a hairy tweed jacket for exposition, then transferred to the right side-pocket (except when dropped on the floor). He readily appeared at student parties, and in 1967, fulfilled a promise to play his bagpipes on the top of the Dundee Law on a Sunday morning, though requiring to be "dragged from his pit" to do so.

After considering staff identities, we turn to the staff experience. That of the part-time, local practitioner staff, in post for decades in some cases, may have been much the same as they and their predecessors had in previous periods. For the full-timers, the experience must have been very different, allowing full concentration upon the subject taught with time to research and reflect, with teaching loads low to modern eyes, and non-existent pressure to publish. The expectation of engagement in published research crystallised slowly, and MacCormick (not unexpectedly) appears to have been the first member of staff in post to have had an article published[200].

There remains little written record of the nature of law teaching at this time, and how it might have changed in the light of the manifold changes over the period. But the lecture, in some cases, in effect dictating notes, remained the normal method of delivery, with little provision for tutorials and the like. (It is relevant that there were few textbooks offering any exposition of the law, other than Gloag and Henderson[201]). However, the increasing numbers of full-time staff, together with a full-time degree from 1961, made initiatives simpler to introduce[202]. When MacCormick took on English Law teaching, a tutorial assistant was hired, which strongly implies tutorials were held in that subject. About the same time, Willock started a voluntary Jurisprudence Discussion Group, whose members wrote papers each week[203]. There may have been other examples.

Incidentally, at this time, the University Grants Committee published a Report on University Teaching Methods[204]. Senate passed this to Faculties to consider, and the Law Faculty response was that a comprehensive university-wide scheme to inculcate good teaching practice was unworkable, though Faculties might provide some instruction for junior staff[205]. What set the cat among the pigeons, however, were the "highly objectionable" suggestions of CCTV surveillance, and criticism by students or, indeed, any external agency (a view scarcely credible today).

We have more information on where lectures took place. Before the Tower Building was open, the Carnegie (Physics) Building in the Geddes Quadrangle, the Carnelley (Chemistry) Building, the Ewing (Engineering) Building, and both the Princess Cinema[206] and Well Road Ballroom off the (old) Hawkhill (near where the Life Sciences buildings are now) were used. None of these had microphones, and the two last-mentioned were sometimes cold enough in winter to require an overcoat under the gown (the wearing of which was then *de rigueur* for staff)[207]. After the Tower Building opened, for a period, most lectures were on the seventh floor, where the Law Faculty was situated, but they later reverted to some of the earlier *venues*, and other lecture-rooms in the Tower[208].

There may have been more social interaction among staff in this period, for recollections of the time include strong friendships based on the common experience of teaching, camaraderie in the Staff Club on the tenth floor of the Tower when that was opened (with Staff Dinners and Dances and a Wine Club[209]), post-Examiners' Meeting lunches in the Queen's Hotel, and Graduation Garden Parties at Vernonholme[210] or Belmont Hall[211], not to mention socialising with students, readily possible with the small class sizes. There was also, from an unknown date, the annual Law Faculties Conference at the Burn at Edzell[212] ("in idyllic surroundings")[213].

How much this conviviality depended upon the arrival of the new, full time, staff is unclear. But from 1964, to join the most friendly Gordon Cowie, were the most clubbable Jim Robertson, the most amicable Jim Ryan, the most entertaining J W R Gray, the most earnest Ian Willock, and the most stimulating Neil MacCormick, which must have changed the atmosphere.

In any case, for Matheson, McDonald and Willock, other sorts of change were certainly considerable. Matheson was translated to the

Mastership, hugely increasing his administrative burdens in the run-up to the creation of the University of Dundee, with the consequence of similarly increasing the burden upon McDonald by bouncing him into the Deanship (as noted in Chapter 5), something he felt he had not signed up for[214], at just the time that he was rarely out of Court Minutes as the person negotiating the deals which created the university campus as it still largely remains. Willock, as the second (and effectively only) full-time Professor, was thrust into the Deanship shortly after arrival in 1965.

Incidentally, a minor irritant for staff at this time, which echoes down the years in Court Minutes, and resonates with 21st-century staff, was examination invigilation. It was difficult to get staff to volunteer, so commonly invigilation was undertaken by ministers[215] and in 1961 there was a proposal to raise the hourly rate of 8/-, as paid for the last thirteen years, to 10/- (although Aberdeen staff did it for free)[216].

Turning to the students, it should be noted that the Universities Central Council on Admissions (UCCA, the predecessor of UCAS) had been set up in 1961 as a centralised applications processor to avoid the difficulties of a separate application to each university. St Andrews University did not join immediately and in 1965 was still discussing full membership (which the Law Faculty opposed)[217]. Only in 1966 did it decide to participate fully, with effect from 1 October 1967 (thus after the achievement of independence by the University of Dundee)[218]. Whether all this had any effect upon entrant numbers is unknown.

The familiar sources of information on students discussed in the Annex on Sources of Information on Students continue, and the difficulties to which they give rise, increase. Numbers of entrants remain of particular interest as, on the one hand, the BL was "suspended" in 1961 (then abolished) and, on the other, the "1961 LLB" was introduced, but rapidly superseded by the "1965 LLB".

BL entrants appear to have continued at a low, if steady, level for the first few years, varying between two and six, before dropping to one, no doubt in anticipation of the abolition of the degree, then zero, reflecting its "suspension". Over the final six years of its life, there were a total of some 18 entrants (an average of, say, three a year). None appear to have been women.

The LLB also seems to have opened the period with low if steady numbers, between two and six. But from 1961-62 (possibly reflecting the February Revolution of the introduction of the "1961 LLB" and consecutive apprenticeship, and the abolition of the BL), it rose rapidly to several times that level, seemingly rising from sixteen to 56. Overall there were more than 220 LLB entrants (averaging perhaps twenty a year over the whole period, though more usefully seen as some six a year from 1956-57 to 1960-61, but some 38 a year from 1962-3 to 1966-67). Together with some eighteen BL entrants, there were thus perhaps 250 graduating law entrants in the period as a whole. Numbers of women LLB entrants remained low, however, seemingly varying between zero and eight, nearly all in the last half-dozen years, and giving a total of some 37 (but, say, 12% in those latter years), nevertheless indicating something of an advance.

Non-graduating entrants numbers seem to have continued the rapid rise of the previous period, shooting up to between 80 and 90 a year from 1956-57 to 1960-61, slipping back thereafter to between twenty and 30 for a couple of years, and then around 50 a year from 1964-65 to 1966-67, thus totalling over 700 (and averaging some 64 a year). Among them, there was appears to have been a remarkable increase in the number of women entrants, varying from twelve to 25 a year from 1956-57 to 1960-61, before dropping back to penny numbers, varying between zero and four. These swings beg an explanation. The sudden increase in non-graduating entrants, including an increase in the number of women entrants, seems to have co-incided with the appointment of a Lecturer in Accountancy. But it also co-incided with the incorporation into the University of the Dundee School of Economics, which might possibly have had a number of women pursuing an accountancy or other professional qualification, requiring a law input. The equally sudden drop in both might have resulted from that group having worked its way out of the system, but is perverse, since it also roughly co-incided with the plan to increase the teaching of accountancy students in response to the change in the Chartered Institute of Accountants in Scotland's professional requirements. The mystery remains, but it is possible that it is explained simply by an unrecorded change in the practice of recording students.

Nevertheless, these numbers must have caused considerable satisfaction in the Law School. After six decades of marginal existence, considerable numbers of graduating students were entering, and on the "superior" degree. Reliance on accountancy students was reduced, and escape velocity reached.

And as to student identities, yet once more, so far as graduating students entrants are concerned, we can say something about certain sub-groups. The women identified include Helen Taylor and Evelyn Gavin (LLB 1956[219]); Enid Marshall (noted below: LLB 1958[220]); Isabelle Brand or Wight (BL 1959[221]); Moyra Cameron and Margaret Murray (LLB and BL, respectively, 1960[222]); Georgina Lyon (LLB 1963[223]); Elspeth Attwool (noted below), Christine Boyd, Joanne Davies, Frances Robertson and Geraldine Tickle (LLB 1964[224]); Marjorie Brand, Diane Caine, Judith Currie, Aileen Crichton, Enid Haley, Margaret Seppings, Pamela Wright and Eve Crowe (LLB 1965[225]); Jennifer Buigholt, Christine Pollock and Cynthia Holme and Marion McFadzean (LLB 1966[226]); and Valerie Cameron, Alison Mackenzie-Wood, Mary McLaughlan, Penelope Nichols and Mary Normanton (LLB 1967[227]).

The high achievers include, in addition to the prize-winners, Dennis Collins and J J Robertson (both LLB 1956)[228], both referred to above, and Alistair Clark (LLB 1957[229]), noted in the previous Chapter as President of the Law Society of Scotland 1989-90. They also include Enid Marshall and Elspeth Attwool (both noted above). The former obtained a PhD in QCD[230], taught law at what is now Abertay University, and Stirling University, and was a prodigious writer of student textbooks and casebooks[231]. The latter taught law at Glasgow University, but was also an MEP 2000-09 and vice-chairman of the European Parliament Fisheries Committee.

They further include from the last cohort under the "1961 LLB" (thus first matriculating in 1964), for which Honours was not available[232], Peter Robson, who became a Professor at Strathclyde University, Len Higson who became Regional Procurator Fiscal for Strathclyde, and Zenon Bankowski. The last-mentioned, however, was enabled to transfer from the "1961 LLB" to the "1965 LLB"[233] (not envisaged in the regulations, but achieved with Ian Willock's help), and thereby start *de novo* on a Honours degree. This allowed him, in 1969, to achieve the first 'First' in Law from the University of Dundee[234] (in Joint Honours Law and Philosophy), as part of the first (1965-68/9[235]) cohort of the 1965 LLB. After a career at Cardiff and Edinburgh Universities, and the production of several influential books, at the time of writing he was Emeritus Professor of Legal Theory at Edinburgh University.

From the first cohort of the "1965 LLB" (thus first matriculating in 1965) for which Honours was available, and also graduating in 1969, was Thomas Briggs[236], the first (and only) "First" in Law from St Andrews University (in Jurisprudence and Scots Law). (The paradox of Firsts in the same year in both Dundee and St Andrews is resolved by noting that this cohort, and the next, were given the choice of graduating with either Dundee of St Andrews degrees because they had first matriculated before Dundee's regained independence, but graduating after it). After attending the Wharton School of Finance in the University of Pennsylvania, Briggs became managing director and chairman of a variety of companies, and was High Sheriff of Cheshire in 2006-07, earning him an MBE, and also becoming a Knight of the Order of St John for his work with the St John Ambulance, and Lord Lieutenant of Cheshire in 2010.

Also from that first cohort, but graduating with an Ordinary degree in 1968, was John Stewart[237]. After qualifying as a solicitor, he practised in Aberdeen, then Dumfries, becoming an advocate in 1978, a Temporary Sheriff in 1985, Sheriff of South Strathclyde, Dumfries and Galloway in Airdrie, then Hamilton, retiring in 2010[238]. Seemingly he was then one of the longest-serving sheriffs, but more to the point, he was probably the first St Andrews or Dundee graduate to become Sheriff.

From the next following cohort (first matriculating in 1966) was Lynda Clark, whose career has been the most stellar of any Dundee or St Andrews law graduate to date[239]. She taught Jurisprudence in Dundee University from 1973 to 1977, taking a PhD at Edinburgh in 1975, then went to the Bar in 1977, taking silk in 1989 (and becoming a barrister in England in 1990). Elected as an MP in 1997, she was appointed to Government in 1999, as first holder of the new office, under the devolution settlement, of Advocate-General (i.e. legal adviser on Scots Law to the United Kingdom Government[240]), continuing to hold it until 2006, being made a life peer, as Baroness Clark of Calton, in 2005. In 2006, she was appointed a Senator of the College of Justice, the first Dundee or St Andrews graduate to achieve this office and, in 2012, Chairman of the Scottish Law Commission. In 2013, she was elevated to the Inner House of the Court of Session.

Turning from names to addresses, those of graduates recorded in Senate Minutes start to be more exotic in this period (as quinquennial plans indicated[241]). Among the BL students, there were some with English addresses, including one out of the four graduating in 1960, three out of the six in 1961, and one out of the four in 1962. This is surprising, since the degree, unloved in Scotland, had no professional advantage in England and Wales, indeed might be unrecognised for professional purposes.

Among the LLB students, there was a similar pattern of increasing exoticism, though starting later and becoming much more marked. Some half of them had non-Scottish addresses, which is unsurprising given a deliberate policy of seeking English students, principally by providing English Law from the mid-1960s. Thus there were one out of six in 1960; two out of five in 1963; eight out of ten in 1964; 23 out of 35 in 1965; and fourteen out of 36 in 1966 (when it was noted that only two-thirds of the 1966-67 entry were from Scottish addresses, which was nevertheless regarded as unproblematic[242]).

In this period, as with the staff experience, and partly for parallel reasons, the student experience contrasts with that of the previous one[243]. For non-graduating and BL students, little had changed from the period covered by the previous Chapter, although by this time, the Law Library was comparatively well-stocked. Likewise, *mutatis mutandis*, for the remaining "1950 LLB" students.

For the "1961 LLB", and then the "1965 LLB" students, the experience was very different. While the 1961 LLB curriculum was the same as for the 1950 LLB, for full-time students taking a part-time curriculum, it was a much easier work-load, though now some tutorials may have supplemented the lectures. And the "1965 LLB", while genuinely full-time, was increasingly taught by full-time staff on a much wider range of subjects and probably with more tutorial work. Both also benefitted from the improved Law Library.

This meant that law students on these two versions of the LLB could fully participate in student sporting, social and other activities, just as the MA students had been able to. As noted in Chapter 5, the Students' Law Society came into existence in 1955, and continued (doubtless with greater or lesser levels of activity, depending upon the enthusiasm of the Committee). An important milestone was passed in 1965, when Court recognised its existence by awarding it £10[244]. Records of its activities from this time are lost, but probably continued to involve visiting speakers, including judges and academics, and organised social events like Gaudie Night (as well as selling Law Society ties and Law Faculty "college scarves").

What was probably the most important change in the student experience however, was that, as a result of the 'Robbins expansion', an increasing proportion of all students were not local, requiring creation of residences, including Airlie, Belmont, Chalmers and West Park Halls, and use of "digs" or flats. Indeed, this increasing non-local proportion generated a new student culture, in some ways more similar to that in St Andrews, based on the residence, the flat and the Students' Union (and public houses[245]). Associated with this, it should be recalled that most of our period falls into the Sixties, when *mores* for young people were changing rapidly, as was audible in music and visible in dress, and noted in sexual liberty[246].

APPENDIX 1

A SIMPLIFIED* VIEW OF THE LLB DEGREE UNDER THE 1893 ORDINANCE AS MODIFIED BY THE 1961 ORDINANCE ("THE 1961 LLB"), SHOWN IN TERMS OF YEARS TAKEN, WITH SOME DETAIL AS TO SYLLABUS AND FORM OF EXAMINATION[247]

Year	Subjects	Weight	Examination
1	Public International Law	40+ lectures	one paper of three hours
	Civil Law	80+ lectures	two papers of three hours
	Constitutional Law & History	80+ lectures	two papers of three hours and an oral
2	Scots law inc: Sources of law Courts and Jurisdiction Obligations and Contracts: Sale of Goods Partnership Company law Insurance Rights in Security; Cautionary Obligations Bankruptcy Negotiable Instruments Ownership of Moveables Hiring, Loan and Deposit Landlord and Tenant Principal and Agent	80+ lectures	three papers of two hours

	Master and Servant Husband and Wife Parent and Child Reparation Criminal law *or*		
	Jurisprudence	75+ lectures	two papers of three hours
	Conveyancing *or*	80+ lectures	three papers of two hours
	Economics	"at least three times a week" (=, say 75 lectures)	two papers of three hours
3	*Three subjects out of*		
	International Private Law	40+ lectures	one paper of three hours
	Administrative law	unspecified	one paper of two and a half hours
	Evidence & Procedure	40+ lectures	one paper of two and a half hours
	Accounting, Taxation and Death Duties	75+ lectures	two papers of three hours
	Comparative law	40+ lectures	one paper of three hours
	Forensic Medicine	40+ lectures	one paper of three hours

or any other approved subject (in practice only Economics)	"at least three times a week" (= say, 75 lectures)	two papers of three hours

* The principal simplifications are:

(i)   no sequence of subjects was required by the Ordinance, and what is shown here is what typically occurred;

(ii)   the 1893 Ordinance specified 80 lectures each for Scots law and Mercantile law: however, there was no separate Mercantile Law class though, as can be seen, the Scots law syllabus in fact largely comprised Mercantile law;

(iii)   eight subjects were required overall by the 1893 Ordinance, but nine were probably invariably taken[248];

(iv)   Jurisprudence and Accountancy were required to have "not less than forty lectures" in the 1893 Ordinance, but the Syllabus of Courses indicates at least 75 and 80 respectively;

(v)   All subjects nominally required an oral examination, but in practice this was usually used only in marginal cases;

(vi)   not all Third Year subjects were available in all years.

APPENDIX 2

A SIMPLIFIED VIEW* OF THE LLB DEGREE UNDER THE 1964 ORDINANCE ("THE 1965 LLB")

Ordinary Degree

Part	Subjects	Weight	Timing	Examination
Part I	Introduction to Law: ie Jurisprudence I Constitutional Law & History I Administrative Law I Public International Law I Scottish Legal System	160 meetings (60) (35) (15) (10) (50)	First two terms of First Year	April, four papers of three hours (plus resit)
Part II	Jurisprudence II	60 meetings	Third term of First Year and whole of Second Year (ie four terms)	June, two papers of three hours (plus resit)
	Scots law	120 meetings	Second and Third terms of First Year and whole of Second Year (ie five terms overlapping Part I)	June, two papers of three hours (plus resit)

Part III	Jurisprudence III	40 meetings	whole of Third Year	June, two papers of three hours (plus resit)
	and one from Conveyancing I *or* Commercial law *or* English law	all 90 meetings	Third term of Second Year, and whole of Third Year	all ditto
Part IV	The equivalent of five single subjects from: *Single subjects:* Administrative Law II Comparative Law Conflict of Laws Constitutional Law & History II Conveyancing II Evidence Forensic Medicine Procedure Public International Law II *Double subjects:* Accounting, Taxation and Death Duties Accountancy Civil law	all 40 meetings	whole of Third Year	June, one paper of three hours (plus resit)

| | Commercial law Conveyancing I English law Economics, *and* two out of Philosophy Logic & Metaphysics Moral Philosophy Political Economy | all 75 meetings, except Conveyancing I, Commercial law and English law, at 90 meetings | whole of Third Year, except Conveyancing I, Commercial law and English law, at Third term of Second Year, and whole of Third Year | June, two papers of three hours (plus resit) |

* there were numerous specific limits upon taking later Parts, and more advanced courses until earlier Parts, and less advanced courses, were passed

Honours Degree*

Subject	Papers	Weight	Timing	Examination
Private law	Heritable rights Moveable rights and Succession Trusts Vesting, *and* 4 unspecified			
Jurisprudence	Prescribed essay Legal Theory with particular reference to Hans Kelsen	at least 50 classes	over two years	May/June (no resit)

	Legal Control of Industrial Relations The Functions of Punishment			
Economics	various			
Modern History	various			
Philosophy	various			
Political Science	various			

* entry selective, depending upon application, successful passing of earlier stages, and being "academically fit".

---

[1] "Unique selling points", a marketing term.

[2] 1 & 2 Eliz II c 40.

[3] Report of the Royal Commission on University Education in Dundee 1951-52 (Cmnd 8514: 1952).

[4] This section summarises Donald G Southgate, *University Education in Dundee* (1982) ch 9. See also Ronald Gordon Cant, *The University of St Andrews: a short history* 3rd ed (1992) 174-180 and Norman H Reid *Ever to Excel: an illustrated history of the University of St Andrews* (2011) 163-165 (which refers to "the experiment of extending the University of St Andrews to its industrial neighbour to the north ...").

[5] Dundee University Archives ("DUA") Recs A/62, UStA Court Minutes 1955-56, Meeting of 13 December 1955; Recs A/64, University of St Andrews ("UStA") Court Minutes 1957-58, Meetings of 10 December 1957.

[6] Although Commissioners' Ordinances created relevant Chairs, the Faculty of Social Science was not, in fact, so created.

[7] Appended to DUA Recs A/65, UStA Court Minutes 1958-59, Meeting of 19 May 1959.

[8] DUA Recs A/64, UStA Court Minutes 1957-58, Meetings of 10 December 1957 & 18 March 1958.

[9] DUA Recs A/66, UStA Court Minutes 1959-60, Meeting of 22 August 1960.

[10] Higher Education: report of the Committee appointed by the Prime Minister under the Chairmanship of Lord Robbins 1961-63 (Cmnd 2154: 1963) (the "Robbins Report"), Chapter II para 31, and Chapter XIX para 24, respectively. James Drever, later first Principal of the University of Dundee, was a member.

[11] By the Universities (Scotland) Act 1966 (1966 c 13) s 13, Schs 5 & 6.

[12] Charter of Incorporation of the University of Dundee 28 June 1967 ..., Dundee University Archives ("DUA"), KLoc F 378.413 1 G 786.

[13] Tedder Report paras 60-63.

[14] But is now owned and occupied by the High School of Dundee.

[15] Until well into the 1970s, the Scottish Universities Law Faculties Conference, the annual long-weekend gathering open to all staff from all law faculties who cared to attend, fitted comfortably into The Burn in Glenesk: personal recollection.

[16] See Alistair R Brownlie, "The Universities and Scottish Legal Education" 1955 *JR* 26-61; David M Walker, "Law as a Liberal Education" 1956 *SLT* 57-63; David M Walker, "The Crisis in Legal Training" (1956) 1 *JLSS* 101-103 (also 186-187); David M Walker, "Legal Studies in the Scottish Universities" 1957 *JR* 21-41 & 151-179 (two parts); J D B Mitchell, "First Principles First" 1959 *SLT* 1-2; DMW[alker], "The New Glasgow Law Degree" 1959 *SLT* 121-133; David M Walker, "Legal Scholarship in Scotland" 1960 *SLT* 10-14; J D B Mitchell, "The Proposed New Law Degree in Edinburgh University" 1960 *SLT* 21-24; ARB[rownlie], "Legal Scholarship in Scotland" 1960 *SLT* 38-40; David M Walker, "Legal Education and Training" 1960 *SLT* 41-46; J Watson, "Legal Education and Training: a practitioners' point of view" 1960 *SLT* 57-60; and also Ian D Willock, "Examinations Re-Examined" 1962 *SLT* 81 (notable as the first article published by someone who would become a Dundee staff member) and R L C Hunter, "Some Reflections on the Relevance of Educational Thought in Scottish Law Teaching" 1971 *JR* 1-19 (by a recently departed Dundee staff member).

[17] David M Walker (1920-2014), MA LLB PhD CBE QC FBA FRSE, appointed to the Chair of Jurisprudence at Glasgow in 1954 and to the Regius Chair of Law there in 1959 (replacing Andrews Dewar Gibb).

[18] Brownlie "Universities and Scottish Legal Education".

[19] Anon [Andrew Dewar Gibb], "A Scots Law School in 1913" 1919 *JR* 267-272 and AD Gibb, "Reform in the Scottish Law School" 1943 *JR* 152-165.

[20] Walker "Legal Studies in the Scottish Universities" (two parts).

[21] David M Walker *Scottish Legal System* 1st ed was published two years later, in 1959, the 8th (and final), in 2001.

[22] Watson "Legal Education and Training".

[23] *Regulations for Examination and Admission of Solicitors ... 19th March 195*7 reproduced in contemporary editions of *Parliament House Book*.

[24] DUA Recs A/78, UStA Senatus Academicus Minutes 1956-58, Meeting of 8 March 1957.

[25] Brian D Hayes, BA MA, holder of the Donaldson Scholarship at Corpus Christi College, Cambridge, was appointed lecturer in Modern Political & Constitutional History (presumably

with a view to him teaching law students as well), with effect from 1 October 1956, but intimated that he would not take up the place, and Donald Southgate from the Department of Political Science at Glasgow University was appointed with effect from 12 November 1956: see DUA Recs A/62 & A/63, UStA Court Minutes 1955-56 and 1956-57, Meetings of 10 July, 21 August & 23 October 1956. No doubt this accounts for the absence of a name for the Constitutional Law course lecturer in the 1956-57 University Calendar (see Recs A/814/2/86, 48-49).

[26] "[S]ubsequently attached to St Salvator's College and was Lecturer in Dark Age Studies at his premature death": Southgate, *University Education* 31 (also DUA Recs A/64 UStA Court Minutes 1957-5, Meeting of 21 January 1958.

[27] DUA Recs A/65, UStA Court Minutes 1958-59, Meetings of 19 May and 28 July 1959. Recs A/64, UStA Court Minutes 1957-58, Meeting of 18 February 1958 records A J W R Coupar, Conveyancing tutor, leaving but in fact he remained in post until 1962: I am grateful to Dennis Collins for this information.

[28] Figuring in Chapter 4 as a recruit to the UCD staff in 1946, and thus already teaching Civil Law for the LLB within the University, while probably still working in the Town Clerk's Department.

[29] Figuring in Chapter 5 as one of the first LLB graduates, and a prize-winner. He remained in post until 1991, and was an Honorary Fellow thereafter: see *Dundee Courier* 31 January 1995.

[30] DUA Recs A/61, UStA Court Minutes 1954-55, Meeting of 25 July 1955.

[31] DUA Recs A/62, UStA Court Minutes 1955-56, Meeting of 22 November 1955.

[32] DUA Recs A/63, UStA Court Minutes 1956-57, Meeting of 9 July 1957.

[33] DUA Recs A/65, UStA Court Minutes 1958-59, Meetings of 20 January & 17 February 1959.

[34] DUA Recs A/68, UStA Court Minutes 1961-62, Meeting of 14 November 1961.

[35] Section 14 entitled to compensation "[a]ny person who suffers loss of office or employment, or loss or diminution of emoluments or pension rights, which is attributable to the coming into effect of any of the provisions of this Act" (deemed to include redundancy through the incorporation of the School into the University), and provided that such compensation be paid by Court "and shall be of such amount as may be agreed between the University Court and the person entitled to compensation or, in default of agreement, as may be determined by an arbiter appointed by the Lord President ...".

[36] DUA Recs A/68, UStA Court Minutes 1961-62, Meeting of 14 November 1961. It is possible that this coincided with him leaving the Town Clerk's Department.

[37] DUA Recs A/62, QCD Council Minutes 1955-56, Meeting of 16 January 1956 & Appendix D. What did Ben Bowman, as Jurisprudence lecturer, think? The list also re-iterated Administrative Law (40 lectures, rising to 80, at £375-£600), and Mercantile Law "within Scots Law" (80 lectures, at £600). For comparison, new full-time pay scales were also approved, with Senior Lecturers at £1725 (with increments to £2050) and Lecturers at £900 (with increments to £1650, via an efficiency bar at £1350). This Minute also records the death of Dr Tudhope of Pathology, whom Christian Bisset had married.

[38] Finally achieved by Social Science Regulations in 1960, too late to be of use, for reasons appearing below: see DUA Recs A/79 & A/80, UStA Senatus Academicus Minutes 1958-60 &

1960-62, Meetings of 27 June 1960 and 12 May 1961. Walker "Legal Studies in the Scottish Universities" at 26, erroneously asserted this to have happened in 1957.

[39] DUA Recs A/62, UStA Court Minutes 1955-56, Meeting of 20 March 1956, Appendix (Senate Memorandum to the UGC) indicated that Dundee should concentrate on Social Science, Law, Physical and Applied Science and Medicine, and Priority DII therein was three lecturers in law, two part-time.

[40] Michael Shafe, *University Education in Dundee 1881-1981: a pictorial history* (1982) 14 & 54-55 contain pictures of them and, at 53, a plan. Most lectures were given in the second house from the west (marked B on this plan), with Forensic Medicine (along with medical students) in a tiered lecture room behind it (enhanced by a voluntary visit to the Police Mortuary in the Bell Street police station), while Civil Law and Public International Law were in the Old Technical Institute behind it (marked G on this plan), which still stands: I am grateful to Dennis Collins for this information. The same plan, appears in Southgate, *University Education* xiv.

[41] DUA Recs A/62, QCD Council Minutes 1955-56, Meetings of 16 January & 8 September (App A) 1956, also Recs A/63, QCD Council Minutes 1956-57, Meeting of 8 April 1957, and Recs A/64, QCD Council Minutes 1957-58 Meeting, Meeting of 2 December 1957. The Tower Building was the first multi-storey building in Dundee.

[42] DUA Recs A/78, UStA Senatus Academicus Minutes 1956-58, Meeting of 7 December 1956.

[43] DUA Recs A/79, UStA Senatus Academicus Minutes 1958-60, Meeting of 7 November 1958.

[44] DUA Recs A/80, UStA Senatus Academicus Minutes 1960-62, Meeting of 10 February 1961.

[45] DUA Recs A/78, UStA Senatus Academicus Minutes 1956-58, Meeting of 8 March 1957.

[46] DUA Recs A/64, UStA Court Minutes 1957-58, Meeting of 21 January 1958, Appendix D.

[47] Presumably the Mercantile Law lecturer.

[48] DUA Recs A/79, UStA Senatus Academicus Minutes 1958-60, Meeting of 7 November 1958.

[49] As noted in Chapter 4, his devil-master, J Randall Philip, who claimed "a share in securing his appointment", noted his "sensitive nature": Fiona Craddock (ed), *The Journal of Sir J Randall Philip, OBE, QC: public and private life in Scotland 1947-1957* (1998) 115, 192.

[50] Southgate *University Education* 235.

[51] DUA Recs A/69, QCD Council Minutes 1962-63, Meeting of 3 December 1962, records him as being in hospital in late 1962.

[52] DUA Recs A/78, UStA Court Minutes 1957-58, Meeting of 17 June 1958.

[53] "... the delightful old house with the curved front door ..." personal communication from Dennis Collins.

[54] DUA Recs A/66, QCD Council Minutes 1959-60, Meeting of 7 March 1960, Appendix B. The position is complicated by the expectation that Law would decline from 92 to 75 in the following year because of commencement of the "Accountants' Academic Year", and would increase modestly thereafter at five extra per year, though it could take more, growth being limited by demand.

[55] DUA Recs A/66, UStA Court Minutes 1959-60, Meeting of 15 March 1960, Appendix A.

[56] Still taught by Matheson, although Master of the College, his Scots Law responsibilities having been reduced by J P Parker Smith's appointment as "supernumerary lecturer".

[57] DUA Recs A/66, UStA Court Minutes 1959-60, Meeting of 17 May 1960.

[58] DUA Recs A/79, UStA Senatus Academicus Minutes 1958-60, Meeting of 6 May 1960.

[59] He was commissioned as a Second Lieutenant in the Royal Pioneer Corps (constituting, since he was MA LLB, and had already completed a Bar apprenticeship, passing advocate in 1962, an egregious example of the Forces' ability to place highly qualified national servicemen in posts where their qualifications were not useful): I am grateful to Mrs Cowie, his widow, and Rev George Cowie, his son, for the above information (though they are not responsible for the comment thereon).

[60] Finally relieving Matheson of the job.

[61] DUA Recs A/66, UStA Court Minutes 1959-60, Meeting of 14 June 1960. Initial lack of permanent Law Faculty accommodation meant his first office was in an upstairs room of a small house in a short lane running south from Small's Lane, which joins Small's Wynd and Park Place (thus, seemingly, between the backs of the Ewing Building and the Dental Hospital). I am grateful to Dennis Collins for this recollection.

[62] Solicitor, Town Clerk, Port Glasgow 1943-48, Member Scottish Committee of Council on Tribunals 1964-?: see Directory of Members of the Society of Public Teachers of Law 1965 (1965).

[63] DUA Recs A/80, UStA Senatus Academicus Minutes 1960-62, Meeting of 11 October 1960; Recs A/67, UStA Court Minutes 1960-61, Meeting of 18 October 1960. Because of existing commitments, he could only give a 40 lecture course in the first year, necessitating an Ordinance change. In 1962 a change of syllabus was sought, to include "the structure and functions of local authorities and public corporations (including those in the National Health Service) and their relations with central authorities" with reference made to "the scope of judicial review of administrative action and to the operation of administrative tribunals and enquiries", with "Miller *Administration and Local Government*, Wade *Administrative Law* [and] Griffith & Street *Principles of Administrative Law* (2nd ed)" as text books, and one examination of two-and-a-half hours, plus an oral: DUA Recs A/81, UStA Senatus Academicus Minutes 1962-62, Meeting of 7 December 1962.

[64] DUA Recs A/66, UStA Court Minutes 1959-60, Meeting of 14 June 1960.

[65] *Ibid.*

[66] DUA Recs A/66, UStA Court Minutes 1959-60, Meeting of 15 July 1960.

[67] He recalled that his appointment just before the start of the academic year meant he was preparing his lectures "virtually the night before", in the "small room at the west end of the western front building which housed the Law Library and had a desk and two or three chairs" described in Chapter 5, which Alastair McDonald found as his initial academic accommodation on arrival in 1953, and that he taught accountancy students, of whom there were about twenty: personal communication.

[68] DUA Recs A/67, UStA Court Minutes 1960-61, Meeting of 22 May 1962.

[69] DUA Recs A/80, UStA Senatus Academicus Minutes 1960-62, Meeting of 28 April 1961, Appendix A.

[70] Although one of them, I M S Robertson, was specifically appointed to Mercantile Law. At least later, he taught the subject to LLB and accountancy students in separate classes, and for accountancy students, the course was extended to include matters taught to LLB students in Scots Law, i.e. trusts and judicial factors, testate and intestate succession and legal rights, fee and liferent, and apportionment, which were dealt with by Dennis Collins: see DUA Recs A/814/2/95, St Andrews University Calendar 1965-66.

[71] NCR was then becoming a major employer in Dundee, in a post-war industrial regeneration.

[72] DUA Recs A/65, UStA Court Minutes 1958-59, Meeting of 20 January 1959; Recs A/64, QCD Council Minutes 1957-58, Meetings of 3 March and 5 May 1959.

[73] DUA Recs A/64, QCD Council Minutes 1957-58, Meeting of 7 March 1960.

[74] Presumably, only Cowie and Matheson required offices of their own, though Matheson also had one elsewhere as Master.

[75] Certainly, the Conveyancing class was: I am grateful to Dennis Collins for this recollection.

[76] "… the biggest job [in moving the Law Faculty to the seventh floor] being the transfer of the Library": personal communication from Dennis Collins.

[77] DUA Recs A/65, UStA Court Minutes 1958-59, Meeting of 16 June 1959.

[78] DUA Recs A/66, UStA Court Minutes 1959-60, Meeting of 6 January 1960, Appendices A & B.

[79] The Glasgow version is described at length in D M W[alker], "New Glasgow Law Degree" , notably introducing a Scottish Legal system course, splitting Scots Law into Parts I (persons and contracts) and II (delict, property, trusts and succession) and Criminal Law, also introducing Comparative Law and Industrial Law as well as half-a-dozen History and Philosophy courses. The Edinburgh version is described in J D B Mitchell, "The Proposed New Law Degree in Edinburgh University".

[80] David M Walker, *A History of the School of Law: University of Glasgow* (c.1990) 74 (also observing that if LLB students were better than BL, it was not necessarily because they had taken an MA). See also David M Walker, "Legal Education in Scotland, 1889-1988" 1988 *JR* 184-204, at 188 n 20.

[81] Walker, *History of the School of Law* 74. He added that the Oxbridge law graduates were "frequently very unsatisfactory as they felt they had learned it already and were merely noting Scottish differences". See also John W Cairns & Hector L MacQueen, *Learning and the Law: a short history of Edinburgh Law School* (2013) 26.

[82] Walker, *History of the School of Law* 74.

[83] Walker, "Legal Studies in the Scottish Universities" 38.

[84] Walker, *History of the School of Law* 75-6. See also Cairns & MacQueen, *Learning and the Law* 26.

[85] Walker, *History of the School of Law* 76.

[86] For draft Aberdeen, Edinburgh and Glasgow Ordinances, and regulations thereunder) see DUA Recs A/66, UStA Court Minutes 1959-60, Meeting of 19 January 1960, Appendix B.

[87] Walker, *History of the School of Law* 77: his critique was foreshadowed in several articles, principally Walker, "Legal Studies in the Scottish Universities".

[88] A fairly general view of the law staff: I am grateful to Alastair McDonald for this information.

[89] DUA Recs A/79, UStA Senatus Academicus Minutes 1958-60, Meeting of 5 February 1960; Recs A/66 & A/67, UStA Court Minutes 1959-60 & 1960-61, Meetings of 19 April & 15 November 1960.

[90] DUA Recs A/66, UStA Court Minutes 1959-60, Meeting of 6 January 1960, Appendix A.

[91] Personal recollection includes amazement in the mid-1960s upon reading a reprinted graduation address by Principal Knox, expressing similar views and including the phrase "I shudder when I hear [the summer vacation] called a holiday".

[92] DUA Recs A/79, UStA Senatus Academicus Minutes 1958-60, Meeting of 6th May 1960; Recs A/66, UStA Court Minutes 1959-60, Meeting of 17 May 1960.

[93] Ordinance No 39 (General No 11) of 1893, discussed in Chapter 1.

[94] (St Andrews Court) Ordinance No 56 (Amendment of Ordinance No 39 (General No 11) ...), 4 January 1961, passed by Privy Council 26 June 1961. This was a Court Ordinance, the "Crown Commissioners" (see Chapter 5) having demitted office.

[95] DUA Recs A/80, UStA Senatus Academicus Minutes 1960-62, Meeting of 12 May 1961; Recs A/68, UStA Court Minutes 1961-62, Meeting of 17 October 1961. (Final approval must thus have almost exactly co-incided with the arrival of the students).

[96] *Alias* "limitation of studies".

[97] Personal recollection.

[98] DUA Recs A/80, UStA Senatus Academicus Minutes 1960-62, Meeting of 28 April 1961, Appendix A.

[99] Jurisprudence had been available to MA students since 1959: DUA Recs A/65, UStA Court Minutes 1958-59, Meeting of 19 May 1959.

[100] Personal recollection of disappointed students.

[101] DUA Recs A/80, UStA Senatus Academicus Minutes 1960-62, Meeting of 26 June 1961, Appendix A.

[102] DUA Recs A/81, UStA Senatus Academicus Minutes 1962-64, Meeting of 7 December 1962.

[103] I am grateful to Alastair McDonald for this information. The late Ian Willock (see below) is usually credited with the policy, but he gave the credit to Ben Bowman: personal communication.

[104] I am grateful to Alastair McDonald for this explanation.

[105] Personal recollection indicates numerous complaints about the amount of Jurisprudence, but the system did produce, *int. al.* a notable Professor of Legal Theory at Edinburgh University (as discussed later).

[106] Ordinance 39 (General No 11) of 1893, s 2(4).

[107] Andrew Dewar Gibb was described as lecturer in English Law at Edinburgh, but this is not mentioned by Cairns & MacQueen, *Learning the Law*. Walker, *History of the School of Law* 26 writes that it was briefly taught in Glasgow in the late eighteenth century.

[108] DUA Recs A/80, UStA Senatus Academicus Minutes 1960-62, Meeting of 26 June 1961, Appendix A. Personal recollection of a few years later suggests that St Andrews and Trinity College, Dublin, were regarded by some as appropriate destinations for those unable to get into Oxbridge. This corroborates a number of sayings attributed to W L Lorimer (successively lecturer in Greek in United College, Reader in Latin in University College, and Professor of Greek back in United College, also translator of the New Testament into Scots), describing St Andrews as "the potting shed of the English rose", which "receives the off-scourings of Oxford", declaring the career path of "nice gels" to be "St Catherine's [a prep school attached to St Leonard's], St Leonard's [a fee-paying school in St Andrews] and St Salvator's [the principal part of United College]", and asserting that St Andrews chairs were being used as "louping-on stanes" for Oxbridge chairs: I am grateful to Dennis Collins, who heard them from the horse's mouth, as the sole member of the Humanity (Latin) class of his year, for this information.

[109] *Admission of Solicitor (Scotland) Regulations 1960* reproduced in contemporary editions of *Parliament House Book*. See also Walker, "Legal Education and Training" and Watson "Legal Education and Training".

[110] Walker, "New Glasgow Law Degree" at 122.

[111] Walker, "Legal Education in Scotland, 1889-1988".

[112] *Admission of Solicitor (Scotland) Regulations 1960* s 15, Second Schedule.

[113] Introduced in the 1938 Second Professional Examination: see Chapter 3.

[114] Introduced in the 1938 First Professional Examination: see Chapter 3.

[115] Also introduced in the 1938 Second Professional Examination.

[116] Walker, "Legal Education and Training (1960)" 41.

[117] *Admission of Solicitor (Scotland) Regulations 1960*, First Schedule, though it is obscurely drafted, referring to "preliminary degrees" without defining the term.

[118] Walker, "Legal Education and Training (1988)" 191.

[119] See D A O Edward, "Faculty of Advocates Regulations as to Intrants" 1968 *SLT* 181. The 1968 Regulations, in effect, removed the general scholarship requirement, but made an apprenticeship, followed by formal "devilling", compulsory.

[120] DUA Recs A/71, QCD College Council Minutes 1964-65 (bound in with Court Minutes), Meeting of 12 October 1964. By this time, Jim Robertson and J W R Gray had been appointed as full-time staff in addition to Cowie and Matheson, and an appointment to the Chair of Jurisprudence and other full-time posts were in anticipation: see below.

[121] DUA Recs A/71, QCD College Council Minutes 1964-65 (bound in with Court Minutes), Meeting of 11 January 1965.

[122] I.e., respectively, the easternmost half of the tenement opposite Small's Wynd, next to Seabraes Lane, and the tenement immediately east of the Duncan of Jordanstone Matthew Building.

Student rumour at the time predicted "We're going to move over above Gray's Funeral Parlour [23-30 Perth Road]": personal recollection.

[123] DUA Recs A/71, QCD College Council Minutes 1964-65 (bound in with Court Minutes), Meeting of 1 March 1965. McDonald relates that he cannot now recall the reason.

[124] DUA Recs A/82, UStA Senatus Academicus Minutes 1964-68, Meetings of 15 January and 12 October 1965.

[125] Although there were only three Professors: it is not clear where all the full-time staff were accommodated.

[126] DUA Recs A/71, QCD College Council Minutes 1964-65 (bound in with Court Minutes), Meeting of 3 May 1965.

[127] Personal recollection.

[128] DUA Recs A/72, QCD College Council Minutes 1965-65 (bound in with Court Minutes), Meetings of 16 January and 12 March 1966.

[129] A year before, a request had been made to the University Library Committee that the two sets of *Session Cases* on the St Andrews site be brought over, which was refused on the ground that the Dundee site had two sets already and (implausibly) that the St Andrews ones were in frequent use, which suggests that two of the four sets were recently acquired from elsewhere: DUA Recs A/81, UStA Senate Minutes 1962-64, Meeting of 8 May 1964.

[130] DUA Recs A/81, UStA Senatus Academicus Minutes 1962-64, Meeting of 8 March 1963.

[131] DUA Recs A/69, UStA Court Minutes 1962-63, Meeting of 21 May 1963.

[132] DUA Recs A/81, UStA Senatus Academicus Minutes 1962-64, Meeting 8 November 1963. A month earlier, it had noted a new Aberdeen LLB Ordinance.

[133] Ordinance No 452 (St Andrews No 75) Regulations for the Degree of Bachelor of Laws (LLB). For the text, see Anon, *University of St Andrews Ordinances* (c1964) which also contains those Commissioners' and Court Ordinances under the Universities (Scotland) Acts 1858 and 1889 still in force at that time, and Commissioners' and Court Ordinances under the University of St Andrews Act 1953.

[134] Sections 4 & 5.

[135] Section 2.

[136] Section 12 (i.e. the 1893, 1911 and 1956 Ordinances *quoad* St Andrews University, "insofar as [not] ... preserved by Section XIV hereof", which is curious as no Section 14 appears). The original 1863 Ordinance 75 (General No 8) (Regulations for Degrees in Law), and the 1919 Ordinance LXXXII (St Andrews No 17) (Institution of a degree in Commerce), had been revoked by Ordinance No 477 (St Andrews No 74) (Revocation of Certain Ordinances) earlier that year.

[137] Section 11.

[138] Published in University Calendars, e.g. DUA RecsA/814/2/95, *St Andrews University Calendar 1965-66*.

[139] See e.g. *ibid.* 360-65.

[140] See e.g. *ibid* 366-70.

[141] "It will deal with the aims of law and its function in society; the evolution of law systems; the creation of law by statute, judicial decision, custom, juristic writings, etc, and the advantages and disadvantages of these sources", with recommended books being "Paton, *Jurisprudence* (third edn., 1964), or Dias, *Jurisprudence* (1964): Lloyd, *The Idea of Law* (1964): Allen *Law in the Making* (seventh edn., 1964)": DUA Recs A/814/2/95, *St Andrews University Calendar 1965-66*, 380-81.

[142] "The course will deal with the analysis of legal concepts, including right, duty, personality, status, civil and criminal liability, punishment, causation, obligation, ownership and possession, and with their changing social functions", with recommended books "Paton, *Jurisprudence* (third edn., 1964), or Dias *Jurisprudence* (1964): Salmond, *Jurisprudence* (eleventh edn., 1957): Friedmann, *Law in a Changing Society* (1959)": DUA Recs A/814/2/95, *St Andrews University Calendar 1965-66*, 381.

[143] "The course will deal with the leading theories on the nature of law; the relationship of law to morality and the state; the nature of justice and other selected topics", recommended books "Lloyd, *Introduction to Jurisprudence* (1959); Bodenheimer, *Jurisprudence* (1962); Hart, *The Concept of Law* (1961): Friedmann *Legal Theory* (fourth edn., 1960)": DUA Recs A/814/2/95, *St Andrews University Calendar 1965-66*, 381.

[144] The Regulations specified "not less than 90".

[145] The Honours Regulations were not fully enacted by 1967, the first cohort under the 1964 Ordinance not reaching Third Year until then.

[146] And did not become common until the 1980s: personal recollection. As it involved an extra year, it may have been regarded as a Master's degree is now.

[147] Personal recollection.

[148] DUA Recs A/814/2/95, *St Andrews University Calendar 1965-66*, 361-62.

[149] DUA Recs A/80, UStA Senatus Academicus Minutes 1960-62, Meeting of 28 April 1961, Appendix A.

[150] Ordinance No 417 (St Andrews No 68) (Foundation of the Chair of Jurisprudence).

[151] Unsurprising, given his later carer, which made him one of the foremost scholars in the world on the subject, having held chairs in several universities and published a dozen books and innumerable articles.

[152] DUA Recs A/70, UStA Court Minutes 1963-64, Meetings of 21 April & 19 May 1964.

[153] Presumably because he became aware that the Douglas Chair of Civil Law at Glasgow, his earliest *alma mater*, was becoming vacant. He was appointed to it in 1965.

[154] And External Examiner in Jurisprudence at Queen's College, alongside, for Scots Law, A J Mackenzie-Stuart, then not even a QC, but a dozen years later the first United Kingdom judge on the European Court of Justice.

[155] DUA Recs A/70, UStA Court Minutes 1963-64, Meeting of 7 July 1964.

[156] DUA Recs A/82, UStA Senatus Academicus Minutes 1964-66, Meeting of 15 January 1965.

[157] DUA Recs A/70, UStA Court Minutes 1963-64, Meeting of 15 October 1963.

[158] *Ibid.*, Meeting of 21 April 1964. JWR Gray was occasionally referred to by students as "Lord Gray of Kampala": personal recollection.

[159] The Quinquennial Estimates anticipated only a part-time lecturer in Conveyancing.

[160] Bizarrely, though, while her Wardenship of Chalmers Hall was approved in 1965 (see DUA Recs A/71, UStA Court Minutes, Meeting of 25 May 1964), her part-time lectureship with effect from 1 August 1965 was retrospectively approved by Court only in 1969 (see DUA RU 162/1/2, UoD Court Minutes 1968-69, Meeting of 27 May 1969). She was made full-time eighteen months later: see RU 162/1/4, UoD Court Minutes 1970-71, Meeting of 18 January 1971.

[161] DUA Recs A/71, UStA Court Minutes 1964-65, Meeting of 20 April 1965.

[162] DUA Recs A/72, UStA Court Minutes 1965-66, Meeting of 24 May 1966,

[163] DUA Recs A/71, UStA Court Minutes 1964-65, Meeting of 24 May 1965. Donald Southgate, still teaching Constitutional Law, was also promoted to Senior Lecturer.

[164] MacCormick, Willock and Bowman all taught Jurisprudence to the last cohort under the 1961 Ordinance (i.e. IN 1965-66): personal recollection.

[165] A hint of this may appear in DUA Recs A/814/2/95, *St Andrews University Calendar 1965-66*, possibly printed before Baker had been appointed, or after it became clear that he was not coming for, at 392 fn, it is recounted that "Although the Law of England is listed as an optional subject above, no tuition is *at present* given in this subject nor can students be examined in it" (emphasis added).

[166] DUA Recs A/71, UStA Court Minutes 1964-65, Meeting of 25 May 1965. He appears to have come from and returned to, Aberdeen University: see Directory of Members of the Society of Public Teachers of Law 1967 (1967).

[167] DUA Recs A/72, UStA Court Minutes 1965-66, Meeting of 19 October 1965. He was formerly Attorney-General of Eritrea 1952, and Senior Resident Magistrate Eritrea and Acting Judge of High Court of Tanganyika 1962-64, and appears to have gone on to the College of Law: see Directory of Members of the Society of Public Teachers of Law 1967 (1967).

[168] DUA Recs A/814/2/95, *St Andrews University Calendar 1966-67,* 381, comprising English Legal System (15 lectures), English Law of Contract (25 lectures), English Law of Torts (25 lectures) and English Criminal Law (25 lectures) with three examination papers, each of two hours.

[169] DUA Recs A/73, UStA Court Minutes 1966-67, Meeting of 22 November 1966.

[170] Personal recollection.

[171] DUA Recs A/72, UStA Court Minutes 1964-65, Meeting of 15 March 1966.

[172] Ordinance 39 (General No 11), Section II(7). No syllabus was ever published in the University Calendar, but personal recollection suggests it covered Contract and Tort only.

[173] Ordinance 39 (General No 11), Section II(4).

[174] DUA Recs A/73, UStA Court Minutes 1966-67, Meeting of 24 January 1967: also personal recollection.

[175] DUA Recs A/73, UStA Court Minutes 1966-67, Meeting of 18 April 1967. The minute-taker miss-spelled his name.

[176] Later Sir Colin Campbell, DL FRSA, Vice-Chancellor of Nottingham University at the age of 43, and member of numerous bodies and committees, including the Standing Advisory Committee on Human Rights for Northern Ireland, the University Grants Committee, the Higher Education Funding Council for England the Human Fertilisation and Embryology Authority, and also notorious for advocating "privatisation" of universities and (re)introduction of fees.

[177] DUA Recs A/73, UStA Court Minutes 1966-67, Meeting of 18 April 1967.

[178] DUA Recs A/73, UStA Court Minutes 1966-67, Meeting of 21 February 1967.

[179] DUA Recs A/83, UStA Senatus Academicus Minutes 1966-67, Meeting of 11 October 1967, Appendix.

[180] Up from 50 in 1965-66 and 30 to 40 in preceding years.

[181] Three or four postgraduates, rising to six were also predicted.

[182] Pay and prospects in England and Wales in some jobs were prejudiced by inability to claim a 2i or better, and the unavailability of Honours regarded in some quarters with disbelief: personal recollection. The contrast with the suspicion with which many Scottish solicitors' firms then regarded Honours degrees is marked.

[183] DUA Recs A/82, UStA Senatus Academicus Minutes 1964-66, Meeting of 12 October 1965.

[184] Anon, "University of Strathclyde" 1967 *SLT* 3, 27.

[185] DUA Recs A/68, UStA Court Minutes 1961-62, Meeting of 10 July 1962.

[186] *Ibid.*

[187] DUA Recs A/70, UStA Court Minutes 1963-64, Meeting of 15 September 1964. The present writer was conducted by him to an admission interview with Matheson, and was the first student admitted by him in October 1964: I am grateful to the late Jim Ryan for this recollection.

[188] DUA Recs A/72, UStA Court Minutes 1965-66, Meeting of 12 July 1966.

[189] DUA Recs A/73, UStA Court Minutes 1966-67, Meeting of 22 November 1966.

[190] See obituary in *The Scotsman* 16 October 2013.

[191] Noted above.

[192] One architect of the original Zimbabwean Constitution and (until falling out with the regime) first Vice-Chancellor of the University of Zimbabwe.

[193] Scourge of H L A Hart and Analytical Jurisprudence: see Nicola Lacey, *A Life of HLA Hart: the nightmare and the noble dream* (2004).

[194] Who, after going to Warwick Law School, held the Drapers' Chair in Law at Queen Mary and Westfield College (1994-97), was Edmund-Davies Professor of Criminal Law and Criminal Justice at King's College London (1997-2009), thereafter returning as a Professor to Warwick, where he was Head of School for a period, and is author of numerous influential books.

[195] See obituary in Dundee City Library Family and Local History Centre *Obituaries Notices 2009-13,* 7 February 2011, also University of Dundee *Contact* magazine vol. 6, no. 4 (June 1981). This account has been read by Mrs Anne Robertson, but she bears no responsibility for what appears in it.

[196] Personal recollection.

[197] I am grateful to Mrs Elspeth Collins and Sheriff Herald for the information from which these paragraphs are constructed. (Note also *Dundee Courier* 1 August 2017).

[198] See e.g. http://www.independent.co.uk/news/obituaries/professor-sir-neil-maccormick-legal-philoso pher-and-politician-who-espoused-a-nationalism-that-was-1672082.html (last accessed 30 July 2018) and H C G Matthew & Brian Harrison *Oxford Dictionary of National Biography* (2004).

[199] Personal recollection.

[200] D Neil MacCormick, "Seabathing, Sunbathing and Sea Coal" 1967 *SLT* 69. (Ian Willock's article, published while he was still at Aberdeen, was remarked on above).

[201] I am grateful to Alastair McDonald for pointing this out. For a comprehensive list of works available around that time, see Walker, "Legal Scholarship in Scotland".

[202] At least in the mid-1960s (as before) there was an enormous range of styles and effectiveness of lectures, and while some lecturers were exemplary, in one subject the content of lectures was identical from year to year, as inherited notes demonstrated (and possibly had been for decades): personal recollection.

[203] Personal recollection, including one on advertising and the law, another on William Golding's *Lord of the Flies* then recently filmed and possibly one on Anthony Burgess' *Clockwork Orange*, then recently published (but still unfilmed).

[204] Report on University Teaching Methods (London, HMSO, 1964): the "Hale Report".

[205] DUA Recs A/82, UStA Senatus Academicus Minutes 1964-66, Meeting of 30 June 1965.

[206] DUA Recs A/66, QCD Council Minutes 1959-60, Meeting of 23 November 1959, records a request to the UGC for funds to buy the Princess Cinema for an examination hall.

[207] I am grateful to Dennis Collins for this information.

[208] Personal recollection.

[209] DUA Recs A/72, QCD Council Minutes 1965-66, Meeting of 11 October 1965, records an agreement with Gloag's of Perth to lay down half a hogshead per year for five year maturity, at £150 per year.

[210] A large house next to the Botanic Garden, then owned by the University.

[211] Then a residence in the traditional, full-board, style.

[212] See note 15.

[213] I am grateful to Dennis Collins for these recollections.

[214] I am grateful to Alastair McDonald for confirming suspicions.

[215] I am grateful to Dennis Collins for this recollection.

[216] See e.g. DUA Recs A/68, UStA Court Minutes 1961-62, Meeting of 14 November 1961.

[217] DUA Recs A/82 UStA Senatus Academicus Minutes 1962-64, Meeting of 14 May 1953; Recs A/71, UStA Court Minutes 1964-65, Meeting of 13 July 1965. The Law Faculty employed an informal interview process with the Dean about this time.

[218] DUA Recs A/72, UStA Court Minutes 1965-66, Meeting of 21 June 1966. See also Ronald Kay *UCCA: its origins and development 1956-1985* (1985) 22, 36 & 47.

[219] DUA Recs A/77, UStA Senatus Academicus, Minutes of 1954-56, Meeting of 3 July 1956, and Recs A/78, UStA Senatus Academicus, Minutes of 1956-58, Meeting of 10 October 1956, respectively (the latter noted in Chapter 5).

[220] DUA Recs A/78, UStA Senatus Academicus Minutes 1956-58, Meeting of 1 July 1958.

[221] DUA Recs A/79, UStA Senatus Academicus Minutes 1958-60, Meeting of 30[t] June 1959. Most unusually, she took an MA after the BL, and was President of the Student Representative Council: I am obliged to her children for this information.

[222] DUA Recs A/79, UStA Senatus Academicus Minutes 1958-60, Meeting of 28 June 1960. Margaret Murray was also belatedly awarded the FPSD Conveyancing Prize in 1961: see Recs A/80, UStA Senatus Academicus Minutes 1960-62, Meeting of 30 June 1961.

[223] DUA Recs A/81, UStA Senatus Academicus Minutes 1962-64, Meeting of 3 July 1963. She also won the Henry Scrymgeour Prize in 1961: see Recs A/80 UStA Senatus Academicus Minutes 1960-62, Meeting of 30 June 1961.

[224] DUA Recs A/81, UStA Senatus Academicus Minutes 1962-64, Meetings of 30 June and 14 October 1964.

[225] DUA Recs A/82, UStA Senatus Academicus Minutes 1964-66, Meetings of 2 July 1966 and A/83, UStA Senatus Academicus Minutes 1966-67, Meeting of 12 October 1966.

[226] DUA Recs A/82, UStA Senatus Academicus Minutes 1964-66, Meetings of 5 July 1966 and 14 October 1964.

[227] DUA Recs A/83, UStA Senatus Academicus Minutes 1966-67, Meeting of 4th July 1967.

[228] DUA Recs A/72, UStA Senatus Academicus Minutes 1954-56, Meeting of 3 July 1956. James Robertson also was awarded the FPSD Scots Law and Conveyancing Prizes: see FPSD Minutes 1887-1960, Meeting of 2 August 1956.

[229] DUA Recs A/78, UStA Senatus Academicus Minutes 1956-58, Meeting of 27 June 1957.

[230] Enid A Marshall, 'An Historical Analysis of the Common Law of Scotland relating to Companies, with Consideration of the Transition from the Common Law to the Statutory Provisions', unpublished PhD thesis (University of St Andrews) (internal examiners Professor AA Matheson and Messrs. IMS Robertson and JJ Robertson, external examiner David Maxwell QC), awarded 1966: see DUA Recs A/82, UStA Senatus Academicus Minutes 1964-66, Meeting of 29 June 1964.

[231] *General Principles of Scots Law* 1st ed (1971), 7th ed (1999); *The Companies (Floating Charges and Receivers) (Scotland) Act 1972* (1972); *Scottish Cases on Agency* 1st ed (1977), 2nd ed (1980); *Scottish Cases on Contract* (1978); *Scottish Cases on Partnership and Companies* (1980); *The Social Work (Scotland) Act 1983* 1st ed (1983), 2nd ed (1984, with Rosemary Gray); *Sale of Goods, Consumer Credit, Bills of Exchange, Cheques and Promissory Notes* (1983); *Scots Mercantile Law* 1st ed (1983), 3rd ed (1993); and *Company Law* 12th ed (1994, with MC Oliver), also Scottish editor of *Charlesworth's Company Law* 11th ed (1977 to 16th ed (1999).

[232] In this cohort, Stephen Campbell obtained a Distinction.

[233] DUA Recs A/82, UStA Senatus Academicus Minutes 1962-64, Meeting of 3 December 1965 (having obtained the Henry Scrymgeour Prize in 1965: see Recs A/82 UStA Senatus Academicus Minutes, Meeting of 2 July 1965).

[234] DUA RU 161/1/2 University of Dundee Senate Minutes 1969-70, Meeting of 9 October 1969.

[235] Those with Ordinary degrees graduated in 1968, those with Honours 1969.

[236] DUA RU 161/1/2 University of Dundee Senate Minutes 1969-70, Meeting of 9 October 1969.

[237] J H Stewart (1944-2015): see Stephen P Walker, *The Faculty of Advocates: a Biographical Directory of Members Admitted from 1 January 1800 to 31 December 1986* (1987), and *The Herald* 17 September 2015, 17.

[238] Records relating to sheriffs are kept in such a way as to make this difficult to know.

[239] DUA RU 161/1/3 University of Dundee Senate Minutes 1970-71, Meeting of 8 October 1970 (but note the elevation to a judgeship of the European Court of Human Rights of Tim Eicke, graduate of 1992.

[240] The Lord Advocate and Solicitor-General for Scotland, previous advisers, became advisers to the Scottish Government.

[241] DUA Recs A/83, UStA Senatus Academicus Minutes 1966-67, Meeting of 11 October 1966, Appendix.

[242] DUA Recs A/83, UStA Senatus Academicus Minutes 1964-66, Meeting of 11 October 1966.

[243] For an instructive comparison, see Callum G Brown, Arthur J McIvor & Neil Rafeek *The University Experience 1945-1975: an oral history of the University of Strathclyde* (2004) chs 3 & 6.

[244] DUA Recs A/71, UStA Court Minutes 1964-65, Meeting of 15 March 1965.

[245] For some cohorts of Law students, particularly the Tavern in the (Old) Hawkhill, its site now covered by the car park next to the Institute of Sport & Exercise: personal recollection.

[246] Drugs were barely known at that time: personal recollection.

CODA

A full account of the period from 1967 to date must await a further volume. However, those 50 years cannot be ignored, so a brief survey of changes over that period is appropriate. It is best approached by asking what students and staff, transported from 1967 to the present day, would find different.

The Student

Students transported from 1967 to today would be pleasantly surprised at the range of subjects available on the LLB, though possibly disappointed by how much the exigencies of professional qualification still constrain that choice.

Nevertheless, the 'Scottish stream' in 1967, expecting to go from an Ordinary degree straight into apprenticeship, would probably also be happy to find that today nearly all students take Honours, and embark upon the postgraduate Diploma in Professional Legal Practice, before a traineeship. And the 'English (and Northern Ireland) stream', who in 1967 had just a couple of English Law options on a Scots Law degree, would be very happy today to see a full-blown Honours English Law degree.

Both streams would no doubt also be very happy to see the 'dual qualification degree' straddling both jurisdictions, the Law with Languages degree, and the possibility of spending up to a year abroad in one of a number of destinations, European, Australian or American.

Both streams would also no doubt welcome the growth of post-graduate studies, not only through the Diploma, but also through LLMs, often in subjects unknown in 1967, from Environmental Law to Oil & Gas Law to Health Care Law & Ethics. They would certainly be surprised at the size of the resulting enterprise, with an undergraduate entry risen from 30 or 40 a year in the late 1960s, to over 150 in the late 2010s, with 40 or more on the Diploma and yet others on the LLMs.

Both steams would be no less surprised by the origins of many undergraduate and postgraduate students, from Europe, North America, Africa and Asia.

Our 1967 students would certainly notice several changes in teaching today. Used to lectures, they would be interested by the importance attached to tutorials, seminars, moots and the like, and associated emphasis upon inculcating skills as well as information, all of which they would no doubt welcome.

They would be amazed by the range of supporting course materials available. Used to brief syllabuses in a Faculty Handbook (not necessarily including reading-lists), few handouts, and in complete ignorance of any 'learning objectives', they relied heavily on 'a good set of notes' which, with luck, accurately reproduced the lecturer's, and contained citations of cases and legislation. They would find extraordinary the range of information, containing all this information and more, now available in course guides.

But what would really astonish them is, of course, the means by which all that information is now available. They would find extraordinary the gadgetry available for the delivery of lectures today, and almost unbelievable the availability, at the press of a button, of course guides and the like, on electronic devices unthought of in 1967, such as university PCs, and even their own laptops, tablets and smartphones, accessed in the privacy of their own homes.

They would also notice certain things about examinations. Used to straightforward two- or three-hour written examinations in 1967, they would be interested to find today not only essays but dissertations, drafting exercises and even moots employed for examining. Perhaps they would be mildly apprehensive at the range of achievement expected of them, though they might be reassured by the much clearer criteria for marking.

Students from 1967 would find the location of today's Law School unfamiliar. Used to the 'Terrapins' (and ignorant of the intervening sojourn in Bonar House from 1969 to the 1978), they would be very pleasantly surprised by the Scrymgeour Building (into which the Law School then moved), and possibly even more by the Dalhousie Building, as a dedicated building for lectures and tutorials across the university. But also used to an 'on-site' Law Library (and though ignorant of its presence within the Scrymgeour Building for most of the intervening half-century), they would be less pleasantly surprised by its translation into a mere section of the Main Library, though greatly cheered by its enormous improvement in holdings.

What would be really unfamiliar is the changed use of the Law Library. Used to spending much time there, the only place at which cases and legislation could be studied (and that in silence), our 1967 students would find that, because those sources can now be read in the university or at home on an electronic device, the Law Library has become a place to hold discussions (possibly accompanied by food and drink), as much as a place to read and write.

They might notice that the Dalhousie Building and the re-location of the Law Library have removed much of the reason for being in the Law building, producing, no doubt, a certain loss of corporate identity.

Amazement, and possibly horror, would also, of course, be directed to changes in student finance. Our 1967 students were used to fees being paid by the Scottish Education Department (or local authorities elsewhere in the United Kingdom), and to receiving their living expenses from the same source (subject to parental contribution), supplemented in a few cases by bursaries from the university or from charities.

Today, if resident in Scotland (or if non-UK EU nationals resident in the EU), they would find fees still being paid, though now by the Students Award Agency for Scotland, and they might also receive bursaries from the same source, or from the university or a charity, but their living expenses would probably come (subject again to parental contribution) from a large loan from the Student Loan Company. And if resident elsewhere in the United Kingdom (or elsewhere abroad), they would also have substantial fees to pay, probably financed through another loan from the Student Loan Company (though not if resident elsewhere abroad).

Many of these changes reflect a more fundamental one. Our 1967 students went to university to be provided with information, and possibly some skills, by people who had the information and skills, but in the way those people chose to impart them.

They would therefore be amazed that today, students are treated, to put it somewhat tendentiously, much as customers seeking value for money in the delivery of information and skills.

Their amazement would be particularly directed to "student feedback". Used to a system in 1967 with no mechanism to discover student views, because they were not regarded as important, they would find a system in 2017 in which no class is complete without feedback forms, which are discussed, and might lead to alterations in the content and delivery of courses.

It would be most particularly directed at the official National Student Survey, which asks questions on teaching, assessment, support, etc, and its results published and forming the basis of 'league tables' which influence a university's reputation and thus the choice made by future students as to where they will study.

Overall, our 1967 students might look at the present day with some apprehension, but much envy.

The Staff

Something which would immediately strike the 1967 staff is that the former Faculty of Law is today officially the Dundee School of Law (oxymoronically within a School of Social Sciences), with offshoots under the wordy titles of the Centre for Energy, Petroleum and Mineral Law & Policy, and the Centre for Water Law, Policy & Science.

They would also be struck by the change from half a dozen full-time, and half a dozen part-time, staff (including a couple of professors), to some twenty full-time on the LLB Degree (including half-a-dozen professors), some 40 part-time on the Diploma, and several more of various statuses teaching oil and gas law and water law.

Our 1967 staff would also notice the enormous changes in teaching and examining which the students noticed. Used to lecturing, they would find teaching more intensive, with the growth of tutorials, etc, and entailing harder work. Used to marking examination essays, they would find examining by other means, including electronic submission of essays, sometimes simpler, sometimes more difficult.

They would be more concerned, however that, today teaching and examining are assessed, not only internally (with the idea of 'peer-review' of teaching possibly causing apoplexy in some of them) but also externally, with the Quality Assurance Agency for Higher Education applying its UK Quality Code for Higher Education, and a Teaching Excellence Framework.

Research is one of two areas where our 1967 staff would be most astonished by the changes. Used to a system in which undertaking research was regarded as an optional extra, they would find today a system with two sorts of lecturer, one expected to teach and engage in scholarship, the other expected to teach and undertake research, preferably funded by government department, quango, research council or charity.

Thus they would find hard to comprehend the considerable pressure upon their colleagues of today to publish, and to have their published works regularly assessed in a Research Excellence Framework operated by the university funding bodies, upon the results of which the Law School is ranked against all other Law Schools.

The other area in which our 1967 staff would be astonished by changes is administration. Some administrative tasks were required of 1967 staff, though chiefly of the Dean, as executive head, assisted by two or three administrators, including a Faculty Secretary. Today, the mere size of the enterprise requires more administration, so there are many more administrators, but much also falls upon academic staff generally.

Course development, teaching and examining arrangements in general are in 2017 subject to internal quality assurance processes operated by Learning and Teaching Committees at various levels, which require procedures and reports. Moreover, they must conform to external quality assurance criteria set down in a UK Quality Code for Higher Education. This covers setting and maintaining academic standards, ensuring and enhancing academic quality (including criteria for "programme design, development and approval", "student engagement", "assessment of students and recognition of prior learning", and so on, all terms meaningless in 1967), the whole enforced through periodic reviews requiring even more documentation in advance, and discussion afterwards. In addition, unlike the position in 1967, today professional bodies impose similar processes for accreditation.

The administration required for research today is no less. Applications to funding bodies must be made, often in lengthy forms with exiguous requirements (and might still be deemed very good, but not good enough to get into the very highest proportion which is all that the available resources can fund). Further, once completed the research may be entered for the Research Excellence Framework noted above, and be judged on originality, significance, rigour and impact, etc. Indeed, since someone has to do the judging, the system further requires enormous input of time by volunteers in reading every item entered.

The amount of effort put into administration might thus be a biggest change for staff in the years since 1967.

Overall, undoubtedly, while many of the changes would be welcomed, the work-load of staff today would shock the staff of 1967.

Success

But the enterprise has been successful.

In 2017, in its half-centenary year, the University as a whole was, for an unprecedented second year running, named "Scottish University of the Year" by *The Times and Sunday Times Good University Guide*; secured a Gold Award, the highest possible rating, in the newly-introduced Teaching Excellence Framework; and was placed second in Scotland (and ninth in the United Kingdom) in the National Student Survey).

And in that year, the Law School itself was ranked tenth out of the 100 law schools in the UK and first in Scotland; in the National Student Survey, it was ranked eighth in the United Kingdom for overall student satisfaction; and in 2014, the most recent Research Assessment Exercise rated all its research activity as "recognised internationally" in terms of originality, significance and rigour, and more than half as "world-leading" or "internationally excellent".

Those scores are certainly better than it would have scored in 1967, and incomparably better than those it would have scored in 1899, 1890, or before. And its graduates include not only numerous solicitors, many advocates, a number of Sheriffs, but also six Senators of the College of Justice (Lady Clark of Calton PC, Lord Turnbull PC, Lord Malcolm PC, Lord Jones, Lord Burns and Lord Summers); a judge of the European Court of Human Rights (Judge Eicke); and a Circuit Judge in England, sitting in the Old Bailey (HH Judge Anuja Dhir), not to mention the Lord Lyon King of Arms (Rev Dr J Morrow CBE).

ANNEX ON SOURCES OF INFORMATION ON STUDENTS

It is clearly desirable to give information and conclusions on student numbers, gender and identity, etc. The text attempts this in broad terms. This annex seeks to show the detail from which the broad information and conclusions were derived.

The sources used are the Minutes of Court and Senate, the Minutes of UCD Council, the annual UCD Calendars, Graduation Programmes, and a *"Register"*. Of these, only the *"Register"* requires explanation. It is a list existing in two versions. One is typescript (entitled *Register of Law Students in U.C.D. from 1897-1947*). It is presumably a source for the relevant part of the other, printed, version covering all disciplines (entitled *University of St Andrews Record of Past and Present Students of University College, Dundee and Senior Medical College 1897-1947*). Both purport to list all law students in the 50 years since the re-affiliation, in tabular form with seven columns headed, respectively, "Present [i.e. 1947] Address", "Date and Year of Study on Entry", Date when Graduated or Left College", "Address on Graduation", "Degree Taken, "If Dead, Date of Decease", "Particulars of Subsequent Career" and "Change of Name were Appropriate".

Unfortunately, while information on identities appears reliable, in relation to numbers and gender, these sources can be unclear as to their meaning, vary in their method of recording, and show discrepancies as between themselves, and be incomplete or simply missing. Thus, the information that can be extracted from them must be subject to error, and the conclusions drawn consequently tentative, as the text tries to make plain.

Reliance has been placed principally upon Court Minutes, the other sources ameliorating their deficiencies.

Table 1

Estimated Numbers, and Gender, of Entrant Law Students

1899-1900 to 1938-39 (Chapter 3)

"Law entrants" numbers for 1899-1900, 1903-04, 1904-05, 1906-07, 1907-08, 1908-09, 1910-11, 1914-15 and 1915-16 are taken from UCD Calendars[1]; for intervening other years, and from 1916-17 to 1926-27, derived from the "*Register*"[2]; and for 1927-28 to 1938-39 taken from "Entrant Students" tables in Court Minutes[3]. "Of whom women" numbers for 1899-1900 to 1930-31 are derived from the "*Register*"[4]; and for 1931-32 to 1938-39 taken from "Entrant Students" tables in Court Minutes[5]. All Scots law and Conveyancing numbers are taken from "Entrant Students" tables[6].

	1899 -00	1900 -01	1901 -02	1902 -03	1903 -04	1904 -05	1905 -06	1906 -07	1907 -08	1908 -09
Law entrants	21	8	5	8	9	10	10	16	23	12
Of whom women	0	0	0	0	0	0	0	0	0	0
	1909 -10	1910 -11	1911 -12	1912 -13	1913 -14	1914 -15	1915 -16	1916 -17	1917 -18	1918 -19
Law entrants	5	10	13	17	13	5	3	2	0	2
Of whom women	0	0	0	1	0	0	0	0	0	0
	1919 -20	1920 -21	1921 -22	1922 -23	1923 -24	1924 -25	1925 -26	1926 -27	1927 -28	1928 -29
Law entrants	8	28	18	17	23	23	17	28	34	28 = 27 Sc 1 Con
Of whom women	0	0	0	0	0	0	0	1	0	0
	1929 -30	1930 -31	1931 -32	1932 -33	1933 -34	1934 -35	1935 -36	1936 -37	1937 -38	1938 -39

Law entrants	30 = 29 Sc 1 Con	33 = 30 Sc 3 Con	25 = 22 Sc 3 Con	39 = 36 Sc 3 Con	43 = 38 Sc 5 Con	32 = 29 Sc 3 Con	45 = 35 Sc 10 Con	38 = 32 Sc 6 Con	30 = 20 Sc 10 Con	32 = 21 Sc 11 Con
Of whom women	1	2	1 = 1 Sc	0	1 = 1 Sc	1 = 1 Sc	0	1 = 1 Sc	1 = 1 Con	0

Table 2

Estimated Numbers, and Gender, of Entrant Law Students

1939-40 to 1949-50 (Chapter 4)

All numbers taken from "Entrant Students" tables in Court Minutes[7], supplemented by (for 1939-40) UCD College Council "Preliminary Statistics"[8], (for 1940-41) the "*Register*"[9] and (for 1941-2) Senate Minute recording examination passes[10]. NB: For 1940-41, numbers and gender of BL and non-graduating students are not disaggregated in any source; for 1942-43, BL entrants include 8 Polish "soldier-students".

	1939 -40	1940 -41	1941 -42	1942 -43	1943 -44	1944 -45	1945 -46	1946 -47	1947 -48	1948 -49	1949 -50
BL entrants	6	?	4	12	1	0	6	12	8	6	6
Of whom women	0	?	0	2	0	0	2	2	0	2	2
Non-graduating law entrants	16	?	14?	7= 7 Sc	5= 4 Sc 1 Con	4= 3 Sc 1 Con	4= 4 Sc	8	18	32	45
Of whom women	0	?	?	1 = 1 Sc 0 Con	2 = 1 Sc 1 Con	3 = 2 Sc 1 Con	2 = 2 Sc 0 Con	2	1	0	3
Total law entrants	22	12	18?	19	6	4	10	20	26	38	51
Of whom women	0	1	?	3	2	3	4	4	1	2	5

Table 3

Estimated Numbers, and Gender, of Entrant Law Students

1950-51 to 1955-56 (Chapter 5)

All numbers are taken from UCD College Council Minutes (occasionally "Preliminary") "Student Statistics"[11]. NB: BL and LLB entrant numbers for 1954-55 are unobtainable.

	1950 -51	1951 -52	1952 -53	1953 -54	1954 -55	1955 -56
BL entrants	4	6	6	3	?	4
Of whom women	0	4	2	2	0	0
LLB entrants	2	3	13	4	?	5
Of whom women	0	0	2	1	0	1
Combined BL and LLB entrants	6	9	19	7	2	9
Of whom women	0	4	4	3	0	1
Non-graduating law entrants	30	23	26	27	17	51
Of whom women	0	1	1	0	0	1
Total law entrants	36	32	45	34	19	60
Of whom women	0	5	5	3	0	2

Table 4

Estimated Numbers, and Gender, of Entrant Law Students

1956-57 to 1966-67 (Chapter 6)

For 1956-57 to 1964-65, BL and LLB entrant numbers arc inferred from Senate Minutes' lists of graduates three years later[12], and, for 1965-6 and 1966-67, from Graduation Programmes lists of Ordinary graduates three years later (and in the latter case, and Honours graduates four years later)[13]. The apparent entrant in 1961, must have been a 1958 entrant who took four years to graduate.

For 1956-57 to 1961-62, non-graduating entrant numbers are taken from Senate Minutes' "Entrant Students" table with total entrant numbers calculated by adding BL and LLB entrant numbers[14]: from 1962-63 to 1966-67, total law entrant numbers are taken from Senate Minutes with non-graduating entrant numbers calculated by subtracting the BL and LLB entrant numbers[15].

	1956 -57	1957- 58	1958 -59	1959 -60	1960 -61	1961 -62	1962 -63	1963 -64	1964 -65	1965 -66	1966 -67
BL entrants	2	4	6	4	1	1	0	0	0	0	0
Of whom women	0	0	0	0	0	1	0	0	0	0	0
LLB entrants	4	6	2	6	6	16	37	36	31	28	56
Of whom women	0	1	0	0	1	5	8	4	5	4	8
BL and LLB entrants	6	10	8	10	7	17	37	36	31	28	56
Of whom women	0	1	0	0	1	6	8	4	5	4	8
Non- graduating entrants	87	83	85	82	93	71	28	21	53	52	46
Of who women	24	12	15	16	25	25	0	3	4	2	3
Total law entrants	93	93	93	92	100	88	65	57	84	80	102

[1] DUA Recs A/814/1/17, /21, /22, /24, /25, /26, /28, /32 & /33, St Andrews University Calendar for the year[s] 1899-1900, 1903-04, 1904-05, 1906-07, 1907-08, 1908-09, 1910-11, 1914-15 and 1915-16 (various pages).

[2] DUA Recs A/665, Register of Law Students in U.C.D. from 1897-1947 (various entries).

[3] DUA Recs A/34 to A/45, UStA Court Minutes 1927-28 to 1938-39, November or December Meetings.

[4] See note 2.

[5] DUA Recs A/37 to A/45, UStA Court Minutes 1931-32 to 1938-39, November or December Meetings.

[6] DUA Recs A/35 to A/45, UStA Court Minutes 1928-29 to 1938-39, November or December Meetings.

[7] DUA Recs A/46 to A/56, UStA Court Minutes 1939-40 to 1949-50, November, December or January Meetings. .

[8] DUA Recs A/108, UCD Council Minutes October 1939-September 1943, Finance Committee Meeting 16 October 1939.

[9] See note 2.

[10] UStAA Recs UY 452/44, UStAA Senatus Academicus Minutes, Meeting of 25th June 1942.

[11] DUA Recs A/112 and A/60 to A62, UCD Council Minutes October 1950-September 1952 to 1955-56, December Meetings.

[12] DUA Recs A/78 to A/82, UStA Senatus Academicus Minutes 1955-58 to 1964-66, June or July and October Meetings.

[13] DUA RU 352/1 to /5, University of St Andrews/University of Dundee, academic Ceremony of Conferral of Degrees, July 1968, July & October 1969, July & October 1970.

[14] DUA Recs A/78 to A/80, UStA Senatus Academicus Minutes 1956-58 to 1960-62, December Meetings.

[15] DUA Recs A/81 to A/83, UStA Senatus Academicus Minutes 1962-64 to 1966-67, December Meetings.

BIBLIOGRAPHY

Archived University material

University of St Andrews Court Minutes 1891-1967

Dundee University Archives: Recs A/415 to A/420 (1891-95 to 1910-11)

Dundee University Archives: Recs A/18 to A/73 (1911-12 to 1966-67)

University of St Andrews Senate Minutes 1891-1967

Dundee University Archives: Recs A/421 to A/436 (1891-95 to 1937-39),

University of St Andrews Archives: UY 452/42 to 452/48 (1939-40 to 1945-46)

Dundee University Archives: Recs A/437-74 (1946-48) and A/74 to A/83 (1948-50 to 1966-67)

University College Dundee Council Minutes 1882-1954

Dundee University Archives: Recs A/98 to A/113 (1882-89 to 1952-54)

Queen's College Dundee Council Minutes 1953-1967

Dundee University Archives: Recs A/60 to A/73 (bound in with University of St Andrews Court Minutes) (1953-54 to 1966-67)

University College Dundee Education Board Minutes 1883-1940

Dundee University Archives: Recs A/114 to A/116 (1883-1940, including some Miscellaneous Papers)

University of Dundee Court Minutes 1967-93

Dundee University Archives: RU 162/1/1 to RU 162/1/29 (1967-68 to 1992-93)

University of St Andrews Calendars 1950-66

Dundee University Archives: Recs A/814/2/80/1 to A/814/2/95 (1950-51 to 1965-66)

University College Dundee Calendars 1883-1940

Dundee University Archives: Recs A/814/1/1 to A/814/1/51 (1883-84 to 1939-40)

University of St Andrews/University of Dundee "Graduation Programmes" (Academic Ceremony of Conferral of Degrees)

Dundee University Archives: Recs 352/1 to 352/6 (2 July 1968, 1 July 1969, 10 October 1969, 6 July 1970 and 16 October 1970).

University of St Andrews General Council Minutes 1859-1983

University of St Andrews Archives: UY/615 (1859-1983) (nb catalogue indicates available to 1953, but later editions are available in unbound form)

Other

Dundee University Archives: A/162: "Law and Conveyancing Students 1932-33" (loose sheet)

Dundee University Archives: RU/191: Faculty of Law Centenary Miscellaneous Papers

Dundee University Archives: Recs A/335/8: University of St Andrews. Lectureships in Law in University College, Dundee

Dundee University Archives: Recs A/337: University College, Dundee, Secretary, Miscellaneous Secretary's papers relating to Department of Law 1885-1927

Dundee University Archives: Recs A/351/17: Law Department Correspondence and list

Dundce University Archives: Recs A/335/8: Law Lectureships. Advertisements and conditions of appointment 1939

Dundee University Archives: Recs A/665: Register of Law Students in UCD from 1897-1947

Dundee University Archives: Recs A/669: University College, Dundee, 1919-20, Faculty of Law: Student Lecture Notes, Edward R Simpson

Dundee University Archives: Recs A/678/46: University of St Andrews. Assistant Quaestor and Factor Files 1966-67

Dundee University Archives: Recs A/759/2: Dundee University, Faculty of Law. Chair of Conveyancing

Dundee University Archives: Recs A/779/6/1: Dundee University, Miscellaneous Secretary's Files

Dundee University Archives: RU 191: Faculty of Law – Centenary. Miscellaneous Papers (1990)

Dundee University Archives: 378.413 3 U 58: University of St Andrews Record of Past and Present Students of University College, Dundee and Senior Medical College 1897-1947

Dundee University Archives: Recs A/680/1 to A/680/45: University College Dundee Student Representative Council, "The College: the official publication of the Student Representative Council, University College, Dundee", 1888 to 1891 (vols I-III), 1903 to 1934 ("New Series" vols I-XXXI), 1940 to 1951 (vols XX [sic] to XXX [sic]) (some missing)

Dundee University Archives: KLoc F 378.413 1 G 786: Privy Council, Grant of Charter [& statutes] to University of Dundee, 1967

Other archived material

Faculty of Procurators and Solicitors in Dundee: Index to Minutes 1846-87

Faculty of Procurators and Solicitors in Dundee: Minutes 1887-1960, 1961-1984

Official Reports

Report made to His Majesty by a Royal Commission of Inquiry into State of the Universities of Scotland 1826-30 (London, H.M.S.O., 1831)

Report of the St Andrews University Commissioners (Scotland) (London, H.M.S.O, 1845)

General Report of the Commissioners under the Universities (Scotland) Act 1858 with an Appendix containing Ordinances, Minutes, Reports on Special Subjects and Other Documents (Edinburgh, H.M.S.O., 1863)

First Report of the Royal Commission on the Courts of Law in Scotland C-175 (Edinburgh, H.M.S.O., 1869)

Report of the Royal Commissioners appointed to inquire into the Universities of Scotland (1876-78) with Evidence and Appendix, volume I (Report with Index of Evidence) C.1935 (Edinburgh, H.M.S.O., 1878)

General Report of the Commissioners under the Universities (Scotland) Act 1889 with an Appendix containing Ordinances, Minutes, Correspondence, Evidence, and Other Documents (Edinburgh, H.M.S.O., 1900)

Report of the Committee on Scottish Universities, with Appendices Cd 5257 (London, H.M.S.O., 1910)

Report of the Inquiry Appointed in February 1949 to Review and Report on the Organisation of University Education in Dundee and its Relationship with St Andrews University (Edinburgh, H.M.S.O., 1949) (the "Cooper Inquiry")

Report of the Royal Commission on University Education in Dundee 1951-52 Cmnd 8514 (Edinburgh, H.M.S.O., 1952) (the "Tedder Commission").

Higher Education: report of the Committee appointed by the Prime Minister under the Chairmanship of Lord Robbins 1961-63 Cmnd 2154 (London, H.M.S.O., 1963) (the "Robbins Report")

Report on University Teaching Methods (London, H.M.S.O., 1964) (the "Hale Report")

Legislation

(Prerogative) primary

Charter of Incorporation of the University of Dundee 28 June 1967 [& statutes] (see above "Archived University materials")

(Parliamentary) primary

Stamp Act 1785 (25 Geo III c 80)

Procurators (Scotland) Act 1865 (28 & 29 Vict c85)

Universities (Scotland) Act 1858 (21 & 22 Vict c 83)

Stamp Act 1870 (33 & 34 Vict c 97)

Law Agents (Scotland) 1873 (36 & 37 Vict c 63)

Universities (Scotland) Act 1889 (52 & 53 Vict c 55)

Law Agents and Notaries Public (Scotland) Act 1891 (54 & 55 Vict c 30)

Law Agents (Scotland) Act Amendment Act 1896 (59 & 60 Vict c 49)

Solicitors' (Scotland) Act 1933 (23 & 24 Geo V c 21)

Chartered and Other Bodies (Temporary Provisions) Act 1939 (2 & 3 Geo VI c 119)

University of St Andrews Act 1953 (1 & 2 Eliz 2 c 40)

Universities (Scotland) Act 1966 (1966 c 13)

delegated (statutory instruments)

Scottish Universities (Temporary Provisions) Order 1940, SI 1940 No 319

University of St Andrews (Appointment of Commissioners) Order 1953, SI 1953 No 1562

University of St Andrews (Extension of Duration of Commissioners' Powers) Order 1956, SI 1956 No 1585

University of St Andrews Act 1953 (Commencement) (No 1) Order 1953, SI 1953 No 1451

University of St Andrews Act 1953 (Commencement) (No 2) Order 1953, SI 1953 No 1898

University of St Andrews Act 1953 (Commencement) (No 3) Order 1953, SI 1954 No 1031

University of St Andrews Act 1953 (Commencement) (No 4) Order 1953, SI 1954 No 1564

University of St Andrews Commissioners (Ordinance No 3) Order (Ordinance (SAC) No 3), SI 1954 No 1034

University of St Andrews Commissioners (Ordinance No 4) Order (Ordinance (SAC) No 4), SI 1954 No 1368

University of St Andrews Commissioners (Ordinance No 5) Order (Ordinance (SAC) No 5), SI 1954 No 1474)

University of St Andrews Commissioners (Ordinance No 10) Order (Ordinance (SAC) No 10), SI 1955 No 247

delegated (Acts of Sederunt)

AS 26 June 1866 (and appended thereto:

(i)   Curriculum and Regulations prepared by the General Council of Procurators in Scotland under the Act 28 & 29 Vict c 85 in regard to curriculum and examination of intending practitioners, and extension of Apprenticeships (dated 8 March 1866);

(ii)　Bye-Laws for the General Council of Procurators in Scotland under the Act 28 & 29 Vict c 85 (dated 8 March 1866); and

(iii)　Approval and Report by the Sheriffs of Scotland (dated 20 June 1866)[1]

AS 20 December 1873

AS 28 January 1874

AS 18 March 1875

AS 20 July 1878

AS 4 November 1886

AS 12 March 1926

delegated (Ordinances not in statutory instruments)

[Commissioners'] Ordinance No 75 (General No 8) of 1862

[Two] Notes of Alteration ... [of Commissioners'] Ordinance 75, General No 8] authorised by Order of Her Majesty in Council of date 6th August 1874

Note of Alteration ... [of Commissioners'] Ordinance No 75, General No 8] authorised by Order of Her Majesty in Council of date 11th August 1884

[Commissioners'] Ordinance No 46 (St Andrews No 5) of 1894

Emergency [Court] Ordinance (St Andrews No 2) (Regulations for Degrees, Diplomas, Certificates, Examinations and Examiners) of 1940

Emergency [Court] Ordinance (St Andrews No 6) (Regulations for Degrees, Diplomas and Certificates) of 1940

[Court] Ordinance No 249 (St Andrews No 45) of 1948 (Foundation of Chair of Scots Law)

[Court] Ordinance No 339 (St Andrews No 52) of 1960 (Faculty of Social Science)

[Court] Ordinance No 365 (St Andrews No 56 (Amendment of Ordinance No 39 (General No 11) of the Commissioners under the Universities (Scotland) Act 1889) of 1961 (Degree of Bachelor of Laws)

[Court] Ordinance No 417 (St Andrews No 68) of 1963 (Foundation of the Chair of Jurisprudence)

[Court] Ordinance No 447 (St Andrews No 74) of 1964 (Revocation of certain Ordinances)

[Court] Ordinance No 452 (St Andrews No 75) of 1964 (Regulations for Degree of Bachelor of Laws)

Legislative compilations

Anon (ed), *Curriculum, Regulations and Bye-Laws prepared by the General Council of Procurators in Scotland, approved of and reported on by the Sheriffs of Scotland, and approved by the Lords of Council and Session, by Act of Sederunt, dated 22d June 1866, all in terms of the "Procurators (Scotland) Act 1865"* (Edinburgh, Neill & Co, 1866)[2]

Anon, *Court of Session: Acts of Sederunt, 1875-1906* (Edinburgh, Court of Session?, 1906)

Anon, *University of St Andrews Ordinances* (St Andrews, University of St Andrews, c1964)

Alan E Clapperton (ed), *Universities (Scotland) Act 1889 together with Ordinances of the Commissioners ... and University Court Ordinances* (Glasgow, James Maclehose & Sons, 1915)

Alan E Clapperton (ed), *Universities (Scotland) Act 1858 together with Ordinances of the Commissioners under said Act ...* (Glasgow, James Maclehose & Sons, 1916)

Alan E Clapperton (ed), *University Court Ordinances made and approved between 1st January 1915 and 31st December 1924 under the Universities (Scotland) Act 1889 ...* (Glasgow, Jackson, Wylie & Co, 1925)

W A Fleming, *University Court Ordinances from 1st January 1925 to 31st July 1947 ... and Emergency Ordinances ... with a General Index* (London, Oliver & Boyd, 1948)

see also:

J Henderson Begg, *A Treatise on the Law of Scotland relating to Law Agents, including the law od costs as between agent and client* (Edinburgh, Bell & Bradfute, 1st ed 1873, 2nd ed 1883) (below), containing relevant Acts of Sederunt

General Report of the Commissioners under the Universities (Scotland) Act, 1889 ... Cd 276 (Edinburgh, HMSO, 1900) (above), containing all Ordinances in force at the time of its publication

Green's Encyclopaedia of the Law of Scotland (Edinburgh, William Green & Sons, 1st ed 1896-1904, 2nd ed 1909-14, 3rd ed 1926-35 & Supplement 1949-51), containing summaries of relevant Acts of Parliament, Acts of Sederunt and Ordinances

Parliament House Book annual volumes (Edinburgh, W Green & Sons, various dates) (above), containing current Acts of Parliament, Acts of Sederunt, and various Regulations

Cases

Hall v Incorporated Society of Law Agents (1901) 3F 1059, (1901) 9 SLT 150 (IH, Whole Court)

Nairn v University of St Andrews and Edinburgh University Courts (1909) SC(HL) 10

Metcalfe & Others v University of St Andrews & Others (1894) 2 SLT 139 (Outer House); (1894) 2 SLT 371 and (1894) 22R 210 (Court of Seven Judges); (1895) 22R (HL) 13 (House of Lords); (1896) 23R 559 (Inner House); (1896) 23R (HL) 60 & [1896] AC 647 (House of Lords)

M'Gregor & Others v University Court of St Andrews & Others (1897) 5 SLT 102 (Outer House); (1897) 5 SLT 215 (Inner House) and (1898) 25 R 1216 (Inner House).

Books

R D Anderson, *Education and Opportunity in Victorian Scotland* (Oxford, Clarendon Press, 1983)

Harold F Andorsen [*sic*] (ed), *Memoirs of Lord Salvesen* (London & Edinburgh, WR Chambers Ltd, 1949)

Anon, *Register of the Society of Writers to Her Majesty's Signet* (Edinburgh, Clark Constable, 1983)

Anon, *The Society of Writers to HM Signet, with a list of members of the Society from 1594 to 1890 and an abstract of the Minutes* (Edinburgh, The Society, 1890)

Anon, *The Society of Writers to HM Signet, with a list of members and abstracts of the Minutes of the Society, the Commissioners and the Council and the early history of the Scottish Signet* (Edinburgh, The Society, 1936)

Anon, *University College, Dundee: the opening ceremony, Professor Stuart's Address, Description of the College Buildings* (Dundee, John Leng & Co, 1883)

J B Barclay, *The SSC Story 1784-1984* (Edinburgh, Edina Press, 1984)

J Henderson Begg, *A Treatise on the Law of Scotland relating to Law Agents, including the law od costs as between agent and client* (Edinburgh, Bell & Bradfute, 1st ed 1873, 2nd ed 1883)

William George Black, *The Law Agents Act 1873: its operation and results as affecting legal education in Scotland* (Glasgow, James Maclehose, 1884)

Callum G Brown, Arthur J McIvor & Neil Rafeek *The University Experience 1945-1975: an oral history of the University of Strathclyde* (Edinburgh, Edinburgh University Press in association with the University of Strathclyde, 2004)

John Malcolm Bulloch, *A History of the University of Aberdeen 1495-1895* (London, Hodder and Stoughton, 1895)

John W Cairns & Hector L MacQueen, *Learning and the Law: a short history of Edinburgh Law School* (Edinburgh, Edinburgh Law School, 2013)

Ronald Gordon Cant, *The University of St Andrews: a short history* (St Andrews, St Andrews University Library, 3rd ed 1992)

Fiona Craddock (ed), *The Journal of Sir J Randall Phillip OBE QC: public and private life in Scotland 1947-1957* (Edinburgh, Pentland Press, 1998)

E Fiddes, *Chapters in the History of Owens College and of Manchester University 1851-1914* (Publications of the Manchester University Press No. CCLIV, Historical Series, No. LXXIV) (Manchester, Manchester University Press, 1937)

John Finlay, *Men of Law in Pre-Reformation Scotland* (Scottish Historical Review Monograph, No 9) (East Linton, Tuckwell Press, 2000)

John Finlay, *The Community of the College of Justice: Edinburgh and the Court of Session 1687-1808* (Edinburgh, Edinburgh University Press, 2012)

John Finlay, *Legal Practice in Eighteenth Century Scotland* (Leiden, Brill Nijhoff, 2015)

J D Ford, *Law and Opinion in Scotland during the Seventeenth Century* (Oxford and Portland, Oregon, Hart, 2007)

Anna Frankiewicz (ed), *Polish Students at the University of St Andrews: lives and times of graduates 1941-1950* (Edinburgh, the Author, 1994)

F J Grant, *The Faculty of Advocates in Scotland 1532-1943 ...* (Edinburgh, Scottish Record Society, 1944)

Rosemary Hannah, *The Grand Designer: Third Marques of Bute* (Edinburgh, Birlinn, 2012)

Robert Kerr Hannay, *The College of Justice: essays on the institution and development of the Court of Session* (Edinburgh & Glasgow, William Hodge & Co, 1933)

F J Hartog (ed), *The Owens College, Manchester: (Founded 1851) A Brief History Of The College And Description Of Its Various Departments* (Manchester, JE Cornish, 1900)

John Alexander Henderson (ed), *History of the Society of Advocates in Aberdeen* (Aberdeen University Studies, No 60) (Aberdeen, University of Aberdeen, 1912)

D B Horn, *A Short History of the University of Edinburgh 1556-1889* (Edinburgh, Edinburgh University Press, 1967)

Mabel V Irvine, *The Avenue of Years: a memoir of Sir James Irvine, principal and vice-chancellor of the University of St Andrews, 1921-1952* (Edinburgh & London, Blackwood, 1970)

Matthew Jarron (ed), *Ten Taysiders* (Dundee, Abertay Historical Society, 2011)

Ronald Kay, *UCCA: its origins and development 1956-1985* (Cheltenham, UCCA, 1985)

William Angus Knight, *A Biographical Sketch with Reminiscences on Sir Thomas Thornton, Dundee, including several estimates of him* (Dundee, William Kidd, 1905)

William Angus Knight, *Early Chapters in the History of the University of St Andrews and Dundee* (Dundee, William Kidd, 1902)

Nicola Lacey, *A Life of HLA Hart: the nightmare and the noble dream* (Oxford, Oxford University Press, 2004)

D S Littlejohn, A Popular Sketch of the Law of Scotland: being an address to the Dundee law apprentices *(Edinburgh, Bell & Bradfute, 3rd ed 1893)*

Charles McKean & David Walker, *Dundee: an illustrated architectural guide* (Edinburgh, Royal Incorporation of Architects in Scotland, 1984)

Charles McKean and Patricia Whatley, with Kenneth Baxter, *Lost Dundee: Dundee's lost architectural heritage* (Edinburgh, Birlinn, 2008)

J D Mackie, *The University of Glasgow 1451-1951* (Glasgow, Jackson, Son, & Co, 1954)

Macmillan (Lord), *A Man of Law's* Tale (London, Macmillan & Co, 1952)

A H Millar (ed), *Roll of Eminent Burgesses of Dundee 1513-1886* (Dundee, Provost, Magistrates and Town Council of Dundee, 1887)

Mary Jane Mossman, *The First Women Lawyers: a comparative study of gender, law and the legal profession* (Oxford & Portland, Hart, 2006)

J Spencer Muirhead, *An Outline of Roman Law* (London, William Hodge, 1st ed 1937, 2nd ed 1947)

D H S Nicholson and A H E Lee (eds), *The Oxford Book of Mystical Verse* (Oxford, The Clarendon Press, 1917)

J M Page, *The Three Elizabeths* (London, Blackie, 1950)

William (Sir) Peterson, *St Andrews and Dundee: a retrospect* (Dundee, John Leng & Co, 1893)

Norman H Reid, *Ever to Excel: an illustrated history of the University of St Andrews* (Dundee, Dundee University Press, 2011)

O F Robinson, T D Fergus & W M Gordon, *European Legal History: sources and institutions* (London, Butterworths, 3rd ed 2000),

Michael Shafe, *University Education in Dundee 1881-1981: a pictorial history* (Dundee, University of Dundee, 1982)

Annette M Smith, *The Guildry of Dundee: a history of the Merchant Guild of Dundee up to the 19th Century* (Dundee, Abertay Historical Society, 2005)

James V Smith, *The Watt Institution Dundee 1824-49* (Dundee, Abertay Historical Society, 1977).

David Swinfen, *The Fall of the Tay Bridge* (Edinburgh, Mercat Press, 1994)

Donald G Southgate, *University Education in Dundee: a centenary history* (Edinburgh, Edinburgh University Press, 1982)

Joseph Thompson, *The Owens College: its foundation and growth; and its connection with the Victoria University, Manchester* (Manchester, JE Cornish, 1886)

John Trayner, *Trayner's Latin Maxims* (Edinburgh, William Paterson, 1st ed 1861)

Various Authors, *An Introduction to Scottish Legal History* (Stair Society Publication, No 20) (Edinburgh, the Stair Society, 1958)

Richard Vinen, *National Service: a generation in uniform 1945-1963* (London, Penguin Books, 2014)

David M Walker, *A History of the School of Law, the University of Glasgow* (Glasgow, the Law School, University of Glasgow, c.1990)

David M Walker, *A Legal History of Scotland*, 7 <u>vols.</u> (Edinburgh, W Green, 1988-2004)

Stephen P Walker, *The Faculty of Advocates: a Biographical Directory of Members Admitted from 1 January 1800 to 31 December 1986* (Edinburgh, The Faculty, 1987)

Chapters in Books

John W Cairns, "The Origins of the Glasgow Law School: the Professors of Civil Law 1714-1761", in Peter Birks (ed), *The Life of the Law: Proceedings of the Tenth British Legal History Conference, Oxford 1991* (London, Hambledon Press, 1993)

John W Cairns, "Importing our Lawyers from Holland: Neherlands Influences on Scots law and lawyers in the eighteenth century", in Grant G Simpson (ed) *Scotland and the Low Countries 1124-1994* (East Linton, Tuckwell Press, 1996)

John W Cairns, "The Civil Law Tradition in Scottish Legal Thought", in DL Carey Miler & R Zimmerman (eds) *The Civilian Tradition and Scots Law: Aberdeen Quincentenary Essays* (Berlin, Dunker & Humblot, 1997)

David L Carey Miller, "A Scottish Celebration of the European Legal Tradition", in David L Carey Miller & Reinhard Zimmerman (eds) *The Civilian Tradition and Scots Law: Aberdeen Quincentenary Essays* (Berlin, Dunker & Humblot, 1997)

Thomas Mackay Cooper, "Legal Education in Scotland: a criticism", in Lord Cooper, *Selected Papers 1892-1955* (Edinburgh, Oliver & Boyd, 1957) (reprinted from TMC "Legal Education in Scotland: a criticism" (1922) XXXVII *Scottish Law Review* 71)

John Durkan, "The early Scottish notary", in Ian B Cowan & Duncan Shaw (eds) *The Renaissance and Reformation in Scotland* (Edinburgh, Scottish Academic Press, 1983)

John Finlay, "The History of the Notary in Scotland", in Mathias Schmoekel & Werner Schubert (eds), *Handbuch zur Geschichte des Notariats der europaeischen Tradition* (Baden-Baden, Nomos, 2009)

John Finlay, "Lawyers in the British Isles", in B Dolemeyer (ed), *Anwaelte und Ihre Geschichte* (Tuebingen, Mohr Siebeck, 2011)

John Finlay, "Legal Education", in Robert Anderson, Mark Freeman & Lindsay Paterson, *The Edinburgh History of Education in Scotland* (Edinburgh, Edinburgh University Press, 2015)

William M Gordon, "A Comparison of the Influence of Roman Law in England and Scotland", in DL Carey Miller & R Zimmerman (eds) *The Civilian Tradition and Scots Law* (Berlin, Duncker & Humblot, 1997).

Neil J D Kennedy, "The Faculty of Law", in P J Anderson (ed) *History of the University of Aberdeen: a quatercentenary tribute* (Aberdeen University Studies, No 19) (Aberdeen, Aberdeen University Press, 1906)

P S Lachs, "Scottish Legal Education in the Nineteenth Century", in E W Ives & A H Manchester (eds) *Law, Litigants and the Legal Profession* (Royal Historical Society Studies in Legal History Series, No 36) (London, Royal Historical Society/New Jersey, Humanities Press Inc, 1983)

Hector L MacQueen, "The Foundation of Law Teaching in Aberdeen", in DL Carey Miler & R Zimmerman (eds) *The Civilian Tradition and Scots Law: Aberdeen Quincentenary Essays* (Berlin, Dunker & Humblot, 1997)

Alan A Paterson, "The Legal Profession in Scotland: an endangered species or a problem case for market theory?", in Richard L Abel and Phillip S C Lewis *Lawyers in Society,* vol 1 "The Common Law World" (Berkeley/Los Angeles/London, University of California Press, c1988)

Alan Rodger, "The Uses of Civil Law in Scottish Courts", in D L Carey Miler & R Zimmerman (eds) *The Civilian Tradition and Scots Law: Aberdeen Quincentenary Essays* (Berlin, Dunker & Humblot, 1997)

Encyclopaedias

Green's Encyclopaedia of the Law of Scotland (Edinburgh, William Green & Sons, 1st ed 1896-1904, 2nd ed 1909-14, 3rd ed 1926-35 & Supplement 1949-51)

Sir T Smith & R Black (Gen Eds), HMcN Henderson, JM Thomson & K Miller (Dep Gen Eds), *Stair Memorial Encyclopaedia of the Laws of Scotland* (Edinburgh, Law Society of Scotland, various dates)

H C G Matthew & B Harrison, *Oxford Dictionary of National Biography* (Oxford, Oxford University Press, 2004)

Articles

Anon, "Admission of Women to Law Classes" (1906-07) 14 *Scots Law Times* 161

Anon, "Appointment of Lecturer on Conveyancing in Dundee College" (1904-5) 12 *Scots Law Times* 190

Anon, "Appointments" (1885) XXIX *Journal of Jurisprudence* 169

Anon, "Bill to amend Law Agents (Scotland) Act" (1887) XXXI *Journal of Jurisprudence* 386

Anon, "Country Agent" (letters) (1893) IX *Scottish Law Review* 148 & 173

Anon, "Dundee Faculty Dinner Dance" 1950 *Scots Law Times* 227

Anon, ("General News") 1948 *Scots Law Times* 32

Anon, "Graduation in Law" (1871) XV *Journal of Jurisprudence* 246

Anon, "The late Mr Henry Hilton Brown: formerly Procurator-Fiscal for Midlothian" 1927 *Scots Law Times* 19

Anon, "James Allison, Esq, solicitor, Dundee" (1909) 17 *Scots Law Times (News and Statutes)* 161

Anon, "James Pattullo, Esq: Solicitor, Dundee" (1902-03) 10 *Scots Law Times* 105

Anon, "Ladies in the Profession" (1903-04) 11 *Scots Law Times* 114

Anon, "Lady Lawyers" (1900-01) 8 *Scots Law Times* 126

Anon, "Law Agents Bill" (1872) XVI *Journal of Jurisprudence* 363 & 430

Anon. "Law Agents' Bill" (1873) XVII *Journal of jurisprudence* 313

Anon, "Law Graduation" 1894 *Scots Law Times* 456

Anon, "Law Lectures in Dundee" (1895-6) 3 *Scots Law Times* 254

Anon, "Lectures to the Dundee Society of Law Clerks" (1868) XII *Journal of Jurisprudence* 97

Anon [J Spencer Muirhead], "Legal Education" [part of the President's Report] (1956) 1 *Journal of the Law Society of Scotland* 95

Anon, "Local Law Societies – Society of Solicitors in the Supreme Court" (1970) 15 *Journal of the Law Society of Scotland* 66

Anon, "Local Law Societies: II – The Advocates of Aberdeen" (1970) 14 *Journal of the Law Society of Scotland* 325

Anon, "Local Law Societies: I – The Royal Faculty of Procurators in Glasgow" (1970) 14 *Journal of the Law Society of Scotland* 295

Anon, "Local Law Societies: IV – The Society of Writers to Her Majesty's Signet" (1970) 15 *Journal of the Law Society of Scotland* 35

Anon, "Lord Trayner" (1893-4) 1 *Scots Law Times* 311

Anon, "Memorial for Additional Sheriffs in Dundee ..." (1860) IV *Journal of Jurisprudence* 135

Anon, "New Queen's Counsel" 1956 *Scots Law Times* 84

Anon, "News" (1901-02) 9 Scots Law Times 13

Anon, "Notes on the Judicature Commission" (1869) XIII *Journal of Jurisprudence* 13

Anon, "Obituary" 1959 *Scots Law Times* 52

Anon, "Professional Reform" (1871) XV *Journal of Jurisprudence* 201

Anon, "Proposed Law School in Dundee" (1867) XI *Journal of Jurisprudence* 91

Anon, (Report of discussion on Law Agents Bill in the Scottish Law Amendment Society) (1872) XVI *Journal of Jurisprudence* 369

Anon, "Sir Thomas Thornton LLD, solicitor, Dundee" (1895-96) 3 *Scots Law Times* 89

Anon, "Solicitors' Examinations" 1938 *Scots Law Times (News)* 90

Anon, "St Mungo's College" (1890) XXXIV *Journal of Jurisprudence* 506

Anon, "St Mungo's College – Faculty of Law" (1889) 1 *Juridical Review* 390

Anon, "The Chair of Law in Aberdeen University" (1907-08) 15 *Scots Law Times* 42 & 50

Anon, "The Education of Scotch Lawyers" (1869) XIII *Journal of Jurisprudence* 124, 177

Anon, "The Hon Lord Trayner" (1904-05) 12 *Scots Law Times* 145

Anon, "The late James Pattullo, Esq, Solicitor Dundee" (1903-04) 11 *Scots Law Times* 159

Anon, "The Late Lord Trayner" 1929 *Scots Law Times (News)* 21

Anon, "The Late Mr JM Hendry, solicitor, Dundee" 1916 *Scots Law Times (News and Statutes)* 81

Anon, "The late Sir Thomas Thornton, LLD, Dundee" (1903-04) 11 *Scots Law Times* 9

Anon, (papers of the Scottish Law Amendment Society) "The Law Agents (Scotland) Bill" (1873) XVII *Journal of Jurisprudence* 353

Anon, "The Legal Profession in Scotland – a survey of the position" (1956) 1 *Journal of the Law Society of Scotland* 10

Anon, "The New Act of Sederunt anent the Admission of Law Agents" (1886) XXX *Journal of Jurisprudence* 644

Anon [Andrew Dewar Gibb], "A Scots Law School in 1913" 1919 *Juridical Review* 267

Anon, "Undaunted ..." (1906-07) 14 *Scots Law Times* 106

Anon, "Uniform Rights for Law Agents in Scotland" (1871) XV *Journal of Jurisprudence* 595

Anon, "University Legal Education" (1889) 1 *Juridical Review* 194

Anon, "University of Strathclyde" 1967 *Scots Law Times* 3 & 27

Anon, "Unlicensed Practitioners" [annual meeting of Incorporated Society of Law Agents AGM] (1885) XXIX *Journal of Jurisprudence* 381

Anon, "William Guthrie, Esq ..." (1893-4) 1 *Scots Law Times* 17

John H Begg, "On the Law Agents Act 1873" (1873) XVII *Journal of Jurisprudence* 449

H H Brown, "Legal Education of Apprentices" (1896-97) 4 *Scots Law Times* 106

R Alex Stark Brown, "The Crisis in Legal Education" [letter] (1956) 1 *Journal of the Law Society of Scotland* 147

Alistair R Brownlie, "The Universities and Scottish Legal Education" 1955 *Juridical Review* 26

ARB[rownlie], "Legal Scholarship in Scotland" 1960 *Scots Law Times* 38

John W Cairns, "The Law, the Advocates and the Universities in Late Sixteenth Century Scotland" (1994) LXXIII *Scottish Historical Review* 171

John W Cairns, "From 'Speculative' to 'Practical' Legal Education: the decline of the Glasgow Law School 1801-1830" (1994) 62 *Tijdschrift voor Rechtsgeschiednis* 331

John W Cairns, "Lawyers, Law Professors and Localities": the Universities of Aberdeen 1680-1750" (1995) 46 *Northern Ireland Legal Quarterly* 304

John W Cairns, "Academic Feud, Bloodfeud, and William Welwood: legal education in St Andrews, 1560-1611" (1998) 2 *Edinburgh Law Review* 158 & 255

John W Cairns, "Advocates' Hats, Roman Law and Admission to the Scottish bar, 1580-1812" (1999) 20 *Journal of Legal History* 24

D A O Edward, "Faculty of Advocates Regulations as to Intrants" 1968 *Scots Law Times* 181

Robin Evans-Jones, "Reception of Law, Mixed Legal Systems and the Myth of the Genius of Scots Private Law" (1998) 114 *Law Quarterly Review* 228

John Finlay, "Pettyfoggers, Regulation, and Local Courts in Early Modern Scotland" (2008) LXXXVII *The Scottish Historical Review* 42

John Finlay, "'Tax the Attornies!' Stamp Duty and the Scottish Legal Profession in the Eighteenth Century" (2014) 34 Journal of Scottish Historical Studies 141

John G Gardiner, "Suggestions for Strengthening the Position of the Legal Profession in Scotland" 1929 *Scots Law Times (News)* 163

John G Gardiner, "The Necessity for a Reformation of Legal Education in Scotland" 1928 *Scots Law Times (News)* 363

Andrew Dewar Gibb, "Reform in the Scottish Law School" 1943 *Juridical Review* 267

Stephen D Girvin, "Nineteenth century Reforms in Scottish Legal Education" (1993) 14 *Journal of Legal History* 127

A R B Haldane, "Local Law Societies: III – The Society of Writers to Her Majesty's Signet" (1970) 15 *Journal of the Law Society of Scotland* 35

R L C Hunter, "Some Reflections on the Relevance of Educational Thought in Scottish Law Teaching" 1971 *Juridical Review* 1

D Neil MacCormick, "Seabathing, Sunbathing and Sea Coal" 1967 *Scots Law Times* 69

J D B M[itchell], "First Principles First" 1959 *Scots Law Times* 1

J D B M[itchell], "The Proposed New Law Degree in Edinburgh University" 1960 *Scots Law Times* 21

J Spencer Muirhead, "Notes on the History of the Solicitor Profession in Scotland" (1952) 68 *Scottish Law Review* 25 & 59

D L Munby, "The Dundee School of Economics: In Memoriam" (1957) 4 *Scottish Journal of Political Economy* 60

James J Robertson, "Random Reflections" (1981) vol. 6 no. 4 *Contact* (University of Dundee house magazine) 289

TBS, "Law and Lectures" 1922 *Scots Law Times (News and Statutes)* 39

T B Smith, "A Meditation upon Scottish Universities and the Civil Law" (1958-59) 33 Tulane Law Review 621

TMC [Thomas Mackay Cooper], "Legal Education in Scotland: a criticism" (1922) XXXVII *Scottish Law Review* 71 (reprinted in Lord Cooper, *Selected Papers 1892-1955* (Edinburgh, Oliver & Boyd, 1957) 3)

David M Walker, "Law as a Liberal Education" 1956 *Scots Law Times* 57

David M Walker, "The Crisis in Legal Training" (1956) 1 *Journal of the Law Society of Scotland* 101

David M Walker, "The Crisis in Legal Education" [letter] (1956) 1 *Journal of the Law Society of Scotland* 186

David M Walker, "Legal Studies in the Scottish Universities" 1957 *Juridical Review* 21 & 151

DMW[alker], "The New Glasgow Law Degree" 1959 *Scots Law Times* 121

David M Walker, "Legal Scholarship in Scotland" 1960 *Scots Law Times* 10

David M Walker, "Legal Education and Training" 1960 *Scots Law Times* 41

David M Walker, "Legal Education in Scotland, 1889-1988" 1988 *Juridical Review* 184

J Watson, "Legal Education and Training: a practitioners' point of view" 1960 *Scots Law Times* 57

Ian D Willock, "Examinations Re-Examined" 1962 *Scots Law Times* 81

J F Wilson, "A Survey of Legal Education in the United Kingdom" (Part E) (1966-67) 9 *Journal of the Society of Public Teachers of Law (New Series)* 1

Other

Directory of Members (London, Society of Public Teachers of Law, various years)

Dundee Courier (and Argus / and Northern Warder) (various dates)

Dundee City Library Family and Local History Centre *Obituaries Notices / Miscellaneous Press Cuttings* (bound volumes with cuttings pasted in or photocopied, various dates, first volume entitled *"Obituary Book, vol 1"*) (undated and unpublished)

Dundee Year Book (Dundee, John Leng & Co, various dates)

Faculty of Advocates *Regulations as to Intrants* (various dates) (reproduced in contemporary *Parliament House Books* (see below), and summarised in *Green's Encyclopaedia,* various editions: see above)

Parliament House Book annual volumes (Edinburgh, W Green & Sons, various dates)

Regulations and Catalogue of the Library belonging to the Society of Writer in Dundee (Dundee, Society of Writers in Dundee, 1826) (unpublished)

Regulations for Examination and Admission of Solicitors (various dates) (reproduced in contemporary *Parliament House Books*, and summarised in *Green's Encyclopaedia,* various editions: see above)

The Scotsman (various dates)

Websites (in order of appearance in the text)

Chapter 1 (all last accessed 27 July 2018)

http://www.fdca.org.uk/1823_JohnBoydBaxter.html)

http://archiveshub.ac.uk/data/gb237-coll-737

http://www.universitystory.gla.ac.uk/biography/?id=WH1693&type=P

http://first100years.org.uk/carrie-morrison-2/

Chapter 2 (all last accessed 28 July 2018)

http://www.railwaysarchive.co.uk/eventsummary.php?eventID=75

http://www.fdca.org.uk/Burgess_List.htm

https://www.scran.ac.uk/database/record.php?usi=000-000-519-986-C&scache=1x8ou8eacp&searchdb=scran

Chapter 3 (all last accessed 29 July 2018)

http://en.wikipedia.org/wiki/Edmund_Robertson,_1st_Baron_Lochee#cite_ref-thepeerage.com_1-0

http://thepeerage.com/p23743.htm#i237426

http://www.dundeewomenstrail.org.uk/jordan-jessie-spy/

Chapter 4 (both last accessed 29 July 2018)

http://www.sln.law.ed.ac.uk/2010/02/25/j-j-hamish-gow-1918-23-february-2009/

http://www.ed.ac.uk/schools-departments/student-funding/current-students/university-prizes-awards/humanities/law.

Chapter 6 (last accessed 30 July 2018)

http://www.independent.co.uk/news/obituaries/professor-sir-neil-maccormick-legal-philosopher-and-politician-who-espoused-a-nationalism-that-was-1672082.html.

---

[1] NB: The Act of Sederunt is clearly dated 26 June 1866, but the title page of the section in Anon. (ed) *Curriculum, Regulations and Bye-Laws prepared by the General Council of Procurators in Scotland ....* (Edinburgh, Neill & Co, 1866) (and bound in the Advocates' Library *Legal Tracts XIV*) containing the Curriculum and Regulations, Bye-Laws, and Approval by Sheriffs dates it as 22 June 1866, as does Anon. "The Education of Scotch Lawyers" (1869) XIII *Jurnal of Jurisprudence* 177 "Procurators in Inferior Courts").

[2] NB: See reference above to AS 26 June 1866.

INDEX

Notes: page numbers in *italics* are in
    endnotes
A
A W Cumming, 91
Aberdeen, University of
    Chair of Law applicants, 88, 123
    establishment, 20, 23
    female law students, first recorded, 35
    law department, 19th Century, *43*
    law teaching, provision, 67
    LLB introduction, 22, *45*
    merger of King's and Marischal
        Colleges, 23
academic dress
    college scarves, 276, 333
    cost, 214
    gowns, wearing in class, 213–214
    Graduation Ceremonials, for, 213
    hoods, 213
    women, for, 213
accounting
    degree requirement, as
        1918-1938, 181, 211
        1950-1955, 260
        1960-1963, 309–310, 336, 339
        1964-1965, 339
        LLB degree, for, 336, 339
    examinations
        1893-1918, 156
        1918-1939, 131, 156–157
    professional qualifications, 294, 298,
        329
    professional requirement, as
        1893-1918, 131, 156–157
        1918-1939, 156–157
    teaching staff
        1950-1951, 257, 259
        1951-1953, 264
        1954-1955, 269
        1956-1959, 296, 298–299
        1960-1963, 301
        1964-1971, 319, 329

Act of Sederunt 1825, *37*
Act of Sederunt 1839, *37*
Act of Sederunt 1866, 15, 17, *38, 92*
Act of Sederunt 1873, 17, *40, 96, 99, 159,
    173*
Act of Sederunt 1874, *96*
Act of Sederunt 1875, *40*
Act of Sederunt 1878, *40*
Act of Sederunt 1886, 17, *40, 99*
Act of Sederunt 1893, 17, *41,* 112, 156,
    159
Act of Sederunt 1926, 13, 17, *41,* 129–
    130, 134, 156–157, *166, 168, 173*
Adam, D K, 191
administration
    Faculty Secretary, appointment, 321
    present day, 360
administrative law
    degree requirement, as
        1956-1959, 296
        1965-1967, 339
        BL degree, for, 154
        LLB degree, for, 152, 336, 339
    teaching staff
        1950-1951, 257
        1951-1953, 265
        1960-1963, 300–301, 335
        1967-1968, 314–315, 318
advocates, 8, 10, 12
agents *see* law agents
Agnew, Alexander, 65, *98*
Aitken, Patrick, 144, *172*
Albert Institute, 29
Alexander, G.W., 79, *102*
Allan, Dawson, Simpson & Hampton
    WS, 270
Allardice, W.D., 89
Allison, James, 116–117, 122–123, 129,
    133–135, 137–140, *165,* 180, 185–
    186, 190, 195, *216–217*
Anderson, Alexander Greig, *280*

Anderson, Gardiner, Hepburn & Co, 91
Anderson, Madge Easton, 18, 33–35, *50–51*
Anderson, Marshall, 144, *172*
Anderson's Institution, Glasgow, 23
Andrew Hendry & Sons, 140–141
apprenticeships
  concurrent law studies, and, 302–304, 313, 329
  devilling, 18, 311
  examinations, need for, 8, 112, 129
  law studies to precede, 293, 303–304
  pay, 276, *287*
  post-qualifying year, as, 309–310
  professional entrance by way of
    benefits of, 302–303
    proportion of, *159*
    requirement, 8–9, 12, 18, 54, 129, 293, 298
  reforms, 1960-1963, 310
  term of, 10, 13–14, *38,* 54, 310
  19th Century, 2–3, 7–8, 13–15, 18, *38,* 54, 112
  validity of, 293
attendance requirements *see* law class attendance requirements
attorneys, 8
Attwool, Elspeth, 330

B
Bachelor of Commerce (BCom) degree
  entrance requirements, 136–137
  proposal, 129, 135–136, 254–255
Bachelor of Jurisprudence (BJur) degree, 304
Bachelor of Law (BL) degree, 1–2
  entry requirements, 21, 124
    Arts, 124, 198–199, 260–261, 303, 305
    Latin, 152–153, *218, 286,* 305, 308
    logic or mathematics, 153
    MA precondition, 186, 260, 293, 303–305
  female students, 272–273
  forms of study, 21–22
  General Ordinances, 180, 259–260
  introduction, 21–22, 61, 177–179, 181–182
  LLB degree, and
    comparison with , 151–155
    proposal for merger with, 304
    transition to, 306
  MA precondition, 186, 260, 293, 303–305
  matriculation fees, 184
  pass rates, 1918-1939, 1
  pass requirements, 21–22
  Polish soldier students, 209–210
  proposals for, 178–181, 211–212
  reforms and revisions
    19th Century, 22, 80–81, 124
    1899-1917, 124
    1918-1939, 131–132
  student numbers
    19th Century, 22
    1942-1945, 195, 205–206
    1951-1955, 264, 267, 272–273, 366
    1964-1967, 328
    non-graduating, 205–206, 273
  subject requirements for
    1899-1917, 125, 127
    1939-1949, 181–182, 186–188, 256–257
    1951-1953, 260–261
    administrative law, 154
    civil law, 113, 124–125, 153, 181–182
    constitutional law, 112, 124–125, 154, 182, 195
    conveyancing, 112–113, 124–125, 153, 182, 199
    evidence and procedure, 124–125, 181–183
    forensic medicine, 154, 181–182
    jurisprudence, 154, 182–183
    mercantile law, 154
    private/ public international law, 154–155

Scots law, 113, 153, 182
suspension and abolition, 2, 132, 305–306, 315
teaching staff, 199
timetabling, 181
transfer provisions, 80–81
transitional arrangements, 306
Bachelor of Laws (LLB) degree
  BL degree, and
    comparison with , 151–155
    proposal for merger with, 304
    transition from, 306
  entry requirements, 21, 297, 305–306
    Arts, 132, 260–261, 303, 305
    Latin, 152–153, *218, 286,* 305, 308
    MA precondition, 186, 260, 293, 303–305, 311, 313
  examinations, 309
    exemptions, 315
  February Revolution, 1960-1963, 300–310
  female students
    1951-1955, 273
    first recorded graduates, 267, 274
  General Ordinances, 259–260
  grades, 313
  Honours degrees, 314–315, 318–319, 340–341
  introduction, 2, 11, 21, 124
  law class attendance requirements, 11, 310
  MA precondition, 31, 186, 260, 293, 303–305, 313
  October Revolution, 1964-1967, 311–319
  pass rates, 1918-1939, 1
  pass requirements, 21, 305–306, 309, 313
  post-qualifying year, 309–310
  reforms and revisions
    19th century, 22, 80–81, 124
    1899-1917, 124–125
    1918-1939, 131–132
    1960-1963, 300–310
    1964-1965, 309–319
    proposals for, 1944, 193–195, 255
    Special Committee deliberations, 194–195
  student numbers
    19th Century, 21–22
    1951-1955, 264, 267, 272–273, 366
    1964-1967, 328–329
    non-graduating, 273
  subject requirements for
    1950-1951, 255–258
    1951-1953, 260
    1961-1964, 333–335
    1964-1967, 314–315, 333, 338–341
    accounting, 335, 339
    administrative law, 152, 335, 339
    civil law, 122, 151, 255, 310, 335, 339
    constitutional law, 255, 335, 338–339
    constitutional law and history, 112, 125, 151, 338
    conveyancing, 112–113, 124, 151, 335, 340
    English law, 151–152, 340
    evidence and procedure, 124, 151, 335, 339
    forensic medicine, 152, 335, 339
    jurisprudence, 152, 255, 335, 339–340
    mercantile law, 151
    private international law, 152, 335
    public international law, 151–152, 335, 338–339
    Scots law, 151, 335–336, 338
  transfer provisions, 80–81
Baker, C.D., 316–317
Bankowski, Zenon, 322, 331, *354*
bankruptcy law, 78
Bar, the, 9
Barnett, Elizabeth, 34–35
Bates, Robert M., 144
Baxter, David, 31
Baxter, George Washington, Sir, *160*

Baxter, John Boyd, 24–26, 28, 31–32, *46, 49,* 58–59, 63, 85, 114–116
Baxter, John William, 28–30
Baxter, May Ann, 25–26, 28, 30–32, *46–47,* 63, 85
Baxter, William, 28, 31, *46–47*
Bell, William, *95*
Berry Bequest, 27, 110
Beveridge, C.R., 89
Bieszczad, Jozef, 210, 215
Bisset, Christian, 34, 92, 145, *172,* 185, 188–189, 193, 202–203, 209, *228,* 262, 264, 271
Bisset, Christopher Johnson, 89–92
Bisset, Isobel, 144, *172*
Black Watch, The, 90, 145, *173*
Blackadder, David, 144, *172*
Blackadders, 324
Boland, John H., 144
Bonar, George, 136–137, *169, 170*
Bonar House, 137, 291, 312
Bond, John Richmond, 134, *168*
book keeping *see* accounting
Bowes-Lyon, Elizabeth, Queen Mother, *278,* 302, 312
Bowman, Bernard Clifford (Ben), 185, 188–189, 191–193, 197, 200–201, 204, 210, 257, 262, 264–265, 308, 317, 324
Bowman, Neil, 201
Bowmans, 200, 324
Boyd, Christine, 330
Brand, Alan Salt, 207, *229*
Brand, David, *229,* 271
Brand, Isabelle, 330
Brand, Marjorie, 330
Brand, Steven, *229*
Briggs, Thomas, 331
Brown, Henry Hilton, 122–124, *164*
BSc (Econ), *281,* 295
Buglass, A.H., 89
Buigholt, Jennifer, 330
Burden, Duncan McNab, 122, *164*
Burns, David Spencer, Lord, 363

bursaries, 184, *228,* 357–358
Bute, 3rd Marquess of, John Patrick Crichton-Stuart, 27, *48–49,* 81, 113, *160*

C
Caine, Diane, 330
Cameron, Moyra, 330
Cameron, Valerie, 330
Campbell, A, H., 316
Campbell, Colin, Vice-Chancellor, 317, 322, *351,* 363
Campbell, Stephen, *354*
Campbell Smith, John, Sheriff , 64, *98*
Carlisle, Alfred Watson, 89, *107*
Carlton, Hugh J., 129, 135, 139–142, 177–180, 185–186, 188, 191–192, 195–197, 204, 255, 257, 262, 264, 268, 272
Carlton & Reid, 141
Carlton Gilruth, 324
Carmichael, D., 91
Carmichael, J., 89
Carnegie Trust , 110, *158,* 196
CCTV surveillance, 327
Centre for Energy, Petroleum, Mineral Law & Policy, 309
Centre for Water Law, Policy & Science, 309
Chalmers, Ivan, 190–193, *219*
chamber practitioners, 12, 16–17
Chlebowski, Wladyslaw, J., 210, 215
Cinoniak, Stanislaw, 215
civil law
  definition, 18, *41*
  degree requirement, as
    1899-1917, 121–127, 151–152, 156
    1918-1939, 129, 132, 156–157, 181–182
    1939-1949, 181–182, 187–188
    1950-1951, 256–257
    1951-1953, 260
    1960-1963, 310, 335
    1965-1967, 339

BL degree, for, 112, 113, 124–125, 153, 181–182
LLB degree, for, 21, *44*, 112, 122–123, 151, 255, 310, 335, 339
MA degree, for, 186
examinations, 131
lectures, 19th Century, 59, 122
professional requirement, as
  examinations, 156–158
  Faculty of Advocates, 17–18
  19th Century, 17–18, 59, 151–152
teaching staff
  1950-1951, 257
  1951-1953, 265
  1956-1959, 296
civil service, 113
Clark, Alistair, 276
Clark, Francis William, 57, *95*
Clark, Lynda, Baroness Clark of Calton, 36, 322–323, 332, 363
Clyde, James Latham McDiarmid, Lord, 267, 284
Cochran, Betty, 144
College of Justice, *9, 37*
college scarves, 276, 333
Collins, Dennis Ferguson, 299, 301, 324–325, 330, *344,* 345
Commentaries on the Law of Scotland (Hume), 78, *103*
commercial law
  see also mercantile law
  degree requirement, as
    1964-1967, 314, 339
  professional requirement, as, 73
  teaching staff
    1956-1959, 295
    1967-1968, 318
company and partnership law, 57, 335
comparative law
  degree requirement, as
    1951-1953, 260
    1961-1964, 336
    1965, 314, 339
  teaching staff

1960-1963, 301
1967-1968, 318
Conference of Scottish Universities on Law Degrees
  Report 1949, 198–199
  Report 1959, 302–303
Conference on General Law Ordinances, 260
conflicts of laws
  degree requirement, as
    1918-1939, 132
    1964-1965, 314
Connelly, David, 321
constitutional law
  see also constitutional law and history
  degree requirement, as
    1899-1917, 112, 124–127, 125–127
    1918-1939, 131, 157, 180, 182
    1939-1949, 180, 182, 187–188, 195, 211
    1950-1951, 255
    1960-1963, 310, 335
    1964-1965, 338, 339
    Arts conflicts, 195
    BL degree, for, 124–125, 154, 182, 195
    LLB degree, for, 255, 335, 338–339
    MA degree, for, 186
  examinations, 131, 156–157
  professional requirement, as
    examinations, 156–157
    19th Century, 17–18
  teaching staff
    1967-1968, 318
constitutional law and history
  degree requirement, as
    1938-1939, 186, *219*
    1950-1951, 256–257
    1951-1953, 260, 264
    1964-1965, 339
    BL degree, for, 112, 125
    LLB degree, for, 112, 125, 151, 339
  professional requirement, as, 17–18
  exemptions, 315

teaching staff
  1938-1939, 184, *219*
  1950-1951, 255, 257
  1951-1953, 265
  1956-1959, 294
conveyancing
  degree requirement, as
    1899-1917, 125, 148–150, 156
    1918-1939, 129–130, 133–135, 143,
      156–157, 182
    1939-1949, 182, 188, 198, 211
    1950-1951, 257
    1951-1953, 260
    1960-1963, 309–310, 335
    1964-1967, 314, 339–340
    BL degree, for, 112–113, 124–125,
      153, 182, 199
    LLB degree, for, 112–113, 124,
      151, 335, 339–340
  examinations, 129
  lectures, 19th Century, 55, 57, 71, 77,
    118–119, 121
  monopoly, 12
  prizes, 196–197, 207, 274–275
  professional requirement, as
    examinations, 156–157
    law class attendance, 61, 71, 73,
      112, 129–130
    19th Century, 10–11, 17–18, 57,
      61, 71, 73, 112
  self-practice, legality of, 12, 16
  teaching staff
    1950-1951, 257
    1951-1953, 268–269, 271
    1960-1963, 302
    1964-1965, 316
    Chair, establishment of, 255, 257–
      258, 266–269, 296
conveyancing agents, 12, 14
Conveyancing Manual (McDonald), 271
Conveyancing Notes (McDonald), 271
Cooper, Mary, 144
Cooper, Thomas Mackay, Baron Cooper
  of Culross, 197, *216*

Cooper Inquiry 1949, *47,* 176, 197–199,
  216, *227,* 249–250, 254, 299
correspondence
  Arts classes proposals 1897, 82
  Circular to FPSD 1890, 75
  Law School founding declaration, 71–
    73, 124
  Letter from Carlton on progress of BL
    1938, 177–179
  Letter from Thain on LCAS lectures
    1868, 59–60
  Letter to University Court 1938, 177–
    178, 255
  Letters to Peterson from Thornton on
    need for law school 1890, 70–74
  Memorandum to UCD 1939, 178
  Memorandum to University Grants
    Council 1944, 193–195
  Memorial sent to FPSD on need for
    law lectures 1885, 63–66
  Memorial sent to Prime Minister
    1907, 125
Coupar, Alexander James Waddell
  Robertson, 192, 207, 264, 301
Couratos, Alexander, 266
Courts of Law (Scotland) Agents Bill
  1872, 12–15, *39, 96*
  Acts of Sederunt, *40, 96*
Cowie, Gordon, 301, 318, 323, 327, *344*
Crawford, Mabel, 144
Crichton-Stuart, John Patrick, 3rd
  Marquess of Bute , 27, *48–49,* 81,
    113, *160*
criminal law
  degree requirement, as , 129, 156–157
  lectures, 19th Century, 60, 78
  professional requirement, as , 157
  teaching staff, 316
Criminal Procedure according to the Law of
  Scotland (Renton and Brown), 122–
  123
Crowe, Eve, 330
Crown Assessors, 251, 290

Crown Commissioners, 252–253, 289–290

Cullen, Kenneth Douglas, Sheriff, 196, *226*

Cumming, Patrick, 185, 189, 192, 257–258

Cunningham, Robert C., 145, *173*

Currie, Judith, 330

Cuthbert, H.V., 145, *172*

D

Dalhousie Building, 357

Davies, Joanne, 330

Day Cards, 79

de Luna, Peter, 276

devilling, 18, 311

Dhir, Anuja, Judge, 361

Diploma in Professional Legal Practice, 309, 355–356

disciplinary matters, 208

dissertations, 356

Donald, George Reid, 89–90

Donald & Ross, 90

Donaldson, Frances, 274

Dorward, William Fyffe, 185, 192, 264, 316

double counting, 186, 257, 273, 305

Dow, David Rutherford, Principal, 267, 299

Drever, James, Principal, 291

Dunbar, William Bishop, 60, *96*

Duncan, Agnes, 206–207

Duncan, David, 56

Dundee, generally, 23, 29, *42*

Dundee, Law School in
  see also Faculty of Law, Dundee
  Advisers of Studies, 188
  Baxter family role, 24–26, 28, 30, *46–47*, 62–63
  Berry Bequest, 27, 110
  Carnegie Trust awards, 110, *158*, 196
  Deed of Endowment and Trust, 25, *278–279*
  development

1899-1917, 113–128
1917-1939, 128–138
establishment, background to, 23–25, 55–58, 61–63
financial donations, 25, 27, 30, 32, 110
founding declaration, 71–73
funding, 25, 27, 30, 32, 110, 125–126, *158–159*, 196
governance arrangements, 25–27
Harkness Foundation donations, 110, *159*
inauguration, 26
independence, 27–28
lectures, 19th Century
  1865-1870, 54–61
  1883-1887, 61–68
  1890-1998, 68–82
  1899-1938, 110–113, 128–139
  fees for, 66
location of, 26, *47*, 137, *161*, 270–271, 300, 302, 311–312, *344, 347*, 357
matriculation/ registration fees
  19th century, 72, 74–75, 79
  1899-1917, 116, 123
  1939, 184
preference lists, 297
private donations, 25, 30, 32
reasons for lack of, 22–23
Royal Commission 1878
  recommendations, 24–25
Statement of Needs 1908, 125–126
student numbers
  19th Century, 77–78, 115
  1899-1917, 117–118, 121, 128, *166*, 364
  1918-1939, 128, 142–146, 187, *217–218*, 364–365
  1939-1949, 189, 205–206, 365
  1950-1959, 365–367
  1960-1963, 300–301, 367
  1964-1967, 328–329, 367
  present day, 355–356

student origins and demographics, 145–146, *220, 278,* 332, *356*
syllabus Committees, 127
teaching staff
19th century, 73–74, 76
1899-1917, 116
unique selling points, 296, 306–309, 312–313
Dundee, University of
see also Dundee, Law School in; Faculty of Law, Dundee
before 1954 (*see* University College Dundee)
between 1954 and 1967 (*see* Queen's College Dundee)
admissions policies, 13, 195, 297, 328
league tables, place in, 361
Royal Charter, 291, *341*
student admissions policies, 297, 328
War Memorial, 145, *173*
Dundee School of Economics, 254, 269, *281*
incorporation into QCD, 137, 251, 291, 294–295, 329
Dundee University Student Law Clinic, 323

E
economics
see also Dundee School of Economics
degree requirement, as, 188, *227,* 337, 339–341
Edinburgh, University of
BL, introduction of, 21–22, *45*
establishment, 23
female law students, first recorded, 35
law department, 19th Century, *43*
LLB, introduction of, 21, *45*
student numbers, 1899-1917, 118
Eicke, Tim, Judge , 361
English law
degree requirement, as
1960-1963, 308–309

1964-1967, 312–317, 340
LLB degree, for, 151–152, 340
teaching staff
1956-1959, 295
1960-1963, 307
1964-1967, 315–317, 326
unique selling points, as, 308–309
equity law
19th Century lectures, 57
Erskine, John, 78, *103*
evidence and procedure
see also forms and process
degree requirement, as
1899-1917, 125, 151–152
1918-1939, 129, 131, 158, 181–183
1939-1949, 181–183, 188, 211
1960-1963, 309, 335
1964-1965, 339
BL degree, for, 124–125, 181–183
LLB degree, for, 124, 151, 335, 339
examinations, 129, 156
professional requirement, as, 11, 156
teaching staff
1950-1955, 271
examinations, generally
19th Century, 10–11, 13–15, 17, *37,* 77–79, 156
1917-1939, 129, 131–132, 144–145, 156–158
Board of Examiners, 13
content, *37, 78*
exemptions from, 11, 13–15, 54, 131, 315
invigilation, 328
obligations to impose, 10–11
obligations to take, 14–15, 17
pass rates, 1918-1939, 132
preliminary examinations, 10, 13
present day, 356
prize-winners
19th Century, 89
1899-1939, 144–145
professional examinations

First Law examinations, 129, 131–132, 156–158, 211, 309
Second Law examinations, 129, 131–132, 156–158, 211, 309
Third Law examinations, 131–132, 156–158, 211, 309
reform of, *39,* 129, 131
executive Commissioners, 68, 252–253, 289–290
executive Commissions, *5, 43–44,* 68, *164,* 252, 290
expenses, 184

F
Faculties and Societies, generally
  see also Faculty of Advocates; Society of Solicitors in the Supreme Courts; Society of Writers to the Signet
  admission requirements, 9–10, 16, *39,* 61, 112
  classes, obligations to provide, 10–11, 54–55
  examinations, exemptions from, 11, 13–15, 54
  examinations, obligations to impose, 10–11
  importance of, 8–9
  incorporation, 10–11
  law class attendance requirements, 11
  law practices outside control of, 12
  lectures, 19th Century, 55–56
  Rights and Privileges, 11, 14–15, *39*
  self-regulation, 9, 16–18
Faculty of Advocates, 8
  admissions policies, 16
  law class attendance requirements, 17–18
  membership, 3
  reforms, 17–18
  regulation, 261
  unification of legal profession, and, 17–18
Faculty of Law, Dundee, 256

see also Dundee, Law School in
departmental expenses, 267
establishment, 263, 266–268
Faculty Secretary, 321
first 'First' in Law, award of, 331
Honorary Graduates in Law (LLDs), 267
location, 26, *47,* 137, *161,* 270–271, 300, 302, 311–312, *344, 347,* 357
Report to the Senate 1955, 267
social interaction, 327
student demographics, 332
student numbers, 1960-1963, 300–301
Faculty of Law and Commerce, 269
proposal for, 197, 254–256
Faculty of Procurators and Solicitors in Dundee, 19, *38,* 53
  admission requirements, 54
  Chair of Scots Law, promotion of, 196–197
  classes, obligation to provide, 54–55
  Conveyancing prizes, 196–197, 207, 274–275
  correspondence, 63–65, 71–75
  Dundee Law School, discussions regarding establishment, 56–57
  female members, first recorded, 202
  General Meetings, 70
  Joint Committee, 64–65, 73–75
  law classes
    attendance requirements, 11, 54
    development of, 54–58, 64–70
  lectures
    lecturers appointments, 73–74, 76
    provision of financial support for, 81
    19th Century, 55–70, 81
  Library, use of, 118, 147, 208
  Minutes, 69–70
  Preses and Vice Preses, 29, 63, 85, *95,* 115
  records, lack of, 3
  Scots Law prizes, 89, 196–197, 207, 274–275

Faculty of Social Sciences, Dundee, 291, 307, *340*
February Revolution, 1960-1963, 300–310
fees
  examiners' expenses, 184
  lecture attendance, 19th Century, 66
  matriculation/ registration
    19th Century, 72, 74–75, 79
    1899-1917, 116, 123
    1939, 184
  Railway lectures, 138, 197
Ferguson, Inez, 274
Ferguson, James Millar, 145, *172*
Ferguson, Mary, 35, *51,* 144
Ferguson & Stephen, 90
Fettes, J., 89
foreign students, *219*
forensic medicine
  degree requirement, as
    1917-1939, 132, 181–182, 184–185, 188
    1950-1951, 256
    1961-1965, 336, 339
    BL degree, for, 154, 181–182
    LLB degree, for, 152, 336, 339
  professional requirement, as
    19th Century, 17–18
  teaching staff
    1918-1939, 185
    1964-1965, 316
forespeakers/ forspeakers, 8
forms and process
  degree requirement, as
    1899-1917, 156
    1917-1939, 159, 178
  lectures, 19th Century, 121, 124
  professional requirement, as, 131, 156
    examinations, 131, 156
    19th Century, 17–18
Front Buildings, 208, 267, 297, 300
Fulton, Angus Robertson, Principal, 175, 191, 193
funding

Baxter family donations, 25, 30, 32
Berry Bequest, 27, 110
Carnegie Trust awards , 110, *158,* 196
Harkness Foundation donations, 110, *159*
Memorial sent to Prime Minister 1907, 125
Fyffe, Mary, 144

G
Gash, Norman, 190
Gaudie Night, 146, 208, 333
Gavin, Evelyn E., 275, 330
General Council of Procurators, 10–11, 18, 29
General Council Regulations 1936, 129–130, 157
General Council Regulations 1938, 129, 131, 157–158, *167,* 178, 182, 211–212, *217,* 261
General Council Regulations 1951, 261
Gibb, Andrew Dewar, Sheriff, 194, *347*
Gibson, Hector James, 274
Gibson, Henry, 59, *96*
Gillan, Archibald Wedderburn, 259, 264, 294
Gilruth, Pollock & Smith, 301, 324
Glasgow, University of
  BL, introduction of, 21–22, *45*
  establishment, 23
  female law students, first recorded, 35
  law classes, 19th Century, 80
  law department size, 19th Century, *43*
  LLB, introduction of, 21, *45*
  Ordinance, 1960, 309
  St Mungo's College, 23, *46,* 80
  student numbers, 1899-1917, 118
Gold Awards, 361
Gordon Stuart, Josephine, 22, 35
Gow, James John (Hamish), 196–197, *226*
gowns, wearing in class, 213–214

Graduation
   academic dress for, 213
   first Ceremony in Caird Hall, 267
Graham, F.B., 133–135, 139, *168*
Grant, James David, 55, 57, 59–60, 89, *107*
Gray, J.W.R., 316, 327, *347*
Gray, Robertson & Wilkie, 185, 200, 324
Guildry Room, 29, *95, 96*
Guthrie, William, 56–58, 86–87
Guthrie Smith, John, Sheriff, 56–60, 72, *94*

H
H & H J Carlton, 135, 141
H Carlton, 135, 141
Haley, Enid, 330
Hall, Margaret, 33–34
Hall v Incorporated Society of Law Agents (1901), 33, *50–51*
Halley, Pamela, 206–207, 274
Hallowhill, *171*
Harari, Abe, 322
Harkness, Edward Stephen, *159*
Harkness Foundation , 110, *159*
Hay, William, Bailie, 57, *94–95*
Hayes, Brian D., *342*
Hean, Helen, 83
Hendry, Andrew, 60, 140–141
Hendry, James, 141
Hendry, John M., 119–122, 139–141
Hendry & Fenton, 141
Henry Scrymgeour prize for Public International Law, 274–275
Heriot, Frederick Maitland, Sheriff, 55–56
Higson Len, 330
Hill Watson, Lawrence , 267, 277
Hird, T.L., 191–193, 197, 205, 258, 264–265, 294–296
Hodge, J.M., 89
Holme, Cynthia, 330

Honorary Graduates in Law (LLDs), 267
Honours degrees, 303–305, 307, 314–315, 318–319, 340–341, *351*
hoods, wearing of, 213
Houston, Louise, 316, *350*
How, Harold, 145, *172–173*
Hughes, Edward, 29
Hume, David, 78, *103*
Hunter, Robin L.C., 316
Hurst, Janet, 35, 274
Husband, Kathleen, 206
Husband, L.W., 135

I
Incorporated Society of Law Agents in Scotland, 18, 79–80
inferior courts, 8
Innes, Peter David, Sir, *280*
inquiries *see* Cooper Inquiry; Royal Commissions; Tedder Commission
Institute of Chartered Accountants in Scotland (ICAS), 294, 298, 329
Institute of the Law of Scotland, An (Erskine), 78, *103*
Irons, J,M., 89
Irvine, James, Sir, Principal, 110, 175–177, 180, 194, 197, 250, 254–255

J
J & H Pattullo, 90
J & H Pattullo & Donald, 90, 192
Jamicson, H., 56
Janigar, Kazimerz, 215
Johnston, Helen, 206–207, *229,* 274
Johnstone, Logie & Millar, 301
Jolly, Kathleen, 274
Jones, Michael, Lord, 363
Journal of Jurisprudence, 87
Juridical Review, 88
jurisprudence
   Chair of, 257, 265, 307–308, 316
   degree requirement, as
      1899-1917, 125, 127

1918-1939, 131, 157, 182–183
1939-1949, 182–183, 187–188, 211
1950-1951, 255, 256
1951-1953, 260
1956-1959, 296
1960-1963, 310, 336, *346*
1964-1965, 312–317, 338–340
BL degree, for, 154, 182–183
Honours degree, for, 340
LLB degree, for, 152, 255, 336,
338–339
DJur degree, 260
examinations, 131, 157
professional requirement, as
examinations, 157
19th Century, 17–18
unique selling point, as, 296

K
Kamba, Walter, 322, *351*
Kerr, R.N., 79
Kerr, R.R., *281*
Kidd, Margaret Henderson, 18, 34
King's College, Aberdeen, 20, 23
Kinmond, Jean, 207
Kinnear, Carlisle & Gillan, 259
Knight, William Angus, *97*
Knox, Thomas Malcolm, Principal, 250,
253, 255, 290, 299, 302
Kosiewicz, Wladyslaw, 215

L
labour law, 295
Laburn, Eve, 206
Lafferty, Austin, 274
Lambton, A.K., 266
land law
degree requirement, as , 318
lectures, 19th Century, 60, 76–77
Lang, J.A., 89–90
Latin, as entry requirement, 152–153,
218, 286, 305, 308
Laurie, R.B., 277
law, generally

university subject, validity as, 292
law agents, 3, 8, 13–15, 14
experience, qualification by way of,
16
impersonating, penalties for, 10, 12,
15, *39*
solicitors, qualification conversion,
128–129
women as, 18
Law Agents (Scotland) Act 1873, 14–15,
33, 130
Act of Sederunt, 13, 17, 129–130, 134
amendments to, 15–16, *99, 101, 103,
104,* 129–130
law class attendance requirements,
17, 61
Law Agents Act 1873 (Amendments) Bill
1887, 15, *41,* 67–68, *99, 101, 103,
104*
Law Agents and Notaries Public
(Scotland) Act 1891, 15, 17, 80
Act of Sederunt, 17, 80
law class attendance requirements,
17, 80
law class attendance requirements
19th Century, 11, 13, 15, 17–18, 61,
68, 74, 79–80, 112
1918-1939, 129–131, 133–134, 310
evening classes, 74, 79
Faculties and Societies rules and
exemptions, 11, 17–18, 54
implementation, 11, 13, 15, 17, 79–80
Law Clerks and Apprentices Society
(LCAS), 63–64
annual meetings, 61
establishment, 56
lectures, 19th Century, 56, 58–61
Letter from J.Thain on lectures 1868,
59–60
Memorial sent to FPSD 1885, 63–66
law degrees, generally
see also Bachelor of Law (BL);
Bachelor of Laws (LLB);
examinations

admission policies, 13, 195, 297
entry requirements
    Arts, 132, 260–261, 303, 305
    Latin, 152–153, *218, 286,* 305, 308
    logic or mathematics, 153
    Faculty and Society admission, not
      needed for, 9
double counting, 186, 257, 273, 305
established by law , 10–11, *38*
full-time degrees, 303–304, 320–321
further degree students, 265–266
Honours degrees, 303–305, 307, 314–
    315, 318–319, 339–340, *351*
law class attendance requirements,
    11, 13, 15, 17
MA precondition for, 186, 260, 293,
    303–305, 311
present day, 355–356
qualifications prior to development of,
    7–8
research degrees, development of,
    265–266
scope of study
    19th Century, 10–11, 17–18, *38, 44,*
      45, 69, 76–77
    1899-1917, 117, 120, 124–125,
      124–127
    BL degrees (*see* Bachelor of Law)
    1939-1949, 181–182, 187–188
    1950-1951, 256–258
    1951-1953, 264–265
    1960-1963, 301–302, 307
    1964-1967, 326–327, 333
    LLB degrees (*see* Bachelor of Laws)
social sciences, and, 307, 312–315
syllabus Committees, 127
triad, 11, 14, 57, 59, 71, 78, 112, 121,
    129, 131, 178
'Law Leaflet,' 196
Law Library
    FPSD library, use of, 118, 147, 208
    holdings, 147, 208, 302, 312, 332–
      333, *348*
    location, 110, 357

Terrapins reading rooms, 312
Law of Scotland, The (Gloag and
    Henderson), 103, 190
Law Society of Scotland, 3, 18, 274, 276
    admission requirements, 293–294,
      298, 303, 309
Lawson, John Graftton, 89, 91
lectures, 19th century
    advertisements for, 76
    attendance fees, 66
    developments, 56–78
    evening classes, classification as, 74,
      79
    financial support for provision of, 81
    FPSD proposals for, 64–66
    joint, for bank and law clerks, 68
    LCAS, provided by, 56, 58–59
    matriculation/ registration fees, 72,
      74–75, 79, 116
      1899-1917, 116
    publication, 69–70
    style, 78
    subjects covered, 54–68, 76–78, 118–
      119, 121- 122
    venue, 76
legal oaths, 60
legal profession, generally
    admission requirements, 7–9, 293–
      294, 298
    chamber practitioners, 12, 16–17
    historical development, 7–9
    right to practice, geographical
      restrictions, 13, *39*
    self-governance, 8–9
    titles used by, 7–9, *36*
    unification, 10–17
legal professional qualifications,
    generally
    apprenticeships, 2–3, 8, 13–15, 18, *38,*
      54
    dual-qualifying degrees, 308
    examination exemptions, 315
    experience, qualification by way of,
      16

historical development, 7
law agents, conversion into solicitors,
    128–129
national legal practioners, 2–3
non-graduate routes, 2
penalties for impersonating law agent,
    10, 12, 15, *39*
post-graduate studies, 309–310
prior to law degree establishment, 7–8
reform of, 128–129
legal scholarship
law, validity as university subject,
    292
law studies, apprenticeship to follow,
    293
Leighton, William A., 144
Leng, John, Sir, 71–73, 85, 88, *106,* 124
Leslie, J.W., 56
libraries
FPSD library, use of, 118, 147, 208
Law Library
    holdings, 147, 208, 302, 312, 332–
        333, *348*
    location, 357
    uses for, 357
Terrapins reading rooms, 312
Lindsay, A., 89
Littlejohn, David Stewart, 69–70, *100–
    101*
LLB *see* Bachelor of Laws (LLB) degree
LLM degrees, 355–356
Loch Tay, trips to, 324
logic, as degree requirement, 153
London and North Eastern Railway
    Company, 137–139, 197
London University external degrees, 26,
    137, 295
Lorrimer, W.L., *347*
Lowden, Gordon Stewart, 269, 274
Lowe, F., 89
Lyon, Georgina, 330

M
McCall, W., 56

MacCormick, Donald Neil, Sir, 316–
    317, 322, 325–326, 327
McCracken, Agnes, 206
McCulloch, William Scott, 207
McDonald, Alexander John (Alastair),
    208, 268–272, 276, 277, *285,* 306,
    308, 312, 323, 327–328
MacDonald, D.F., 266
McFadzean, Marion, 330
MacGregor Mitchell, Robert, 178–180,
    217
McIntyre, P., 56
Mackay, John Yule, Principal, 114,
    118–119
Mackenzie-Wood, Alison, 330
McKerchar, Anne, 206–207, *229*
MacKinnon, Rudolf, Sheriff, 194, 196
MacLaren, Eveline, 22, 35
McLaren, Joseph, 145, *173*
McLaughlin, Mary, 330
MacLennan, John Ferguson, 66, *98*
McManus Art Gallery and Museum,
    Dundee, 29
Malcolm, Elizabeth, 206
man of law, 8
Marischal College, Aberdeen, 20, 23
Marshall, Enid, 330
Masson, James Irvine, *280*
Masters degrees (MA)
degree requirements
    1939, 186
    1950, 255, 258
introduction, 21
precondition for BL/ LLB degrees, as,
    186, 260, 293, 303–305, 311, 313
mathematics, as degree requirement,
    153
Matheson, Arthur Alexander, Principal,
    196–197, 201, 203–205, 254–255,
    257–259, 262, 266, 272, *281,* 298–
    299, 301, 327
matriculation fees
    19th Century, 66, 72, 74–75, 79
    1899-1917, 116

1939, 184
present day, 357–358
Matthews, Nigel F., 317
Maxwell-Fyffe, David, Viscount
    Kilmuir, 277
Medical Act 1858, *37*
Meldrum, Catherine, 144
Melville, Phyllis, 144
Memorialists, 63–66
Menzies, Charles Andrew Richmond,
    274
mercantile law
    see also commercial law
    degree requirement, as
        1899-1917, 125
        1918-1939, 129, 133, 136, 156, *166*
        1951-1953, 265
        1956-1959, 296, 298
        1964-1967, 314
        BL degree, for, 154
        LLB degree, for, 151
    examinations, 156
    lectures, 19th Century, 57, 78
    professional requirement, as, 156
    teaching staff
        1960-1963, 301
Merry, James R., 144
Methven, Norman A.P., 317
Middleton, Bruce, 196
Miller, J. Bennett, 252, *279–280*
Miller, John, 89
Mitchell, David E., 144
Mitchell, William Low, 191–192
Moore, John Alexander, 134, *168*
Moore, Robert, 301, 316
moots, 356
More, John Shank, 60
More, William, 196
Morgan, Moira, 206–207
Morrison, James, 144, *172*
Morrow, J.J., Rev Dr, Lord Lyon King
    of Arms, 361
Mount, W.B., 89
Muirhead, J. Spencer, Sir, 252, 267, *279*

Munro, Marjory, 206
Murray, Margaret, 330

N
*Nairn v University of St Andrews and
    Edinburgh University Courts* 1909,
    33, *50*
National Service (Armed Forces) Act
    1939, *230*
National Student Survey, 358, 361
Nethergate, *47, 161, 162,* 267, 271, 277,
    297, 300
Nichols, Penelope, 330
Nicholson, Badenoch, Mrs, 312
Nicholson, George, 144
Nicol, J., 90
Noble, F.S., *216*
Normanton, Mary, 330
Norrie, Alan, 322, *351*
notaries public, 3, 7–8, 10, 12–14, 16
Novellae Constitutiones, 275

O
October Revolution, 1964-1967, 311–
    319
Ogilvy, Ramsay, Sheriff, 55
oil and gas law, 309
Orchardson, W.Q., 83
Ordinance 1862, 21, *44,* 124, 151–152
Ordinance 1874, *45,* 124, 152–155
Ordinance 1892, *44*
Ordinance 1893, *45, 104,* 124, 152–155,
    260, 305
Ordinance 1894, *49*
Ordinance 1911, 124, 151–155, *164,*
    211–212, *218,* 260
Ordinance 1954, 252, 260, 266, *280,* 302
Ordinance 1959, *280*
Ordinance 1960, 309
Ordinance 1961, 335–337
Ordinance 1963, 316
Ordinance 1964, 312–313, 316, 338–
    341, *348*

Origins and Development of the Jury in Scotland, The (Willock), 321
Orme, Elizabeth, *51*
Owens College, Manchester, 25–26
Oxbridge graduates, 113, *345*

P
Page, Jess M., 35, 206–207
Park Place, 26, 271
Parker Smith, James Pearce, 274–275, 295–296, 299, 301
partnership law, 57, 335
Paton, James Malcolm, 275
Patrick, D.W., 144
Pattullo, James, 65–66, 83, *105*
Pattullo & Agnew, 65
Pattullo & Thornton, 83, *105,* 270
Patullo, Henry A., 80, *98*
Pearson, John, 89–91
peer-review, 359
Perth Road, 311
Peterson, William, Principal, 65–66, 73
Petrie, Allan & Robertson, 294
Piotrowski, Bronislaw, 210
Pirie, George R., 144
Polish soldier-students, 189, 205, 207–210, 215, *231*
Political Sciences, 300
Pollock, Christine, 330
Pollock & Smith, 324
postgraduate studies
    see also Masters degrees (MA)
    Diploma in Professional Legal Practice, 309, 355–356
    LLMs, 355–356
prelocutors, 8
Principles of the Law of Scotland (Erskine), 78, 87–88, *103,* 190
Pritchard, Kenneth J., 274
private international law
    degree requirement, as
        1899-1917, 125, 127
        1918-1939, 136
        1938-1949, 199

1951-1953, 265
1956-1959, 296
1961-1964, 336
1964-1965, 314
BL degree, for, 154–155
LLB degree, for, 152, 336
professional requirement, as, 17–18
teaching staff
    1950-1951, 257
    1960-1963, 300–301
Private Members' Bills, *105*
prizes
    Conveyancing, 196–197, 207, 274–275
    examinations, 1899-1939, 144–145
    examinations, 19th Century, 89
    Henry Scrymgeour, public international law, 274–275
    Scots Law, 96, 196–197, 207, 274–275
    won by women, 275
procurators, 2–3, 7–8, 10–14, 13–14
Procurators (Scotland) Act 1865, 10, 54
    Acts of Sederunt, 17, *37*
    criticism of, 12
    law class attendance requirements, 11, 17
    law degree examinations, 10–11
    law degree syllabus, 10–11, *38*
    qualifications, unification of, 10–11
    Royal Commission 1869 , 12–13, 15
professional qualifications, generally
    see also legal professional qualifications
    chartered accountants, 294, 298, 329
prolocutors, 8
Provosts, 251
public international law
    degree requirement, as
        1899-1917, 125, 127
        1918-1939, 132, 136, 182, 186
        1939-1949, 199
        1950-1951, 255–259
        1951-1953, 260

1956-1959, 296
1961-1964, 335
1965-1967, 296, 338–339
BL degree, for, 154–155
LLB degree, for, 151–152, 335,
    338–339
prizes, 275
professional requirement, as
    19th Century, 17–18
teaching staff
    1950-1951, 258–259
    1960-1963, 300–301
    1964-1967, 317
    1967-1968, 319

Q
quality assurance, 359–360
Queen Mother Building, 312
Queen's College Dundee, 2, 28
    Dundee School of Economics,
        incorporation, 137, 251, 294–295
    establishment, 250, 252–253
    independence, calls for, 299
    student admissions policies, 297
Quinquennial Estimates, 318
    syllabus 1962-1967, 301–302
    teaching staff 1962-1967, 306–307,
        315–316

R
Railway Lectures, 1923-1932, 129, 137–
    139, 197
Railway Lectures, 1946-1951, 197
Raisin Monday, 146, 208
Randall Phillip, J., Sir, 203, 227
reading lists, 78
redundancies, 295–296, 342
Regent Scheme, 189
Report on University Teaching Methods
    1964, 326–327
research
    administration, 360
    beginnings, 266
    trends, 359

Research Excellence Framework, 359–
    360
Rettie, W. Phillip, 145, 173
Robbins Committee on Higher
    Education 1963, 2, 113–114, 290
Robertson, Edmund, 88, 121–122, 163
Robertson, Frances, 330
Robertson, Fred J., 172
Robertson, I.M.S., 294, 299, 301, 345
Robertson, James Joseph (Jim), 276,
    316, 321, 323–324, 327, 347
Robertson, John B., 144–145
Robertson, John, 56
Robertson, John, 64, 98
Robertson, Theora, 144
Robson, Peter, 331
Roll, Edgar Franciszek Tadeusz, 210,
    215
Roman law, 122, 157, 211
    see also civil law
Roscoe, H.E., 47
Ross, Isobel, 206, 229
Royal Commissions
    on Courts of Law in Scotland 1869 ,
        12–13, 15, 29, 39
    on Universities of Scotland 1826-30,
        20, 42–44
    on Universities of Scotland 1876-78,
        20, 24–26, 42–44
    on University Education in Dundee
        1951-1952 (Tedder), 2, 62, 97,
        198, 217, 250–253, 260–263, 289–
        290
Rushton, Donald, 316
Russell, James, 134
Ryan, Jim, 321

S
Sacra Romana Rota, 323
St Andrews, University of
    Affiliation Order 1890, 26–27, 48
    College Councils, 44, 252
    Colleges, structure and management,
        24

Commissioners, 252–253
Commissions and Inquiries
    1878 Royal Commission, 24–25
    Cooper Inquiry 1949, *47,* 176, 197–
        199, 216, 249–250, 254, 299
    Tedder Report, 2, 198, 250–253,
        260–263, 289–290
Dundee, University College, and
    affiliation with, 2, 26–27, *48–49,*
        67–69, 80, 109–110
    as campus of, 113–114
    conflicts between, 24–27, 109–110,
        175–176, 198
    separation from, 113–114, 251, 291
    establishment, 22–23, 276–277
female law students, first recorded,
    35
funding
    Berry Bequest, 27
    Harkness Foundation , 110, *159*
    Memorial sent to Prime Minister
        1907, 125
    Statement 1908, 126
histories of, 3–4
law teaching at, 2
LLB introduction, 22
Mackintosh Hall, 202
Masters, 252–253
Provosts, college, 252–253
Rector of, 3rd Marquess of Bute, 27,
    48–49, 81, 114
St Mary's College, 22, 176, 251, *278–
    279*
Statement of Needs 1908, 125–126
student numbers, 19th Century, 2, 24
United College of St Salvator and St
    Leonard, 24, 176, 251, *278–279*
St Mary's College, 22, 176, 251, *278–279*
St Mungo's College, Glasgow, 23, *46,* 80
Scanlan, Thomas, 144
scholarships *see* bursaries
Scolag, 323
Scots law
    definition, 18, *41*

degree requirement, as
    1899-1917, 125, 148, 156
    1918-1939, 129–130, 132–133,
        181–182
    1939-1949, 181–182, 187–188, 211
    1950-1951, 256
    1951-1953, 260
    1960-1963, 310, 335–336
    1964-1965, 314, 338
    BL degree, for, 113, 153, 182
    history of law, 260
    LLB degree, for, 151, 335–336, 338
    lectures, 19th Century, 57, 59, 76, 78,
        118–119
    prizes, 89, 196–197, 207, 274–275
    professional requirement, as
        examinations, 157
        Faculty of Advocates, 17–18
        law class attendance, 61, 129–130
        19th Century, 17–18, 61
    teaching staff
        1950-1951, 257
        1954-1955, 268
        1956-1959, 298
        1960-1963, 302, 307
        1971-1972, 318
        Chair of, 190, 193, 203, 254, 268,
            318
Scott, D.R., *169*
Scott, Patricia, 274
Scott, Vivien, 206
Scott Chalmers, R., 144
Scottish Congregational College,
    Glasgow, *50*
Scottish Legal Action Group, 323
Scottish Legal System (Walker), 323
Scottish Universities Law Institute, 292
Scrimgeour, Catherine, 144, *172*
Scrymgeour Building, 357
Scrymgeour prize for Public
    International Law, 275
Scrymgeour-Wedderburn, Henry
    (Harry), 11th Earl of Dundee, 274–
    275, *286*

Secretary, of Law Faculty, 321
Secretary of State for Scotland, The (Smith),
88
Senate, generally
delegated powers, 313–314
functions of, 20–21
Seppings, Margaret, 330
Sercukzewski, Czeslaw, 210, 215
Sex Discrimination (Removal) Act 1919,
33, 35, *50*
Shaw, Thomas, 66, *98*
Shiell & Small, 64, *97–98*
Sikorski, Wladyslaw, General , 209
Sim, Lindsay, 301
Simpson, Alan, 185–186, 189–191
Simpson, Edward Reginald, 133, *167*
Simpson, G.B., 89
Simpson, J. Gordon, 194
Simpson, N.D., 134
Small, David, *97–98*
Small's Lane, *344*
Small's Wynd, 26, *347*
Smith, Edith Philip, 189
Smith, Joan, 266
Smith, Robert C., 145
Smith, T.B., 203
Smith, William Charles, 73–74, 76–78,
81, 87–88, *104*
Smith & Bennet, 90
smoking, 213–214
Sobieraj, Stanislaw, 215
social and industrial law, 295
Social Government for Scotland (Smith), 88
social sciences
collaboration with law, as USP, 263,
289, 290–291, 307, 312–313, 315
law degree, studying as part of, 307,
312–315
Society of Solicitors in the Supreme
Courts, 9, 112
examination exemptions, 11, 13–15
Society of Writers in Dundee, 19
Society of Writers to the Signet, 9, 11,
13–15, 112

solicitors, 8
General Council Regulations 1936,
129–130, 157
General Council Regulations 1938,
129, 131, 157–158, *167,* 178, 182,
211–212, *217,* 261
General Council Regulations 1951,
261
law agents, conversion into, 129–130
Solicitors (Scotland) Act 1933, 12, 129–
130
Solicitors (Scotland) Act 1949, 261
Soutar, J.M., 89
Souter, James Macarthur, *107*
Southgate, Donald, 175–176, 294, *341*
Staff Club, *228,* 327
Staff Society, 323
Stamp Act 1870, 12, *39*
Stamps Act 1785, *36*
Steven Harvey S., 145, *173*
Steven Sidney H., 145, *173*
Stewart, J.N., 144
Stewart, John, 331
Stewart, Joyce, 274
Stewart, R.B., 316
Stewart Committee on Alternatives to
Prosecution, 323
Still, Robert, 84
Stoddart & Ballingall, 90
Strathclyde, University of, 23
BA Law, introduction, 319
Stuart, Ian David, 207, 274
student behaviour
academic dress, 213–214
smoking, 213–214
student feedback, 358
student finance, 357–358
student grants, 276
student life, 145, 207–208, 275–277, 327,
333
Student Loan Company, 357–358
student numbers
1899-1917, 117–118, 121, 128, *166,*
364

1918-1939, 128, 142–146, 187, *217–218,* 364–365
1939-1949, 189, 205–206, *217–218,* 365
1950-1959, 365–367
1960-1967, 300–301, 318, 367
Aberdeen, 1899-1917, 118, 123
BL degree
   19th Century, 22
   1942-1945, 195
   1964-1967, 328
   1951-1955, 264, 267, 272
Dundee School of Economics, *281*
Edinburgh, 1899-1917, 118
female law students, first recorded, 22, 33, 35, *51,* 144
Glasgow, 1899-1917, 118
LLB degree
   1951-1955, 264, 267, 272–273
   1964-1967, 328–329
   19th Century, 21–22
non-graduating entrants, 273, 328
present day, 355–356
St Andrews, 19th Century, 2, 24
19th Century, 21–22, 77–78, 115
WWII impact on, 189–190, 205–206
student residences, 333
Students Award Agency for Scotland, 357
Students' Law Society, 276–277, 333
Students Union, 110, 146, 208, 333
Sturrock, Bernard S., 145, *173*
succession, law of
   degree requirement, as
      1918-1939, 129, 157–158, 211
      1956-1959 (proposal), 298
      1960-1963, 309–310
   lectures, 19th Century, 60, 76
   professional requirement, as, 157–158
Succession (Scotland) Act 1964, 202
Summers, Alan, Lord, 363
Swinton, Ken, *229*
Swinton, R.S., 207
syllabus Committees, 127

T
taxation
   degree requirement, as, 133, 156–157, 309–310, 336, 339
   professional requirement, as, 157
   teaching staff, 1967-1968, 318
Taylor, Douglas, 145, *172*
Taylor, Helen, 330
Teaching Excellence Framework, 359, 361
teaching methods
   accreditation, 360
   present day, 356, 359–360
   quality assurance, and, 359–360
   tutorials, 78, 191, 207–208, 315, 356
teaching staff, appointments
   1899-1917, 116, 119–123, 140
   1918-1939, 133–135, 142, 185
   1939-1949, 185, 188, 190–191, 199–202
   1950-1951, 257–259
   1964-1965, 316–317
   Conveyancing, Chair of, 255, 257–258
   Jurisprudence, Chair of, 257, 307
   public practice, recruitment from, 199, 319–320
   redundancies, 295–296, *342*
   Scots Law, Chair of, 190, 193, 196–197, 203, 254
   19th Century, in, 73–74, 76
teaching staff, generally
   BL degree, for, 1938-1949, 199
   department size
      1950-1955, 269
      1964-1967, 315–316, 319–320
      present day, 359
   length of service, 199–200, 269, 320
   present day, 358–360
   Railway Lectures, 197
   women, first, 35
teaching staff, salaries
   1899-1917, 117, 119–120, 125–126

1938-1939, 177, 183–184, *219*
1939-1949, 191–193, 197–198
1950-1951, 254–255, 257
1951-1953, 263–265, 267–268
1956-1959, 294, 298, *342–343*
1960-1963, 301
1964-1967, 317
fee fund allocation, 117
redundancy payments, 295–296, *342*
Tedder, Arthur William, Marshall of
 Royal Air Force, *278*
Tedder Commission 1952, 2, 62, *97,*
 198, *217,* 250–253, 260–263, 289–
 290
Tehrani, Ahmed, 265–266, *283*
Terrapins, The, 312, 357
Thain, James, 56–57, 59–60, 89
Theological Hall, 31, *50*
Thomas Thornton, Son & Coy, 84
Thoms, George , 57, *95*
Thomson, James, 127–128, 136, *165, 166*
Thornton, John, 71–73, 84, 124
Thornton, Thomas, Sir, 5, 25–27, 53,
 55–60, 63–64, 71–78, 81–86, 114–
 116, 140
Thornton, William, 84
Thorntons, *105,* 270
Tickle, Geraldine, 330
Tocsin, The, 91
Tounis College, Edinburgh, 23
Tower Building, 110, 297, 300, 302, 311,
 327
Traynor, John, Lord , 29, 57, 75–77, *102*
trusts law
 degree requirement, as, 129, 156–157,
 211
Tudhope, Mrs *see* Bisset, Christian
Tulloch, John, 63, *97*
Turnbull, Alan, Lord, 363
tutorials
 19th Century, 78
 1939-1949, 191, 207–208
 1964-1965, 315
 present day, 356

Tweedie, David Hamilton, 274–275

U
UK Quality Code of Higher Education,
 359–360
ultra vires legislation, 15, *40–41*
unique selling points
 desirability of, 306–307
 English law as, 308–309
 jurisprudence as, 296
 oil and gas law, 309
 social science collaboration as, 263,
 289, 290–291, 307, 312–313, 315
United College of St Salvator and St
 Leonard, St Andrews, 24, 176, 251,
 278–279
universities, generally
 civic universities, development of, 23–
 24, *46*
 establishment, reasons for, 22–23
 female students, first, 22, 33, 35, *51,*
 143–144
 General Council, establishment, 20–
 21
 Law Society, relationship with, 293–
 294
 league tables, 358–359, 361
 main aims of, 20
 reforms, 19–21
 Scottish universities, differences from
 English, 23–24
 Senates, functions of, 20–21
 session dates, *101*
Universities (Scotland) Act 1858, 20–21,
 25, 27
Universities (Scotland) Act 1889, 20–21,
 26–27, *43–44*
 see also Ordinances
Universities (Scotland) Act 1966, *341*
Universities Central Council on
 Admissions, 328
University Air Squadron, 208
University College Dundee (UCD)

see also Dundee, Law School in;
Faculty of Law, Dundee
Constitution, 27, 176–177
degree-awarding powers, 26
establishment, 1–2
Royal Commission 1878
recommendations, 24–25
St Andrews University, and
affiliation with, 2, 26–28, *48–49,*
67–69, 80, *109–110*
as campus of, 113–114
conflicts between, 24–27, 109–110,
175–176, 198
separation from, 113–114, 251, 291
Statement of Needs 1908, 125–126
student admissions policies, 13, 195
War Memorial, 145, *173*
University Courts, 20
University of St Andrews Act 1953, 252,
280, 289, 291, 295
University of St Andrews (Appointment
of Commissioners) Order 1953, SI
1953 No. 1562, *279*
University of St Andrews (Extension of
Duration of Commissioners'
Powers) Order 1956, SI 1956 No.
1585, *279*

V
Valentine, George G., 145

W
W B Dickie & Sons, 270, *285*
Wainwright, Frederick, 190, 192–193,
257, 262, 265–266, 294
Walker, David M., 292, *341*
Walker, Margaret, 35, 206–207
Wanless, Alexander, 207
Watson, Alan, 316, *349*
Watson, Frederick J., 145, *173*
Watson, Stanley L., 145, *173*
Watt, Alexander L., 145, *173*
Watt, Bisset & Co, 90–91
Watt, Donald & Co, 90–91

Watterston, W.A., 89
Weker, Casmir, 215
Wighton, James D., 145
will-writing, regulation, 12, 16–17
Willock, Ian, Dean of Law, 311–312,
316–317, 321–323, 327–328
Wilson, Douglas, 321
Wilson, Garnet, Sir, *170,* 196, *226*
Wimberley, Douglas Neil, Major
General, Principal , 176, 190, 193,
196, *216,* 253, 290
women
academic dress, 213
law students
1899-1939, 143–144, 364
1939-1949, 206, 210, 365
1950-1955, 267, 272–275, 366
1956-1967, 327, 330, 367
first BL graduate, 207
first LLB graduate, 267, 274
first recorded, 22, 33, 35, *51,* 144
lawyers, first recorded, 18, 33–34, 202
prizes won by, 275
students, pastoral care, 188–189
teaching staff
1938-1949, 202–203, *228*
first appointments, 35
universities founded by, 30, 32
World War I
student numbers, impact on, 110–111,
123–124, 128
War Memorial, 145, *173*
World War II
Polish soldier-students, 189, 205,
207–210, 215, *231*
student numbers, impact on, 189–190,
205–206
Wright, Frederick, 254–255
Wright, James, 144
Wright, Pamela, 330
writers, 8, 112
Wrobel, Ryszard, 210, 215

Y
Yule, Anne, 206

Z
Zawilski, Mieczyslaw, 215
Zolna, Jan, 215

The Abertay Historical Society

The Society was founded in May 1947 and exists to promote interest in local history. For further information, please visit our website at **www.abertay.org.uk**

Publications of the Abertay Historical Society
currently in print

No 37 Michael St John, *The Demands of the People, Dundee Radicalism 1850-1870.* (1997) ISBN 978 0 900019 33 3

No 39 Lorraine Walsh, *Patrons, Poverty & Profit: Organised Charity in Nineteenth Century Dundee.* (2000) ISBN 978 0 900019 35 7

No 41 Ian McCraw, *Victorian Dundee at Worship.* (2002) ISBN 978 0 900019 37 9

No 42 Andrew Murray Scott, *Dundee's Literary Lives vol 1: Fifteenth to Nineteenth Century.* (2003) ISBN 978 0 900019 38 7

No 43 Andrew Murray Scott, *Dundee's Literary Lives vol 2: Twentieth Century.* (2004) ISBN 978 0 900019 39 5

No 45 Annette M. Smith, *The Guildry of Dundee: A History of the Merchant Guild of Dundee up to the 19th century.* (2005) ISBN 978 0 900019 42 5

No 46 Mary Verschuur, *A Noble and Potent Lady: Katherine Campbell, Countess of Crawford.* (2006) ISBN 978 0 900019 43 2

No 47 Kenneth Cameron, *The Schoolmaster Engineer: Adam Anderson of Perth and St Andrews 1780-1846.* (2007) ISBN 978 0 900019 44 9

No 48 Sarah F. Browne, *Making the Vote Count: The Arbroath Womens' Citizens Association, 1931-945.* (2007) ISBN 978 0 900019 45 6

No 49 Ann Petrie, *The 1915 Rent Strikes: An East Coast Perspective.* (2008) ISBN 978 0 900019 46 3

No 51 Matthew Jarron, *et al* (editors), *Ten Taysiders: Forgotten Figures from Dundee, Angus and Perthshire.* (2011) ISBN 978 0 900019 48 7

No 52 Susan Keracher, *'Dundee's Two Intrepid Ladies: A Tour Round the World by D.C. Thomson's Female Journalists in 1894'*. (2012) ISBN 978 0 900019 49 4

No 54 Julie S Danskin, *A City at War. The 4th Black Watch, Dundee's Own.* (2013) ISBN 978 0 900019 51 7

No 55 Catherine Rice *"All their Good Friends and Neighbours": the Story of a Vanished Hamlet in Angus.* (2014) ISBN 978 0 9000019 548

No 56 Matthew Jarron *"Independent and Individualist": Art in Dundee 1867–1924.* (2015) ISBN 978 0 9000019 562

No 57 Jean Dundas & David Orr (editors) *"Quite Happy": The Diary of James Fyfe, Cattle Dealer 1836-1840.* (2016) ISBN 978 0 900019 579

No 58 Matthew Jarron (editor) *Growing and Forming: Essays on D'Arcy Thompson.* (2017) ISBN 978 0 900019 586

No 59 William Kenefick & Derek Patrick (editors) *Tayside at War.* (2018) ISBN 978-0-900019-65-4

All publications may be obtained via www.abertay.org.uk where selected out-of-print titles are also available in pdf form.